Origins and Development of Recollection

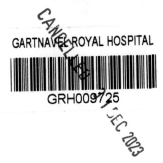
Origins and Development of Recollection

Perspectives from Psychology and Neuroscience

EDITED BY SIMONA GHETTI AND PATRICIA J. BAUER

OXFORD
UNIVERSITY PRESS

OXFORD
UNIVERSITY PRESS

Oxford University Press, Inc., publishes works that further
Oxford University's objective of excellence
in research, scholarship, and education.

Oxford New York
Auckland   Cape Town   Dar es Salaam   Hong Kong   Karachi
Kuala Lumpur   Madrid   Melbourne   Mexico City   Nairobi
New Delhi   Shanghai   Taipei   Toronto

With offices in
Argentina   Austria   Brazil   Chile   Czech Republic   France   Greece
Guatemala   Hungary   Italy   Japan   Poland   Portugal   Singapore
South Korea   Switzerland   Thailand   Turkey   Ukraine   Vietnam

Published by Oxford University Press, Inc.
198 Madison Avenue, New York, New York 10016
www.oup.com

Library of Congress Cataloging-in-Publication Data

Origins and development of recollection : perspectives from psychology and
neuroscience / edited by Simona Ghetti and Patricia J. Bauer.
  p. cm.
 Includes bibliographical references and index.
 ISBN 978-0-19-534079-2 (hbk. : alk. paper)
1. Recollection (Psychology) 2. Memory. I. Ghetti, Simona. II. Bauer, Patricia J.
 BF371.O75 2011
 153.1'23—dc23   2011036649

9 8 7 6 5 4 3 2 1

Printed in USA
on acid-free paper

CONTENTS

PREFACE

For millennia, philosophers, scientists, and lay people alike have sought an understanding of how we remember the past. In his *Confessions*, Saint Augustine wondered how one "discern(s) the breath of lilies from violets, though smelling nothing . . . but remembering only." He likened memory to a "spacious palace" in which is stored "the treasures of innumerable images, brought into it from things of all sorts perceived by the senses . . . for thought to recall . . ." (Saint Augustine, ~401 CE). Since Saint Augustine wrote these words, our explanations of memory and how it functions have moved beyond the poetic metaphor of a "spacious palace" to the more concrete realities of modern psychological and neural sciences. However, what has remained the same is the nature of the phenomenon we are attempting to explain. In his time, Saint Augustine wondered how physical entities such as flowers could be "discerned" based not on the chemicals in the air that give rise to smell, but through memory alone. Present-day psychologists and neuroscientists are asking essentially the same question as we ponder how the roughly 1500 grams (3½ pounds) of tissue that sits in the bony case atop our shoulders manages to vividly recreate—and even allows us to relive—events and experiences from the past. The modern day developmental scientist further questions how the material substrate and the processes it subserves develop from infancy through childhood.

It is clear that the ability to use memory alone to vividly recreate experiences from the past begins to develop early in ontogeny. By early in the second year of life, preverbal infants can reenact action sequences, in accurate order, months after original exposure. Over the course of the second year, the length of time over which memory for sequences is apparent increases dramatically. Once verbal, children become more and more sophisticated at describing their past experiences, such that by middle childhood, their memories not only include surprising levels of detail but also precise assessments of their subjective experience ranging from feelings of memory vividness to reports of emotional content. It is therefore clear that from early ages children are capable of remembering a great deal about their past, and this ability continues to develop throughout childhood.

Current models of adult memory identify recollection as the process designated to allow for reexperiencing our past in vivid detail. Work grounded in these models has elucidated the functional principles of recollection, and recent advances in cognitive neuroscience have further clarified the neural architecture supporting its functioning. The present volume represents our effort to integrate these recent advances with a growing literature on the typical and atypical development of recollection, from infancy into adolescence. Much of the discussion is in terms of the neural systems and basic mnemonic processes that permit memories to be formed, retained, and later retrieved. Yet, a satisfying solution to the puzzle of memory also entails consideration of "higher level" influences such as the social forces that shape what children come to view as important to remember and even how they express their memories. These far-reaching, complementary perspectives are necessary because memory is a complex, multidimensional process. Indeed, an assumption common to the chapters between these covers is that memory is not a unitary construct. Rather, there are different types of memory that involve different processes and that are subserved by different neural substrates. Each of the chapters in the volume illuminates a portion of the larger picture that we recognize as *recollection*. Here we describe the organization of the volume and highlight the motivation behind each contribution.

WHAT IS RECOLLECTION?

In the first section, we included two chapters that provide necessary background for the rest of the volume. In Chapter 1, Andrew Yonelinas asks, "What is recollection?," and offers a comprehensive overview of theoretical and methodological approaches grounded in dual-process models of memory to address his question. From this perspective, the process of recollection is specifically devoted to the retrieval of qualitative detail about the past; its contribution to memory performance can be formally estimated, and its neurological underpinnings specified. In Chapter 2, Katherine Nelson engages in a thoughtful analysis of how biological, psychological, and cultural bases of recollection make it possible to remember over time, preserve meaning of life experiences, and form autobiographical memories. Although Nelson's analysis focuses on child development, it is clear that the unique function of recollection outlined in the chapter extends beyond childhood. Together, these chapters reflect the rich theoretical discourse surrounding the construct of recollection and its development.

THE DEVELOPMENT OF RECOLLECTION

In this second section, we include four chapters that provide an overview of current theories and empirical evidence regarding the psychological mechanisms involved in the development of recollection. In Chapter 3, Tracy Riggins offers a comprehensive analysis of evidence of development of memory in infancy and early childhood. In doing so, she addresses pressing questions about whether and when recollection is present in infancy and reflects on the methodological approaches and the conclusions that these approaches afford about early recollection. Adhering to the definition of recollection as the capacity to remember events in their spatiotemporal context, Riggings provides a careful examination of recent research differentiating among spatial, temporal, and other attributes of episodic recollection.

In Chapter 4, Nora Newcombe, Marianne Lloyd, and Frances Balcomb examine the development of one fundamental feature of episodic recollection, namely, the capacity to bind different features of an event into an integrated representation. This capacity is distinguished from the operation of strategies and other forms of controlled mechanisms that promote and monitor binding operations. Newcombe and colleagues examine the development of binding during childhood and integrate this knowledge with a lifespan perspective and investigations with nonhuman animals. The authors offer a series of insightful comments on how binding might affect the emergence and development not only of episodic memory, but also of other faculties conceptually linked to episodic memory, such as mental travel time and imagining the future.

In Chapter 5, Charles Brainerd, Valery Reyna, and Robyn Holliday provide a compendium on the development of recollection from a fuzzy-trace theory perspective. Brainerd and colleagues acknowledge the long tradition of mathematical models in the study of adult recollection and the limited use of such an approach in the field of child development. They convincingly use their rich empirical work to argue for the importance of model estimation in the development of memory and provide extensive evidence on the developmental dissociation between recollection and familiarity trajectories.

In Chapter 6, Simona Ghetti, Kristen Lyons, and Dana DeMaster identify the key components of the development of episodic recollection in the binding and controlled processes that are necessary to form, store, and reinstate episodic memories. The authors then proceed to emphasize the development of the subjective experience of recollection. Despite a general agreement that episodic recollection is accompanied with subjective feelings of vividness, little research has examined the development of this component; Ghetti and her colleagues review a nascent literature on the topic.

Overall, these four chapters draw from a variety of theoretical perspectives to provide a comprehensive base from which to examine the phenomenon of recollection and its development, from infancy to adolescence.

NEURAL BASIS OF RECOLLECTION AND ITS DEVELOPMENT

In this section, we include four chapters that document recent advances in the cognitive neuroscience of recollection and its development. Chapters 7 and 8 examine the neural correlates of adult recollection, and Chapters 9 and 10 examine the development of the neural substrates supporting this capacity during childhood.

In Chapter 7, Rachel Diana and Charan Ranganath present an extensive overview of state-of-the-art knowledge about the contribution of medial temporal lobes, prefrontal, and parietal regions to episodic recollection. They do so by discussing the wealth of evidence gathered from patients with brain lesions, electrophysiological, and neuroimaging research. In addition, the authors take a closer look at functional specialization of media temporal subregions: they propose an intriguing neurocognitive model that accounts for a wealth of data and discriminates between MTL substrates of recollection and familiarity.

In Chapter 8, Peggy St. Jacques and Roberto Cabeza examine the neural substrates of autobiographical memory. The authors masterfully communicate the unique defining features of autobiographical memory by reflecting on similarities and differences with other relevant constructs such as episodic and semantic memory. Similarly, as they review experimental paradigms used to examine neural substrates of autobiographical memory, they successfully raise awareness of the unique complexities one faces when developing methods that appropriately capture the richness of the autobiographical memory construct. This richness is further reflected in their thorough discussion of factors affecting autobiographical construction and retrieval.

In Chapter 9, Kathleen Thomas and Lyric Jorgenson offer a meticulous overview of the principles of brain development that provide a critical foundation to appreciate changes in brain-behavior associations during development. Furthermore, these authors discuss the most recent empirical evidence documenting the role of changes in prefrontal regions and medial temporal structures in the development of recollection.

In Chapter 10, David Friedman reviews an impressive body of research conducted in his laboratory examining the event-related potentials correlates of the development of recollection. By comparing the correlates of recollection to those of familiarity, and by probing the processes (semantic processing, monitoring) thought to influence recollection, Friedman begins to clarify their nature and interaction during development. Together these four chapters give true justice to the breadth and depth of current understanding of the neural substrates of memory development.

IMPAIRMENTS IN THE DEVELOPMENT OF RECOLLECTION

In this last section, we include two chapters that provide an overview of how development of recollection is altered in child patients who have suffered neurological insult. In Chapter 11, Michelle De Haan reviews the literature on developmental amnesia and other alterations of recollection following injury to the medial temporal lobes. De Haan examines the variety of conditions that might result in this type of injury, outlines the nature of memory deficits while highlighting areas of preserved functioning, and provides new insight on the relations between type and time of injury, as well as consequences for memory functioning.

In Chapter 12, Gerri Hanten and Harvey Levin discuss the consequences of frontal lesions on memory functioning, with a focus on traumatic brain injury— one of the most common and potentially debilitating conditions that result in frontal damage. The authors examine domains of deficits and preserved function, as well as factors affecting potential for recovery during development and ideas about rehabilitation. Though the literature on atypical development of recollection is still relatively sparse, these two chapters provide excellent insight into the conditions that not only hinder memory functioning in children, but also alter its developmental trajectory.

This volume brought together an impressive group of contributions that provide an in-depth analysis of recent advances in the behavioral and neural basis of the development of episodic recollection. We hope that the ideas and empirical evidence discussed in this volume will provide fruitful insight for future investigations. We are indebted to our publisher, Oxford University Press, for its unwavering support, and to Paola Castelli for outstanding technical assistance.

Simona Ghetti

Patricia J. Bauer

CONTRIBUTORS

Frances Balcomb
Department of Psychology
Temple University
Philadelphia, PA, USA

Patricia J. Bauer
Department of Psychology
Emory University
Atlanta, GA, USA

Charles J. Brainerd
Department of Human
    Development
Cornell University
Ithaca, NY, USA

Roberto Cabeza
Center for Cognitive Neuroscience
Department of Psychology and
    Neuroscience
Duke University
Durham, NC, USA

Michelle De Haan
Institute of Child Health
University College London
London, UK

Dana DeMaster
Department of Psychology and Center
    for Mind and Brain
University of California, Davis
Davis, CA, USA

Rachel A. Diana
Department of Psychology and
    Center for Neuroscience
University of California, Davis
Davis, CA, USA

David Friedman
New York State Psychiatric
    Institute
Columbia University
New York, NY, USA

Simona Ghetti
Department of Psychology
    and Center for Mind and Brain
University of California, Davis
Davis, CA, USA

Gerri Hanten
Department of Physical Medicine
    and Rehabilitation
Baylor College of Medicine
Houston, TX, USA

Robyn E. Holliday
School of Psychology
University of Leicester
Leicester, UK

Lyric Jorgenson
Center for Neurobehavioral Development
University of Minnesota
Minneapolis, MN, USA

Harvey Levin
Department of Physical Medicine
    and Rehabilitation
Baylor College of Medicine
Houston, TX, USA

Marianne E. Lloyd
Department of Psychology
Seton Hall University
South Orange, NJ, USA

Kristen E. Lyons
Institute of Child Development
University of Minnesota
Minneapolis, MN, USA

Katherine Nelson
City University of New York
    Graduate School and
    University Center
New York, NY, USA

Nora S. Newcombe
Department of Psychology
Temple University
Philadelphia, PA, USA

Charan Ranganath
Department of Psychology and
    Center for Neuroscience
University of California, Davis

Davis, CA, USA

Valerie F. Reyna
Department of Human
    Development
Cornell University
Ithaca, NY, USA

Tracy Riggins
Department of Psychology
University of Maryland
College Park, MD, USA

Peggy L. St. Jacques
Department of Psychology
Harvard University
Cambridge, MA, USA

Kathleen M. Thomas
Institute of Child Development
University of Minnesota
Minneapolis, MN, USA

Andrew P. Yonelinas
Department of Psychology
University of California, Davis
Davis, CA, USA

Origins and Development of Recollection

1

Remembering

Thoughts on Its Definition, Measurement, and Functional Nature

ANDREW P. YONELINAS

> I enter a friend's room and see on the wall a painting. At first I have the
> strange, wondering consciousness, "surely I have seen that before," but
> when or how does not become clear. There only clings to the picture a sort
> of penumbra of familiarity,—when suddenly I exclaim: "I have it, it is a
> copy of part of one of the Fra Angelicos in the Florentine Academy—
> I recollect it there!"
>
> —WILLIAM JAMES, THE PRINCIPLES OF PSYCHOLOGY (1890, p. 658)

The capability to remember our past is perhaps one of the most remarkable and
mysterious cognitive abilities we possess. Despite the fact that it has been studied
by neuroscientists for decades, by psychologists for over a century, and by philosophers for 2000 years before that, its inner workings remain largely unex-
plained. One thing we do know about remembering or recollection—I will use the
term *recollection* to refer to the process that gives rise to the phenomenological
experience of remembering—is that it is but one of the many different forms of
memory that we possess. As illustrated above, William James differentiated
between familiarity-based recognition and recollection, which for James reflected
the "recall" or "bringing back into consciousness" of past experiences. This distinction can be traced back to Aristotle who described recollection as a special
type of memory that involves a search or recall process whereby we retrieve into
awareness the sensory details about prior events. Aristotle thought that sensory
information passed through the blood stream to the heart where the memory
traces of these events were stored. James, in contrast, thought that "currents"

passed from the sensory organs through the nerves to the brain and that memory reflected the creation and modification of neural associations in the brain.

A number of prominent cognitive psychologists such as Richard Atkinson, George Mandler, Larry Jacoby, and Endel Tulving further explored the functional nature of recollection and familiarity and provided theoretical frameworks for understanding how these two processes operate (for reviews of this earlier work, see Yonelinas, 2002). In addition, based on neuropsychological findings indicating that damage to the medial temporal lobes causes severe memory impairments (Scoville & Milner, 1957), recent theories of memory have focused on understanding how regions within the medial temporal lobes support recollection and familiarity (e.g., Aggleton & Brown, 1999; Eichenbaun, Otto, & Cohen, 1994; Norman & O'Reilly, 2003).

In the current paper, I will begin by discussing how recollection has been defined and separated from familiarity-based recognition, and briefly describe the methods that have been developed to measure these two forms of memory. I will then provide a selective review of the behavioral literature and discuss some of the more well-established findings that have informed us about the functional nature of these processes. Finally, I will describe some recent neuropsychological work that has revealed how different regions within the medial temporal lobe support these two processes.

WHAT IS RECOLLECTION?

The simple answer to this question is that *recollection* is the process of retrieving qualitative information about a past experience. As illustrated by the quote from James, perceiving an object as familiar is not sufficient for recollection, rather one must retrieve information that links that item to a specific past experience. So recollection is necessarily an associative form of memory. Thus, simply recognizing or retrieving an "item" such as a word, image, color, concept, or idea is not sufficient, rather, the item must be associated with something else such as another item, or a temporal, physical, or mental context that links it to a previous event. Nonetheless, the retrieval of associative information in itself is not sufficient for remembering, rather that information must effectively link the item to a past experience, so that the memory is "about" or is "attributed to" some past event. Thus, a painting may lead one to think of many complex and vivid associations, but they would simply reflect passing thoughts rather than an act of remembering unless those associations are perceived as reflecting a memory for a past experience.

What types of associative information are sufficient to support recollection? Some have argued that recollection must support controlled or discriminative responding (Jacoby, 1991). Thus, if one remembers where or when the information was learned, then one can chose to use that information or withhold it depending on one's intentions. Others have argued that the most important aspect of recollection is the retrieval of information linking the memory to the person or to the self (Conway, 2005; Tulving, 1985). So for example, William James argued that recollection has a certain warmth and intimacy, and it "must be dated to *my* past. In other words, I must think that I directly experienced its occurrence." Tulving used the term *autonoetic consciousness* to refer to this special type of self-awareness associated with remembering. This differentiates remembering from other types of memory that are associated with different forms of conscious experience, such as the sense of familiarity one might experience when encountering a familiar painting (i.e., noetic consciousness), or a variety of implicit forms of memory that may occur with little or no conscious awareness.

HOW DO WE MEASURE RECOLLECTION?

Essential in measuring recollection is separating it from other forms of memory such as familiarity. Various different approaches have been developed, and each has its advantages and disadvantages. An early approach was to use task dissociation methods, in which one contrasts performance on tests thought to rely preferentially on one or the other process. So, for example, free recall or cued recall tasks have been used as a measure of recollection, whereas item recognition has been used as a measure of familiarity (e.g., Aggleton & Brown, 1999; Mandler, 1980). However, a shortcoming of this method is that neither of these tasks provides a "process pure" measure of recollection or familiarity. For example, both recollection and familiarity are expected to contribute to item recognition. Thus, one may fail to find differences between recall and recognition simply because both tests may be relying heavily on recollection. In addition, performance differences in recall and recognition tests might be related to the different retrieval cues used on those tests, rather than the differential contribution of recollection and familiarity.

A similar approach is to measure recollection using tests of source or associative recognition in which subjects must retrieve some specified qualitative information about a particular study event (e.g., Was it in list 1 or list 2? Where was it located? Was it paired with this item?) and measure familiarity using tests of item recognition. An advantage of this approach is that the retrieval cues can be held constant in the different tests. However, it still relies on the assumption that these two types of tests are "process pure." Note that some have argued that this problem might be improved on by using forced-choice item recognition tests that presumably provide a purer measure of familiarity than yes/no tests (e.g., Holdstock, Mayes, Gong, Roberts, & Kapur, 2005: Holdstock et al., 2002), although studies directly contrasting these test procedures have not always supported this claim (e.g., Khoe, Kroll, Yonelinas, Dobbins, & Knight, 2000).

An alternative approach is to rely on "process estimation methods" that are designed to estimate the contribution of recollection and familiarity to performance by contrasting performance on two or more very similar test conditions. For example, Jacoby (1991) developed the process dissociation procedure in which he examined source and item recognition. This method estimates *recollection* as the ability to remember when or where an item was encountered, whereas *familiarity* is estimated on the basis of items that were recognized but that were

not recollected. Another approach is to separate these two processes using a subjective report method in which subjects in a recognition test are instructed
to indicate when they remember qualitative information about a previous
event, or whether they recognize items on some other basis such as familiarity
(the "remember/know" procedure of (Gardiner, 1988; Tulving, 1985)). Finally,
recognition confidence responses (or response bias manipulations) can be used to
plot receiver operating characteristics (ROCs). Because the shape of the ROC is
determined by recollection and familiarity, by quantifying the shape of the ROC,
one can estimate the extent to which recognition performance relies on recollection and familiarity (Yonelinas, 1994; for a comparison of these various methods
see Yonelinas, 2002).

Although these estimation methods overcome several of the potential difficulties related to the task dissociation methods, they do make strong assumptions
that can in some cases be violated. For example, subjective reports of remembering and knowing can be notoriously susceptible to individual biases in the sense
that whether an item is treated as having been remembered will depend on several
factors such as how the term is understood by the subject, the subject's willingness
to provide such a report, and the specific retrieval conditions (e.g., Baddeley,
Vargha-Khadem, & Mishkin, 2001; Bodner & Lindsay, 2003). In my opinion,
without other more objective methods to verify these subjective reports of remembering (e.g., using source or associative recognition tests), these methods alone
cannot serve as the basis for a mature science of memory.

Tests of source or associative recognition are less susceptible to subjective
report biases, but they too can provide distorted views of recollection. For example, they can be too restrictive in the sense that subjects may remember aspects
of the study event that do not support the discrimination required by the test
(e.g., in a test of object location, subjects may remember having seen the object,
but may be unable to remember its initial location). Conversely, associative tests
can be too inclusive in the sense that accurate associative discriminations can be
made even when recollection fails. For example, in a test of temporal order, subjects may find the object to be very familiar, and thus might correctly infer that it
was presented in the most recent study list. So familiarity may be used to support
associative or source recognition. Moreover, whether a test requires the retrieval
of associative information depends on the subject's past experience with the particular test materials, as well as the manner in which they process the incoming
stimuli (e.g., Cohen, Poldrack, & Eichenbaum, 1997; Yonelinas, Kroll, Dobbins, &
Soltani, 1999). For example, a string of letters may be treated as a set of associations between separate parts or as a single word, depending on whether the individual has experience with that particular word, and whether they are processing
it as a word or as separate components. In addition, associative recognition for
randomly paired works may require recollection if the items were encoded as two
separate words, but it may rely on familiarity if they were encoded as a unified
novel compound word (Quamme, Yonelinas, & Norman, 2007). Thus, accurate
performance on associative tests cannot serve as a litmus test for recollection.

The ROC method does not require the use of different types of memory tests, and it does not require that the subjects understand complex subjective report instructions, thus it is useful in a broad range of research settings from studies of rats to studies of children and brain-injured patients. However, this method too relies on important assumptions that can sometimes be violated. For example, ROCs are particularly susceptible to floor and ceiling effects, and the method requires a large number of responses per subject-condition, which may not be practical in some situations (Yonelinas & Parks, 2007).

One can, and should, design experiments to avoid the potential problems associated with each method. However, because one can never be absolutely sure whether a method's assumptions have been met in a particular experimental context, only a convergent operations approach can ensure that our understanding of recollection is not biased by a specific measurement method. It is encouraging that we are now seeing fewer studies that focus exclusively on a single measurement methodology and an increase in the number of studies that examine recollection and familiarity using a variety of different methods. In addition to increasing one's confidence in the validity of the parameter estimates, the convergent operations approach is also useful in helping rule against alternative interpretations of the results, as is often problematic in single-paradigm studies.

There is one final point about converging operations that may be particularly relevant to the current volume. Prior studies in adults have shown that these various different measurement methods do converge on the same general conclusions about recollection and familiarity. This is important in developmental studies because not all methods may be equally appropriate for infants or very young children. For example, the remember/know procedure relies on understanding a complex set of verbal instructions, which are obviously not appropriate for infants. However, if a subject group cannot use that method, then various other methods, such as the associative recognition and ROC methods, can be used to serve exactly the same purpose (e.g., see Fortin, Wright, & Eichenbaum, 2004; Yonelinas, 2002).

WHAT HAVE WE LEARNED ABOUT RECOLLECTION AND FAMILIARITY?

Our knowledge of recollection and familiarity is growing at an ever-increasing rate, so it is not possible to provide a thorough review of that literature here (for prior reviews, see Diana, Reder, Arndt, & Park, 2006; Rugg & Curran, 2007; Yonelinas 2002). Fortunately, the current volume contains excellent papers discussing the most recent neuroimaging and developmental work related to this topic. In the current chapter, I will limit myself to briefly reviewing some of the more well-established behavioral findings and some of the neuropsychological findings from adult patients, with the aim of highlighting some of the general theoretical implications of these results.

RECOLLECTION IS A RELATIVELY SLOW RETRIEVAL PROCESS

One of the core assumptions of a number of behavioral dual-process models is that familiarity is faster than recollection (Atkinson & Juola, 1974; Jacoby, 1991; Mandler, 1980; Yonelinas, 1994). This assumption is also consistent with neuro-anatomical models that assert that familiarity is based on brain regions earlier in the processing stream than those regions supporting recollection (Aggleton & Brown, 1999; Norman & O'Reilly, 2001; Tulving & Markowitsch, 1998; Yonelinas, 2001). A variety of empirical results support this assumption. For example, results from response deadline and response signal procedures indicate that familiarity is available earlier than recollection (Toth, 1996; Yonelinas & Jacoby, 1994). In addition, studies of event-related potentials have indicated that the electro-physiological correlates of familiarity are observed earlier than those associated with recollection (for reviews, see Rugg & Curran, 2007; Rugg & Yonelinas, 2003). It should be noted, however, that these methods indicate *when the products of these processes are available*, not necessarily when the subject will make use of this information. So, for example, it is generally the case that remember responses are made more quickly than knowing responses are (e.g., Dewhurst & Conway, 1994). Thus, although familiarity is generally available earlier than recollection is, familiarity may be used as a basis for responding only once the subject determines that recollection has not been successful.

RECOLLECTION GENERALLY OPERATES INDEPENDENTLY OF FAMILIARITY

Most dual-process models assume that recollection and familiarity function inde-pendently (Mandler, 1980; Jacoby, 1991; Tulving & Markowitsch, 1998; Yonelinas, 1994). In line with these models, the empirical evidence indicates that the two processes are independent under most standard test conditions, but there are test conditions under which this assumption does not appear to hold. To deter-mine whether recollection and familiarity are operating independently, it is nec-essary to assess whether they can be functionally dissociated. That is, if the two processes are fully independent, it should be possible to produce double dissocia-tions (e.g., find variables that have selective effects on one process, and other vari-ables that have selective effects on the other process). The behavioral literature indicates that recollection and familiarity can be doubly dissociated by a variety of manipulations. For example, response-speeding and dividing attention during time of test reduce recollection but leave familiarity unaffected (e.g., Gruppuso, Lindsay, & Kelley, 1997; Yonelinas & Jacoby, 1994). Conversely, relaxing response criterion and increasing processing fluency lead to changes in familiarity, but they have little effect on recollection (Rajaram, 1993; Yonelinas 1994). Similarly, forget-ting over intermediate retention intervals selectively influences familiarity (Yonelinas & Levy, 2002), and changing the presentation modality of words between study and test also appears to selectively affect familiarity (Gregg & Gardiner, 1994; Toth, 1996).

Another line of evidence indicating that the two processes operate independently comes from the observation that the results of the process-estimation methods are verified by the results from the task-dissociation methods. The estimation methods all assume that recollection and familiarity are independent, whereas the task-dissociation methods do not make any explicit assumption about how the two processes are related. The fact that the task-dissociation methods verify the results of the estimation methods suggests that the assumptions underlying the estimation methods were not violated (for a further discussion of this issue, see Yonelinas, 2002).

Finally, event-related potentials correlates of recollection and familiarity are found to be spatially and topographically distinct, such that recollection is associated with a late positive component, whereas familiarity has been associated with an earlier bifrontal component (for reviews, see Diana & Ranganath, Chapter 7 this volume; Rugg & Curran, 2007; Rugg & Yonelinas, 2003).

Although recollection and familiarity generally do appear to operate independently, there may be special cases in which they do not operate independently. For example, in studies in which performance levels are extremely high, the estimation methods produce patterns of results that are inconsistent with the results from studies in which such ceiling effects were avoided. For example, most studies of aging indicate that healthy aging disrupts recollection but not familiarity. However, in studies in which estimates of recollection are extremely high (e.g., studies in which more than 60% of the studied items are recollected, and thus, overall recognition performance is close to ceiling), aging appears to disrupt both recollection and familiarity (for review, see Yonelinas, 2002). Although these ceiling effects may simply reflect a methodological limitation associated with the estimation methods, it is possible that when performance levels are extremely high, the two processes no longer operate independently. For example, if subjects remember a large proportion of the test items, and thus find only a few items to be familiar in the absence of recollection, this may affect how subjects map their subjective experiences onto remember and know responses, or how likely they are to endorse nonrecollected items in source recognition tests, and thus the two processes may no longer independently contribute to performance. In either case, the important methodological implication is that one needs to be careful to avoid ceiling effects when examining recollection and familiarity.

RECOLLECTION AND FAMILIARITY ARE WELL DESCRIBED AS THRESHOLD AND SIGNAL DETECTION PROCESSES, RESPECTIVELY

Most dual-process models assume that familiarity reflects the assessment of a continuous memory strength index, whereas recollection reflects the retrieval of qualitative or associative information about a study event (Atkinson & Juola, 1974; Jacoby, 1991; Mandler, 1980; Yonelinas, 1994). Moreover, in quantitative models, familiarity has been formalized using signal detection theory, whereas recollection has been formalized as a threshold process (Atkinson & Juola, 1974;

Norman & O'Reilly, 2001; Yonelinas, 1994). Treating familiarity as a signal detection process is to assume that everything is familiar to some extent, but that studied items are simply more familiar on average than nonstudied items are. Because the familiarity distributions of old and new items overlap, subjects have no direct way of determining whether an item was old or new, rather they can only use familiarity to make an educated guess as to whether an item was or was not studied. In contrast, treating recollection as a threshold process means that not everything is recollected. That is, for some items, one might not recollect anything at all about having studied it before. These items are said to fall below the recollective strength threshold.

The empirical evidence generally supports these two claims. That is, ROCs observed in a wide variety of different types of recognition tests, such as item, source, remember/know, exclusion, and associative recognition are best described by models including both signal detection and threshold processes and are poorly described by pure signal detection or pure threshold models alone (for review, see Yonelinas & Parks, 2007). For example, under conditions expected to rely heavily on recollection, such as source recognition and associative recognition, ROCs plotted in z-space typically exhibit a pronounced U-shape, a finding that is problematic for pure signal detection models. Conversely, under conditions expected to reflect primarily familiarity-based recognition, such as item recognition judgments in amnesic patients, the ROCs in z-space are linear with a slope of 1.0 as expected if performance reflects a classical equal variance signal detection model. Such a finding is problematic for pure threshold models. Dual-process models provide a nature account for both types of findings.

Although there are alternative models that have been developed to account for some of these findings (e.g., the variable recollection dual-process model of Sherman, Atri, Hasselmo, Stren, & Howard, 2003; and the mixture model of DeCarlo, 2002), they reflect extensions of the basic dual-process account, and they assume two independent processes contributing to recognition, one of which is a signal detection process and other which is a threshold process. So the models tend to parallel the conclusions drawn by the dual-process models, but they provide a somewhat different interpretation of those processes. Experiments that more directly contrast these various dual-process approaches will be important in future studies.

RECOLLECTION AND FAMILIARITY TEND TO BE PREFERENTIALLY SENSITIVE TO CONCEPTUAL AND PERCEPTUAL MANIPULATIONS, RESPECTIVELY

One of the central assumptions of the early dual-process models (Atkinson & Juola, 1974; Mandler, 1980) was that recollection reflected a conceptual or elaborative process, whereas familiarity reflected a more sensory or perceptual process. The empirical results provide some support for this claim in showing that recollection and familiarity are preferentially sensitive to conceptual and perceptual manipulations, respectively. For example, recollection increases more with semantic compared with perceptual encoding conditions than does familiarity (Gardiner, 1988; Yonelinas, 2001). Moreover, other elaborative encoding manipulations such as generation compared with read conditions (Gardiner, 1988; Jacoby, 1991) and full compared with divided attention conditions (Gruppuso, Lindsay & Kelley, 1997; Yonelinas, 2001) are also found to increase recollection to a greater extent than familiarity. In contrast, perceptual fluency manipulations influence familiarity but not recollection (Rajaram, 1993), supporting the claim that familiarity is more sensitive to perceptual manipulations than recollection. Similarly, changing the presentation modality of words between study and test leads to decreases in familiarity, but it does not influence recollection (Gregg & Gardiner, 1994; Toth, 1996).

However, both recollection and familiarity are sensitive to conceptual manipulations to some extent, and thus the results are consistent with models that propose that familiarity can support conceptual as well as perceptual information (Jacoby, 1991). For example, as just described, although deep compared with shallow processing, full compared with divided attention, and generate compared with read conditions tend to increase recollection more than familiarity, in all of these cases, familiarity is found to increase to some extent. Moreover, conceptual fluency manipulations lead to increases in familiarity, suggesting that familiarity is sensitive to conceptual manipulations (Rajaram & Geraci, 2000).

So, although there is support for the claim that recollection and familiarity are differentially sensitive to conceptual and perceptual manipulations, the conceptual/perceptual distinction does not provide a completely satisfactory characterization of these processes. These results indicate that familiarity cannot be described as reflecting the activation of entirely presemantic or lexical representations, as Mandler and Atkinson had initially proposed, but it must reflect in part conceptual fluency (Jacoby, 1991) or the products of a semantic memory system (Tulving, 1985).

FAMILIARITY IS LESS ATTENTION DEMANDING THAN RECOLLECTION, BUT NEITHER PROCESS IS COMPLETELY AUTOMATIC

Jacoby (1991) has argued that familiarity is more automatic than recollection. Thus, the two processes are expected to be differentially sensitive to variables that have different effects on controlled and automatic processes (see Hasher & Zacks, 1979; Shiffrin & Schneider, 1977). In general, as already discussed, familiarity is more automatic than recollection in the sense that during time of test, familiarity is less demanding of attention, faster, and more perceptual than recollection. It should be pointed out, however, that familiarity is not automatic in an absolute sense. For example, familiarity does appear to decrease with extremely short response deadlines and when subjects are told to ignore the study items. Moreover, familiarity is not automatic in the sense that the subject is unable to control whether that process leads to a behavioral response. There are numerous examples indicating that subjects have control over whether familiarity is used as a basis of responding. For example, recollection can be used to oppose the effects of familiarity (e.g., Jacoby, 1991), familiarity-based responses can be withheld until recollection is completed (e.g., in remember-know conditions), subjects can vary their response criterion on familiarity-based responses (Yonelinas, 1994), and fluency effects on familiarity can be reduced if subjects become aware that fluency is being manipulated (Jacoby & Whitehouse, 1989). Thus, it appears that although the products of familiarity, compared with recollection, are available relatively automatically, the use of familiarity information is not obligatory.

AT VERY SHORT RETENTION INTERVALS FAMILIARITY DECREASES MORE RAPIDLY THAN RECOLLECTION DOES

Several models assume that familiarity should decrease more rapidly than recollection. For example, models that assume that familiarity reflects temporary item activation (Atkinson & Juola, 1974; Mandler, 1980) lead to the expectation that familiarity should decrease rather rapidly, and Eichenbaum et al. (1994) proposed that the parahippocampal region, which supports familiarity-based responses, reflects an intermediate-term storage system that, at least initially, should exhibit a faster forgetting rate than recollection should. In agreement with the latter claim, the results suggest that over short retention intervals (i.e., 8 to 32 intervening items), familiarity does decrease rapidly, whereas recollection is relatively unaffected (Yonelinas & Levy, 2002). However, across longer-term delays (i.e., across minutes to months), both recollection and familiarity are found to exhibit considerable forgetting (Gardiner, 1988).

The finding that familiarity decreases more rapidly over short-term retention intervals than does recollection provides support for the notion that familiarity reflects temporary activation. However, familiarity and recollection often remain well above chance after 6 months, indicating that this "activation" can be quite long-lived. Thus, even though familiarity does initially decrease rapidly, it appears to be more than simply an "intermediate-term" storage.

FAMILIARITY CAN SUPPORT NOVEL LEARNING

Several influential models have assumed that familiarity reflects the activation of preexisting representations (Atkinson & Juola, 1974; Cary & Reder, 2003; Mandler, 1980). As such, familiarity should not support learning of novel items or of novel associations between items. However, it is now quite clear that familiarity does support memory for new items such as random geometric shapes, nonwords, and unfamiliar faces (Gardiner & Java, 1990; Parkin, Gardiner, & Rosser, 1995; Yonelinas & Jacoby, 1995). These results indicate that familiarity is not limited to item activation, at least as described by these early models. In addition, although familiarity often does not support the learning of random associations between items (Yonelinas, 1997), there are some conditions in which it does appear to be useful in supporting memory for new associations (Yonelinas et al., 1999).

To account for familiarity-based learning of novel associations, two different accounts have been proposed. First, by the "unitization account" (Yonelinas et al., 1999), associative recognition should not be supported by familiarity if the two paired items are treated as separate items that are simply associated with one another. However, if the two items are processed as a single unit, then that "item" can become more familiar, and thus, familiarity can be used to support memory for that association. In line with this hypothesis is the finding that familiarity does support associative recognition between different parts of faces when the faces are presented in an upright orientation and thus are processed as a single coherent face, whereas it does not support associative recognition when the faces are presented upside-down and thus processed as separate components (Yonelinas et al., 1999; also see Jäger & Mecklinger, 2009). In addition, familiarity does not support word-word associations when the words are encoded as separate items, but it does support performance when the words are processed as new compound words. In addition, amnesic patients with selective recollection impairments do have pronounced impairments on tests of word-word associative recognition, but these impairments are significantly reduced if the word pairs form existing compound words (Giovanello, Keane, & Verfaellie, 2006). In addition, the associative recognition impairments in these patients are reduced even for random word pairs, as long as the word pairs are encoded as if they formed new compound words (Quamme et al., 2007).

A related account is the "processing domain" account that assumes that familiarity can support memory for novel associations as long as the two items are processed in the same cortical regions, whereas recollection is needed to associate items that are processed in different cortical regions (Mayes et al. 2004; Mayes, Mantaldi, & Migo, 2007). Results supporting this account include the finding that amnesic patients sometimes do exhibit a greater impairment in associative recognition when the items are from different processing types (e.g., faces-words), than when they come from the same processing domain (face-face, e.g., Mayes, Mantaldi, & Migo, 2007; Vargha-Khadem et al., 1997). Future work that more directly contrasts these two accounts will be useful in further understanding exactly when familiarity will support novel learning.

RECOLLECTION DEPENDS CRITICALLY ON THE HIPPOCAMPUS, WHEREAS FAMILIARITY DEPENDS ON THE PERIRHINAL CORTEX

Neuropsychological studies of memory are important in determining which brain regions are necessary for a given cognitive function. Since the early reports on amnesic patients such as HM who suffered damage to the medial temporal lobes, it became clear that these regions play an essential role in supporting episodic memory. Early work by Huppert and Peircy indicated that medial temporal lobe patients can discriminate between old and new items relatively well, but they are profoundly impaired at discriminating between recently and frequently presented items (e.g., Huppert & Piercy 1978; Mayes, Baddeley, Cockburn, & Meudell, 1989; Meudell, Mayes, Ostergaard, & Pickering, 1985). Based in part on these results, several dual-process models have assumed that the medial temporal lobes are particularly important for recollection (Tulving, Mandler, Jacoby, Yonelinas). Subsequent studies using the remember-know procedure (e.g., Blaxton & Theodore 1997; Kishiyama, Yonelinas, & Lazzara, 2004; Knowlton & Squire, 1995; Moscovitch & McAndrews, 2002; Schacter, Verfaellie, & Pradere, 1996), the process dissociation procedure (Verfaellie & Treadwell, 1993), and the ROC procedure (Yonelinas, Kroll, Dobbins, Lazzara, & Knight, 1998) have verified that recollection is more impaired by medial temporal lobe damage than is familiarity. Although, in all these studies, familiarity was slightly reduced as well, suggesting that familiarity is not entirely independent of the medial temporal lobes.

More recently, a number of models have made more specific assumptions about regions within the medial temporal lobe that may be functionally specialized to support recollection and familiarity (Brown & Aggleton, 2001; Eichenbaum et al., 1994; Norman & O'Reilly, 2001). Namely, it has been argued that the hippocampus is responsible for binding together arbitrary associations necessary to support recollection, whereas the anterior parahippocampal gyrus (including the perirhinal, entorhinal, and possibly the parahippocampal cortex) is critical for supporting item familiarity. These models predict that hippocampal damage should disrupt recollection but not familiarity, whereas damage to surrounding medial temporal lobe regions should lead to deficits in familiarity. These models can account for the pattern of severely impaired recollection and mildly deficient familiarity in the amnesic studies described here, because these studies included patients with damage to the hippocampal and the surrounding medial temporal lobes. However, the strongest prediction of these models is that patients with selective hippocampal damage should exhibit a selective impairment in recollection.

More recent research has tested these theories by attempting to dissociate recollection and familiarity in patients with selective hippocampal damage. Typically, these patients developed memory loss following transient cerebral hypoxia (oxygen deprivation). The hippocampus is particularly vulnerable to hypoxic-ischemic damage, and postmortem studies as well as structural imaging studies have demonstrated that mild hypoxia results in neuronal loss confined largely to the hippocampus (e.g., Gadian et al., 2000; Hopkins, Kesner, & Goldstein, 1995; Zola-Morgan, Squire, & Amaral, 1986). An important caveat about these studies is that it is difficult to rule out damage to regions outside the hippocampus, particularly in cases in which the hypoxic event is severe. Notably, structural magnetic resonance imaging scans can fail to reveal neuronal loss that is apparent in histological examinations (Rempel-Clower, Zola, Squire, & Amaral, 1996).

Studies using estimation methods have largely confirmed that recollection can be selectively impaired in hypoxic patients. For example, in one study, we examined recognition confidence ROCs and found that mildly hypoxic patients exhibited severe deficits in recollection but demonstrated normal familiarity (Yonelinas et al., 2002). The results were verified by using remember-know measures in the same patients. Moreover, the covariation between recall, recognition, and hypoxic severity (as indexed by coma duration) was examined using structural equation modeling methods in a large sample of hypoxic patients and indicated that hypoxic severity predicted the degree to which recollection, but not familiarity, was impaired. A similar pattern of deficient recollection and preserved familiarity was reported in a patient with selective hippocampal atrophy related to meningitis (Aggleton et al., 2005).

However, some studies of severely impaired hypoxic patients have found decreases in both recollection and familiarity (Cipolotti et al., 2006; Manns, Hopkins, Reed, Kitchener, & Squire, 2003). Although, the familiarity deficits observed in these patients could be due to damage outside the hippocampus (in some cases, parahippocampal atrophy has been documented, whereas in others, either no magnetic resonance imaging data was reported or data was not reported for regions known to be involved in recognition memory). In addition, because these subjects were selected to have low memory scores, it is perhaps not surprising that they had low recollection and familiarity scores. Nonetheless, the results do highlight the importance of looking for convergent results from animal lesion studies, where one has direct control over the lesion location. In fact, recent ROC results from rats performing item recognition tasks indicate that selective hippocampal lesions do lead to a selective deficit in recollection (Fortin et al., 2004). In addition, in associative recognition tasks, ROC results indicate that control rats base performance on recollection, whereas after selective hippocampal lesions, recollection was effectively eliminated (Sauvage, Fortin, Owens, Yonelinas, & Eichenbaum, 2008). The animal lesion results are further supported by human neuroimaging results, indicating that the hippocampus is involved in recollection, whereas the perirhinal cortex is involved in familiarity (for a recent review see Diana & Ranganath, Chapter 7 of this volume).

One important question, however, is whether it is possible to find lesions that can selectively impair familiarity. By some models, the perirhinal cortex provides a gateway to the hippocampus such that damage to the perirhinal cortex will necessarily disrupt both recollection and familiarity (Fernandez & Tendolkar, 2006). However, the hippocampus also receives projections from various regions such as the parahippocampal cortex, thus it is possible that damage to the perirhinal cortex may selectively impair familiarity. Two recent studies support the latter possibility. First, we recently examined a patient with relatively selective damage to the perirhinal cortex (Bowles et al., 2007). Based on the results from a variety of different measurement methods, including remember-know, ROC, and response-speed procedures, we found that the patient exhibited a deficit in familiarity, whereas recollection was normal. In addition, we examined memory and brain changes in a group of 157 normal aged adults (Yonelinas et al., 2007). We found that age-related reductions in hippocampal volume were more highly correlated with recall than recognition, whereas decreased entorhinal volumes were more directly related to recognition than recall. Structural equation modeling indicated that hippocampal volume was directly related to recollection, whereas entorhinal volume was directly related to familiarity. Together the results leave little doubt that the hippocampus is most critical for recollection, whereas the surrounding medial temporal lobe is most critical for familiarity.

CONCLUSIONS

If Aristotle were to see what we have learned about recollection over the past 2000 years, I wonder what he would think. The recent work linking these processes to regions in the medial temporal lobe might not fit well with his ideas that memory was stored in the heart, but in some ways, much of the recent work examining the nature of recollection and familiarity can be seen as a direct continuation of his writings on memory and recollection. My guess is that he would be happy to see that the questions he concerned himself with have led to such a productive field of scientific study, and he may well take some pride in realizing that the questions he contemplated are sufficiently deep that they will keep us busy for a long time to come.

REFERENCES

Aggleton, J. P., & Brown, M. W. (1999). Episodic memory, amnesia, and the hippocampal-anterior thalamic axis. *Behavioral and Brain Sciences, 22*, 425–89.

Aggleton J. P., Vann, S. D., Denby, C., Dix, S., Mayes, A. R., Roberts, N., & Yonelinas, A. P. (2005). Sparing of the familiarity component of recognition memory in a patient with hippocampal pathology. *Neuropsychologia, 43*, 810–23.

Atkinson, R. C., & Juola, J. F. (1974). Search and decision processes in recognition memory. In D. H. Krantz, R. C. Atkinson, R. D. Luce & P. Suppes (Eds.), *Contemporary developments in mathematical psychology (Vol.1): Learning, memory and thinking* (pp. 243–293). San Francisco: Freeman.

Baddeley, A., Vargha-Khadem, F., & Mishkin, M. (2001). Preserved recognition in a case of developmental amnesia: Implications for the acquisition of semantic memory? *Journal of Cognitive Neuroscience, 13*, 357–69.

Blaxton, T. A., & Theodore, W. H. (1997). The role of the temporal lobes in recognizing visuospatial materials: Remembering versus knowing. *Brain and Cognition, 35*, 5–25.

Bodner, G. E., & Lindsay, D. S. (2003). Remembering and knowing in context. *Journal of Memory and Language, 48*, 563–80.

Bowles, B., Crupi, C., Mirsattari, S. M., Pigott, S. E., Parrent, A. G., Pruessner, J. C., . . . Köhler, S. (2007). Impaired familiarity with preserved recollection after anterior temporal-lobe resection that spares the hippocampus. *Proceedings of the National Academy of Sciences of the United States of America, 104*, 16382–7.

Brown, M. W., & Aggleton, J. P. (2001). Recognition memory: What are the roles of the perirhinal cortex and hippocampus? *Nature Review Neuroscience, 2*, 51–61.

Cary, M., & Reder, L. M. (2003). A dual-process account of the list-length and strength-based mirror effects in recognition. *Memory and Language, 49*, 231–48.

Cipolotti, L., Bird, C., Good, T., Macmanus, D., Rudge, P., & Shallice, T. (2006). Recollection and familiarity in dense hippocampal amnesia: A case study. *Neuropsychologia, 44*, 489–506.

Cohen, N. J., Poldrack, R. A., & Eichenbaum, H. (1997). Memory for items and memory for relations in the procedural/declarative memory framework. *Memory, 5*, 131–78.

Conway, L. N. (2005). Memory and the self. *Journal of Memory and Language, 53*, 594–628.

DeCarlo, L. T. (2002). Signal detection theory with finite mixture distributions: Theoretical developments with applications to recognition memory. *Psychological Review, 109*, 710–21.

Dewhurst, S. A., & Conway, M. A. (1994). Pictures, images, and recollective experience. *Journal of Experimental Psychology: Learning, Memory, and Cognition, 20*, 1088–98.

Diana, R. A., & Ranganath, C. (2011). Neural basis of recollection: Evidence from neuroimaging and electrophysiological research. In S. Ghetti & P. J. Bauer (Eds.), *Origins and development of recollection: Perspectives from psychology and neuroscience* (pp. 168–87). New York: Oxford University Press.

Diana, R. A., Reder, L. M., Arndt, J., & Park, H. (2006). Models of recognition: A review of arguments in favor of a dual-process account. *Psychonomic Bullettin Review, 131*, 1–21.

Eichenbaum, H., Otto, T., & Cohen, N. J. (1994). Two functional components of the hippocampal memory system. *Behavioral and Brain Sciences, 17*, 449–517.

Fernández, G., & Tendolkar, I. (2006). The rhinal cortex: "Gatekeeper" of the declarative memory system. *Trends in Cognitive Science, 10*, 358–62.

Fortin, N. J., Wright, S. P., & Eichenbaum, H. (2004). Recollection-like memory retrieval in rats is dependent on the hippocampus. *Nature, 431*, 188–91.

Gadian, D. G., Aicardi, J., Watkins, K. E., Porter, D. A., Mishkin, M., & Vargha-Khadem, F. (2000). Developmental amnesia associated with early hypoxic-ischaemic injury. *Brain, 123*, 499–507.

Gardiner, J. M. (1988). Functional aspects of recollective experience. *Memory and Cognition, 16*, 309–13.

Gardiner, J. M., & Java, R. I. (1990). Recollective experience in word and nonword recognition. *Memory and Cognition, 18*, 23–30.

Giovanello, K. S., Keane, M. M., & Verfaellie, M. (2006). The contribution of familiarity to associative memory in amnesia. *Neuropsychologia, 44*, 1859–65.

Gregg, V. H., & Gardiner, J. M. (1994). Recognition memory and awareness: A large effect of study-test modalities on "know" responses following a highly perceptual orienting task. *European Journal of Cognitive Psychology, 6*, 131–47.

Gruppuso, V., Lindsay, D. S., & Kelley, C. M. (1997). The process-dissociation procedure and similarity: Defining and estimating recollection and familiarity in recognition memory. *Journal of Experimental Psychology: Learning, Memory, and Cognition, 23*, 259–78.

Hasher, L., & Zacks, R. T. (1979). Automatic and effortful processes in memory. *Journal of Experimental Psychology: General, 108*, 356–88.

Holdstock, J. S., Mayes, A. R., Roberts, N., Cezayirli, E., Isaac, C. L., O'Reilly, R. C., & Norman, K. A. (2002). Under what conditions is recognition spared relative to recall after selective hippocampal damage in humans? *Hippocampus, 12*, 341–51.

Holdstock, J. S., Mayes, A. R., Gong, Q. Y., Roberts, N., & Kapur, N. (2005). Item recognition is less impaired than recall and associative recognition in a patient with selective hippocampal damage. *Hippocampus, 15*, 203–15.

Hopkins, R. O., Kesner, R. P., & Goldstein, M. (1995). Item and order recognition memory in subjects with hypoxic brain injury. *Brain and Cognition, 27*, 180–201.

Huppert, F. A., & Piercy, M. (1978). The role of trace strength in recency and frequency judgments by amnesic and control subjects. *Quarterly Journal of Experimental Psychology, 30*, 347–54.

Jacoby, L. L. (1991). A process dissociation framework: Separating automatic from intentional uses of memory. *Journal of Memory and Language, 30,* 513–41.

Jacoby, L. L., & Whitehouse, K. (1989). An illusion of memory: False recognition influenced by unconscious perception. *Journal of Experimental Psychology: General, 118,* 126–35.

Jäger, T. & Mecklinger, A. (2009). Familiarity supports associative recognition memory for face stimuli that can be unitized: Evidence from receiver operating characteristics. *European Journal of Cognitive Psychology, 21,* 35–60.

James, W. (1890). *The principles of psychology.* New York: Dover Publications Inc.

Khoe, W., Kroll, N. E. A., Yonelinas, A. P., Dobbins, I. G., & Knight, R. T. (2000). The contribution of recollection and familiarity to yes-no and forced-choice recognition tests in healthy subjects and amnesics. *Neuropsychologia, 38,* 1333–41.

Kishiyama, M. M., Yonelinas, A. P., & Lazzara, M. M. (2004). The von Restorff effect in amnesia: The contribution of the hippocampal system to novelty-related memory enhancements. *Journal of Cognitive Neuroscience, 16,* 15–23.

Knowlton, B. J., & Squire, L. R. (1995). Remembering and knowing: Two different expressions of declarative memory. *Journal of Experimental Psychology: Learning, Memory, and Cognition, 21,* 699–710.

Mandler, G. (1980). Recognizing: The judgment of previous occurrence. *Psychological Review, 87,* 252–71.

Manns, J. R., Hopkins, R. O., Reed, J. M., Kitchener, E. G., & Squire, L. R. (2003). Recognition memory and the human hippocampus. *Neuron, 37,* 171–80.

Mayes, A. R., Baddeley, A. D., Cockburn, J., & Meudell, P. R. (1989). Why are amnesic judgments of recency and frequency made in a qualitatively different way from those of normal people? *Cortex, 25,* 479–88.

Mayes, A. R., Holdstock, J. S., Isaac, C. L., Montaldi, D., Grigor, J., Gummer, A., . . . Norman, K. A. (2004). Associative recognition in a patient with selective hippocampal lesions and relatively normal item recognition. *Hippocampus, 14,* 763–84.

Mayes, A., Montaldi, D., & Migo, E. (2007). Associative memory and the medial temporal lobes. *Trends in Cognitive Science, 11,* 126–35.

Meudell, P. R., Mayes, A. R., Ostergaard, A., & Pickering, A. (1985). Recency and frequency judgments in alcoholic amnesics and normal people with poor memory. *Cortex, 21,* 487–511.

Moscovitch, D. A., & McAndrews, M. P. (2002). Material-specific deficits in "remembering" in patients with unilateral temporal lobe epilepsy and excisions. *Neuropsychologia, 40,* 1335–42.

Norman, K. A., & O'Reilly, R. C. (2003). Modeling hippocampal and neocortical contributions to recognition memory: A complementary-learning-systems approach. *Psychological Review, 110,* 611–46.

Parkin, A. J., Gardiner, J. M., & Rosser, R. (1995). Functional aspects of recollective experience in face recognition. *Consciousness and Cognition, 4,* 387–98.

Quamme, J. R., Yonelinas, A. P., & Norman, K. A. (2007). Effect of unitization on associative recognition in amnesia. *Hippocampus, 17,* 192–200.

Rajaram, S. (1993). Remembering and knowing: Two means of access to the personal past. *Memory and Cognition, 21,* 89–102.

Rajaram, S., & Geraci, L. (2000). Conceptual fluency selectively influences knowing. *Journal of Experimental Psychology: Learning, Memory, and Cognition, 26,* 1070–74.

Rempel-Clower, N. L., Zola, S. M., Squire, L. R., & Amaral, D. G. (1996). Three cases of enduring memory impairment after bilateral damage limited to the hippocampal formation. *Journal of Neuroscience, 16*, 5233–55.

Rugg, M. D., & Curran, T. (2007). Event-related potentials and recognition memory. *Trends in Cognitive Science, 11*, 251–7.

Rugg, M. D., & Yonelinas, A. P. (2003). Human recognition memory: A cognitive neuroscience perspective. *Trends in Cognitive Science, 7*, 313–9.

Sauvage, M. M., Fortin, N. J., Owens, C. B., Yonelinas, A. P., & Eichenbaum, H. (2008). Recognition memory: Opposite effects of hippocampal damage on recollection and familiarity. *Nature Neuroscience, 11*, 16–8.

Schacter, D. L., Verfaellie, M., & Pradere, D. (1996). The neuropsychology of memory illusions: False recall and recognition in amnesic patients. *Journal of Memory and Language, 35*, 319–34.

Scoville, W. B., & Milner, B. (1957). Loss of recent memory after bilateral hippocampal lesions. *Journal of Neurology, Neurosurgery and Psychiatry, 20*, 11–21.

Sherman, S. J., Atri, A., Hasselmo, M. E., Stern, C. E., & Howard, M. W. (2003). Scopolamine impairs human recognition memory: Data and modeling. *Behavioral Neuroscience, 117*, 526–39.

Shiffrin, R. M., & Schneider, W. (1977). Controlled and automatic human information processing: II. Perceptual learning, automatic attending and a general theory. *Psychological Review, 84*, 127–90.

Toth, J. P. (1996). Conceptual automaticity in recognition memory: Levels-of-processing effects on familiarity. *Canadian Journal of Experimental Psychology, 50*, 123–38.

Tulving, E. (1985). Memory and consciousness. *Canadian Psychology, 26*, 1–12.

Tulving, E., & Markowitsch, H. J. (1998). Episodic and declarative memory: Role of the hippocampus. *Hippocampus, 8*, 198–204.

Vargha-Khadem, F., Gadian, D. G., Watkins, K. E., Connelly, A., Van Paesschen, W., & Mishkin, M. (1997). Differential effects of early hippocampal pathology on episodic and semantic memory. *Science, 277*, 376–80.

Verfaellie, M., & Treadwell, J. R. (1993). Status of recognition memory in amnesia. *Neuropsychology, 7*, 5–13.

Yonelinas, A. P. (1994). Receiver-operating characteristics in recognition memory: Evidence for a dual-process model. *Journal of Experimental Psychology: Learning, Memory, and Cognition, 20*, 1341–54.

Yonelinas, A. P. (1997). Recognition memory ROCs for item and associative information: The contribution of recollection and familiarity. *Memory and Cognition, 25*, 747–63.

Yonelinas, A. P. (2001). Components of episodic memory: The contribution of recollection and familiarity. *The Philosophical Transactions of the Royal Society, Series B, 356*, 1363–74.

Yonelinas, A. P. (2002). The nature of recollection and familiarity: A review of 30 years of research. *Journal of Memory and Language, 46*, 441–517.

Yonelinas, A. P., & Jacoby, L. L. (1994). Dissociations of processes in recognition memory: Effects of interference and of response speed. *Canadian Journal of Experimental Psychology, 48*, 516–34.

Yonelinas, A. P., & Jacoby, L. L. (1995). The relation between remembering and knowing as bases for recognition: Effects of size congruency. *Journal of Memory and Language, 34*, 622–43.

Yonelinas, A. P., Kroll, N. E. A., Dobbins, I., Lazzara, M., & Knight, R. T. (1998). Recollection and familiarity deficits in amnesia: Convergence of remember-know, process dissociation, and receiver operating characteristic data. *Neuropsychology, 12,* 323–39.

Yonelinas, A. P., Kroll, N. E. A., Dobbins, I. G., & Soltani, M. (1999). Recognition memory for faces: When familiarity supports associative recognition. *Psychonomic Bulletin and Review, 6,* 418–661.

Yonelinas, A. P., Kroll, N. E., Quamme, J. R., Lazzara, M. M., Sauvé, M. J., Widaman, K. F., & Knight, R. T. (2002). Effects of extensive temporal lobe damage or mild hypoxia on recollection and familiarity. *Nature Neuroscience, 5,* 1236–41.

Yonelinas, A. P., & Levy, B. J. (2002). Dissociating familiarity from recollection in human recognition memory: Different rates of forgetting over short retention intervals. *Psychonomic Bulletin Review, 9,* 575–82.

Yonelinas, A. P., & Parks, C. M. (2007). Receiver operating characteristics (ROCs) in recognition memory: A review. *Psychologic Bulletin, 133,* 800–32.

Yonelinas, A. P., Widaman, K., Mungas, D., Reed, B., Weiner, M. W., & Chui, H. C. (2007). Memory in the aging brain: Doubly dissociating the contribution of the hippocampus and entorhinal cortex. *Hippocampus, 17,* 1134–40.

Zola-Morgan, S., Squire, L. R., & Amaral, D. G. (1986). Human amnesia and the medial temporal lobe region: Enduring memory impairment following a bilateral lesion limited to field CA1 of the hippocampus. *Journal of Neuroscience, 6,* 2950–67.

2

Development of Meaning-Conserving Memory

KATHERINE NELSON

> Regulatory actions provide a threshold for memory storage, presumably
> to ensure that only important, life-serving experiences are learned.
> —KANDEL, *IN SEARCH OF MEMORY* (2006, p. 264)

Based on his studies of cellular and molecular processes of basic learning and
memory functions, Nobel prize-winner Eric Kandel (in this quotation) emphasized the *meaning* of memory for organisms from the simple to the complex:
namely, the preservation of *life-serving* experiences. Such preservation necessitates distinguishing among possible information sources and their specific
contents in terms of their meanings for the organism. In this chapter, I consider
ways that memory as a *meaning-preserving system* develops in human infancy and
early childhood. In addressing how changes in meaning affect memory and the
process of recollection, I consider the nature of *experience* in the social and cultural world of childhood and the related developing meaning system of the child
(Nelson, 2007; Nelson & Fivush, 2004). I further explore the idea that functional
changes in memory accompany an expansion of consciousness, a product of *interlocking systems* of the developing child and social and cultural transactions during
the critical early years.

The chapter is organized as follows. First, I sketch the systems involved in basic
memory and consider how recollection may relate to that construct. Next I discuss the general outlines of experience and memory within dynamic developmental systems (based on Nelson, 2007), noting constraints on early developments
of the meaning and memory system. Finally I describe how the scope of consciousness expands from the intersection of experiential and social-cultural
change and its relation to the developing personal memory system.

MEMORY AS A MEANING-CONSERVING SYSTEM

The narrow claim consistent with the quotation from Kandel is that memory in general conserves learning that is life-serving for the organism, where what is life-serving is dictated by the biological systems and states of the organism. The broader claim is that memory is an experience-conserving system in which meaning serves as a filter for long-term conservation. It follows that how we understand memory is necessarily tied to *how we understand the experience of the organism* (in this case, the growing infant-child). This view inevitably challenges the usual conception of memory as an information processing system by its emphasis on the dynamics of *organismic meaning*. By definition, *information* exists in infinite varieties and forms in the world, but from the view of any specific organism at any given point of time, only a minute fraction of the possible information available is potentially meaningful to the organism and, therefore, a potential component of an ongoing experience. Meaning can then be thought of as a *filter* for experience, and for any resulting experience-conserving memory.

This conception requires further unpacking of the notion of "meaning for the organism." For the simple organisms studied by Kandel, life-preserving seems a simple biologically-based concept, and to a considerable extent, this is true for all organisms: the urgency of sufficient food and other necessities are clearly meaningful. What is meaningful for complex creatures like humans goes beyond simple necessities, including many inherent interests, but also limits. Our kind values the sight, sound, and close contact of other people from birth, but is restricted in terms of some of the possible information to be derived from our senses in comparison with other mammals. Some of what we find meaningful or life-serving is biologically set, but much of what humans find meaningful are products of experience, just as experience is a filtered product of meaning. Thus the study of memory, experience, and meaning are intertwined (Nelson, 2007). What a particular experience *means for the organism*, for example, its value in seeking food or avoiding predators, is the basis for memory retention or for its oblivion. Therefore, to understand memory in its most basic as well as derivative forms, it is critical to identify the potential activities, experiences, functions, and values of the organism that determine meaning for each individual. In addition, meaning changes with development for any organism, and this is particularly true for human development: What is meaningful for the infant is unlikely to be so for the older child. The reverse is true as well: What an older child or adult finds meaningful is unlikely to be seen in the same way by the infant.

Basic Memory

The kind of memory that we share with others in our phylogenetic line (i.e., primates, or more generally, mammals) and that, at least from early infancy, is available to human infants, I term here "basic memory" without any qualification as to whether it is implicit or explicit, procedural or declarative. It may be appropriate to designate some of this memory as declarative (Bauer, 2007; Mandler, 2004), and it may be that some memory originally implicit or procedural later becomes accessible to voluntary recall, as Donald (1991) argued with respect to the hominid evolutionary scale. I begin here with the proposition that basic adaptive memory is focused on conserving meaningful patterns from the perceptual analysis of experienced events (Donald, 1991; Nelson, 1993, 2005a). Such patterns in memory function as predictors of the course of events that the organism can expect to experience in future encounters in the world. In this functional system, *meaning*, identified as significant information relevant to maintaining life and to taking action, determines the retention or loss of memory contents. The sequence and composition of recurrent events are especially meaningful for this purpose and are conserved in schematic representations (scripts or routines), together with alternative components and pathways that depend on specific conditions.

Bauer (2007) describes the early development of memory as involving the same processes as later (adult) memory but with less effectiveness and efficiency, specifically in the process of consolidation. This is a very important point. However, knowledge of the neural processes involved in memory do not illuminate the *selection* of information to be preserved through consolidation. As argued here, selection for memory is necessary and is not random at any age. What is selected changes with development because what is meaningful at successive points in development differs from what was meaningful at an earlier point or in a different context. For this reason, it would not be surprising to discover that basic memory is quite chary with regard to what is entered into long-term memory and what is retained there over a long time span. Old memories may be replaced by new findings that differ from the old, or they may be updated with additional information. In such a basic system, generalized memory configurations (schemas and scripts) may contain alternate possible entries, whereas a singular happening may be discarded if it is not repeated or is deemed irrelevant to ongoing life functions (Nelson, 1993).

Adult human memory in contrast seems to be almost inexhaustible and is often filled with detailed episodic remnants, suggesting a watershed in the evolution of humans and the ontogeny of memory that requires different or additional explanations from early basic memory. As adults, we keep general knowledge (semantic memory), much of it held in nonconscious structures that guide daily life, and we also hold onto useless as well as useful stuff, when viewed from the perspective of life-serving information. Although we may try to keep our knowledge base updated, we also hang onto old memories for a very long time. We tend to remember the layouts of all the houses we have lived in since childhood, for example, and some middle-aged adults can recite telephone numbers of high school friends whose numbers have long since been deleted from telephone circuits. Many theories have addressed the discrepancy between the apparent fragility of early memory and the persistence of later memories in terms of "infantile amnesia." The account here proposes that social and cultural uses of past and future have revised the *function* of memory in human lives and thus its *meaning* for older individuals, producing changes in memory process and structure itself during the preschool and school years. The basis for this account lies in the relation of experience and its changing forms to meaning and resulting memory systems, as discussed in the following sections.

Developing Memory

The topic of this volume is *recollection*, which I take to be conscious remembering for some purpose. Bauer's (2007) masterful review of early and later memory concludes that very young children have established long-term declarative memories that may be recollected in or out of their original context. Delayed imitation has been cited as evidence of recollection and thus of declarative memory in children as young as 9 months. Because few children are capable of verbalizing their memories prior to about 2 years of age, the attribution of such early recollection raises important questions. Is it different from memory that exists in other animals, as well as in very young infants? In my understanding, recollection implies that the memory is "brought to mind," and I am not convinced that delayed imitation is evidence of this state, whereas verbalization of the memory does appear to be evidence of having the memory "in mind" or in recollection. Recollection involves conscious awareness, *specificity, subjectivity*, and *reflection*. *Specificity* distinguishes memories of specific persons, places, or events from general knowledge. The difference can be seen in varying reports such as the following (perhaps in response to a question "Do you remember the park?" in a discussion of childhood scenes):

> I remember the merry-go-round.
> I remember riding on the merry-go-round.
> I remember riding on the merry-go-round in the park on my third birthday when . . . (further detailed episode).

Whereas all of these statements might occur *within* a recollection, referring to a specific item (*the* merry-go-round), the first and second statements have a vague and general quality, perhaps referring to a general script for an activity that was not specific with respect to time or episodic features. The third statement, however, is clearly "recollecting" a specific episode. Unfortunately, determining how specific a memory is for a preverbal child (or for a nonhuman) can be very difficult; evidence derived from recognition of items or imitated action may point to either specific memory or generalized knowledge (Nelson, 1994).

Subjectivity distinguishes between general knowledge (e.g., knowing a merry-go-round by sight or by verbal reference) and reports of personal experience from a first-person (rather than a third-person) perspective. All of the preceding examples reflect subjectivity ("I remember"), but like specificity, subjectivity is also very difficult to establish for pre- or nonverbal individuals who cannot make their actions or reports reflect these distinctions. All early memory is subjective in the sense of being private to the self, but the sense of subjectivity changes over developmental time as the distinction between self-memory and others' memory becomes salient (see section Private Minds). The subjectivity of recollection then develops over the preschool years as the child becomes increasingly aware of the self as a distinctive perspective that differs in multiple internal as well as external ways from that of others. The internal ways gradually become revealed through the medium of verbal exchanges, including those of conversations about shared experiences, about events from the past not experienced by the child, and cultural narratives of many kinds, including stories.

Reflection characterizes recollection to the extent that the function of recollection is to *represent* what is in memory in a new conscious form, for oneself or for and with others, for the purpose of enjoyment (reminiscing), problem solving, or other interests. To some degree, the reflective function is defining of recollection. There is considerable overlap between the process of recollection and Tulving's construct of episodic memory (Tulving, 1993). Episodic memory is specified as memory for personally experienced episodes, although recollection may involve others' reports or other sources. Reminiscing is bringing episodic memory into public view and overlaps with the more general idea of recollecting. All these kinds are involved in what Suddendorf and Corballis (2007) call "time travel,"[1] and all these forms are products of development, with functions that go beyond those of "basic memory" as it exists in many animals from simple to complex, and presumably in the young infant (on the basis of the generally accepted assumption that episodic memory involves autonoetic awareness not developed in the first years of life).

RECOLLECTION AT 2 YEARS

When in early development recollecting begins is like so many similar questions in depending on our measures as well as on our understanding of recollection as a distinct function of memory. Given the limitations on experience and memory during the first years of life, we can be certain that recollection is less rich in the early years, more focused on a narrower sense of self and a less informed sense of the participation of others. The interconnectedness of these constructs appeared vividly in the study of presleep monologues by the 2-year-old Emily (Nelson, 1989b).[2] The original motivation for gathering data from a verbal 2-year-old talking to herself before falling asleep was to track what she might verbalize about her daily experiences as an indication of her experiential memory. I hoped thereby to gain insight into the nature of her perspective on the events of her everyday life; this hope was richly rewarded. As reported elsewhere, at the outset, when she was just 21 months, her verbalizations were mostly scattered across many different events. By 2 years of age, her recounts were more topic-focused, but also reflected

1. Tulving (1983) deserves credit for initiating this construct in the first paragraph of his 1983 book: "members of no other species possess quite the same ability to experience again now, in a different situation and perhaps in a different form, happenings from the past, and know that the experience refers to an event that occurred in another time and in another place. Other members of the animal kingdom . . . cannot travel back into the past in their own minds" (p. 1).

2. This research was carried out more than 25 years ago and published in part as *Narratives from the Crib* (Nelson,1989b; 2006).

a concentration on "what happens" sometimes in a puzzling way, at other times in a decisive "that's the way it is" format (e.g., "If ever we go to the airport we have to get some luggage." Nelson, 1989a, p. 68). At this young age, the child was clearly recollecting experiences from her life, both repeated and novel. Two other points are of interest: (a) The meaning for the child focused on the everyday, the how of things, not the when or why or even who. Close analysis of her use of pronouns and verb forms indicated, however, that she was making a distinction between those (few) activities under her own control and those in which she was a more passive participant (Gerhardt, 1989). (b) Memory was reflective in that the monologues consisted of fragments of episodes from her life, as well as fragments repeated from her parents' talk about future happenings. But throughout the third year, there were few examples of a specific memory for an event that had happened more than a day previously. The most extensive recounts were amalgams of routines, for example, the routine of getting up, having breakfast, and going to nursery school, in which a particular piece might come from a single episode but the entire construction was organized as an elaborate script or perhaps a model narrative.

Emily's memory musings at the age of 21 months brought the limitations of the perspective of self and personal meaning to light and made it available for examination (Nelson, 1989a). In one extended sequence, she seemed to be recollecting an account of "Daddy and Emmy" focused on washing in the basement that included the following statements: "That Daddy brings down basement washing," "so, Daddy brings down the, the washing on the basement," "My daddy went on a big free washing," "Emmy went down the, down cellar" among 46 other utterances in 1 night's monologue. This excerpt alone compels the conclusion that Emily was engaged in recollection of a reflective mode, externalizing her memory of experiences, possibly serving as a way of coming to better understanding of them. An evocative monologue at 2 years focused on sleeping at Tanta's house (her babysitter), being awakened by Mommy, and going home to sleep in her "regular" bed. This account was repeated several times in different forms of which the following is one version (Nelson, 1989a, p. 71–72):

> My sleep,
> Mommy came
> And Mommy get,
> Get up, time go home.
> . . .
> time to go ho-o-ome.
> Time to go home.
> Drink P-water.
> Yesterday did that.
> Now Emmy sleeping in regular bed.

This monologue includes temporal markers (e.g., came, time, yesterday, now) indicating it is "not now" in contrast to "now sleeping." However, there is no mention of thinking, knowing, or feeling as there would be months later at 33 months, 9 days in the following selection:

> We bought a baby, cause
>
> . . .
>
> we thought it was for Christmas
> but when we went to the store we didn't have our jacket on,
> but I saw some dolly,
> and I yelled at my mother and said
> I want one of those dolly.
> So after we were finished with the store,
> We went over to the dolly and she bought me one.
> So I have one.

In this monologue there is much language of consciousness (wanting, thinking, seeing, yelling, cause). There are also indications of narrative in the use of the language of time, the formal "my mother" rather than "mommy" and the concluding evaluation in terms of satisfaction of having what she asked for. The first example expressed feeling through prosody and episodic movement, but not directly through symbolic forms. The second example used both. At the latter point—not quite 3 years old—Emily was clearly capable not only of recollecting, but of narrativizing her memory into a coherent account of actions in relation to feelings and expression.[3]

For this 2-year-old, recollection of events was well established both for herself and in collaboration with her parents. However, no episode from this period of her life (21 months to 3 years) was retained until the age of 6 years (probed at that age by her mother), nor has she retained any memories from this period (age 2 to 3 years) into adulthood (Oster, 2006).[4] The omission of memories from this period of Emily's life, in spite of her very strong verbal capacities, raises the question of what the relation is of recollective memory development and the phenomena of infantile amnesia, if any. Recollection is critical to autobiographical memory, but it may not be sufficient for retention over the very long term. If it were, the highly verbal Emily should have had many memories from the age of 2 years, but these did not persist. Many of the questions surrounding the development of memory in infancy and early childhood have been resolved, indicating a long period of maturation of the neural systems involved that accounts for many limitations on its early functioning (see Bauer, 2007). Yet the richness of

---

3. Not all the monologues were as well-formed as these. See Nelson (1989b) for further elaboration and more examples, as well as analyses from different perspectives.

4. As was emphasized in the original report (Nelson, 1989b), Emily was an exceptionally verbal child from an academic family with a higher than average use of language in daily life. These characteristics enabled us to attain a view through her own language to her perspective on her experience. However, both that experience and her verbalization were unique. I approach any generalization from these observations with caution.

2-year-old Emily's recollections, reflections, and representations, in conjunction with the failure of their long-term retention imply the need for an additional account, given the current assumption that language is involved in long-term retention. In the next section I propose that memory considered in its functional contexts accounts for at least some of the developmental puzzles remaining.

EXPERIENCE, MEANING, AND MEMORY

This section expands on the relation between meaning and memory from the experiential perspective. The focus on experience, rather than learning, for example, has the important advantage that it recognizes the reality that experience, meaning, and memory are individuated for each child and adult. No two see a situation in exactly the same way, and no two acquire exactly the same things from exactly the same encounters. Variation is rampant, within and across ages, genders, classes, and cultures, as well as situations, times, and physical health. The idea of conserving meaningful experience in memory focuses on the individual's interests as a determiner of what aspect of an encounter may be retained. *What* is remembered from different encounters in different situations and contexts depends on a set of intersecting and interacting conditions of the organism and the world.

Experience

Experience is conceptualized here in terms of contextualizing sources that in combination bear on how any particular encounter is meaningfully interpreted by a given person.[5] Figure 2.1 distinguishes six sources, with biological conditions of the organism found on the left side of the diagram and social and cultural conditions of the environment on the right. At the top of the diagram, ongoing situational conditions (e.g., the physical setting of the encounter) are sited, whereas at the bottom, the constantly changing memory relevant to the present ongoing experiential encounter is found. Under some converging conditions, some meaningful aspects of experiences will be remembered by a person and become part of "past experience," entering in a spiral fashion into the conditioning of the next experiential encounter. The orientation of this hexagram is not intended to indicate dominance or precedence of any one constraint source; all are omnipresent, but in any given case, one or more might become more significant than others because of past experience, biological demands, social pressure, or other variable forces.

   We can think of each of these labeled dimensions as systems in continuous dynamic change. The *evolved state* of the organism, that is, its particular "evo-devo" human constitution, affects aspects of meaning/experience, including those of general species restrictions and potentials. For example, children's temperaments differ and affect how they meet and accept new experiences; sense systems

5. This account is a variant on that presented in Nelson (2007).

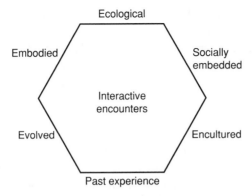

Figure 2.1. Contextualizing sources influencing personal interpretation of experiences

vary in how sensitive they are; and so on. These biological aspects vary in their organismic influence over time as well, such as different sex-determined growth patterns that affect children's specific experiences and become focal at puberty. *Embodiment* is conceived as individually variant, representing a dynamic system that changes rapidly in the first five years of life in ways that are familiar to everyone. In addition to physical growth and attained sensory and motoric capacities, the embodied brain, and more generally the nervous system as a whole, grows and matures over these years. The *ecology* of experiences may seem stable when considered in terms of definite locations such as home and school, yet conditions such as seasons and weather make clear that *when* a particular experience takes place, as well as *where*, may affect its memory. Over time, important new places are encountered (e.g., preschool) that must be explored and new routines enter memory to accommodate them.

The systems of most concern to the present consideration of meaning in memory include the *social* and *cultural*, the latter specifically including language and other symbolic systems. The social world of caretaking and guidance is paramount in terms of direct interaction with the growing child. These interactions undergo continuous change both in response to the subtle changes in the developing infant/child, and as social interactors provide new activities for the infant/child to experience. In addition, the circle of social interactors widens for the infant as new players (e.g., babysitters, teachers, child-care workers, extended family, and friends) enter the child's life and provide new experiences.

The critical characteristic of social conditions is that they may be directed specifically to the child, requiring attention and interaction in a way that other sources do not. The social factor is then the main intermediator for ecological and cultural conditions and messages. The symbolic world of cultural experience is always there, but it is not always available for the child's meaningful interpretive experience. It takes several years for the child to fully engage in verbal experiences, and more years still to comprehend the meaning of many of the cultural conditions of her own life. For example, contemporary cultural norms support differential treatment of male and female infants and young children in terms of toys provided and activities encouraged, as well as the clothing used to distinguish them. Preschool children do become aware—even hyperaware—of some of these differentiating signals, but the degree to which they are perceived as natural or culturally imposed may not enter consciousness until much later, if at all.

Experiential Change

To envision development within this experiential model is to view it in terms of *interlocking dynamic systems*, each system undergoing continuous change but at different paces or tempos. The idea of interlocking systems encompasses a theoretical partitioning of an active social organism—the person—without disturbing its unity, while simultaneously emphasizing the ongoing and changing interdependence of the parts of the whole. In addition, because this model includes externalities (social, cultural, and ecological) and does not remake them simply as mental representations, it implies that the biophysical boundary of the person is not the boundary of the whole person-system. This theoretical position is laid out more directly in the last section of this chapter on the expansion of consciousness.

Within any organism (including human infants and older persons) multiple systems interconnect; for example, systems of physical growth and change—the various life-sustaining organs, sensory systems, neural systems, perceptual and cognitive systems, including those of memory and knowledge systems. The brain functions to integrate internal systems to determine the meanings extracted from encounters with the dynamics of the social, cultural, and ecological interactions. What we call the *mind* serves as intermediator between the symbolic external and internal systems. As a result of these intermediations, self-systems emerge from interactive experiences. This is consistent I believe with Rubin's (2005) view that multiple sensory, perceptual, and cognitive systems enter into autobiographical memory. Rubin argues that "the self is not a single entity" but is distributed among these systems. "The continuity of the self emerges from the continuity of these separate systems and their interaction with each other and the world" (Rubin, 2005, p. 79).

Not only do the various semi-independent systems of the individual organism interconnect, but the resulting whole system interconnects with that of the ongoing independent systems of social interactors, such as parents, who are themselves changing over time in ways that interact with, and thus perturb, the child system. Changes in the child over time elicit responsive changes in parent behavior, and at other times, parent behavior changes in anticipation of expected changes in the child as growth and development proceed. Of greatest significance in child development, both (or all three) major personal systems (i.e., parents and child) are in flux; they are also in interlocking relationships that demand that changes in one be recognized and adapted to by changes in the other. This combination constitutes an *interlocking system* of two or more self-organizing dynamic systems as whole interactors. As suggested previously, it also implies that the child self-system extends beyond its physical boundaries to include interpretations of parental behavior and attitudes.

The psychological and social are thus interlocked in the sense that changes in one require adjustments in the others, while both are undergoing change at different rates. For example, as the child grows from infant to toddler to preschooler different expectations of gender roles, a cultural system component, enter the experiential milieu, indicating different clothes and toys for the child. At the same time, parents envoice new rules and routines as well as providing new cultural experiences, such as visits to a zoo where different sexes may be highlighted in animal activities or to a museum where paintings from different historical periods emphasize gender in different costumes and settings. A major point here is that the child's meaningful experience is in constant flux, the result of his or her own growth in body and mind, as well as the social and cultural conditions surrounding him or her.

Experience and Memory

How does this conception bear on the issues of memory? To consider this question, it is necessary to look at the ways in which experience changes over the first few years of life a bit more closely. Not surprisingly, some of the cognitive conditions of infancy and the early years are similar to those of the conditions of life experiences of nonhuman animals, but they change radically with the unique social and cultural—particularly the symbolic—conditions of human experience. One of these limiting conditions is basic memory, which, as previously noted, may focus on general knowledge to the relative neglect of preserving specificity of experience, as illustrated in the Emily monologues. Basic adaptive memory is limited in retention time and subjected to constant updating and discarding of old information; for example, information relevant to nursing and diapering. In function, basic memory is well adapted to forecasting what is expected to happen, automatically called up in a particular situation, and is not adapted to focus on the past in the reflective mode of recollection, as Tulving and his colleagues have emphasized (Tulving, 1993; see also Nelson, 1993, 2005). Two other considerations play a notable role in limiting experience and memory in the early years: private minds and source blindness.

PRIVATE MINDS

The initial two- to three-year period of mostly preverbal life (up to 3 years of age) structures the "private mind" of the infant and toddler. Adults have private minds in the sense that no other person can directly read what is in our minds. But infants have private minds in a much more restricted way, indeed in much the same way that other members of the animal kingdom do. The restriction works two ways: the infant cannot import information directly from another's mind, nor can she directly provide information from her own mind for someone else's use. Infants may "read" behavioral signs, including facial expressions while engaging in social activities. Some of these signs may be biologically specified, as human interpretations of facial expressions of emotions appear to be, whereas others may be learned through experience. Thus the young mind may "read" goals and intentions, as well as emotions, but in limited forms. This privacy barrier begins to be breached through social learning, based on imitation and collaborative action, prior to learning language during the second and third years of life. However, it is only when a child acquires a *symbolic system* for communicating with others—spoken language, sign language, or graphic or written language— that private *mental contents* can be effectively articulated and exchanged, enabling the sharing of memories, thoughts, knowledge, plans, imagination, and feelings on an explicit level that is not possible through other means. Development of these capacities for the *externalization* of mind contents importantly affects the child's development of memory as well as other cognitive functions, as argued in Nelson (1996, 2007).

SOURCE BLINDNESS

Related to the private mind, "source blindness" is an additional constraint on basic memory and experience in the early years. Prior to the point where children are open to understanding verbal reports from someone else, all memory is a distilla- tion of their own experience. (This is true for nonhuman animals as well.) In this period, there is no contrast between "my" mind or memory and "your" mind or memory, as "I" have no access to "your" mind.[6] A cognitive revolution then must take place when the child can use language to interpret others' reports as repre- sentations of happenings in the world that she did not experience herself, whether these appear as stories or personal narratives or as more abstract narratives such as myths, fables, or religious parables. However, such reports may be viewed by the child as "common knowledge" similar to her own knowledge gained through direct personal exploration of the world; as such, there would be no value in attributing this new knowledge to any particular other source.

Indeed, a large body of research (e.g., Roberts & Blades, 2000) suggests that children may first take in verbal accounts as having the same evidentiary status as that from one's own experience, with no distinction being made between the two. It is not that the child generally confuses your experience with his or her own, but that the source of the account is not noted in memory. Four- or 5-year- olds given new information may claim after even a brief delay to "have always known it" (Taylor, Esbensen, & Bennett, 1994). Both adults and children generally share the intuitive feeling that knowledge (rather than personal memory) is a gen- eral possession in common: that is, "if I know it, so do you and I have always known it."[7] This appears to be the stance of the young child who in exploring the world acquires a great deal of new knowledge in everyday life. The idea here is that the child intuitively feels that the knowledge is "out there" to be picked up, and once picked up, it is not distinguished in terms of source from all the other

6. This inference is based on the reasoning that if there is no contrast to my mind, then there is no concept of my mind.

7. A related phenomenon observed among adults as well as children has been dubbed "the curse of knowledge" or "the hindsight bias" in that individuals with knowledge about a topic overesti- mate the knowledge of others, who may in fact be ignorant (Birch & Bloom, 2007).

known things. Acquiring knowledge from others via language is then simply another way of "picking it up." Young children's suggestibility—including cases in which a child's own experience is readily replaced with a more dramatic account supplied in conversation by another person (Ceci & Bruck, 1993)—may well result from source blindness of this kind.

However, as we know from empirical research, as well as from general experience, adults (and presumably older children) typically do make a distinction between personal experiential memory and knowing about events derived from another source. Some languages (e.g., Turkish) in fact require that a speaker indicate grammatically whether a report comes from personal experiential knowledge or from some other source (Aksu-Koc, 1988). Note that source blindness is not an issue in very early development because, as discussed previously, direct experience is the source of all memory; it becomes a problem only when sources are indirect through other people's communication (or later from written or printed sources).

Overcoming Initial Constraints

Language both ameliorates and complicates these constraints. Overcoming source blindness requires discriminating between direct experience and verbal discourse as the source of one's information.[8] Gaining access to others' expressions of knowing, thinking, feeling, and remembering, and their reasons for making requests and demands, provides the child with the basis for a multitude of new insights into the nature of the self and the social world, as well as incidental information about the way the world works. Much of this comes through conversation, and one important topic of conversation concerns shared and unshared memories, studied extensively in recent years (see, e.g., Fivush & Nelson, 2006; Nelson & Fivush, 2004). Here the interlocking systems of the psychological self and social interactors become crucial to the child's insight that different sources affect meaning values in the memory system. Social and cultural accounts from different times (past, future, and counterfactual or fiction) and places (here, there, unknown, and imaginary) present challenges to the child's unitary memory system, to be resolved by differentiating self-acquired knowledge from other sources. The child's attentiveness to these narrative sources in turn contributes importantly to the expanding scope of consciousness, which I consider next.

---

8. In the languages in which it is a requirement of the grammar that the speaker specify whether the content of a statement is personally known or is hearsay, children may learn to make the distinction in memory at an earlier point than others do. However, it is possible that children learn to use the forms appropriately before learning their full semantics (see Aksu-Koc, 1988 for details; Levy & Nelson, 1994, for "use without meaning"; also Nelson, 1996, 2007). Even in languages that do not make this distinction, adults often require children to report where they heard the information they are repeating. Various other social experiences might encourage the child to note the specific source of information–such as interaction with adults for whom it is critical, or expansion of the child's own view of the world, as indicated in the next section.

EXPANDING CONSCIOUSNESS

Consciousness is basically directed attention writ large (Kandel, 2006). Indeed, consciousness is critical to determining what is attended, and in this respect, it is strongly linked to social interactions and activities from the beginning of life outside the womb. It is thus critically important to meaning; as consciousness expands, so meaning extends into new territory, and consciousness thereby affects what aspects of experience in an activity are noticed and then remembered. Considering the interrelations of background memory/knowledge, meaningfulness, social experience, and expanding levels of consciousness, can shed light on the development of recollective memory.

It is important to clarify what facet of consciousness is in focus here. Consciousness has been studied and disputed by many scholars in philosophy, neuroscience, and cognitive science in recent years, and it poses important questions in those fields that are not easily resolved or agreed upon (e.g., Dennett, 1991; Donald, 2001; Edelman & Tononi, 2000; Searle, 1992; Zelazo, Moscovitch, & Thompson, 2007). Among these questions are those of what the function of consciousness is for the mind in general; what function it serves in human cognitive processing; what it means to be conscious at all; and how conscious processing changes in child development (Zelazo, Gao, & Todd, 2007). It is assumed by most that the conscious mind attends selectively to aspects of the world relevant to the present concerns of the organism and engages in conscious processes that enable taking actions or solving problems to achieve goals, whereas the nonconscious mind (brain) carries out operations necessary to these processes or engages in "offline" operations of other kinds.

A different sense of consciousness relates the self to the world of meaningful social and physical events, evoking the notion of the *scope* of consciousness. To a large degree, the *scope of consciousness determines what is meaningful* for the individual, and thus for what may become remembered of an experience. Whereas the notions of conscious *state* or conscious *process* concern the functioning of consciousness, *scope* concerns how its function expands over time as meaning for the child changes with development. How the self is understood and what aspects of the world are in the scope of consciousness are both relevant to this relation. The sense of self is clearly an important component, but the other side of the coin is the *sense of the world* that the child encounters and this sense, I suggest, is dramatically affected by changes in social and cultural narratives, as much so as changes in direct experience in the world.

Damasio (1999) took the perspective that consciousness first arises phylogenetically in relation to the organismic self, organizing and recognizing the products of self-maintenance systems, including those of perception, for example, pain. He claimed that consciousness next tracks action in the world and thereafter (among humans) engages in a "continuous narrative" that is extended to new aspects of experience as individuals mature. Damasio's idea of the "continuous narrative" includes the possibility of extended consciousness open to developmental expansion. The present account takes up this notion of expansion.

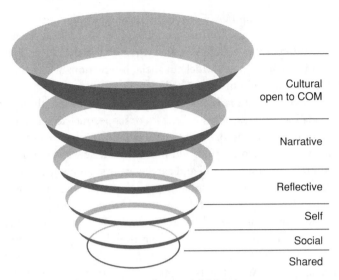

Cultural
open to COM

Narrative

Reflective

Self

Social

Shared

Figure 2.2. Expansion of consciousness during child development

The scope of consciousness depends on how a person is able to view and interpret the world of experience, and this in turn depends to some extent on how social coactors guide attention to novel aspects of encounters. The idea of consciousness here is as a succession of higher level relations of self and world mediated through social and cultural agents. See Figure 2.2 (see also Nelson, 2007).

Expansion of Consciousness Birth to 6 Years

At birth, the baby awakes to a reality previously unseen. Being awake and conscious at this point is being aware of limited aspects of the inhabited world of faces and comforting bodies, as well as spaces and sights and sounds that take on greater definition as persons and things over months of exploring the boundaries of self and nonself in both social and nonsocial forms. The post-birth beginning state is highly constrained by the limits of sensory and motor systems and the dependence of the infant on others to provide movement and place. Thus it is labeled in Figure 2.2 as "shared" (or it could be "attached"), indicating that attention to aspects of the environment is to a large degree under the control of adult caregivers. Meaning-tracking, largely predetermined at this early point, is hard work; it is not surprising that most neonates spend the majority of their time in unawareness, that is, in sleep or near-sleep states. As the infant develops schemata of surroundings and events, she also tunes in more to the verbal and active interactions of those around her, leading into the expansion of social awareness and shared attention, the second phase of *social consciousness* (Carpendale & Lewis, 2004; Hobson, 1993, 2004). In this second phase at the end of the first year and into the second, the child begins to recognize herself as a person-object who may share attention with another, and also actively and intentionally to *externalize* some of what is meaningful to herself, acting out schemas in play, using words to effect action and to comment on her own action. These mark the entry into the third phase of *self-object or personal consciousness*. She sees that others see her and also that they see things from a different view than she does. Now independently mobile, the child engages more widely in social interactions with a variety of different people, with or without the use of language.

As suggested by the dimensions of the figure, these first three phases are short-lived, shallow, and restricted in breadth of scope, but each enables a broader degree of exploration alone or in interaction with adults and other children. With the acquisition of words, the child moves into a new level of *sharing meanings* with others, bringing the child and caregivers into a new social space.

Interaction around words is a first step toward the linguistic cognition that will begin when language is more fully mastered, especially in its *receptive understanding* mode. Consciousness of self and other, externalization of mental contents, and the use of words together enable the child to move into a level of *reflective consciousness*. It is at this level that the child may engage, alone or with others, in reflecting on what has been put into public space, through language, action, or other means (e.g., art). The previous discussion of Emily's reflective monologues provides a sample of this mode. Reflective consciousness is a particularly important human move. It requires not just operating with representations but examination of representations to extract meaning, and possibly to amend or transform, to re-present or reconstruct for self or others what was previously held in private space. When matters are put into public space, they become available for mutual reflection on meaning, thus making accessible to the child's extended consciousness a range of matters that were previously unknowable.

These experiences, often taking place through conversations about the child's activities, past, present, and future, and on other occasions through stories or personal narratives, lay the groundwork for the development of the fifth phase of *narrative consciousness*, which further broadens the space of conscious exploration. Narrative thinking is one of a few basic structural modes of human thought (Bruner, 1990). A full understanding of narrative experience is achieved through linguistic articulation of times, persons, and causal sequences, and this requires practice of receptive and expressive language skills. Narrative consciousness is integrative. It weaves the content of a story or a memory into a whole construction in terms of its temporal and causal relations, the people involved in actions and activities, their motivations, knowledge, and goals. Through narrative practices, the child may come to a broader understanding of the different perspectives of self and others, as well as of the self in different times, as personal memory also expands from the episodic past to the unknown future. The private mind becomes shareable in this phase, and others' past and future experiences are recognized as different from one's own. As other times and other places come into mental view, the peopled world expands exponentially from those that are family to all those whose stories can be told in fact or fiction, or constructed imaginatively.

Reflection on personal memory brings into consciousness the differentiation of others' stories and one's own stories or views on a common story, thus the other's memory and "my" memory, with the potential for overcoming the pervasive problems of source. The differential perspectives of other social and temporal "minds" is manifest in narratives, revealing secrets of social life, including motivations, successes, failures, deception, and generosity. The child's own personal experience may be limited, but through narrative sharing with adults, the realm of consciousness is vastly increased, and in the next phase has no limits. By way of narrative practices of personal reminiscing, cultural storytelling and reading narrative consciousness leads into the larger scope of cultural consciousness, referred to here and elsewhere as the process of "entering the community of minds" (Nelson, 2005b, 2007). This process expands the consciousness perspective to an infinite variety of people in the world, of possible experiences and fantasies undreamt of in the child's past, and of domains of knowledge to be explored in and out of school.

The expansion of consciousness described here is essentially the expansion of the potential for meaningful experience of new and different kinds. The levels reflect initially biological (neurological, bodily) constraints, limitations on experience, learning, and accumulated memory, as well as "meaning sharing" potentials in the different periods of development. The constraints and limitations on the child's experience inevitably place limits on our interpretations of the child's "umweldt" or experience of the world. Exploiting the possibilities of each new vista is what drives development into broader horizons of consciousness, a process that can become lifelong, or may be stunted at any point. New possible perceptions appear through the interaction of "external" and "internal" factors, including through the "outside" opportunities that social interactions, language use in conversations, and other symbolic forms provide in conjunction with the experiential and memory characteristics of the current consciousness state.

Social transactions are often critical to the move from one broad level of consciousness to the next and to the consequences that the move to a new level has for perceiving new relationships. These are complexes that the child does not control, and consequently, opening up to expanded views of the world at each level takes place very gradually. As each level is exploited, established meanings of world and self may conflict with new experiences as these come into awareness, thus motivating the move to the next level of consciousness. Such moves may take place slowly or rapidly; they are not tied to specific ages, and individual patterns are to be expected.

CONSCIOUSNESS, EXPERIENCE, AND MEMORY

At this point, I return to the question of restricted memory in the early years and ask again why Emily's early memories did not persist into later childhood or adulthood. As Robyn Fivush and I have argued, one result of increases in experience with verbal social transactions around memories is that memory changes and both the significance and structure of memory are transformed. We proposed that the experience of sharing memory narratives with others exposes children to a variety of new perspectives that are only available through social interactions (Fivush & Nelson, 2006). These include the cultural notions of time: the division of temporal intervals by hours, days, weeks, and so on; and the ways that a culture uses spatial metaphors to express the passage of time. They include as well the cultural construction of personal relationships, for example, kinship structures and institutional roles. The ways that motivations, emotions, and mental states such as remembering and knowing are characterized in these verbal forms bring out aspects that the child may have experienced but had not previously thought about or conceptualized. The verbal expressions themselves scaffold the child's restructuring of experience in much the way that Vygotsky (1987) anticipated.[9]

Robyn Fivush and I presented the case that these developments during the preschool years were especially significant for the emergence of autobiographical memory toward the end of that period, basically as a self-narrative serving reflective functions (Nelson & Fivush, 2004). We emphasized the contributions of conversations with parents and others about shared past events as providing the context within which young children learn the function and narrative structure for both conversational recollection (reminiscing) and for self-remembering. We also emphasized that it is within such contexts that children come to a new awareness of the distinctive self with a continuous past and future. Cultural differences in the emphasis on self and others in memory talk and in the age of onset of autobiographical memory, as well as its contents, imply that variations in specific kinds of experiences affect these developments and their outcomes. The extent of these influences is wide-ranging: not only do the functions and long-term extension of large numbers of memories emerge in autobiographical memory, but the same processes change the child's knowledge about and perspective on self and other, as well as time past and future.

Autobiographical memory itself serves distinctive social and self functions. These functions cohere with the cultural narratives that different societies provide, such as religious mythologies and political histories, either emphasizing the central role of self-autonomy and -expression or deemphasizing the self and projecting the group or the hierarchical structure of society as preeminent (Nelson, 2003). Our contemporary Western culture is one that puts special emphasis on self-expression through self-narratives. Such expression is won only through emphasis on the distinctiveness of the self in comparison to others. This perspective suggests caution in universalizing our observations in our own culture and extending them to others (see also Leichtman, Wang & Pillemer, 2003; Wang, 2004). The implication is that, as social experience in the symbolic world expands, the self becomes understood in new ways, with new meanings determining the contents and functions of memory.

The experiential framework of the present chapter adds a personal layer to this account. The hypothesis that emerges is that the expansion of consciousness made possible through the guidance of parents and other adults toward the

9. See also Carey (2009) on the process of "Quinean bootstrapping" as a mode of developmental change. The idea here is that language itself serves as a bootstrapping mechanism, implying that the relevant language, while available as a formal tool is not really understood until the bootstrapping is complete. See also Tomasello (1999) for a related view of "cultural bootstrapping."

representation of a specific personal past and possible future, within the cultural framework of the pasts and futures of other people known and unknown, is critical to changing the meaning value of personal experiences. Recollecting for oneself and with others then becomes a "life-serving" experience in itself.

I began this chapter with a quotation from Eric Kandel, whose work has focused on the biological processes involved in memory in the simplest organismic systems. I am ending with the conclusion that a new form of memory—the autobiographical—emerges only in human children in response to social and cultural values conveyed through the symbolic powers of verbal narratives. But the story cannot be told without both ends in mind—the biological and the cultural. In between, it has been important to emphasize how experience, meaning, and memory work together; how meaning in biological terms comes to be supplemented and transformed through social values; and how consciousness becomes expanded and more complex in response to social and cultural influences as these interlocking systems move forward in development. It is my contention that although separate accounts of the different strands involved in these developments are important to understanding the whole, no simpler account can adequately describe the emergence of autobiographical memory in human lives.

REFERENCES

Aksu-Koc, A. (1988). *The acquisition of aspect and modality: The case of past reference in Turkish*. New York: Cambridge University Press.

Bauer, P. J. (2007). *Remembering the times of our lives: Memory in infancy and beyond*. Mahwah, NJ: Lawrence Erlbaum Associates Publishers.

Birch, S., & P. Bloom (2007). The curse of knowledge in reasoning about false beliefs. *Psychological Science, 18*, 382–6.

Bruner, J. S. (1990). *Acts of meaning*. Cambridge, MA: Harvard University Press.

Carey, S. (2009). *The origin of concepts*. New York: Oxford University Press.

Carpendale, J. I. M., & Lewis, C. (2004). Constructing an understanding of mind: The development of children's social understanding and social interaction. *Behavioral and Brain Sciences, 27*, 79–151.

Ceci, S. J., & Bruck, M. (1993). Suggestibility of the child witness: A historical review and synthesis. *Psychological Bulletin, 113*, 403–39.

Damasio, A. (1999). *The feeling of what happens: Body and emotion in the making of consciousness*. New York: Harcourt, Inc.

Dennett, D. C. (1991). *Consciousness explained*. Boston: Little, Brown, & Co.

Donald, M. (1991). *Origins of the modern mind: Three stages in the evolution of culture and cognition*. Cambridge, MA: Harvard University Press.

Donald, M. (2001). *A mind so rare: The evolution of human consciousness*. New York: Norton.

Edelman, G. M., & Tononi, G. (2000). *A universe of consciousness: How matter becomes imagination*. New York: Basic Books.

Fivush, R., & Nelson, K. (2006). Parent-child reminiscing locates the self in the past. *British Journal of Developmental Psychology, 24*, 235–51.

Gerhardt, J. (1989). Monologue as a speech genre. In K. Nelson (Ed.), *Narratives from the crib* (pp. 171–230). Cambridge, MA: Harvard University Press.

Hobson, R. P. (1993). *Autism and the development of mind.* Hillsdale, NJ: Lawrence Erlbaum Associates.

Hobson, R. P. (2004). *The cradle of thought: Exploring the origins of thinking.* New York: Oxford University Press.

Kandel, E. R. (2006). *In search of memory: The emergence of a new science of mind.* New York: Norton.

Leichtman, M. D., Wang, Q., & Pillemer, D. B. (2003). Cultural variations in interdependence and autobiographical memory: Lessons from Korea, China, India, and the United States. In R. Fivush & C. Haden (Eds.), *Autobiographical memory and the construction of a narrative self: Developmental and cultural perspectives* (pp. 73–98). Mahwah, NJ: Erlbaum.

Levy, E., & Nelson, K. (1994). Words in discourse: A dialectical approach to the acquisition of meaning and use. *Journal of Child Language, 21,* 367–89.

Mandler, J. M. (2004). *The foundations of mind: Origins of conceptual thought.* New York: Oxford University Press.

Nelson, K. (1989a). Monologue as representation of real-life experience. In K. Nelson (Ed.), *Narratives from the crib* (Paperback, pp. 27–72). Cambridge, MA: Harvard University Press.

Nelson, K. (Ed.). (1989b). *Narratives from the crib.* Cambridge, MA: Harvard University Press. Paperback 2006.

Nelson, K. (1993). The psychological and social origins of autobiographical memory. *Psychological Science, 4,* 1–8.

Nelson, K. (1994). Long-term retention of memory for preverbal experience: Evidence and Implications. *Memory, 2,* 467–75.

Nelson, K. (1996). *Language in cognitive development: Emergence of the mediated mind.* New York, NY: Cambridge University Press.

Nelson, K. (2003). Self and social functions: Individual autobiographical memory and collective narrative. *Memory, 11,* 125–36.

Nelson, K. (2005a). Evolution and development of human memory systems. In B. Ellis & D. Bjorklund (Eds.), *Origins of the social mind: Evolutionary psychology and child development* (pp. 319–45). New York: Guilford Publications, Inc.

Nelson, K. (2005b). Language pathways to the community of minds. In J. W. Astington & J. Baird (Eds.), *Why language matters to theory of mind* (pp. 26–49). New York: Oxford University Press.

Nelson, K. (2007). *Young minds in social worlds: Experience, meaning, and memory.* Cambridge, MA: Harvard University Press.

Nelson, K., & Fivush, R. (2004). The emergence of autobiographical memory: A social cultural developmental theory. *Psychological Review, 111,* 486–511.

Oster, E. (2006). Foreword. In K. Nelson (Ed.) *Narratives from the crib.* (pp v–vii). Cambridge, MA: Harvard University Press.

Roberts, K. P., & Blades, M. (Eds.). (2000). *Children's source monitoring.* Mahwah, NJ: Erlbaum Associates.

Rubin, D. (2005). A basic systems approach to autobiographical memory. *Current Directions in Psychological Science, 14,* 79–83.

Searle, J. R. (1992). *The rediscovery of mind.* Cambridge: MIT Press.

Suddendorf, T., & Corballis, M. C. (2007). The evolution of foresight: What is mental time travel, and is it unique to humans? *Behavioral and Brain Sciences, 30,* 299–351.

Taylor, M., Esbensen, B. M., & Bennett, R.T. (1994). Children's understanding of knowledge acquisition: The tendency for children to report that they have always known what they have just learned. *Child Development, 65,* 1581–604.

Tomasello, M. (1999). *The cultural origins of human cognitions.* Cambridge, MA: Harvard University Press.

Tulving, E. (1983). *Elements of episodic memory.* New York: Oxford University Press.

Tulving, E. (1993). What is episodic memory? *Current Directions in Psychological Science, 2,* 67–70.

Vygotsky, L. S. (1987). *The collected works of L. S. Vygotsky: Vol. I. Problems of general psychology* (N. Minick, Trans.). R. Rieber & A. Carton (Eds.). New York: Plenum Press. (Original work published 1934).

Wang, Q. (2004). The emergence of cultural self-constructs: Autobiographical Memory and self-description in European American and Chinese children. *Developmental Psychology, 40,* 3–15.

Zelazo, P. D., Gao, H. H., & Todd, R. (2007). The development of consciousness. In P. D. Zelazo, M. Moscovitch, & E. Thompson (Eds.), *The Cambridge handbook of consciousness* (pp. 405–34). Cambridge: Cambridge University Press.

Zelazo, P. D., Moscovitch, M., & Thompson, E. (Eds.). (2007). *The Cambridge handbook of consciousness.* Cambridge: Cambridge University Press.

3

Building Blocks of Recollection

TRACY RIGGINS

WHAT IS RECOLLECTION?

In adults, the term *recollection* refers to the cognitive process that allows individuals to retrieve information about distinct features associated with an event (Yonelinas, 2002). It is through recollection that individuals are able to recover "qualitative" information, such as the temporal or spatial context surrounding an event or the novel associations between different components of an event. In everyday memory tasks, recollection is apparent when individuals are able to recall not only that a specific person looks familiar, but also their name, the place they first met them, and the last time they had an encounter with them (e.g., "That's Simona. I met her in 2005 at UC Davis. I saw her at a conference in Berkeley, California last summer."). In laboratory examinations of memory, recollection is apparent when participants judge that they specifically "remember" items from a study list versus that they simply "know" the items were on the list (e.g., "I remember the word *pizza* was on the list because the word before it was *eggplant*. I was hungry and thought an eggplant-pizza would be a very interesting meal.")

In adults, recollection has been examined from experimental, computational modeling, neuropsychological, neuroimaging, and individual difference perspectives. Evidence from these studies has specified the nature of recollection, its role in the retrieval of specific contextual information, and its neural substrates (Yonelinas, 2002, Chapter 1 this volume). Taken together, these findings provide ample support for the notion that memory in adults is subserved by multiple separable processes, one of which is recollection.

WHY IS THE DEVELOPMENT OF RECOLLECTION IMPORTANT?

One relatively unexplored aspect of recollection is its development. Examination of how recollection is assembled and the factors that influence this process is both necessary and beneficial. First, knowledge regarding the development of recollection will contribute to a more complete understanding of the structure, function, and organization of recollection in adults. Similar to understanding any complex structure, such as a skyscraper, one gains a better understanding of the final formation by observing how it is constructed over time (e.g., Elman et al., 1996). Such complete understanding of psychological phenomena is viewed as a fundamental endeavor in science.

Second, knowledge regarding the development of recollection may also improve our current understanding of "failures" or "disorders" in memory, including information on how and when they arise, why they exist, and possible avenues for intervention or enhancement. For example, increased understanding of memory development in general has helped explain why children perform as well as adults on some memory tasks and why they fall short on others (e.g., Chi, 1978; Schneider, 1993). This information is not only descriptive but also practical as it can be applied in clinical, educational, and classroom settings to improve memory performance.

Finally, from a phenomenological perspective, recollection provides richness and detail to our memories for the past. These details become especially significant when one considers how they contribute to our autobiographies or memories for personally relevant events in our own lives (e.g., graduations, weddings, vacations). Perhaps because of this importance at a personal level, for almost a century (Freud, 1905/1953), researchers have been struck by the lack of detail included in our memories from early childhood. Empirical research has shown that this phenomenon is not simply due to forgetting because of the passage of time, but is rather a ubiquitous form of amnesia referred to as *infantile* or *childhood amnesia* (for recent reviews see Bauer, 2007b, 2008). Even in light of this persistent interest, a variety of questions remain, including: Why do adults show so few, if any, memories from infancy and early childhood? Because recollection underlies our ability to retrieve information about events and their distinct features, examining its development may begin to shed light on phenomena such as infantile or childhood amnesia.

One logical place to begin examining the development of recollection is by asking *when* recollection, or the "building blocks" of recollection, can be detected during ontogeny. The goal of this chapter is to address this question, by reviewing findings from a variety of paradigms in school-aged children, preschoolers, toddlers, and infants. By starting with research in older children and working backward in developmental time, it is hoped that a greater connection can be made between what is currently known about recollection in adults and the roots of this ability. Paradigms used to examine recollection (and memory in general) change drastically over the lifespan. This is mostly due to the large differences in verbal, motor, and attentional capabilities of participants at various ages. By progressively examining younger age groups, it is hoped that the rationale and justification for modifications to traditional adult recollection paradigms will become more readily apparent. Finally, such sequential description may also contribute to increased understanding of what changes in recollection from infancy to adulthood.

Overall, the data reviewed in this chapter suggest that the roots of recollection can be identified in all age groups. However, these abilities are rudimentary and fragile, especially during the first year of life and undergoe substantial developmental change as children transition from infancy, through childhood, and into adulthood. Part of the challenge for future investigations will be to identify the mechanisms underlying this change and the factors that influence this process. Comments on this challenge and particular approaches that may prove especially useful in this endeavor are highlighted throughout.

EVIDENCE FOR RECOLLECTION IN SCHOOL-AGED CHILDREN

Over the last decade, several studies have examined recollection in school-aged children. Typically, these investigations have borrowed paradigms from the adult literature (e.g., the remember/know and signal detection procedures) to isolate the process subserving retrieval of "qualitative" information (i.e., temporal or spatial context surrounding an event or the novel associations between different components of an event). In general, these memory tasks include the administration of a study list followed by a test phase in which children are required to: (a) make a memory judgment and (b) verbally reflect on that response and/or provide subjective ratings of confidence regarding their response (Anooshian, 1999; Billingsley, Smith, & McAndrew, 2002; Brainerd, Reyna, & Howe, 2009; Ghetti & Angelini, 2008; Holliday, 2003; Piolino et al., 2007). In one of the earliest studies, Billingsley and colleagues (2002) used the "remember/know paradigm" (Tulving, 1985) to examine recollection in a group of 8- to 19-year-old participants. Similar to studies in adults, children were first required to remember a series of pictures and words. At test, they were asked to recall if specific stimuli had been on the previous study lists. For each item that children identified as being from the study list, they were also asked to indicate whether they *remembered* the item (i.e., had a specific memory of it, such as memory for the other words with which it was paired, how it appeared on the screen, or another specific detail about the encounter with the item) or *knew* the item was on the study list (i.e., knew they had encountered it without having a specific or detailed memory of the experience). Results indicated all participants were able to complete the task and make distinctions between remembering and knowing. Although know responses were equivalent between age groups, remember responses increased with age (for both the picture and word tasks). These findings suggested that although recollection can be detected in school-aged children, the development of this process continues at least through the adolescent years.

One limitation of this investigation was that no direct evidence was provided indicating that 8-year-olds used the remember/know options in the same manner as 12-year-olds and adults. To address this issue, Ghetti and Angelini (2008) recently employed the dual-process signal detection model commonly used in adult research (Yonelinas, 1994) and examined recollection in 6-, 8-, 10-, 14-, and 18-year-old participants. In their study, children were asked to remember colored line drawings and indicate at test whether or not they had seen the drawing during study and provide a confidence rating for each judgment (i.e., very sure, kind of sure, not sure). Receiver operating curves were obtained by combining the memory and confidence responses (i.e., plotting hits in relation to false alarms as confidence changed). Similar to the study by Billingsley and colleagues (2002), results revealed evidence of recollection in all age groups. Recollection also showed continued development from childhood (6 to 8 years) into early adolescence (10 years and up), whereas familiarity showed no development over this time (once processing time was equated; Ghetti & Angelini, 2008).

Overall, studies in school-aged children strongly suggest that recollective processes can be detected using adult paradigms, although continued development occurs at least until the adolescent years. What remains unclear is whether this development is due to changes in recollection per se or in other cognitive abilities required by these paradigms (e.g., the ability to successfully monitor one's memory performance). In an attempt to address this question, Brainerd and colleagues (2009) recently sought to examine whether evidence for recollection could be obtained in school-aged children using data from paradigms that were cognitively less demanding (i.e., ones that did not require subjective judgments regarding memory or confidence). If changes in recollection are observed under these conditions, it can more confidently be concluded that recollective processes are developing, as opposed to cognitive abilities associated with demand characteristics. Toward this end, Brainerd and colleagues (2009) used data from list recall paradigms (e.g., paired-associates, recall, free recall, or cued recall conditions) that present similar types of stimuli as the adult memory paradigms (e.g., words or pictures that must be remembered) but do not require performance monitoring (e.g., confidence ratings for each memory judgment). They applied a computational modeling approach to a large sample of data from children (7 to 8 years) and young adolescents (11 to 12 years) in order to examine whether recollection-type processes (i.e., those that directly access memory traces and provide vivid restoration of realistic details that are sensitive and labile) could be identified. Indeed, their results showed evidence that recollection, familiarity, and reconstruction were all detectable in childhood, even under conditions with a low cognitive burden in terms of performance monitoring, and that substantial developmental change occurred between childhood and young adulthood, again suggesting the prolonged development of recollection (see Brainerd et al., 2009, for elaboration).

Neural Bases of Recollection in School-aged Children

The neural bases of recollection have been identified in adults using both functional magnetic resonance imaging (fMRI) and event-related potentials (ERPs). Functional MRI provides information about what spatial regions in the brain may be contributing to these processes, whereas ERPs provide information regarding the timing of these processes. Because the brain undergoes considerable developmental change throughout childhood and adolescence (e.g., Giedd et al., 1999; Giedd et al., 1996), it is unclear whether the same circuitry that is engaged when adults complete tasks requiring recollective processing also underlies recollection in school-aged children. A few studies have begun to examine this issue (see Thomas & Jorgenson, Chapter 9 this volume).

FMRI

Functional MRI examines changes in regional blood flow that occur in response to a stimulus or set of stimuli. fMRI studies in adults have revealed changes in blood flow in regions of the medial temporal lobe (MTL) and prefrontal cortex (PFC) during tasks that require recollection (Diana & Ranganath, Chapter 7 this volume; Eichenbaum, Yonelinas, & Ranganath, 2007; Ranganath et al., 2004; Yonelinas, 2002; Yonelinas et al., 2002; cf. Squire, Wixted, & Clark, 2007). In particular, recollection has been shown to involve the hippocampus, a structure located deep in the MTL that is characterized by a protracted developmental course (see "Potential mechanisms of change" section for elaboration), whereas other memory processes (e.g., familiarity) do not (Ranganath et al., 2004). These findings, coupled with data from patients with brain damage to these regions, have been taken to suggest that a relatively specific MTL-PFC circuit underlies the encoding and retrieval of distinct features associated with the context of the event (i.e., recollection).

In one of the first developmental studies, Ofen and colleagues (2007) investigated which brain regions were involved in the formation of memories in a sample of 49 children and adults (ages 8 to 24). Individuals viewed pictures of scenes during fMRI scanning and made judgments as to whether they were indoor or outdoor scenes. Upon completion of scanning, a remember/know paradigm was used to evaluate recognition memory. Results revealed that both MTL and PFC were active during the encoding phase of the memory task (see also Ghetti, DeMaster, Yonelinas, & Bunge, 2010; Menon, Boyett-Anderson, & Reiss, 2005; Thomas & Jorgenson, Chapter 9 this volume). Consistent with reports in adults, activation in these regions was greater for scenes that were subsequently remembered than for scenes that were forgotten. Moreover, the extent to which these regions were recruited was associated with recollection (i.e., remember) responses as opposed to familiarity (i.e., know) responses. These findings suggest that, in school-aged children, the circuitry engaged during encoding memory tasks involving recollective processes may be similar to that in adults (Thomas & Jorgenson, Chapter 9 this volume).

Age-related changes in the extent of activation of these regions were also reported. For instance, Ofen and colleagues (2007) reported increases with age in specific PFC, but not MTL, regions during encoding and that these changes were correlated with developmental gains in recollection. In contrast, Ghetti and colleagues (Ghetti, DeMaster, et al., 2010) recently reported age-related changes in activation profiles of MTL structures (both hippocampus and posterior parahippocampal gyrus), suggesting that these regions become more selective for recollection processes during development, regardless of behavioral performance. Finally, Menon, Boyett-Anderson, and Reiss (2005) reported both changes (i.e., decreases) in MTL activation with age (regardless of performance) as well as increases in effective connectivity between MTL and left, dorsolateral PFC. Thus, although a similar circuit may be involved during recollection in school-aged children, considerable development continues within and between these regions throughout the adolescent years (Thomas & Jorgenson, Chapter 9 this volume).

ERPS

ERPs represent the activity of large populations of neurons that have been synchronously activated in response to a discrete stimulus. When responses elicited by a certain class of stimuli are averaged together (e.g., all responses to novel items versus responses to previously learned items), differences in the spatiotemporal properties of the resulting waveforms allow for the inference of differences in neural processing related to cognition. To date, adult ERP studies have used a wide variety of tasks to examine recollection, ranging from the remember/know paradigm to paradigms that explicitly ask participants to recollect specific details of the study context (e.g., the original color of the stimulus, or when it occurred within a study session). Regardless of the paradigm used, results from these investigations suggest that recollection is associated with a distinct spatiotemporal topography characterized by distributed, positive-going activity that occurs late in the waveform and is maximal over left parietal regions (Duarte, Ranganath, Winward, Hayward, & Knight, 2004; Friedman & Johnson, 2000; Diana & Ranganath, Chapter 7 this volume; Rugg & Yonelinas, 2003). Thus far, ERP investigations in school-aged children have largely used the latter type of paradigm, that examines how retrieval of specific details relates to the study context (Cycowicz, Friedman, & Duff, 2003; Czernochowski, Mecklinger, Johansson, & Brinkmann, 2005; Friedman, Chapter 10 this volume; Friedman, de Chastelaine, Nessler, & Malcolm, 2010).

For example, Cycowicz and colleagues used ERPs to examine memory for items and their context in 10- and 12-year-old children and adults (Cycowicz et al., 2003). During the task, participants viewed line drawings in either red or green ink. ERPs were collected during memory retrieval when individuals made recognition memory judgments about individual drawings (drawn in black ink) and the original color in which they were presented. Results indicated that all age groups showed similar ERP responses. However, ERPs generated when subjects retrieved information about the contextual details (i.e., presumably reflecting recollection) showed age-related changes associated with improvements in memory performance. These results suggest that although school-aged children are able to recollect contextual details, and this process generates an ERP response similar to that observed in adults, this ability and its ERP correlate shows prolonged development during late childhood/adolescence. These authors suggest that this continued development is primarily due to changes in PFC, which they argue contribute to the successful postretrieval monitoring of source information (Cycowicz et al., 2003).

Czernochowski and colleagues (2005) also used ERPs to examine memory for items and their context (spoken words vs. photos, red vs. blue background color, and first vs. second study block) and included a slightly younger group of children

(6- to 8-year-olds, 10- to 12-year-olds, and adults). They used an exclusion paradigm that required children to make old/new memory judgments and indicate whether the item had been shown in a given target context before or not. Consistent with findings from Cycowicz et al. (2003), ERP components related to retrieval of contextual details were present in all age groups and these components showed functional characteristics similar to those in adults. However, in the youngest age group (6 to 8 years), these ERP components were only found in the subgroup of 6- to 8-year-olds whose performance levels were sufficiently high, suggesting there may be a lower age limit for which the exclusion paradigm can be used effectively.

In sum, current empirical evidence suggests that recollection can be identified in school-aged children (and dissociated from other mnemonic processes, such as familiarity), yet it shows continued development during this time period (see also Brainerd, Reyna, & Holliday, Chapter 5 this volume; Ghetti, Lyons, & DeMaster, Chapter 6 this volume; Newcombe, Llyod, & Balcomb, Chapter 4 this volume). This developmental change may be related to brain development occurring during this period that is tractable via fMRI or ERP methodologies (Diana & Ranganath, Chapter 7 this volume; Thomas & Jorgenson, Chapter 9 this volume); however the exact nature of the developmental course and the mechanisms contributing to such change remain largely unknown.

EVIDENCE FOR RECOLLECTION IN PRESCHOOL CHILDREN

Studies of recollection in preschool children are exceedingly rare due to the fact that the demands of most adult paradigms are too cognitively complicated (i.e., they require reliable subjective judgments regarding memory or confidence). One exception is the process dissociation procedure (Jacoby, 1991), which was used by Anooshian (1999) to examine recollection in preschoolers (mean age: 4 years, 6 months, range: 3 years, 11 months to 5 years, 3 months) in comparison to college students. In their task, participants viewed two sets of pictures. One set was seen in the context of hearing a story and the second set (that was perceptually similar) was not associated with the story (participants were told that a filmmaker was saving the second set of pictures for a different film). Following a brief delay, participants were asked to identify pictures under two separate instructional conditions. In the first condition (exclusion condition), participants were asked to identify only pictures they saw in the context of the story (thus excluding any pictures that they had seen but were not associated with the story as well as any new pictures). In the second condition (inclusion condition), participants were asked to identify any picture they had seen previously, regardless of whether it was associated with the story or not. The comparison of hit and false alarm rates in the inclusion and exclusion conditions allows for estimates of recollection and familiarity. Their results showed that children and adults performed above chance, suggesting that both recollection and familiarity were contributing to the recognition memory judgments. As in studies of school-aged participants, adults obtained higher estimates for recollection than did preschool children despite comparable estimates of familiarity between the two groups.

Although this study was successfully conducted with preschoolers and suggests the existence of recollective processes in this age range, 25% of preschoolers were excluded from analysis because they could not understand and/or follow task instructions (i.e., they selected more story pictures with the exclusion vs. the inclusion instructions). In addition, the authors also reported that extensive pilot testing was necessary to develop the task scenario and that great effort was made to ensure the procedure made sense to young children. Clearly there is a lower bound to which paradigms of this nature can be used with young children.

A possible alternative paradigm can be found in the source memory literature. Source memory paradigms differ from the process dissociation procedure in that evidence for recollection is derived directly from the correct recall of a contextual detail on a given trial, thus eliminating the cognitive demands required by two separate instructional conditions. In source memory paradigms, individuals are presented with items in two (or more) contexts (e.g., line drawings presented in either green or red ink) and, at test, are required to make judgments regarding the original context for items they encountered previously (e.g., did they originally see a particular drawing in red or green ink). A correct judgment regarding the contextual details of an item (such as the color it was originally presented in) is, by definition, recollection (i.e., "qualitative" information regarding contextual details). Therefore, one can begin to examine recollection (albeit indirectly or objectively as opposed to subjectively) using these source memory paradigms (e.g., Schacter, Harbluk, & McLachlan, 1984). The primary advantage is that these paradigms are less cognitively demanding than the process dissociation procedure, as they involve fewer instructional conditions and, presumably, can be used reliably with preschool-aged children. Thus, these paradigms may be especially useful in shedding light on the early development of recollection.

Evidence supporting the feasibility of administering source memory paradigms in preschool children comes from a study by Drummey and Newcombe (2002). In this study, children (aged 4, 6, or 8 years) learned novel facts (e.g., "a giraffe cannot make any sounds") from one of two different sources (i.e., a puppet or an experimenter). After a 1-week delay, children were asked to recall (a) the novel fact (e.g., "What animal cannot make any sounds?") and (b) the source from who the fact was learned ("Who did you learn that from?," see Rybash & Colilla, 1994; Schacter et al., 1984, for a similar paradigm). Results indicated that all three age groups showed evidence for recollection in that they could recall the source from whom the facts were learned. Consistent with the findings reported in the preceding discussion, performance on this measure increased as a function of age. However, given that all 4-year-old children understood the task and were able to complete it even after a delay of 1 week suggests that this paradigm may be especially effective for younger children (see also Lindsay, Johnson, & Kwon, 1991).

Evidence from Other Verbal Paradigms

The evidence just reviewed suggests that even 4-year-old children show memory for contextual details associated with events, but what about younger preschool children (e.g., 3-year-olds)? As previously mentioned, most empirical paradigms designed to examine recollection directly have not included children this young due to their high cognitive demands. Moreover, new or alternative paradigms have not been developed because, to date, dual-process models of memory have largely been ignored in developmental literature (Brainerd et al., 2009; Newcombe & Crawley, 2007). In general, most research that has been conducted on the development of memory in younger preschool-aged children has focused on the distinction between procedural and declarative memory. Data from these investigations may provide evidence of recollection (or the roots of recollection) in younger children. Using the definition provided by Yonelinas (2002), findings from empirical research are presented showing young children's ability to recall details related to (a) spatial or (b) temporal context surrounding events or (c) memory for arbitrary associations between components of events.

Research on children's autobiographical memory provides one area in which there is rich data to explore, as these tasks require children to verbally describe unique events in their lives. Until the 1980s, it was largely believed that young children could not form memories about life events, or, if formed, that these memories were fragile, unorganized, and short-lived. However, pioneering work by several developmental psychologists has indicated that young children can remember and verbally report on such events (e.g., Nelson & Gruendel, 1986; Todd & Perlmutter, 1980). Perhaps one of the most well-known studies examined 3- and 4-year-old children's memory for a trip to Disney World (Hamond & Fivush, 1991). In this study, children who visited Disney World at either 3 or 4 years of age were asked to recall their experience. Half of the children were interviewed 6 months after their trip and half were interviewed after 18 months. All children recounted a great deal of accurate information about their Disney World experience, including specific and rich information regarding contextual details of the event. For example, children's memory narratives contained information about activities (e.g., "I went to the Tea Cup ride"), descriptions of the environment surrounding these events ("The tunnel was dark"), as well as information on affect ("I was scared"), animatrons ("The witch on the Snow White ride laughed loudly"), and explanations for events ("My Mom said it was too crowded"). Given the specificity of the contextual details provided, these narratives provide evidence for recollection as defined by Yonelinas (2002). This is not to say there were no differences between the age groups; older children's reports were more detailed and spontaneous than those from younger children. However, age (and retention interval) did not influence the amount of information recalled. Thus, even children as young as 3 years of age were able to recollect their experience after delays as long as 18 months!

Peterson and Rideout (1998) used a similar paradigm to examine children's recall for events that occurred even earlier in their lives. In this study, children were interviewed after experiencing injuries that required them to visit the emergency room (e.g., a laceration on the leg requiring stitches). The children fell in three age ranges: 13 to 18 months, 20 to 25 months, or 26 to 34 months at the time of the incident. Children were interviewed about the event within days of its occurrence (if they were verbal) and after 6, 12, and 18 or 24 months. Most of the children in the oldest group (26 to 34 months) who had narrative skills at time of injury demonstrated good verbal recall 2 years later (e.g., "It was bleeding all down my leg," "Then I went to the hospital," "I got 4 needles in my knee," "I got 14 stitches," "[The] nurse gave me a yellow popsicle;" Peterson & Rideout, 1998). Although their findings suggested that verbal abilities at the time of the event were an important predictor of subsequent verbal memory reports, even children in the intermediate age group (20 to 25 months), who could not narrate about past events at the time of injury, were also able to verbally recall aspects of the target events even after delays of 18 months. Thus, memories reflecting recollective processes likely exist in the minds of children even in the absence of the ability to verbally report on them.

Evidence from Nonverbal Paradigms

Given evidence suggesting that qualitative details surrounding an event are encoded (and subsequently recalled) in preverbal children, examination of children's responses on behavioral memory paradigms may provide a rich source in which to examine the development of recollection. Data from behavioral paradigms have reliably shown that representational competence is present in children as early as the first year of life (Mandler, 1998) and that the capacity to recall certain aspects of events is also in place at this time (Bauer, 2006; Hayne, 2004; Nelson, 1997; Rovee-Collier, 1997).

Returning to the definition of recollection provided by Yonelinas (2002), recollection involves retrieval of "qualitative" information about an event, such the (a) spatial or (b) temporal context or (c) the novel associations between different components of an event. Thus, data from a subset of behavioral paradigms that examine memory for spatial location, memory for temporal order, or memory for novel associations may begin to reveal whether memory for this type of information is reliability present in preverbal children. In these tasks, children are required to recall contextual details in the absence of perceptual support. In order to do this successfully, information regarding the context must be encoded during the presentation of the event and subsequently retrieved from the memory representation, as no perceptual cues exist to support retrieval (see Bauer, DeBoer, & Lukowski, 2007, for elaboration).

Evidence that young children are able to recall "qualitative" details about previously experienced events would, at the very least, suggest that the raw materials of recollection are present early in development. However, because recollection would be inferred by memory for "qualitative" details (as opposed to being assessed directly), there may be no direct evidence—one way or the other—that this retrieval is also accompanied by a recollective experience. However, it is still critically important to examine these abilities because, at minimum, they represent the "building blocks" that will ultimately develop into true recollection over time. Future research will need to adapt the nonverbal paradigms reviewed in the following sections to definitively conclude that there is an accompanying recollective experience.

MEMORY FOR SPATIAL LOCATION

Hayne (2007) has examined memory for location in young children using a unique spatial memory task. In this task, 3- and 4-year-old children were asked to remember where 3 to 5 objects (stuffed animals of characters children knew, e.g., Mickey Mouse, Bert, Ernie) were hidden in different locations in their homes. Following a 5-minute delay, children were required to recall one of the rooms in which objects were hidden (e.g., bedroom), the identity of the object in that room (e.g., Bert), and the specific hiding place in that room (e.g., under the bed). Results indicated that both 3- and 4-year-old children were able to recall information regarding spatial context (i.e., where the items had been hidden) and there was no difference between 3- and 4-year-olds' performance. Furthermore, when asked to do so, children could also recall the order in which the items had been hidden, indicating that they remembered something about the temporal context as well (see Horn & Myers, 1978, for similar paradigm).

MEMORY FOR TEMPORAL ORDER

Memory for temporal order has been examined using the deferred imitation paradigm (Bauer, Wenner, Dropik, & Wewerka, 2000). This technique is borrowed from infant research and capitalizes on young individuals' propensity to imitate others' actions. Memory is inferred when children observe another person's actions and then reproduce those specific actions in the same temporal order after a delay. In the laboratory, these paradigms typically consist of an adult using a set of props to create a series of novel actions. For example, the adult may "make a gong" by placing a bar across a support to form a crosspiece, hang a metal disk from the crosspiece, and use a mallet to hit the disk and make it ring. After a pre-specified delay (ranging from minutes to months), children's memory can be measured in two ways: (a) the number of actions they imitate, and (b) the number of actions they imitate in the correct temporal order.[1] The true advantage of this paradigm is that neither verbal instructions nor verbal report are required.

Bauer has convincingly argued that the imitation paradigm provides a measure of declarative memory, even in preverbal children (Bauer, 2007b; Bauer et al., 2007). Supporting evidence includes the following: the remembered information (a) is accessible to language once children acquire linguistic capacity (Bauer, Kroupina, Schwade, Dropik, & Wewerka, 1998; Cheatham & Bauer, 2005), (b) can be learned in a single trial (Bauer & Hertsgaard, 1993), (c) is subject to forgetting (Bauer, Cheatham, Strand Cary, & Van Abbema, 2002; Bauer, Van Abbema, & de Haan, 1999), (d) is flexible across changes in retrieval context[2] (Barnat, Klein, & Meltzoff, 1996; Bauer & Dow, 1994; Hanna & Meltzoff, 1993), and (e) is impaired

---

1. In most investigations, only the first instance of each action is recorded to control for problem solving or success due to trial and error (see Bauer et al., 2000).

2. Flexibility across changes in retrieval context may only be true for infants older than 12 months of age as there are some data to suggest that 6-month-old infants do not generalize if they are exposed to sequences in one context (e.g., their home) and are asked to recall them in another (e.g., the lab; Hayne, Boniface, & Barr, 2000).

in individuals who suffer damage to the hippocampus (Adlam, Vargha-Khadem, Mishkin, & de Haan, 2005; DeBoer, Wewerka, Bauer, Georgieff, & Nelson, 2005; McDonough, Mandler, McKee, & Squire, 1995; Riggins, Miller, Bauer, Georgieff, & Nelson, 2009a). Finally, the content of the information recalled is similar to that recalled in verbal declarative memory tasks (e.g., *what* happened, *where*, *when*, and *why*). For example, when making a gong, children show memory that in order to make a ringing sound with the mallet, first a crosspiece needs to be put in place and then a disk needs to be suspended from it.

Relevant to the issue of recollection, we discuss evidence from imitation para-digms showing that preschool children can recall *when* items occur in events, as this provides evidence that they are able to recall details regarding the temporal context. Recently, Riggins, Miller, Bauer, Georgieff, and Nelson (2009b) used the imitation paradigm to examine temporal order memory in a sample of typically developing 3- and 4-year-old children. Children were asked to remember nine dif-ferent actions in a specified order. All actions were related to a common theme and used a distinct set of props (e.g., in the "camping" event sequence, children baited a fishing hook, caught a fish, set up a tent, played a guitar, drank hot cocoa etc . . .). Memory for the temporal order of the actions was assessed immediately and after a 1-week delay. Results revealed that both 3- and 4-year-old children were able to recall temporal order information, suggesting memory for "when" items occurred in the event sequence (although performance was better in the older age group).

In addition to the behavioral recall measures at the 1-week delay assessment, this study (Riggins et al., 2009b) also used ERPs to examine the neural representa-tion associated with the memory trace. In this portion of the experiment, children viewed pictures of the props used in the event sequences and pictures of new props they had never seen before. Consistent with previous studies, differences between processing of old and new stimuli was reflected in two ERP components: (a) an early component that has been previously related to attention and memory processes in infants (Carver, Bauer, & Nelson, 2000; Courchesne, Granz, & Norcia, 1981; de Haan & Nelson, 1997; Nelson & Collins, 1991), and (b) a later compo-nent that has previously been related to memory or context updating in infants (Nelson, 1994). Recall of individual actions in the event sequences was correlated with peak amplitude of the early component but not the later component. In con-trast, recall of temporal order information was correlated with the later compo-nent and not the early component. It was suggested that retrieval of contextual information (i.e., temporal order) was related to differences in distributed activ-ity late in the electrophysiological response, which may be reflective of recollec-tion processes. Although speculative, this result is similar to findings in ERP literature in adults and school-aged children (reviewed in the "ERPs" section under "Neural bases of recollection in school-aged children" in this chapter) that report a temporal dissociation between early components that reflect familiarity and later components that reflect recollection (Cycowicz et al., 2003; Czernochowski et al., 2005; Duarte et al., 2004; Friedman et al., 2010; Friedman & Johnson, 2000). Also consistent with this suggestion are results from source analysis in infant ERP studies that have linked late components similar to the one observed in this study to brain regions in the right temporal cortex (see Reynolds & Richards, 2005, for elaboration).

MEMORY FOR NOVEL ASSOCIATIONS

Previous research provides evidence supporting the notion that imitation paradigms measure an individual's recollection for the original demonstration of the event sequence as opposed to more general semantic knowledge regarding how the objects work (see Bauer, 2007b; Bauer et al., 2000). One example is provided by studies showing children's recall of temporal order information for event sequences that only contain arbitrarily ordered items. Although some event sequences in imitation paradigms contain enabling relations between items (which serve to conceptually constrain the order in which the individual actions should be completed in order to achieve the desired end state; e.g., baiting the hook before catching the fish), other sequences contain completely arbitrary associations between the actions (i.e., achieving the desired end state is not dependent on performing the actions in the correct temporal order; e.g., playing the guitar before or after drinking hot cocoa). If children were simply encoding information about how the objects worked, it would not be necessary to also encode the temporal order of arbitrary events because the desired end state could be achieved regardless of the order; in fact it is a matter of personal preference which should be done first. If, on the other hand, children recall the order of the arbitrary sequences, this suggests more than just a semantic representation was formed. Both types of event sequences were included in the study by Riggins and colleagues (2009b). Results indicate that both 3- and 4-year-olds were able to remember temporal order information (at slightly lower levels) even for sequences that only contained arbitrary relations, suggesting true recollection of the original demonstration was present (Bauer et al., 2007).

Impairments in Imitation Performance in Patients with Hippocampal Damage

If the hippocampus is preferentially involved in recollection, then it follows that individuals with damage to this region should show impairments on tasks requiring recollection. Indeed, this logic has been referred to by some as the "amnesia test" and has been argued to provide some of the strongest support that imitation paradigms rely on hippocampally mediated memory systems. For example, in the earliest of these investigations, McDonough and colleagues (1995) used an age-appropriate version of the deferred imitation paradigm to compare memory performance in seven adult patients with amnesia (approximately half of whom had confirmed damage to the hippocampus), patients with frontal lobe damage, and control participants. After a 24-hr delay, adults in the control group and those with frontal lobe damage showed evidence that they recalled both the individual actions and the temporal order of the actions in the event sequences; however, patients with amnesia did not. Adlam and colleagues (2005) also used a deferred imitation paradigm to examine memory in 12 patients (ages 10 to 26 years) with developmental amnesia, a condition associated with bilateral hippocampal volume reduction caused by hypoxic-ischemic events during the perinatal period (see section on "Potential mechanisms of change" for elaboration). Like the adult-onset cases of amnesia (McDonough et al., 1995), patients with developmental amnesia recalled fewer actions and less temporal order information than the age-, sex-, and IQ-matched control group after a 24-hr delay. DeBoer and colleagues (2005) used the deferred imitation paradigm to examine memory in a group of 13 infants of diabetic mothers (at 12 months of age) who were at-risk for hippocampal damage due to exposure to multiple neurologic risk factors during the prenatal period (chronic hypoxia, hyperglycemia/reactive hypoglycemia, and iron deficiency), which have been shown to disproportionately alter hippocampal development. Infants of diabetic mothers demonstrated a selective deficit in the ability to recall the temporal order of event sequences after a 10-minute delay, even after statistically controlling for differences in gestational age and global cognitive abilities. Finally, a recent longitudinal follow-up of this sample of infants of diabetic mothers (Riggins et al., 2009a) revealed that these memory deficits continued to persist into the third year of life and also altered the late ERP component described previously that is proposed to reflect hippocampally mediated recollective memory processes. Together, these findings from patient populations in adulthood, childhood, and infancy suggest that successful performance on behavioral imitation paradigms is dependent on the integrity of the hippocampus in infancy, childhood, and adulthood. Given that this brain structure is essential for recollection (Eichenbaum et al., 2007; Ranganath et al., 2004; Yonelinas et al., 2002), these results support the view that imitation paradigms can be used to assess recollection abilities across the lifespan.

EVIDENCE FOR RECOLLECTION IN TODDLERS AND INFANTS

Memory for Spatial Location

Empirical evidence exists that both toddlers and infants show memory for spatial context. For example, DeLoache and Brown (1979) examined young children's memory for spatial location using a motivating game of hide-and-seek. In the task, 18- and 30-month-old children were told that a small stuffed animal (e.g., Big Bird) was going to hide and that they should remember where the stuffed animal was hiding in order to find him later. Children then watched while the toy was concealed in some natural location in their own home (e.g., under a couch cushion, behind a door, inside a cabinet), and after a prespecified delay (ranging from 3 minutes to 24 hr) children were asked to retrieve the toy. Both 18- and 30-month-old children demonstrated robust memory (>72% errorless retrieval) for the location of the hidden toy, regardless of the delay. These findings are impressive in that 18-month-olds remembered the spatial location just as well as the 30-month-olds in this simple search task. Although there is some evidence that older children may use spatial cues more effectively (DeLoache & Brown, 1983), the fact that spatial context could be reliably recalled suggests evidence of recollection for the past hiding experience.

Using naturalistic observational methods (i.e., parental diary studies), Ashmead and Perlmutter (1980) have reported several instances in everyday life in which 7- to 9-month-old infants recalled the location of objects (such as a favorite toy) after long delays. Newcombe, Huttenlocher, and Learmonth (1999) extended these findings to 5-month-old infants using a series of looking-time studies examining the ability to code the location of an object hidden in a sandbox. Results from this investigation revealed that infants looked longer when objects appeared in locations that violated their expected locations, suggesting that they recollected the original spatial location. Finally, a unique study by Myers, Clifton, and Clarkson (1987) suggested that not only can infants recall details regarding spatial context, but that these memories may be quite robust. They examined long-term memory in 5 children who had participated 15 to 19 times between 6 to 40 weeks of age in a laboratory study of the perception of auditory space in both a lighted and darkened room. When children returned to the lab 2 years later, they provided evidence that they retained memory of the unique objects and actions from the experiment in which they had participated during early infancy. Specifically, compared with a control group they played more with objects from the earlier experiment in a lighted room and in a darkened room they were more likely to grasp and hold onto invisible objects (which was the behavior tested in the earlier experiment). Taken together, these findings suggest that even very young infants show memory for spatial location suggesting that these memories may involve recollection of specific contextual details.

Memory for Temporal Order

There is a great deal of evidence that toddlers and infants show memory for temporal context using the elicited and deferred imitation paradigms. This ability has been reported in infants as young as 6 months of age. For example, Barr, Dowden, and Hayne (1996) used the deferred imitation paradigm in a group of 6-month-old infants to examine recall of a three-action event sequence. The infant's task was to pull a mitten off a puppet's hand, shake the mitten, and replace the mitten on the puppet's hand. One quarter of the infants in the study showed evidence for recall of temporal order after a 24-hr delay. Although only present in a small subset of infants, these individuals did show evidence suggesting memory for temporal order. One limitation of this study that may have underestimated infant's abilities was that the actions in the sequence were physically constrained, such that it was necessary to complete the first action before the second or third actions could even be attempted. Thus, not only did infants have to recall the first action (remove the mitten) but had to successfully complete it in order to begin to recall and attempt the second (shaking) and third (replacing) actions.

To address this limitation, Bauer and colleagues have conducted a series of systematic studies examining memory for temporal order using two-step action event sequences with props that do not have this constraint (e.g., making a gong as described previously). These studies have shown that approximately 50% of 9-month-old infants are able to recall temporal order information after a 5-week delay (Bauer, Wiebe, Carver, Waters, & Nelson, 2003; Bauer, Wiebe, Waters, & Bankston, 2001; Carver & Bauer, 1999). Although only half of the sample shows evidence for recollection, this finding is impressive given the long delay (5 weeks) over which the information is recalled.

These studies show that although memory for temporal order is present in some infants at 9 months of age, there are also data to suggest that there is great improvement in this ability across the next year of life. First, the ability to recall temporal order becomes more reliable across individuals: at 10 months of age, 80% of infants evidence recall of temporal order information after a 1-month delay (Bauer et al., 2006), and by 20 months of age, 100% of children recall order information after a 1-month delay (using age-appropriate sequences with four actions; Bauer et al., 2000). Second, this ability also becomes more robust, as 10-month-old infants are able to recall temporal order information after longer delays (e.g., 3 months as opposed to 1 month, Carver & Bauer, 2001) and 20-month-olds show memory for portions of the events as long as 1 year later (Bauer et al., 2000).

Bauer and colleagues have linked these differences in ordered recall to differences in representation at the neural level using ERPs. Specifically, these studies have shown differences in the processing of old and new stimuli in the two ERP components previously described (i.e., the early component related to attention and memory processes and the later component related to memory updating and perhaps recollection). These differences in ERP responses are evident at both the group and individual levels. In one study, differences in both ERP components were reported, although these differences were only found in the group of 9-month-old infants who showed evidence of memory for temporal order following a 1-month delay (i.e., they were not present in those who did not recall the event sequences; Carver et al., 2000). In subsequent studies, the amount of information recalled has been shown to be correlated with the magnitude of differential processing in both ERP components, such that greater recall is associated with greater differences in processing (Bauer et al., 2006; Bauer et al., 2003). Bauer and colleagues (2006, 2003) have used these ERP findings to suggest that individual differences in both brain development and mnemonic processes (i.e., encoding, consolidation, and storage) contribute to the variability in temporal order memory described previously (see the section on "Potential mechanisms of change" for expansion on the issue of brain development).

In sum, memory for temporal order has been observed in infants as young as 6 months of age. However, this ability is not reliably observed in all infants and, when it is observed, appears fragile as it fades quickly over periods of delay. Thus, although present early in life, memory for temporal order improves dramatically over the first two years of life (Bauer et al., 2000). ERPs have been shown to provide an additional level of analysis that is related to memory performance and may be useful for examining the neural bases of this developmental change (Bauer, 2007a).

Memory for Novel Associations

Most of the imitation studies described herein have used event sequences that are constrained by enabling relations (i.e., relations that serve to conceptually constrain the order in which the individual actions should be completed in order to achieve the desired end state). For example, when making a rattle out of two nesting cups and a bell, one must (a) put the bell into one of the cups, (b) cover this cup with the second cup, and (c) then shake the cups to make a rattle (e.g., Bauer & Dow, 1994). The steps need to be completed in this order to achieve the desired end state; however, it is indeed possible to complete all steps despite the order (i.e., one could cover the second cup and then shake the cups without the bell inside). One reason these sequences have been used so often in infant memory paradigms is that they bolster performance. As is the case for older children and adults, infants show superior ordered recall for events that contain enabling relations between items, compared with events that contain arbitrary associations between items (for review see Bauer, 1997, 2002). Thus, for research questions regarding the reliability and robustness of memory in early childhood, which has predominated the infant literature, the use of these types of events that support memory performance is critically important.

However, more relevant to the discussion of the emergence of recollection, is whether infants and toddlers are also able to recall events in which relations between events are arbitrary (i.e., when it is not necessary to complete the actions in a specified order to achieve the desired end state), as this is more of a direct test of whether the original demonstration was truly recollected. An example of a sequence with arbitrary relations is making a party hat. In this sequence, one can complete the following steps in any order and still achieve the desired end state: (a) put a pom-pom in the top of a cone-shaped base, (b) attach a sticker to the front of the cone, (c) attach a colored band to the base of the cone (e.g., Bauer & Dow, 1994). Indeed, several investigations have shown that both infants and toddlers are able to recall sequences that only contain arbitrary relations between items (Bauer & Dow, 1994; Bauer & Hertsgaard, 1993; Bauer & Travis, 1993; Mandler & McDonough, 1995). For example, Bauer and Hertsgaard (1993) report that both 13.5- and 16.5-month-olds were able to recall the temporal order of sequences with arbitrary relations immediately (on 81% and 67% of trials, respectively) and after a 1-week delay (on 60% and 65% of trials). Thus, evidence exists that memory for novel associations between components of events is present even in preverbal infants.

EVIDENCE FOR RECOLLECTION IN INFANTS YOUNGER THAN 6 MONTHS?

The data reviewed herein suggests that the building blocks of recollection may be present in infants as young as 6 months of age, but what about infants younger than 6 months? Unfortunately, due to the physical and motor maturity required by behavioral imitation paradigms, these methods have not been used with infants younger than 6 months of age. Paradigms that have typically been used to examine memory in infants less than 6 months primarily include: visual paired comparison tasks, habituation procedures, and the mobile conjugate reinforcement task. All of these paradigms have been instrumental in providing evidence that infants can and do form memories during this period. However, these methods do not typically provide data relevant to the question as to which mnemonic processes are contributing to the memory representations. For example, in looking-time studies, longer fixation on certain stimuli can indicate recognition; however, whether this recognition is due to recollection or another mnemonic process (e.g., familiarity) is unknown. Moreover, without measures of recall, it becomes increasingly difficult to determine what "qualitative" aspect of the event (i.e., spatial context, temporal context, or novel associations) is remembered.

Unfortunately, at present, there does not seem to be body of literature or comprehensive set of data available to answer the question as to whether recollection (or its building blocks) is present in infants younger than 6 months of age. One fruitful avenue for future research will be to develop paradigms that will begin to address this question. These tasks may use modifications to commonly used behavioral methods and/or use recordings of brain activity (e.g., ERPs, fMRI, or near-infrared spectroscopy, NIRS) to probe neural events associated with behavior observed during these behavioral assessments. However, until these studies are conducted, the issue of whether infants aged 6 months and younger show evidence for recollection remains largely unaddressed.

DEVELOPMENT

Although there is evidence that the building blocks of recollection are present as early as the sixth month of life, compared to data in adults, this support is rather sparse and thus remains speculative. One reason such speculation is necessary is that in infancy and toddlerhood all available data comes from paradigms that were not specifically designed to examine recollection or separate recollection from other processes, such as familiarity. This is unfortunate and clearly illustrates the need for dual-process models of memory to be recognized and incorporated into the developmental literature.

However, one lesson learned from the history of research on infant memory is not to assume that young children lack a cognitive ability simply due to a methodological impediment. Just because infants and young children are not able to participate in the paradigms of choice for adult memory researchers (e.g., namely, verbal recall) does not mean they lack the ability to remember! The last 30 years of research has generated ample evidence to contrary (see Bauer, 2006; Bauer, 2007b; Hayne, 2004; Rovee-Collier, 1997, for comprehensive reviews). In light of this, alternative datasets were used in the present chapter to begin to address the question of whether recollection may be apparent early in life. This evidence was inferred from tasks in which infants and children showed memory for: (a) objects in specific spatial locations, (b) the temporal order of events, and (c) novel associations between components of arbitrary events. One justification for applying such a "rich" interpretation to these datasets is that evidence for recollection was present in the youngest group (4-year-old preschoolers) tested with traditional paradigms (i.e., process dissociation procedure, see Anooshian, 1999). Thus, it is at least reasonable to suggest that children a few months younger in age also have the ability.

However, one potential pitfall of this rich interpretation is that it may be used (incorrectly) to assert that because recollection may be detectable early in life, no subsequent development occurs. This is certainly not the case. Even in school-aged children, in whom there is clear evidence of recollection (e.g., Ghetti & Angelini, 2008), there is also ample evidence that this ability is not adultlike; in fact, much development occurs. An important avenue for future research will be to examine this developmental change and explain the mechanisms underlying it.

If a more conservative approach is taken regarding the appearance of recollection, conclusions drawn from the evidence reviewed in this chapter would be that recollection is not present in infancy and toddlerhood because paradigms are not able to verify that a recollective experience occurred. One challenge associated with such a conservative interpretation is that then the need arises to identify precisely *when* recollection comes "online." This presents additional obstacles in that it would require evidence showing that a qualitative transition occurs at some point in development (i.e., verification that children do not have the ability to recollect at age *X*, but subsequently have the ability to recollect at age *Y*). To obtain evidence for this, age-appropriate paradigms would still need to be developed to examine recollection using the same techniques across multiple age groups in infancy and toddlerhood. In addition, after indentifying "the age" at which recollection appears, it will then be to necessary to explain why a wide gulf exists between children who do not have recollection abilities and those that do. As pointed out in other cognitive domains, under these circumstances, developmental change becomes a rare or exotic event that requires an equally exceptional explanation. Because such explanations are exceedingly elusive, conceptualizing developmental change in this light may actually be detrimental to scientific progress (Siegler, 1994).

Potential Mechanisms of Change

One mechanism that may account for the "rich" interpretation that recollective processes exist in infancy, yet continue to develop throughout childhood, is the prolonged development of the neural circuitry underlying recollection. Prolonged brain development has been reported in multiple regions, including portions of the MTL and PFC (Giedd et al., 1999; Giedd et al., 1996). Because studies in adults have suggested that recollection (as opposed to familiarity) relies preferentially on the hippocampus, the developmental course of this structure may be of particular relevance especially early in development.[3]

The neural network underlying recollection can only be expected to function at adult levels when each component and all connections between components have reached maturity (Bauer, 2007b). Maturity can be conceptualized on at least two levels: structural and functional. The former refers to when, during ontogeny, a variety of parameters regarding structural elements (e.g., number of cells, cell

---

3. It is acknowledged that simply because a task involves the hippocampus does not make it recollection.

body size, length of dendrites) become adultlike. The latter refers to when organizational and functional parameters become adultlike, both within individual structures and across integrated networks. It is important to recognize that structural maturity does not imply functional maturity. For example, a brain structure (such as the hippocampus) may have adultlike numbers of neurons at birth (or shortly after). However, simply having adult numbers of neurons does not indicate they are performing like mature neurons. As an analogy, one can think of a new company, which may be considered "mature" once it has hired 100 employees to complete the work. However, just because 100 people have been hired does not mean the company is functioning in a "mature" manner. These employees need to take on specialized jobs, learn how to work together, communicate with each other, and correspond with customers and other companies. Similarly, within the brain it is not only required that a "mature" number of cells be present, but these cells must also function in a "mature" manner (i.e., become specialized, function together as a unit, and communicate effectively and efficiently with each other as well as with other regions). Currently, knowledge regarding structural development of the hippocampus and memory circuitry in general far exceeds knowledge regarding functional development.

Neuroanatomical data regarding structural development of the hippocampus have been obtained primarily from nonhuman primate tissue samples. These data suggest that there is prolonged growth of multiple elements within this structure including the formation and migration of neurons as well as proliferation of its afferent and efferent connections; it is the latter that is most prolonged and dramatic. Specifically, within the hippocampus, although adult numbers of neurons in the dentate gyrus are present by the end of the first year of postnatal life, dendritic development and synapse formation persists until at least 5 years of age (Eckenhoff & Rakic, 1991; Serres, 2001). Thus, although the hippocampal formation of young infants may have the necessary number of cells for rudimentary memory formation at 1 year of age, the number of postnatal morphological changes suggests a significant modification of this circuitry between the first year of life and early childhood (Serres, 2001). For instance, between the third to fifth years of life (in the human), neuronal connections between granule cells of the dentate gyrus and pyramidal neurons of Ammon's horn form, which not only alters the structural circuit, but the function of the hippocampus as well. Because this circuitry is critical for adultlike memory formation, this profile suggests that "mature" memory should not be expected before the fifth postnatal year (Serres, 2001). Data from structural MRI studies of children are consistent with the findings reviewed previously and suggest that within the MTL significant development of the hippocampus occurs even between 4 and 25 years of age. In fact, dissimilar trajectories have recently been shown in posterior versus anterior subregions (Gogtay et al., 2004; Gogtay et al., 2006), which parallel differences in their functional development (Giedd et al., 1996). However, this latter suggestion has not yet been examined empirically.

Such prolonged development of the hippocampus stands in stark contrast to the development of other structures in the MTL, such as the entorhinal cortex (which has been related to other mnemonic processes, i.e., familiarity, see Ranganath et al., 2004; Yonelinas et al., 2002). At the time of birth, the basic gross anatomic features and topological relationships of the human entorhinal cortex are present, and postnatal development is complete by the end of the first post-natal year (Grateron et al., 2002). However, it is difficult to evaluate the func-tional importance of such development in human infants and children (Eriksson et al., 1998).

At present, there are no direct data available relating structural and functional development of the hippocampus in humans. However, some researchers have suggested that knowledge of brain development should be used to constrain and inform expectations regarding behavioral performance and have begun to relate changes at the behavioral level to presumed structural changes at the neural level (e.g., Bauer et al., 2007). In an elegant line of research, Patricia Bauer has been relating early changes in brain development to behavioral memory performance in infancy in an effort to evaluate the "fit" between age-related changes in memory behavior and development of the neural substrate responsible for it (Bauer et al., 2006). Specifically, she draws on Goldman-Rakic's (1987) sug-gestion that characteristic functions of a cortical area should begin to emerge as the number of synapses reaches its peak, whereas attainment of adult levels or mature levels of function should coincide with the period of synapse elimination (Bauer, 2007b). The dentate gyrus of the hippocampus shows increases in synap-tic connectivity beginning around 8 months and reaches adult levels around 20 months (Eckenhoff & Rakic, 1991). This region provides an essential link in the trisynaptic circuit that connects the hippocampus with the balance of the temporal-cortical network supporting long-term declarative memory (Zola & Squire, 2000), which ultimately, increases the effectiveness and efficiency of com-munication between parahippocampal structures and the hippocampus (and the hippocampus and neocortex as well). In short, it is the major "route in" to the hippocampus, where new memory traces are consolidated for long-term stor-age. Given the developmental timeline and function of the dentate gyrus, Bauer hypothesized that the late development of this structure would mirror development of memory behavior (Bauer, 2007b). In fact, as reviewed previously, her behavioral work with infants has shown dramatic increases in memory for temporal order between 9 and 20 months of age. These improvements have been observed both in terms of the number of infants who are able to recall tem-poral order (50% at 9 months, 100% at 20 months) and in the length of time over which events can be recalled (9-month-olds remember for 1 month, whereas 20-month-olds remember for up to 12 months). Individual differences in rates of brain development may be reflected in 9-month-olds' recall performance: infants who have increased numbers of synapses in this region may show memory for temporal order early. However, as more infants enter this stage of brain devel-opment, more show memory for temporal order. In sum, near the end of the first year of life, coincident with increases in synaptogenesis in dentate gyrus, increases in reliability and robustness of temporally ordered recall are observed (Bauer, 2007b).

Evidence supporting this view of continuity in the role of the hippocampus in recollection across development comes from cases in which early damage to the hippocampus alters recollective processing later in development. These data come primarily from individuals with developmental amnesia (see also work on children with Type 1 diabetes and infants of diabetic mothers, e.g., Ghetti, Lee, Sims, DeMaster, & Glaser, 2010; Nelson, 2007). Developmental amnesia results from hypoxic or ischemic episodes suffered early in life that significantly reduce hippocampal volume bilaterally (Bachevalier & Vargha-Khadem, 2005) and impair episodic memory while leaving semantic memory largely intact. Specific to the purpose of this chapter, detailed studies of one patient with developmental amnesia (Jon) with perinatal-onset bilateral hippocampal pathology (~50% volume reduction) revealed impairments in recollection exclusively. For example, in recognition memory tests requiring remember versus know judgments, Jon demonstrated a preserved ability to make familiarity, but not recollection judgments (Baddeley, Vargha-Khadem, & Mishkin, 2001). Electrophysiological studies of word recognition with Jon revealed normal modulation of familiarity ERP components, but not recollection ERP components (i.e., the late positive component over parietal leads, Duzel, Vargha-Khadem, Heinze, & Mishkin, 2001). Finally, fMRI studies with Jon have shown different patterns of activation in hippocampal-cortical connectivity when he recalled autobiographical events (which likely requires some amount of recollection, Maguire, Vargha-Khadem, & Mishkin, 2001). Based on cases of developmental amnesia such as Jon's, it appears that early onset of selective pathology to the hippocampus impairs recollection during adulthood, suggesting that this ability is crucially dependent on this region throughout life (Bachevalier & Vargha-Khadem, 2005; see also Ghetti, Lee, et al., 2010; Nelson, 2007).

This view, which suggests that memory is attributable to the onset of functioning in the hippocampus, is largely maturational in nature (Johnson, 2001). If the hippocampus is both structurally and functionally mature by 5 years of age (in the human), then what could account for the developmental change reported in behavioral studies with older children (Billingsley et al., 2002; Brainerd et al., 2009; Ghetti & Angelini, 2008; Holliday, 2003; Piolino et al., 2007)?

An alternative to this maturational view is one of interactive specialization (Johnson, 2001), in which postnatal functional brain development involves a process of organizing interregional interactions. According to an interactive specialization account, the onset of behavioral competencies (such as recollection) would be associated with changes in maturity of several regions, not just one region. In the case of recollection, the hippocampus is not the only region involved. An entire memory network is required, involving both MTL and PFC (Ranganath et al., 2004; Yonelinas et al., 2002). The PFC is most notably known for its protracted developmental course (Gogtay et al., 2004). Although increases in synaptogenesis begin in the PFC between 8 to 24 months (Huttenlocher, 1979; Huttenlocher & Dabholkar, 1997), this region continues to develop well into the adolescent years (Gogtay et al., 2004). If functional maturity of the entire neural network underlying recollection is only reached once each component and all connections between components are mature, then the changes observed during school-age years may be attributable to continued development of the PFC portion of the network and/or its connections with the hippocampus (which is consistent with the fMRI and ERP studies in school-aged children, Cycowicz et al., 2003; Menon et al., 2005; Ofen et al., 2007).

Recollection in the Context of Other Developmental Change

Determining what mechanism(s) contribute to developmental change is a complex process and becomes increasingly intricate when the viewing lens is expanded and we are reminded that recollection does not develop in isolation. Within the domain of memory, we also know that general semantic memory processes improve with age, as do metamemory abilities, memory strategy use, etc . . . (Gathercole, 1998). Changes in more general cognitive abilities are also occurring simultaneously (e.g., attention, cognitive control, executive functioning) as are changes in social abilities and motivation. Finally, children's experience in the world is accumulating and feeds back to shape functioning. For example, Hayne and colleagues have shown that when chronological age is held constant, the ability to locomote independently (i.e., crawl) influences memory performance (Gross & Hayne, 2004, June; as cited in Newcombe & Crawley, 2007). Specifically, crawlers show increased flexibility in their memory performance and are able to exploit a wider variety of retrieval cues during a deferred imitation task. Thus, future research should not only examine the development of recollection, but the development of recollection in the context of the whole child (see Bauer, 2007b; Nelson & Fivush, 2004, for similar arguments).

CONCLUSIONS

Based on the empirical studies reviewed in this chapter, evidence exists that the building blocks of recollection are present at least in infants as young as 6 months of age. Data from a variety of paradigms have shown that infants and young children are able to recall "qualitative" information, such the temporal and spatial context surrounding an event and novel associations between different components of the event. These abilities are, by definition, evidence of recollection. However, because this evidence is derived from tasks used to investigate general memory abilities (as opposed to recollection per se) it cannot be definitively concluded that true recollective experiences occur during this time period. Yet, these skills, even in their most rudimentary form, will prove vitally important to investigate as they will ultimately develop into true (or adultlike) recollection over time. When the empirical evidence is constrained to only include data from traditional paradigms that separate recollection from other mnemonic processes, it is apparent that recollection is present in the youngest age group tested to date (i.e., 4-year-olds; Anooshian, 1999). Although recollective abilities are detectable, evidence from all paradigms reviewed overwhelmingly shows that much development occurs in recollection and its building blocks over the first two decades of life (Billingsley et al., 2002; Brainerd et al., 2009; Ghetti & Angelini, 2008; Holliday, 2003; Piolino et al., 2007).

Many challenges remain for the future of research on the development of recollection. First, dual-process models of memory must be incorporated into developmental literature, both theoretically and empirically. Future investigations must work to design novel tasks in which recollection can be examined directly in younger samples. These paradigms should contain features similar to those found in adults and strive to isolate recollection from other processes (e.g., familiarity). Importantly, nonverbal paradigms will need to be modified in ways that allow for assessment as to whether true recollective experiences are present. It is also important that paradigms be developed for use in infants younger than 6 months in order to examine if the building blocks of recollection are also present during this period of life. One potential methodology that may prove useful in these endeavors is ERPs, which have been shown to be sensitive to recollective processes in adults (and are suggested to reflect the same in both childhood and infancy). Because ERPs can be used across a wide range of ages, this evidence would not only allow for detection of recollection in young age groups, but also perhaps a common metric on which development of recollective processes could be examined from infancy to adulthood. Second, across all ages (including school-aged children and adolescents) the mechanisms underlying developmental change at both behavioral and neural levels need to be examined further and better understood. Finally, studies investigating the development of individual differences in recollective abilities and the consequences of this in other domains (such as social functioning) are needed as they will not only enhance our understanding of recollection per se but will also serve to increase the significance of the development of recollection in the field overall. In closing, much work is needed to improve our understanding of the development of recollection. By delineating how this complex system is assembled, we will ultimately achieve not only a better understanding of recollection itself but also a better understanding of memory in general.

REFERENCES

Adlam, A. L., Vargha-Khadem, F., Mishkin, M., & de Haan, M. (2005). Deferred imitation of action sequences in developmental amnesia. *Journal of Cognitive Neuroscience*, *17*, 240–8.

Anooshian, L. J. (1999). Understanding age differences in memory: Disentangling conscious and unconscious processes. *International Journal of Behavioral Development*, *23*, 1–17.

Ashmead, D. H., & Perlmutter, M. (1980). Infant memory in everyday life. In M. Perlmutter (Ed.), *New directions for child development: Children's memory* (pp. 1–16). (No. 10) San Francisco, CA: Jossey-Bass.

Bachevalier, J., & Vargha-Khadem, F. (2005). The primate hippocampus: Ontogeny, early insult and memory. *Current Opinion in Neurobiology*, *15*, 168–74.

Baddeley, H., Vargha-Khadem, F., & Mishkin, M. (2001). Preserved recognition in a case of developmental amnesia: Implications for the acquisition of semantic memory? *Journal of Cognitive Neuroscience*, *13*, 357–69.

Barnat, S. B., Klein, P. J., & Meltzoff, A. N. (1996). Deferred imitation across changes in context and object: Memory and generalization in 14-month-old infants. *Infant Behavior and Development, 19*, 241–51.

Barr, R., Dowden, A., & Hayne, H. (1996). Developmental changes in deferred imitation by 6- to 24-month-old infants. *Infant Behavior and Development, 19*, 159–71.

Bauer, P. J. (1997). Development of memory in early childhood. In N. Cowan (Ed.), *The development of memory in childhood* (pp. 83–112). Sussex, England: Psychology Press.

Bauer, P. J. (2002). Early memory development. In U. Goswami (Ed.), *Blackwell handbook of childhood cognitive development* (pp. 127–46). Oxford, England: Blackwell.

Bauer, P. J. (2006). Event Memory. In R. M. L. W. Damon, D. Kuhn, & R. S. Siegler (Eds.), *Handbook of child psychology: Vol. 2. Cognition, perception, and language* (6th ed., pp. 373–425). New York: Wiley.

Bauer, P. J. (2007a). Recall in infancy: A neurodevelopmental account. *Current Directions in Psychological Science, 16*, 142–6.

Bauer, P. J. (2007b). *Remembering the times of our lives: Memory in infancy and beyond.* Mahwah, NJ: Lawrence Erlbaum Associates.

Bauer, P. J. (2008). Infantile amnesia. In M. M. Haith & J. B. Benson (Eds.), *Encyclopedia of infant and early childhood development* (pp. 51–61). San Diego, CA: Academic Press.

Bauer, P. J., Cheatham, C. L., Strand Cary, M., & Van Abbema, D. (2002). Short-term forgetting: Charting its course and its implications for long-term remembering. In S. Shohov (Ed.), *Perspectives on cognitive psychology* (pp. 93–112). Huntington, NY: Nova Science Publishers.

Bauer, P. J., DeBoer, T., & Lukowski, A. F. (2007). In the language of multiple memory systems, defining and describing developments in long-term explicit memory. In L. M. Oakes, & P. J. Bauer (Eds.), *Short- and long-term memory in infancy and early childhood: Taking the first steps towards remembering* (pp. 240–70). New York: Oxford University Press.

Bauer, P. J., & Dow, G. A. (1994). Episodic memory in 16- and 20-month-old children: Specifics are generalized but not forgotten. *Developmental Psychology, 30*, 403–17.

Bauer, P. J., & Hertsgaard, L. A. (1993). Increasing steps in recall of events: Factors facilitating immediate and long-term memory in 13.5- and 16.5-month-old children. *Child Development, 64*, 1204–23.

Bauer, P. J., Kroupina, M. G., Schwade, J. A., Dropik, P. L., & Wewerka, S. S. (1998). If memory serves, will language? Later verbal accessibility of early memories. *Development and Psychopathology, 10*, 655–79.

Bauer, P. J., & Travis, L. L. (1993). The fabric of an event: Different sources of temporal invariance differentially affect 12-month-olds' recall. *Cognitive Development, 8*, 319–41.

Bauer, P. J., Van Abbema, D. L., & de Haan, M. (1999). In for the short haul: Immediate and short-term remembering and forgetting by 20-month-old children. *Infant Behavior and Development, 22*, 321–43.

Bauer, P. J., Wenner, J. A., Dropik, P. L., & Wewerka, S. S. (2000). Parameters of remembering and forgetting in the transition from infancy to early childhood. *Monographs of the Society for Research in Child Development, 65 (4, Serial No. 263)*.

Bauer, P. J., Wiebe, S. A., Carver, L. J., Lukowski, A. F., Haight, J. C., Waters, J. M., & Nelson, C. A. (2006). Electrophysiological indices of encoding and behavioral indices of recall: Examining relations and developmental change late in the first year of life. *Developmental Neuropsychology, 29,* 293–320.

Bauer, P. J., Wiebe, S. A., Carver, L. J., Waters, J. M., & Nelson, C. A. (2003). Developments in long-term explicit memory late in the first year of life: Behavioral and electrophysiological indices. *Psychological Science, 14,* 629–35.

Bauer, P. J., Wiebe, S. A., Waters, J. M., & Bankston, S. K. (2001). Reexposure breeds recall: Effects of experience on 9-month-olds' ordered recall. *Journal of Experimental Child Psychology, 80,* 174-200.

Billingsley, R. L., Smith, L. M., & McAndrews, P. T. (2002). Developmental patterns in priming and familiarity in explicit recollection. *Journal of Experimental Child Psychology, 82,* 251–77.

Brainerd, C. J., Reyna, V. F., & Holliday, R. E. (2011). Development of recollection: Episodic memory and binding in young children. In S. Ghetti & P. J. Bauer (Eds.), *Origins and development of recollection: Perspectives from psychology and neuroscience* (pp. 101–43). New York: Oxford University Press.

Brainerd, C. J., Reyna, V. F., & Howe, M. L. (2009). Trichotomous processes in early memory development, aging, and cognitive impairment: A unified theory. *Psychological Review, 116,* 783–832.

Carver, L. J., & Bauer, P. J. (1999). When the event is more than the sum of its parts: Nine-month-olds' long-term ordered recall. *Memory, 7,* 147–74.

Carver, L. J., & Bauer, P. J. (2001). The dawning of a past: The emergence of long-term explicit memory in infancy. *Journal of Experimental Psychology: General, 130,* 726–45.

Carver, L. J., Bauer, P. J., & Nelson, C. A. (2000). Associations between infant brain activity and recall memory. *Developmental Science, 3,* 234–46.

Cheatham, C. L., & Bauer, P. J. (2005). Construction of a more coherent story: Prior verbal recall predicts later verbal accessibility of early memories. *Memory, 13,* 516–32.

Chi, M. T. H. (1978). Knowledge structure and memory development. In R. Siegler (Ed.), *Children's thinking: What develops?* (pp. 73–96). Hillsdale, NJ: Erlbaum.

Courchesne, E., Granz, L., & Norcia, A. M. (1981). Event-related brain potentials to human faces in infants. *Child Development, 52,* 804–11.

Cycowicz, Y. M., Friedman, D., & Duff, M. (2003). Pictures and their colors: What do children remember? *Journal of Cognitive Neuroscience, 15,* 759–68.

Czernochowski, D., Mecklinger, A., Johansson, M., & Brinkmann, M. (2005). Age-related differences in familiarity and recollection: ERP evidence from a recognition memory study in children and young adults. *Cognitive, Affective, & Behavioral Neuroscience, 5,* 417–33.

de Haan, M., & Nelson, C. A. (1997). Recognition of the mother's face by 6-month-old infants: A neurobehavioral study. *Child Development, 68,* 187–210.

DeBoer, T., Wewerka, S., Bauer, P. J., Georgieff, M. K., & Nelson, C. A. (2005). Neurobehavioral sequelae of infants of diabetic mothers: Deficits in explicit memory at 1 year of age. *Developmental Medicine and Child Neurology, 47,* 525–31.

DeLoache, J. S., & Brown, A. L. (1979). Looking for Big Bird: Studies of memory in very young children. *The Quarterly Newsletter of the Laboratory of Comparative Human Cognition, 1,* 53–7.

DeLoache, J. S., & Brown, A. L. (1983). Very young children's memory for the location of objects in a large scale environment. *Child Development, 54,* 888–97.

Diana, R. A., & Ranganath, C. (2011). Neural basis of recollection: Evidence from neuroimaging and electrophysiological research. In S. Ghetti & P. J. Bauer (Eds.), *Origins and development of recollection: Perspectives from psychology and neuroscience* (pp. 168–87). New York: Oxford University Press.

Drummey, A. B., & Newcombe, N. S. (2002). Developmental changes in source memory. *Developmental Science, 5*, 502–13.

Duarte, A., Ranganath, C., Winward, L., Hayward, D., & Knight, R. T. (2004). Dissociable neural correlates for familiarity and recollection during the encoding and retrieval of pictures. *Cognitive Brain Research, 18*, 255–72.

Duzel, E., Vargha-Khadem, F., Heinze, H. J., & Mishkin, M. (2001). Brain activity evidence for recognition without recollection after early hippocampal damage. *Proceedings of the National Academy of Sciences of the United States of America, 98*, 8101–6.

Eckenhoff, M. F., & Rakic, P. (1991). A quantitative analysis of synaptogenesis in the molecular layer of the dentate gyrus in the rhesus monkey. *Developmental Brain Research, 64*, 129–35.

Eichenbaum, H., Yonelinas, A. P., & Ranganath, C. (2007). The medial temporal lobe and recognition memory. *Annual Review of Neuroscience, 30*, 123–52.

Elman, J. L., Bates, E. A., Johnson, M. H., Karmiloff-Smith, A., Parisi, D., & Plunkett, K. (1996). *Rethinking innateness: A connectionist perspective on development.* Cambridge, MA: Massachusetts Institute of Technology Press.

Eriksson, P. S., Perfilieva, E., Bjork-Eriksson, T., Alborn, A.-M., Norborg, C., Peterson, D. A., & Gage, F. H. (1998). Neurogenesis in the adult human hippocampus. *Nature Medicine, 4*, 1313–7.

Freud, S. (1905/1953). Childhood and concealing memories. In A. A. Brill (Ed.), *The basic writings of Sigmund Freud* (pp. 62–8). New York: The Modern Library.

Friedman, D. (2011). The development of episodic memory: An event-related brain potential (ERP) vantage point. In S. Ghetti & P. J. Bauer (Eds.), *Origins and development of recollection: Perspectives from psychology and neuroscience* (pp. 242–64). New York: Oxford University Press.

Friedman, D., de Chastelaine, M., Nessler, D., & Malcolm, B. (2010). Changes in familiarity and recollection across the lifespan: An ERP perspective. *Brain Research, 1310*, 124–41.

Friedman, D., & Johnson, R. (2000). Event-related potential (ERP) studies of memory encoding and retrieval: A selective review. *Microscopy Research and Technique, 51*, 6–28.

Gathercole, S. E. (1998). The development of memory. *Journal of Child Psychology and Psychiatry, 39*, 3–27.

Ghetti, S., Lyons, K. E., & DeMaster, D. M. (2011). The development of episodic memory: Binding processes, controlled processes, and introspection on memory states. In S. Ghetti & P. J. Bauer (Eds.), *Origins and development of recollection: Perspectives from psychology and neuroscience* (pp. 144–67). New York: Oxford University Press.

Ghetti, S., & Angelini, L. (2008). The development of recollection and familiarity in childhood and adolescence: Evidence from the dual-process signal detection model. *Child Development, 79*, 339–58.

Ghetti, S., DeMaster, D. M., Yonelinas, A. P., & Bunge, S. A. (2010). Developmental differences in medial temporal lobe function during memory encoding. *Journal of Neuroscience, 30*, 9548–56.

Ghetti, S., Lee, J. K., Sims, C. E., DeMaster, D. M., & Glaser, N. S. (2010). Diabetic ketoacidosis and memory dysfunction in children with type 1 diabetes. *Journal of Pediatrics, 156,* 109–14.

Giedd, J. N., Blumenthal, J., Jeffries, N. O., Castellanos, F. X., Liu, H., Zijdenbos, A., . . . Rapport, J. L. (1999). Brain development during childhood and adolescence: A longitudinal MRI study. *Nature Neuroscience, 2,* 861–3.

Giedd, J. N., Snell, J. W., Lange, N., Rajapakse, J. C., Casey, B. J., Kozuch, P. L., . . . Rapaport, J. L. (1996). Quantitative magnetic resonance imaging of human brain development: ages 4–18. *Cerebral Cortex, 6,* 551–60.

Gogtay, N., Giedd, J., Lusk, L., Hayashi, K. M., Greenstein, D. K., Vaituzis, A. C., . . . Thompson, P. M. (2004). Dynamic mapping of human cortical development during childhood through early adulthood. *Proceedings of the National Academy of Sciences, 101,* 8174–9.

Gogtay, N., Nugent, T. F. I., Herman, D. H., Ordonez, A., Greenstein, D., Hayashi, K. M., . . . Thompson, P. M. (2006). Dynamic mapping of normal human hippocampal development. *Hippocampus, 16,* 664–72.

Goldman-Rakic, P. S. (1987). Circuitry of primate prefrontal cortex and regulation of behavior by representational memory. In F. Plum (Ed.), *Handbook of physiology; the nervous system* (pp. 373–401). Bethesda, MD: American Physiological Society.

Grateron, L., Insausti, A. M., Garcia-Bragado, F., Arroyo-Jimenez, M. M., Marcos, P., Martinez-Marcos, A., . . . Insausti, R. (2002). Postnatal development of the human entorhinal cortex. In M. P. Witter & F. G. Wouterlood (Eds.), *The Parahippocampal Gyrus* (pp. 21–31). Oxford: Oxford University Press.

Gross, J., & Hayne, H. (2004, June). *Is there a relation between motor performance development and cognitive development in human infants?* Paper presented at the International Society for Developmental Psychobiology, Aix-en-Provence, France.

Hamond, N. R., & Fivush, R. (1991). Memories of Mickey Mouse: Young children recount their trip to Disneyworld. *Cognitive Development, 6,* 433–48.

Hanna, E., & Meltzoff, A. N. (1993). Peer imitation by toddlers in laboratory, home, and day-care contexts: Implications for social learning and memory. *Developmental Psychology, 29,* 701–10.

Hayne, H. (2004). Infant memory development: Implications for childhood amnesia. *Developmental Review, 24,* 33–73.

Hayne, H. (2007). Infant memory development: New questions, new answers. In L. M. Oakes & P. J. Bauer (Eds.), *Short- and long-term memory in infancy and early childhood: Taking the first steps towards remembering* (pp. 209–39). New York: Oxford University Press.

Hayne, H., Boniface, J., & Barr, R. (2000). The development of declarative memory in human infants: Age-related changes in deferred imitation. *Behavioral Neuroscience, 114,* 77–83.

Holliday, R. E. (2003). Reducing misinformation effects in children with cognitive interviews: Dissociating recollection and familiarity. *Child Development, 74,* 728–51.

Horn, H., & Myers, N. A. (1978). Memory for location and picture cues at ages two and three. *Child Development, 49,* 845–56.

Huttenlocher, P. R. (1979). Synaptic density in human frontal cortex: Developmental changes and effects of aging. *Brain Research, 163,* 195–205.

Huttenlocher, P. R., & Dabholkar, A. S. (1997). Regional differences in synaptogenesis in human cerebral cortex. *Journal of Comparative Neurology, 387,* 167–78.

Jacoby, L. L. (1991). A process dissociation framework: Separating automatic from intentional uses of memory. *Journal of Memory and Language, 30*(5), 513–41.

Johnson, M. H. (2001). Functional brain development in humans. *Nature Reviews Neuroscience, 2,* 475–83.

Lindsay, D. S., Johnson, M. K., & Kwon, P. (1991). Developmental changes in memory source monitoring. *Journal of Experimental Child Psychology, 52,* 297–318.

Maguire, E. A., Vargha-Khadem, F., & Mishkin, M. (2001). The effects of bilateral hippocampal damage on fMRI regional activations and interactions during memory retrieval. *Brain, 124,* 1156–70.

Mandler, J. M. (1998). Representation. In W. Damon, D. Kuhn & R. S. Siegler (Eds.), *Handbook of child psychology: Cognition, perception, and language* (5th ed., pp. 255–308). New York: Wiley.

Mandler, J. M., & McDonough, L. (1995). Long-term recall of event sequences in infancy. *Journal of Experimental Child Psychology, 59,* 457–74.

McDonough, L., Mandler, J. M., McKee, R. D., & Squire, L. R. (1995). The deferred imitation task as a nonverbal measure of declarative memory. *Proceedings of the National Academy of Sciences, 92,* 7580–4.

Menon, V., Boyett-Anderson, J. M., & Reiss, A. L. (2005). Maturation of medial temporal lobe response and connectivity during memory encoding. *Cognitive Brain Research, 25,* 379–85.

Myers, N. A., Clifton, R. K., & Clarkson, M. G. (1987). When they were very young: Almost-threes remember two years ago. *Infant Behavior and Development, 123,* 123–32.

Nelson, C. A. (1994). Neural correlates of recognition memory in the first postnatal year of life. In G. Dawson & K. Fischer (Eds.), *Human behavior and the developing brain* (pp. 269–313). New York: Guilford Press.

Nelson, C. A. (1997). The ontogeny of human memory: A cognitive neuroscience perspective. *Developmental Psychology, 31,* 723–38.

Nelson, C. A. (2007). A developmental cognitive neuroscience approach to the study of atypical development: A model system involving infants of diabetic mothers. In G. Dawson, K. Fischer, & D. Coch (Eds.), *Human behavior and the developing brain* (2nd ed., pp. 1–27). New York: Guilford Press.

Nelson, C. A., & Collins, P. F. (1991). Event-related potential and looking time analysis of infants' responses to familiar and novel events: Implications for visual recognition memory. *Developmental Psychology, 27,* 50–8.

Nelson, K., & Gruendel, J. (1986). Children's scripts. In K. Nelson (Ed.), *Event knowledge: Structure and function in development* (pp. 21–46). Hillsdale, NJ: Lawrence Erlbaum Associates.

Nelson, K. D., & Fivush, R. (2004). The emergence of autobiographical memory: A social cultural developmental theory. *Psychological Review, 111,* 486–511.

Newcombe, N. S., Lloyd, M. E., & Balcomb, F. (2011). Contextualizing the Development of Recollection: Episodic Memory and Binding in Young Children. In S. Ghetti & P. J. Bauer (Eds.), *Origins and development of recollection: Perspectives from psychology and neuroscience* (pp. 73–100). New York: Oxford University Press.

Newcombe, N. S., & Crawley, S. L. (2007). To have and have not: What do we mean when we talk about long-term memory development? In L. M. Oakes & P. J. Bauer (Ed.),

Short- and long-term memory in infancy and early childhood: Taking the first steps toward remembering (pp. 291–313). New York: Oxford University Press.

Newcombe, N. S., Huttenlocher, J., & Learmonth, A. E. (1999). Infants' coding of location in continuous space. *Infant Behavior and Development, 22,* 483–510.

Ofen, N., Kao, Y. C., Sokol-Hessner, P., Kim, H., Whitfield-Gabrieli, S., & Gabrieli, J. D. E. (2007). Development of the declarative memory system in the human brain. *Nature Neuroscience, 10,* 1198–1205.

Peterson, C., & Rideout, R. (1998). Memory for medical emergencies experienced by 1- and 2-year-olds. *Developmental Psychology, 34,* 1059–72.

Piolino, P., Hisland, M., Ruffeveille, I., Matuszewski, V., Jambaqué, I., & Eustache, F. (2007). Do school-age children remember or know the personal past? *Consciousness and Cognition, 16,* 84–101.

Ranganath, C., Yonelinas, A. P., Cohen, M. X., Dy, C. J., Tom, S., & D'Esposito, M. (2004). Dissociable correlates for recollection and familiarity within the medial temporal lobes. *Neuropsychologia, 42,* 2–13.

Reynolds, G. D., & Richards, J. E. (2005). Familiarization, attention, and recognition memory in infancy: An event-related potential and cortical source localization study. *Developmental Psychology, 41,* 598–615.

Riggins, T., Miller, N. C., Bauer, P. J., Georgieff, M. K., & Nelson, C. A. (2009a). Consequences of maternal diabetes mellitus and neonatal iron status on children's explicit memory performance. *Developmental Neuropsychology, 34,* 762–79.

Riggins, T., Miller, N. C., Bauer, P. J., Georgieff, M. K., & Nelson, C. A. (2009b). Electrophysiological indices of memory for temporal order in early childhood: Implications for the development of recollection. *Developmental Science, 12,* 209–19.

Rovee-Collier, C. (1997). Dissociations in infant memory: Rethinking the development of implicit and explicit memory. *Psychological Review, 104,* 467–98.

Rugg, M. D., & Yonelinas, A. P. (2003). Human recognition memory: A cognitive neuroscience perspective. *Trends in Cognitive Science, 7,* 313–9.

Rybash, J. M., & Colilla, J. L. (1994). Source memory deficits and frontal lobe functioning in children. *Developmental Neuropsychology, 10,* 67–73.

Schacter, D. L., Harbluk, J. L., & McLachlan, D. R. (1984). Retrieval without recollection: An experimental analysis of source amnesia. *Journal of Verbal Learning and Verbal Behavior, 23,* 593–611.

Schneider, W. (1993). Domain-specific knowledge and memory performance in children. *Educational Psychology Review, 5,* 257–73.

Serres, L. (2001). Morphological changes of the human hippocampal formation from midgestation to early childhood. In C. A. Nelson & M. Luciana (Eds.), *Handbook of developmental cognitive neuroscience* (pp. 45–58). Cambridge, MA: MIT Press.

Siegler, R. S. (1994). Cognitive variability: A key to understanding cognitive development. *Current Directions in Psychological Science, 3,* 1–5.

Squire, L. R., Wixted, J. T., & Clark, R. E. (2007). Recognition memory and the medial temporal lobe: a new perspective. *Nature Review Neuroscience, 8,* 872–83.

Thomas, K. M., & Jorgenson, L. (2011). Brain development and neuroimaging evidence. In S. Ghetti & P. J. Bauer (Eds.), *Origins and development of recollection: Perspectives from psychology and neuroscience* (pp. 219–41). New York: Oxford University Press.

Todd, C. M., & Perlmutter, M. (1980). Reality recalled by preschool children. *New Directions for Child Development, 10,* 69–85.

Tulving, E. (1985). Memory and consciousness. *Canadian Psychologist, 26*, 1–12.

Yonelinas, A. P. (1994). Receiver-operating characteristics in recognition memory: Evidence for a dual-process model. *Journal of Experimental Psychology: Learning, Memory, and Cognition, 20*, 1341–54.

Yonelinas, A. P. (2002). The nature of recollection and familiarity: A review of 30 years of research. *Journal of Memory and Language, 46*, 441–517.

Yonelinas, A. P. (2011). Remembering: Thoughts on its definition, measurement, and functional nature. In S. Ghetti & P. J. Bauer (Eds.), *Origins and development of recollection: Perspectives from psychology and neuroscience* (pp. 3–19). New York: Oxford University Press.

Yonelinas, A. P., Kroll, N. E., Quamme, J. R., Lazzara, M. M., Sauve, M. J., & Widaman, K. F. (2002). Effects of extensive temporal lobe damage or mild hypoxia on recollection and familiarity. *Nature Neuroscience, 5*, 1226–41.

Zola, S. M., & Squire, L. R. (2000). The medial temporal lobe and the hippocampus. In E. Tulving & F. I. M. Craik (Eds.), *The Oxford handbook of memory* (pp. 485–500). New York: Oxford University Press.

4

Contextualizing the Development of Recollection

Episodic Memory and Binding in Young Children

NORA S. NEWCOMBE, MARIANNE E. LLOYD, AND
FRANCES BALCOMB

Building an adapted mind requires a solution to the problem of how to select and organize the many kinds of information in the world. We need to select which kinds of information to encode at all, from among the overwhelming amount of information potentially available in the world. Even once the information has been selected, however, we need to organize it, considering which kinds of information are mutually relevant and belong together. Both the selection and the organization problems can be addressed at several levels of processing: sensory, perceptual, attentional, and mnemonic. In addition, each of the problems can be addressed in phylogenetic or in ontogenetic development. For example, in evolutionary time and at the sensory level, the problem of which kinds of information to encode can be simplified by natural selection of the sensory apparatus, so that bats end up equipped with sonar, certain birds with a magnetic sense, and humans with excellent vision in color and in depth. In developmental time and at the perceptual level, initial sensory capabilities are refined by environmental tuning, as when the language environment in which children are reared leads to the consolidation or the elimination of the ability to make phonemic distinctions among the continuously varying acoustic elements that compose human speech (Kuhl et al., 2006; Werker & Tees, 1984).

Fascinating as the selection problem is, however, this chapter does not concern it. Rather, we focus on the organizational question of which kinds of information belong together. This challenge, which can be called the *binding problem* (Garson, 2001;

Roskies, 1999; Treisman, 1996), is as important as the initial problem of selection. At any given point in time, many kinds of information are present in the world that we can sense and process. For example, flickering shadows created by the wind in the trees may co-occur with bird song, with the presence of certain flowers, apprehended both visually and by their scent, with a particular air temperature, and so on. But which of these correlations are important and which are coincidental? Sorting this issue out is fundamental to causal analysis, the formation of categories, and the acquisition of knowledge about the world.

In evolutionary time, some of the binding problem is simplified by natural selection, as when we see *prepared learning* of some associations more easily than others, for example, taste with nausea but vision with electric shock (Garcia & Koelling, 1966). In developmental time, it is likely that infants possess an overall preparedness to compute temporal and spatial correlations for the detection of lawful correspondences. So, for example, dynamic spatial information is central to defining objects, both developmentally (Rakison, 2005; Xu & Carey, 1996) and for adults (Fiser, Scholl, & Aslin, 2007; Mitroff & Alvarez, 2007; Treisman & Gelade, 1980) but, as development proceeds, and as motor development allows for greater experience with grasping objects, static characteristics such as color and texture can also be taken into account (Barrett, Traupman, & Needham, 2008; Wilcox, Woods, Chapa, & McCurry, 2007).

Clearly, determining how to put together the recurring and causally related information in the world is vital to adaptation. In light of the emphasis that must be placed on lawful relations, it is remarkable that we do not focus exclusively on those relations that are lawful and predictive. Even though some co-occurrences are coincidental, or at least only loosely and probabilistically associated, we retain them anyway, to form those memories of our lives that we call *episodic* or *autobiographical*. Adult humans possess an excellent (although not infallible) ability to recall contingent co-occurrences and linked episodes, each of which contain multiple sensory components. As we discuss, some other species may have this ability as well, for example, scrub jays (Clayton, Yu, & Dickinson, 2003; De Kort, Dickinson, & Clayton, 2005). Whether or not human infants have this kind of binding ability, and if not, when and how it is acquired during childhood, is the central focus of this chapter.

There is an interesting paradox in the development of semantic (lawful) and episodic (contingent) binding. The adaptive emphasis for the young child needs to be on learning what is true in general about the world. Does eating certain berries generally produce nausea? Are parrots likely to bite? Children are voracious in their acquisition of knowledge of this semantic kind, beginning in the first year of life. As one example, already mentioned, they learn through visual and manual experience what kinds of attributes other than temporal-spatial coherence define the probable existence of attached solids that constitute objects in the world. As a second example, they learn 10 words per day as toddlers (Bloom, 2001), as well as learning event schemata (Nelson, 2007). Building of this kind of semantic (or crystallized) knowledge in fact continues over the life span, with elderly adults continuing to add to their vocabulary (Rogers & Fisk, 2000).

Learning general facts about the world along with the vocabulary that captures this knowledge is, however, in tension with memory for *specific* instances and events, that is, learning about relations that are *not* lawful or particularly likely to occur again. Most parrots are unlikely to bite, and yet there was the memorable occasion when Aunt Gertrude was nipped by her normally well-behaved bird as she fed Polly seeds from her hand. Furthermore, although it was not causally relevant to the nipping event that Aunt Gertrude was wearing a striped apron, that she was in her kitchen on a hot afternoon in July, or that Cousin Billy was present but Uncle Ernest was playing golf, these aspects of the event may all be bound together. In fact, it is exactly the binding of these elements that makes a memory *episodic* rather than semantic (Tulving, 1972). Episodic memory adds rich texture to our lives, lying at the heart of autobiographical memory although not completely identical to it. (For discussion, see Conway & Pleydell-Pierce, 2000; Johnson, Hashtroudi, & Lindsay, 1993; Klein, German, Cosmides, & Gabriel, 2004; Tulving, 1993; Wheeler, Stuss, & Tulving, 1995.)

In this chapter, we will examine the development of episodic memory from the perspective that, at its heart, it is the development of the ability to bind together information co-occurring at a particular time in a particular spatial context, when such co-occurrences are unique or at least not lawful. This discussion gains considerable interest from recent proposals that episodic memory may overlap considerably with other human faculties such as imagining the future (Addis, Wong, & Schacter, 2007; Buckner & Carroll, 2007; Hassabis, Kumaran, Vann, & Maguire, 2007; Schacter, Addis, & Buckner, 2007) and understanding other people's thoughts (Buckner & Carrroll, 2007; Perner, Kloo, & Gornik, 2007; but see also Rosenbaum, Stuss, Levine, & Tulving, 2007), as well as with faculties that are shared across species such as spatial memory (Eichenbaum, 2007; Shapiro, Kennedy, & Ferbinteanu, 2006). All of these abilities develop, and there have been proposals that they develop together in principled ways (e.g., theory of mind and episodic memory, see Howe & Courage, 1997; or Perner & Ruffman, 1995; for spatial memory and episodic memory, see Newcombe, Lloyd, & Ratliff, 2007).

We begin with a note on what we mean by the term *binding*. We proceed to consider descriptive developmental facts, arguing that there is no good evidence of the kind of binding that lies at the heart of episodic memory until the age of 1.5 to 2 years, and that there is likely to be a period of rapid growth in such binding ability between the ages of 2 and 6 years (Bauer, 2005; Hayne, 2007; Klossek, Russell, & Dickinson, 2008). Thus prepared, we review the current studies focused on the development of binding, beginning with studies of aging humans, where this work is further along, and then turning to studies of children. Aging is not simply early development turned on its head, because the elderly have semantic knowledge and mnemonic strategies that young children lack. However, aging differentially affects the hippocampal and frontal areas that are involved in episodic memory and that are immature in children (Bauer, 2007; Burke & Barnes, 2006; Kersten, Earles, Curtayne, & Lane, 2008; Huttenlocher & Dabholkar, 1997; Kramer et al., 2007) Thus, similarities and differences between the mnemonic abilities of children and the elderly can be very informative. We then situate this developmental discussion in regard to two other literatures. First, there are exciting recent studies of binding in nonhuman animals. This work addresses the question of whether episodic memory is specific to our species or more widely shared across species. In addition, the work may offer tools for understanding of human memory development—techniques devised to work with nonlinguistic animals may offer excellent paradigms, properly adapted, for understanding the capabilities of infants and toddlers (for example, see Balcomb & Gerken, 2008; Klossek et al., 2008). Second, we discuss current theorizing about the relation of episodic memory to spatial memory, envisioning the future, and theory of mind. We conclude with an overview of what is known that highlights frontiers for research in this emerging field.

TWO (OR MORE) BINDING PROBLEMS

It can be confusing to read the literature on binding because the term has been used to refer to at least two different phenomena. First, the term has been used extensively in the literature on initial perceptual processing of objects and the storage of information in visual short-term memory (e.g., Luck & Vogel, 1997; Treisman & Gelade, 1980; Treisman & Zhang, 2006). In this context, *binding* means the assembly of features of an object such as form, color, and location that have initially been separately processed but that must be brought together to create a unified conscious percept. Feature integration theory (Treisman, 1998) suggests how this is accomplished using a master map of locations, dependent on the parietal lobe and disrupted by parietal damage (Coslett & Lie, 2008; Robertson & Treisman, 2006). This kind of binding appears to develop across the first year of life, reflecting changes in parietal cortex and associated changes in capacity for focused attention (Oakes, Ross-Sheehy, & Luck, 2006). At first glance, binding in visual short-term memory would seem to be prerequisite to any further processing and thus prerequisite to memory—we remember the shiny pink purse on the actress's makeup table, not shininess and pinkness and so on as separate entities. However, the relations between visual short-term memory and long-term memory (as well as working memory) are currently open to debate (see review by Luck, 2008). In any case, this kind of binding is not at the heart of the kind of binding that we have in mind when we consider episodic memory and recollection.

Second, once the phenomenal world has been parsed, selected, sensed, and assembled, we may or may not bind together those bound entities to form events, and we may or may not retain those assembled events over time. This kind of binding lies at the heart of Tulving's (1999) conception of autonoetic memory, which brings together the what-where-when-how of the world to allow for "mental time travel." This kind of binding is central to recollection and to experiences of "remembering" as opposed to "knowing" (e.g., Meiser, Sattler, & Weisser, 2008). This kind of binding is also central to source memory, which includes information such as sex or tone of voice with which a statement was pronounced, or the emotional state of the listener (Chalfonte & Johnson, 1996). Last, this kind of binding is an associative process and has been studied recently using paradigms that are fundamentally the paired-associate techniques used for decades in the study of memory (e.g., studies of the elderly by Naveh-Benjamin, 2000).

Within the kind of binding that lies at the heart of episodic memory and recollection, further distinctions may also be important. First, intraobject (or intrinsic) binding links the shape, function, or name of an object to other characteristics, such as an arbitrary color (e.g., a green whistle) whereas interobject (or extrinsic) binding links different objects together (e.g., a paired association of whistle and cheese). A particularly important kind of interobject binding involves linking an object to a context, such as a setting or background. Extrinsic binding may be more relevant to episodic memory than intrinsic binding (Ecker, Zimmer, & Groh-Bordin, 2007). Further distinctions are also possible. Bindings can be across rather than within modality (e.g., the sound of the whistle that we also see). Indeed, cross-modality linkages may be especially relevant to episodic memory (Meiser et al., 2008). Furthermore, bindings can be studied both in working memory and in long-term memory. Studying binding in working memory is relevant to recollection because deficits in long-term binding in the elderly seem to be caused at least in part by difficulty in initial binding in working memory (Mitchell, Johnson, Raye, Mather, & D'Esposito, 2000).

DEVELOPMENT OF EPISODIC MEMORY

The first step in understanding development is delineating what happens when. Research of this kind is fundamentally descriptive, but establishing age norms goes beyond the preoccupations of Arnold Gesell, the developmental psychologist who began to tabulate such norms a century ago. Age norms suggest causal explanations and constrain those theories that have been proposed. Thus, it is important to establish the time course of the development of episodic memory. There have been three methodologies used for this purpose: (a) investigations of children's and adults' autobiographical recall, often related to the phenomenon called infantile or childhood amnesia, (b) experiments using classic laboratory measures of episodic memory such as free recall or paired association, and (c) experiments using techniques tailored to be especially useful with infants and toddlers, such as visual paired comparison, conjugate reinforcement, and delayed imitation.

We argue that these lines of investigation converge to suggest three developmental periods. Before 2 years of age, although there is evidence of explicit memory in a semantic form, and the beginnings of binding, there is as yet no convincing demonstration of episodic memory. Between 2 and 6 years of age, episodic memory is clearly evident, but qualitatively distinct from adult functioning. After 6 years of age and continuing through the elementary school years, episodic memory strengthens, but changes in this age range depending chiefly on the acquisition of successively better and smoother-operating mnemonic strategies (for a review see Schneider & Bjorklund, 1998), as well as on the acquisition of semantic knowledge (Ghetti & Angelini, 2008).

Autobiographical Memory

Autobiographical memories are essentially self-related episodic memories.[1] There are several techniques that have been used to elicit autobiographical memories of childhood and hence to assess the developmental course of episodic memory. First, people have been asked to recall childhood events that come to mind given specific cue words, such as *pencil*, and then asked to date the memories (Crovitz & Quina-Holland, 1976; Crovitz & Schiffman, 1974; Waldfogel, 1948; Wetzler & Sweeney, 1986). The overall distribution of age to frequency of memories from such studies, based on about 11,000 childhood memories, shows very few auto-biographical memories predating the age of 2 years, with a rising but still small number of memories evident in the interval between turning 2 and turning 3, increasing steeply from 3 to 5 years, then leveling off and reaching mature levels by around 7 years of age (Rubin, 2000). That is, adults remember events from later elementary school at about the levels predictable from the time elapsed since the events, but they remember earlier events more poorly than would be predicted from delay time alone. Similar findings have now emerged from studies in which school-aged children recall events from earlier childhood (Bauer, Burch, Scholin, & Guler, 2007).

Other techniques also support the hypothesis that autobiographical memories are not evident before the age of 2 years. For example, people have been asked about single specific events likely to be memorable, such as birth of a younger sibling or a hospitalization, with verified recall beginning at around the age of 2 years (Crawley & Eacott, 1999, 2006; Eacott & Crawley, 1998, 1999; Sheingold & Tenney, 1982; Usher & Neisser, 1993; Winograd & Killinger, 1983). Studies that ask people to recall and date their earliest memory estimate around 3 years as the onset of episodic memory, although there are variations depending on age, gender, and culture (Fiske & Pillemer, 2006; Kihlstrom & Harackiewicz, 1982; MacDonald, Uesiliana, & Hayne, 2000; Matsumoto & Stanny, 2006; Mullen, 1994; Peterson, Grant, & Boland, 2005; Wang, 2001) and children report earlier first memories than do adults (Peterson et al., 2005.)

We also have other kinds of evidence concerning the offset of the period in which autobiographical memories are sparse and fragmentary. People have been asked to judge whether events in their early childhood were simply known from others' reports or actually remembered. The median age of remembered events is around 6 years (Bruce, Dolan, & Phillips-Grant, 2000; Bruce et al., 2005; Multhaup, Johnson, & Tetirick, 2005).

---

1. There are also self-related semantic facts ("I had blond hair as a child") and these may be considered autobiographical in some ways. But note that such facts are not necessarily based on what most people would term "memories." There are also episodic memories that are not self-relevant (quintessential examples of which are classic laboratory tasks as discussed in the next section).

Classic Laboratory Measures

Most studies using classic laboratory measures of episodic recall, such as free recall and paired associate learning, involve children at least 6 years of age (e.g., Schneider, Kron, Hunnerkopf, & Krajewski, 2004). There is a good reason for this concentration on school-aged children, namely that younger children find such tasks very difficult to engage in at all. Getting above-chance performance from preschoolers requires the use of simple tasks with engaging cover stories, for example, remembering items to buy in a toy grocery store (Mistry, Rogoff, & Herman, 2001; Smirnov, Istomina, Mal'tseva, & Samokhvalova, 1969). While toddlers may show use of extremely simple mnemonic strategies such as staring at a location where an object was hidden (Baker-Ward, Ornstein, & Holden, 1984; DeLoache & Brown, 1984; Schneider, 1999), the use of strategies as simple as rehearsal or increasing looking time with task difficulty is rare before 6 years (Flavell, Beach, & Chinsky, 1966; Rogoff, Newcombe, & Kagan, 1974). Investigators have occasionally argued that recognition is an exception to this rule (Werner & Perlmutter, 1979). However, recognition is a task that may tap familiarity as well as recollection and hence not be clearly episodic (e.g., Yonelinas, 2002, for a review; for developmental work, see Ghetti & Angelini, 2008). Furthermore, and supporting this analysis, recognition shows clear age-related differences when foils are similar to correct pictures except in specific details (e.g., Newcombe, Rogoff, & Kagan, 1977) or when there are substantial delays between exposure and test (Drummey & Newcombe, 1995).

Infant Memory Measures

Most studies of infant memory have used special techniques that do not require linguistic skills. The leading methods are visual paired comparison, conjugate reinforcement, and delayed imitation. There are, however, disagreements regarding the first two methodologies concerning whether or not the memory tapped by the technique is explicit or implicit (see chapters in Oakes & Bauer, 2007). There is widespread agreement that delayed imitation relies on explicit memory, and success in delayed imitation is observed as young as 6 months (Barr, Dowden, & Hayne, 1996; Barr, Rovee-Collier, & Campanella, 2005). Early success in delayed imitation does not preclude developmental change, however, and such change is in fact considerable (Bauer, 2007).

More important for present purposes, it is not clear whether delayed imitation tasks rely on semantic or on episodic memory. Data that show developmentally increasing generalization of memory for event sequences to new props or contexts (e.g., Cuevas, Rovee-Collier, & Learmonth, 2006, Hayne, Boniface, & Barr, 2000; Hayne, MacDonald, & Barr, 1997; Herbert, Gross, & Hayne, 2007) suggest the likelihood that the representations that children have formed are primarily semantic. For example, they learn that if you put a hard round object into a container that you can close and then shake, you have made a rattle. This fact is an interesting one, but not an episodic memory of the time they performed this action with a specific person in a specific room accompanied by a specific emotion.

Balcomb, Newcombe, Ferrara, and Funk (2010) have recently done work on the early underpinnings of episodic memory, i.e. the ability to bind the arbitrary elements that comprise a context, that support the idea that its earliest origins are toward the end of the second year. The paradigm was based on work with nonhuman animals by Eacott and Norman (2004). Children were shown the same four distinctive containers in two different rooms, but the containers were arranged differently in the two rooms and there were different experimenters in each room. A toy was hidden in one of the four containers, but in a different container in the two different rooms, requiring children to remember the unique context to find the toy. In Experiment 1, children were cued upon entering the room with a reminder of which toy was hidden there; for example, they were asked, "Where are the bubbles?" Children older than 20 months did quite well, but younger children were unable to cope with the demands of this episodic task. In Experiment 2, children were only given a general prompt such as, "Where are the toys?" In this case, children under the age of 2 years did uniformly badly. Their well-developed semantic memory skills allowed them to remember which two of the four containers were generally associated with toys, but episodic memory requires more specific associations. Thus, this work suggests the emergence of true episodic memory begins around 20 months in its very simplest form and continues past 24 months to a firmer form.

Summary

There is little doubt that the dawning of explicit memory occurs as early as 6 months, and it may be earlier. There is also little doubt that explicit memory strengthens over the first years of life. However, most research has failed to find convincing evidence of episodic memory. Autobiographical memories have not been seen before then; no one would think to attempt to ask children that young to do classic laboratory measures; and infant-friendly measures do not yet show episodic rather than semantic characteristics. Between the ages of 2 and 6 years, there is a strengthening of autobiographical memory and the dawning of the ability to engage in very simple laboratory episodic tasks. After 6 years, an extensive literature has documented the quantitative strengthening of the episodic memory system.

This progression may have adaptive significance. Semantic knowledge is vital for understanding the world and provides the backdrop against which episodic memories can be structured and take on meaning (Ghetti & Angelini, 2008). The developmental rule may be: Learn first how things usually work and later how events unfolded in some particular instance.

BINDING IN HUMAN AGING

Before we discuss how binding changes across childhood, we will discuss the work that inspired many of the studies of children: evidence that older adults are more susceptible to problems with memory binding than younger adults. A large

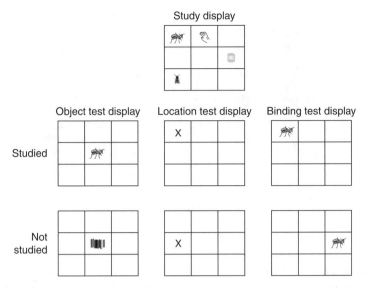

Figure 4.1. Example of typical paradigm, including sample study and test items, used to study binding deficits in aging

body of this work comes out of research conducted by Johnson and colleagues (e.g., Chalfonte & Johnson, 1996; Mitchell, Johnson, Mather, & D'Esposito, 2000; Mitchell, Johnson, Raye, Mather, & D'Esposito, 2000). In these studies, individuals study common objects that also vary in color or spatial location. During a memory test, participants answer questions about individual features or the combinations of features.

In general, older and younger adults perform equally well on features but older adults perform more poorly on combination items (e.g., Chalfonte & Johnson, 1996; Mitchell, Johnson, Mather, & D'Esposito, 2000). This finding is an important one, as it suggests that the deficits are not a general memory failure but rather a specific failure in the memory for how items are related to one another. Further, much of these deficits in memory binding seem to be due to an increased level of false alarms to rearranged combination items. That is, older adults have a difficult time rejecting items made of two familiar components that did not originally appear together (see Figures 4.1 and 4.2).

These findings are similar to studies that focus on verbal materials. Some of this work uses compound words that can be re-paired (e.g., *ladybug* and *bedroom* can be re-paired to form *bedbug*); false alarms to words such as *bedbug* are called conjunction errors (e.g., Underwood & Zimmerman, 1973). Although young adults make conjunction errors at a higher rate than false alarms to novel items (e.g., Jones, 2005; Jones & Jacoby, 2001; Reinitz, Lammers, & Cochran, 1992), this finding is even more dramatic with older adults (e.g., Castel & Craik, 2003). Related work by Naveh-Benjamin and colleagues (2000; Naveh-Benjamin, Guez,

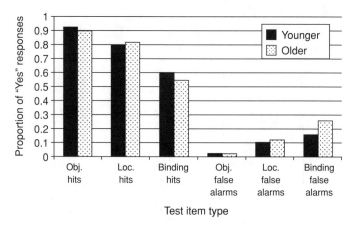

Figure 4.2. Typical results of binding and feature memory in aging studies

Kilb, & Reedy, 2004; Naveh-Benjamin, Guez, & Marom, 2003; Naveh-Benjamin, Hussain, Guez, & Bar-On, 2003) has used verbal materials to compare inter-item (e.g., paired associates) and intraitem (a word and its font color) binding. The major conclusion of this work is that both types of binding are impaired in older adults. The authors argue that this deficit represents a broad problem of remembering associations. Broadly, both lines of work with verbal materials suggest that a binding deficit in memory is not limited to simple pictorial stimuli but rather may represent a general impairment in relational memory. Such theorizing is very consistent with the idea that recollection is more impaired with aging than familiarity (Bishara & Jacoby, 2008; Jennings & Jacoby, 1993, 1997; Kersten et al. 2008; Pierce, Sullivan, Schacter, & Budson, 2005).

To summarize, there is good evidence that many of the deficits in memory with age may be related to deficits specifically in forming associations across features. In the next section, we will review work on similar paradigms across childhood. That is, we will investigate the evidence that children have deficits in binding memory that are similar to those of older adults.

RECENT WORK ON THE DEVELOPMENT OF BINDING

In order to examine the development of memory binding, several studies have been conducted that focus on when children can successfully remember the co-occurrence of features in an environment. Certainly, binding of information is important for good semantic memory as well as for episodic memory. When we remember that Harrisburg is the capital of Pennsylvania, we have established a connection between the name of a city and the name of a state. However, the association is a necessary not a contingent one. Unless the state legislature votes to move its sessions to another city, this fact will always be true. The question that experiments on binding in episodic memory are attempting to answer is instead about contingent associations—when will a child remember first holding his infant female cousin in a bright pink blanket at a family reunion picnic? After all,

Figure 4.3. Example of complex stimuli used in Sluzenski et al. (2006)

the blanket might have been yellow, or the occasion could have been Christmas morning.

Whether children have unique difficulties with this type of binding has only been investigated to a limited degree. Most of this work is similar to that described in the aging section, where memory for individual features is compared with the memory for correctly versus incorrectly paired features. Returning to the preceding example, when do children remember they first held their cousin at a family reunion and not on Christmas morning? In order to fairly answer this question, a first step is making sure that memory for the elements of the event are equally likely to be remembered. That is, deficits in binding need to be separated from deficits in remembering that which is to be bound. Most of the research to date suggests that between the ages of 4 and 6 years dramatic improvements in the use of memory binding processes occur when memory for the features is equated.

Sluzenski, Newcombe, and Kovacs (2006) investigated memory binding across early childhood by testing interitem binding of animals and backgrounds. Children studied an animal as well as its associated background and then were shown the item paired together (Experiment 2, see Figures 4.3 and 4.4).

For example, a child might be shown a picture of a tiger, then a picture of a swimming pool, and finally a picture of the tiger at the swimming pool. In addition, she might also see a turtle, a library, and a picture of a turtle in a library. Later, the participants were given a memory test in which they had to discriminate studied animals (e.g., a tiger) from novel animals (e.g., a seal) and also between studied backgrounds (e.g., a swimming pool) and novel backgrounds (e.g., a freeway), as well as correct (tiger in a swimming pool) and rearranged pairings (tiger in a library). The children performed equally well on the feature memory tasks (animals and backgrounds) but 4-year-olds performed more poorly on the binding task. Although the analysis did not focus on this specifically, it seems that the

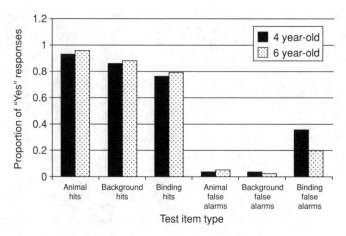

Figure 4.4. Results of Sluzenski et al., Experiment 2 (2006)

poorer performance was a function of an increased false alarm rate for rearranged items (see Figure 4.4). That is, 4- and 6-year-olds were equally good at recognizing the items that had occurred together initially (hit rates of 0.76 and 0.79, respectively) but 4-year-olds had greater difficulty than the 6-year-olds did in rejecting items that were rearranged (false alarm rates of 0.36 and 0.20, respectively). Such a finding is very consistent with the development of episodic memory discussed here. That is, when children false alarm to rearranged pairs, they are doing so to items that are familiar from previous occurrence while failing to recognize the context in which they originally appeared. Such a finding is also compatible with a delayed development of recollection relative to familiarity (e.g., Ghetti & Angelini, 2008).

The work by Sluzenski et al. (2006) leaves uncertain the nature of these binding deficits. That is, do younger children simply encode less information? Do they have more difficulty with retrieval? Do they have difficulty with both? In order to address this question, some of the authors (Lloyd, Doydum, & Newcombe, 2009) investigated memory performance on binding tasks as a function of list length. In this study, participants were tested on objects, backgrounds and combinations of objects and backgrounds. Like the results of Sluzenski et al., 2006), in comparison to 6-year-olds, 4-year-olds were significantly worse at remembering bound items. However, this only occurred when there was a long list of items to be remembered. Again, this was a function only of an increased false alarm rate to repaired items. When the list was short, performance was equivalent for both ages on all types of items. This suggests that at least some of the binding deficits before the age of 6 may be explained by deficits at retrieval.

A retrieval explanation for binding deficiencies is very consistent with the idea that the development of recollection supports memory binding (e.g., Ghetti & Angelini, 2008). That is, in order to successfully reject impaired items, one must be able to overcome the familiarity associated with the previous presentation and instead correctly recollect how items were put together. Again, in the adult memory literature, re-pairings are often referred to as *conjunction errors* and many theoretical accounts of successful avoidance rely on the idea of recollective processes (e.g., Jones, 2005; Lloyd, 2007; Odegaard, & Lampinen, 2004). To the extent that these processes are impaired, such as by speeding responses, errors tend to increase (Jones & Jacoby, 2001). However, it is important to note that the probability of recollection is also a function of the type of material that is encoded. Pairing an item with a picture, repeating it several times, or studying low compared with high frequency words (Gallo, 2004; Jacoby, Jones, & Dolan, 1998; Joordens & Hockley, 2000; Reder et al., 2000) have been shown to support higher levels of recollection at test in comparison with studying a word only once. Because of the practical fact that young children do not read, memory studies using 4-year-olds have relied on items that are pictorial in nature. Thus, it is uncertain whether there are binding memory tasks that would be less susceptible to relying on recollection and whether these change across development.

Whereas the binding work of Sluzenski et al. (2006) and Lloyd et al. (2009) studied preschool children, other binding research has focused on binding later in childhood. For example, Lorsbach and Reimer (2005) compared the memory performance of 9-, 12-, and 21-year-old students on object, location, and binding memory. The design of this study is similar to that used in many studies on binding changes in aging (e.g., Chalfonte & Johnson, 1996; Mitchell, Johnson, Mather, & D'Esposito, 2000). In such tasks, a grid is presented on a screen. Objects then appear in some of the cells. The task of the participant during the recognition test is to decide whether or not an object was presented, whether any object was presented in a cued location or whether a given object was presented in a specific location (see Figure 4.1). Their results showed that feature and binding memory both improved across childhood and into adulthood. However, the changes for binding were greater and were significant after accounting for the influence of feature memory. Again, the difference in memory performance is greater for the false alarm rates than for hit rates. Although the analyses used d' rather than recognition scores, examination of the data shows a similar pattern to Sluzenski et al. (2006). The 12-year-olds had a hit rate that was 7% higher for the two types of features and one that was 6% higher for combination items. In contrast, the false alarm rates for feature items were nearly identical (1% or no difference), whereas the false alarm rate was 14% higher for the 9-year-old children. These findings suggest that memory binding is not always at adult levels by the age of 6 years, as suggested by Sluzenski et al. (2006). However, one potentially important difference exists between the methodologies of the studies. Items were presented serially in the Sluzenski et al. (2006) study as compared to Lorsbach and Reimer (2005), who presented at one time several object-location pairings to be bound. Future research should study the effect of sequential and simultaneous presentation on memory binding processes.

To date, we are aware of only one study that directly compared performance across the lifespan for feature and binding memory performance using nonverbal materials (Cowan, Naveh-Benjamin, Kilb, & Saults, 2006; see also Shing, Werkle-Bergner, Li, & Lindenberger, 2008, for a study using verbal stimuli). In this study, the two features were colors and locations. Like the work by Lorsbach and Reimer (2005), this lifespan study used older children. The participants were children of two ages (8–10 and 11–12 years), college students, and older adults. The study found that children had particular difficulty with binding trials in all testing conditions. Older adults, however, only had significantly greater trouble when binding trials were intermixed with feature trials during the test. Such a finding suggests that the decay of memory in aging is not identical to the growth during childhood. That is, older adults could be having difficulty with task switching, whereas younger children might have a specific deficit in recollection.

The studies described here have all focused on binding problems that occur between an object and its location either directly (remembering that the pumpkin was presented in the top right square of a grid [Lorsbach & Reimer, 2005]) or indirectly (remembering that a tiger was paired with a basketball court [Lloyd et al., 2009; Sluzenski et al., 2006]). Such pairings are arbitrary in nature and likely to involve features that are changeable (especially in the case of mobile creatures like tigers). To date, we are unaware of any published work that has tested the impact of feature binding on less changeable features. For example, whereas one's outfits are likely to change daily, features such as voice remain relatively stable. Whether the distinction of inter-versus intraitem binding yields different developmental patterns in children has yet to be determined. As previously described, there is some evidence that both types of change are subject to memory deficits in older adults. If changes in memory binding do follow a mostly U-shaped pattern, as has been suggested by Cowan et al. (2006), then it seems plausible that intraitem binding would improve across childhood as well.

To conclude, there is good evidence to suggest that memory for bound information achieves adult levels of performance later in development than memory for featural information does. There is also some evidence that much of the differences are due to younger children having difficulty rejecting items that have been rearranged rather than a deficit in recognizing previously seen pairings. Such a finding is consistent with dual-process models of recognition that suggest that recollection may be used to avoid making such errors (e.g., Odegard & Lampinen, 2004). However, there are still several questions about memory binding that remain unanswered. These include the difference between inter-and intraitem binding, the age at which memory performance for children and adults is equated, and the conditions under which binding deficits are a function of encoding or retrieval. Answers to these questions will help in better understanding memory binding, as well as better understanding the development of rich episodic memories. Currently, neuropsychological and neuroscience research suggest that the development of the hippocampus and prefrontal cortex are particularly important for the functioning episodic memories (e.g., Newcombe et al., 2007). Both of these structures develop across childhood (e.g., hippocampus: Lavenex, Lavenex, & Amaral, 2006; prefrontal cortex: Giedd et al., 1999; Huttenlocher & Dabholkar, 1997; Sowell, Delis, Stiles, & Jenigan, 2001) and will likely be essential for describing the changes in binding described herein. Further, changes in the prefrontal cortex have already been cited as important for understanding the aging deficits in binding (e.g., Mitchell, Johnson, Raye, & Greene, 2004). In addition to the development in brain structures, changes in representational abilities may also be an important consideration for explaining improvements in memory binding (Ceci, Fitneva, & Williams, 2010). The two hypotheses are not mutually exclusive.

EPISODIC MEMORY IN NONHUMAN ANIMALS

The original concept of episodic memory, as defined by Endel Tulving (1972) consisted of *what, where,* and *when* components. Recent definitions include aspects of *autonoetic* consciousness, that is, personal awareness of an autobiographical component to the memory. However, demonstrating autonoetic consciousness in nonhuman (and therefore nonverbal) animals has proven to be an elusive goal. Therefore, the question of whether animals can demonstrate episodiclike memory has had to be approached more indirectly through examining nonverbal behavior.

A large amount of research has been conducted to explore the level of detail animals can represent about past events. This research suggests that some animals, such as birds and perhaps rats, have quite sophisticated representations of episodiclike memories; representing and binding multiple components of experienced events. In experiments on episodiclike memory, animals typically encounter multiple stimulus events, each of which has a unique combination of time-sensitive what and where components (often a food reward in a unique situating context). Subsequently, the animals are tested after varying delays to see whether their memory includes information about the differential what–where components and whether they appear to be selectively bound in unique combinations. For example, animals may encounter foods stored in locations differentiated by surrounding context (e.g., tray color or location in a maze) and at a later time are tested for retrieval after different time delays, requiring the animal to remember all three aspects of the original encoding event.

The strongest case for episodiclike memory in nonhuman animals may come from the research with western scrub jays initiated by Clayton and Dickinson (1998). Western scrub jays have a natural inclination to store food and later return to retrieve that food. In an elaborate series of manipulations, Clayton and her colleagues have demonstrated that scrub jays are not only able to satisfy the content requirements of episodic memory, but they also can meet a more stringent criteria, demonstrating that this information is integrated (it is structured) and can be accessed and updated to affect future behavior (it is flexible) (Clayton, Bussey, & Dickinson, 2003; Clayton, Bussey, Emery, & Dickinson, 2003; Clayton & Dickinson, 1998; De Kort et al., 2005). The authors argue that this is a strong demonstration of episodiclike memory in the absence of autonoetic consciousness. For example, in one study, jays were allowed to cache wax worms, which degrade over a short time course, and peanuts, which remain unspoiled, in trays that were situated in unique contexts (each tray was surrounded by a unique configuration of blocks.) The birds were allowed to search for the hidden stashes after a short delay (in which case, the wax worms would be fresh and preferred over peanuts) or long delay (in which case, the wax worms would be degraded and less preferred). Jays differentially searched for the wax worms after a short but not a long delay, suggesting that they remembered what (caching worms and peanuts), where (in different locations), and when (a short time ago or a long time ago), and that these memories were bound together, such that, when presented with relevant stimuli (caching trays) at different time intervals they could differentiate them based on the unique combination of all three aspects (Clayton & Dickinson, 1998). In subsequent experiments, Clayton and colleagues demonstrated that scrub jays could update their memory for a stashing event based on encountering new information. In this study, after jays had encountered a novel food (crickets) and learned to expect a certain time course before degradation, they were allowed to stash food in three contexts (block configurations), and then encountered information contrary to their expectations in one of the contexts (encountering degraded food when they expected it to be fresh). They were able to apply this new information to previously existing memory representations in the absence of the stimuli to alter their foraging behavior for the remaining contexts, suggesting that not only did the birds have memories that bound multiple aspects of the contexts, but that these memories were functionally accessible similarly to how human episodic memory is accessible (Clayton, Yu, & Dickinson, 2003; De Kort et al., 2005).

Other work with pigeons using a different paradigm suggests that they can encode what, where, and when information, as evidenced by their ability to respond at test to unexpected questions about varying contextual aspects of a previously encountered stimulus, although it is unclear that the information is bound into a cohesive representation (Singer & Zentall, 2007; Skov-Rackette, Miller, & Shettleworth, 2006). In one series of experiments, pigeons saw colored shapes in various locations on a computer screen, and after a variable time delay, they were given the task of responding to one of three different aspects of each item; what (identification of the previously viewed stimulus), where (identification of the location on the screen in which the stimulus had appeared), or when (delay length). With no previous information about which aspect of the stimulus memory would be tested, success on this experiment suggested that animals encoded all three types of information on learning. However, when pigeons were tested on multiple aspects of one stimulus item, their accuracy in responding to one aspect of the stimulus was not strongly related to their accuracy in responding about other aspects, suggesting that their memories for different aspects were not bound (Skov-Rackette et al., 2006). This intriguing work suggests that in experimental manipulations that do not rely on birds' natural behavior, they may demonstrate some of the required content of episodiclike memory, but they may not encode such content into a cohesive and flexible memory.

Work with other species, such as rats, has revealed similar findings to the findings from work with birds. Rats appear able to demonstrate event memories that have a what–where component, and further, that these components are bound (Eacott, Easton, & Zinkivskay, 2005; Crystal, 2009; Kart-Teke, De Souza Silva, Huston, & Dere 2006; Nemati & Whishaw, 2007). However, the important question of whether temporal information is incorporated into these episodiclike memories is under debate, with older studies failing to find evidence of when components, in contrast to recent findings in the affirmative (Babb & Crystal, 2006; Naqshbandi, Feeney, McKenzie, & Roberts, 2007). For example, rats have been found to demonstrate episodiclike memory for food locations in radial arm maze, using a paradigm similar to that used in the work by Clayton, Yu, and Dickinson (2003) with scrub jays. Rats entered a radial arm maze with eight arms, four of which were closed, three of which held food pellets, and one of which held preferred chocolate chips. After a delay, which was either short or long, rats reentered the maze to forage again, this time with all eight arms open. The arm containing the chocolate was either empty or full, depending on whether the delay was long or short. Therefore, rats had to remember the what (preferred reward), where (which arm of the maze), and when (time since last search in the maze) in order to determine whether or not to search for the chocolate. Rats demonstrated performance that is consistent with episodiclike memory, that is, searching for the chocolate after one delay type, but not after another (Naqshbandi et al., 2007). In a similar paradigm, rats learned the location of the chocolate, and then later learned to associate the chocolate with nausea. At test, rather than seeking the arm with the chocolate at the appropriate delay, they avoided that arm, suggesting that they were able to access the contextual information and update it, providing evidence for binding (Babb & Crystal, 2006).

In summary, the findings from animal research suggest that some animals may indeed have quite detailed representations of previously experienced events, which they can access and use flexibly, fitting the description of episodiclike memory. Whether or not this ability is equally present within or across species, and to what extent it can be applied in various domains is an ongoing research question. Further, the question of to what extent animals have episodic memory in the way that humans have episodic memory remains unclear. The claim of episodic memory in nonhuman animals has been contested by researchers in the field (e.g. Suddendorf & Busby, 2003a, 2003b), who stipulate that mental time travel is a critical component of episodic memory, and that the animal research thus far has failed to provide a compelling case that animals can project themselves into a different time (either past or present.) According to this view, demonstration of what–where memory shows only that animals are capable of one-time learning of detailed information, but does not necessarily imply mental time travel, (the subjective reexperience of the event itself). For example, it is possible for humans to recall detailed information about an event without reexperiencing the event itself, and therefore, animals might recall what food was hidden where and when, without actually recalling the stashing event itself. In order to test episodicness of episodic memory, the authors suggest, there needs to be evidence, in some form, of mental time travel, requiring research paradigms that enable animals to report on their memory states. Finally, if autonoetic consciousness is an essential component, then, for now, episodic memory is limited to human experience. However, the compendium of research suggests that a variety of nonhuman animals may have episodiclike memories, that is, memories that are very similar in content and structure to those of humans, and that may function similarly, interacting with semantic knowledge to guide future behavior.

The research on episodiclike memory in nonhuman animals, designed for a nonverbal population and revealing quite complex memory representations in the absence of verbal access, suggests possible methodologies for exploring the development of episodic memory in young children whose memories are not easily tested through verbal report. Research thus far has relied on reenactment of events and verbal recall of earlier occurring memories at much later dates, when children are able to reflect and discuss their memories. The animal research, in controlling the learning events and testing recall at a relatively short time course, has been able to explore different aspects of memory, including which types of information are remembered and bound together. These paradigms, if adapted to young children, might reveal information about the developmental character of episodiclike memory, and the transition to what is recognized as true episodic memory. As an example of an experiment adapted from animal research that revealed intriguing memory findings, Klossek et al. (2008) designed a study, adapted from previous work with animals, to test young children's abilities to selectively learn the rewards associated with different specific stimuli. In this study, children aged 18 to 48 months were presented with two different icons on a computer touch screen, and learned that touching each of the icons resulted in one of two video sets of clips appearing. Each stimulus was associated with a different set of video clips. After children had learned to touch the icons for the videos, the reward for one, but not both, of the icons was devalued. Critically, this devaluation occurred in the absence of the icons. Without either of the stimulus icons present, children passively watched one of the associated video sets repeated four times, such that this video series would be comparatively less valued than the contrasting video series. At test, children were again presented with both icons. If they had learned to associate each icon with its specific reward (video set), then they would be expected to touch the icon for the comparatively higher value reward than the icon with the devalued reward. Interestingly, children 27–37 and 37–48 months old behaved accordingly, selecting the icon associated with the higher value significantly more often, whereas children 16–27 months old failed to do so, and in fact showed a lower rate of response to both icons, as if they had learned the devaluation, but generalized it to both icons, rather than selectively associating it with the specific icon. This age difference is in general agreement with other developmental episodic memory research that suggests a change at around 18–24 months of age. Perhaps by adapting the other comparative paradigms, a fuller picture of episodic memory in the early years might be gained. In addition, in adapting and equating, as much as possible, methods across species and age groups, a more fully developed picture of episodic memory itself can be gained.

EPISODIC MEMORY AND OTHER MENTAL FUNCTIONS

Thus far, we have discussed episodic memory as a tool for thinking about the past. However, recently, there has been enormous excitement surrounding the idea that episodic memory may be good for much more than remembering the past—it may also form the basis for imagining hypothetical events or projecting oneself into future. The idea is that the same skills and brain areas involved in remembering our family picnic in Estes Park are involved in thinking about a future company picnic to be held in Montgomery Park. In fact, the "Back to the Future" hypothesis was ninth on *Science*'s list of the 10 scientific breakthroughs of the year 2007 (The News Staff, 2007). The evidence for the linkage is wide ranging and focuses on the hippocampus as the neural basis of imagining the future. In normal individuals studied with functional magnetic resonance imaging, there is considerable overlap between brain regions activated when they remember the past and when they imagine the future, centering on the left hippocampus (Addis et al., 2007). Patients with hippocampal amnesia have difficulty imaging new experiences (Hassabis et al., 2007). Elderly individuals generate fewer distinct details for future events, as well as for past events, than younger adults do, and the number of such details is correlated with relational memory abilities (Addis, Wong, & Schacter, 2008). Even rats may imagine their future: When they are running a maze, hippocampal place cells associated with areas of the maze that they might choose to visit sometimes fire, suggesting that they are considering future routes (Johnson & Redish, 2007). That is, rats seem to use the same brain structures to plan their future (or at least, which way to turn to reach food) as they use to store memories of their past experiences in an environment. For a recent overview of this literature, see Spreng, Mar, and Kim (2009).

It should be noted that there are some disagreements concerning the nature of these linkages. Some investigators stress the spatial bases of the linkage, arguing that scene construction and spatial memory are crucial to both episodic memory of the past and any simulated experience, whether imagined in a general way or specifically engaged with a future (Byrne, Becker, & Burgess, 2007; Hassabis & Maguire, 2007). Other investigators deemphasize the spatial linkage, focusing more simply on the association between memory of the past and projection into the future (Schacter et al., 2007). In addition, there are proposals that the common brain network also engages conceiving the viewpoint of others, as in theory of mind (Buckner & Carroll, 2007), whereas others argue that theory of mind is an independent faculty (Rosenbaum et al., 2007).

In the context of developmental work, these proposed linkages are intriguing. First, in nice agreement with the proposal, the ability to construct a spatial context seems to appear at around the age of 2 years, coincident with the ability to exhibit the first documented episodic memories (Newcombe et al., 2007; Sluzenski, Newcombe, & Satlow, 2004). Second, our attention is drawn to the relative lack of knowledge about how well young children can imagine the future. In one early study, it was not until the age of 8 years that children seemed to engage in future planning in the context of preparing for a memory task (Rogoff et al., 1974). However, this behavior might be more linked to the development of mnemonic strategies than to the development of imagination of the future. The kinds of open-ended "imagine the future" tasks that have been implemented with adults have yet to be attempted with young children. We do know that children as old as

4 years show some difficulty in distinguishing imagined from experienced events (Sluzenski, Newcombe & Ottinger, 2004), suggesting that, at an age when episodic memory is still fragile, dealing with imagined events is also under development. Third, we are also reminded of two proposed developmental linkages: between the development of self in the second year of life and the dawn of episodic memory (Howe & Courage, 1997), and between the development of theory of mind-and episodic memory at around 4 years (Perner & Ruffman, 1995). Further work on both linkages is needed. Recent evidence that sense of self of the kind that emerges at 2 years has as its neural basis a temporal-parietal area (Lewis & Carmody, 2008) may suggest that language is more important and memory less important to this development than has been suggested. And, in agreement with the data of Rosenbaum et al. (2007), developmental linkages between theory of mind and episodic memory have been elusive (Drummey & Newcombe, 2002; Kovacs & Newcombe, 2006).

CONCLUSION AND FUTURE DIRECTIONS

Although the time course of early developmental binding and episodiclike memory is beginning to be understood, questions still remain as to the nature of such emergent memory. How does episodic memory arise in children? Does it emerge from binding, first through visual paired associates, gaining complexity to include binding of what, where, and when components, until, as a child develops autonoetic consciousness, it emerges as true episodic memory? Further, what other cognitive skills are requisite for episodic memory to be present and useful as a cognitive skill in making sense of the world by binding together meaningful information and discarding irrelevant information? Language is often proposed to be an important tool, allowing access to memories, sharing of information in memory, and external symbolic manipulation of memories. Yet, how does that idea square with observations of episodic memory in nonlinguistic species? Certain brain structures, such as the hippocampus, which appears to have significant changes in early childhood, may be necessary for children and other animals to achieve a certain level of complexity in binding information and acting on information. Finally, the nature of binding, and how it functions as a tool in other cognitive processing such as learning from the past, understanding the present, and planning the future is an exciting question that is only beginning to be understood.

REFERENCES

Addis, D., Wong, A. & Schacter, D. (2007). Remembering the past and imagining the future: Common and distinct neural substrates during event construction and elaboration. *Neuropsychologia, 45,* 1363–77.

Addis, D., Wong, A., & Schacter, D. (2008). Age-related changes in the episodic simulation of future events. *Psychological Science, 19,* 33–41.

Babb, S., & Crystal, J. (2006). Episodic-like memory in the rat. *Current Biology*, *16*, 1317–21.

Baker-Ward, L., Ornstein, P., & Holden, D. (1984). The expression of memorization in early childhood. *Journal of Experimental Child Psychology*, *37*, 555–75.

Balcomb, F., & Gerken, L. (2008). Three-year-old children can access their own memory to guide responses on a visual matching task. *Developmental Science*, *11*, 750–60.

Balcomb, F., Newcombe, N. S., Ferrara, K., & Funk, A. (2010). *Changes in context-bound memory may provide the foundations for episodic memory*. Poster presented at the International Conference on Infancy Studies, Baltimore, MD.

Barr, R., Dowden, A., & Hayne, H. (1996). Developmental changes in deferred imitation by 6- to 24-month-old infants. *Infant Behavior & Development*, *19*, 159–70.

Barr, R., Rovee-Collier, C., & Campanella, J. (2005). Retrieval protracts deferred imitation by 6-month-olds. *Infancy*, *7*, 263–83.

Barrett, T., Traupman, E., & Needham, A. (2008). Infants' visual anticipation of object structure in grasp planning. *Infant Behavior & Development*, *31*, 1–9.

Bauer, P. (2005). Developments in declarative memory decreasing susceptibility to storage failure over the second year of life. *Psychological Science*, *16*, 41–8.

Bauer, P. (2007). Recall in infancy: A neurodevelopmental account. *Current Directions in Psychological Science*, *16*, 142–6.

Bauer, P., Burch, M., Scholin, S., & Guler, E. (2007). Using cue words to investigate the distribution of autobiographical memories in childhood. *Psychological Science*, *18*, 910–7.

Bishara, A. J. & Jacoby, L. L. (2008). Aging, spaced retrieval, and inflexible memory performance. *Psychonomic Bulletin & Review*, *15*, 52–7.

Bloom, P. (2001). Précis of how children learn the meanings of words. *Behavioral and Brain Sciences*, *24*, 1095–1103.

Bruce, D., Dolan, A., & Phillips-Grant, K. (2000). On the transition from childhood amnesia to the recall of personal memories. *Psychological Science*, *11*, 360–4.

Bruce, D., Wilcox-O'Hearn, L. A., Robinson, J., Phillips-Grant, K., Francis, L., & Smith, M. (2005). Fragment memories mark the end of childhood amnesia. *Memory & Cognition*, *33*, 567–76.

Buckner, R., & Carroll, D. (2007). Self-projection and the brain. *Trends in Cognitive Sciences*, *11*, 49–57.

Burke, S., & Barnes, C. (2006). Neural plasticity in the ageing brain. *Nature Reviews Neuroscience*, *7*, 30–40.

Byrne, P., Becker, S., & Burgess, N. (2007). Remembering the past and imagining the future: A neural model of spatial memory and imagery. *Psychological Review*, *114*, 340–75.

Castel, A. D. & Craik, F. I. M. (2003). The effects of aging and divided attention on memory for item and associative information. *Psychology of Aging*, *18*, 873–85.

Ceci, S. J., Fitneva, S. A., & Williams, W. M. (2010). Representational constraints on the on the development of memory and metamemory: A developmental-representational theory. *Psychological Review*, *117*, 464–95.

Chalfonte, B. L., & Johnson, M. K. (1996). Feature memory and binding in young and older adults. *Memory & Cognition*, *24*, 403–16.

Clayton, N., & Dickinson, A. (1998). Episodic-like memory during cache recovery by scrub jays. *Nature*, *395*, 272–4.

Clayton, N., Bussey, T., & Dickinson, A. (2003). Can animals recall the past and plan for the future? *Nature Reviews, 4,* 685–91.

Clayton, N., Bussey, T., Emery, N., & Dickinson A. (2003). Prometheus to Proust: The case for behavioural criteria for "mental time travel." *Trends in Cognitive Sciences, 7,* 436–7.

Clayton, N., Yu, K., & Dickinson, A. (2003). Interacting cache memories: Evidence for flexible memory use by scrub-jays. *Journal of Experimental Psychology: Animal Behavior Processes, 29,* 4–22.

Conway, M. A., & Pleydell-Pearce, C. W. (2000). The construction of autobiographical memories in the self-memory system. *Psychological Review, 107,* 261–88.

Coslett, H., & Lie, G. (2008). Simultanagnosia: When a rose is not red. *Journal of Cognitive Neurosciece, 20,* 36–48.

Cowan, N., Naveh-Benjamin, M., Kilb, A., & Saults, J. S. (2006). Life-span development of visual working memory: When is feature binding difficult?. *Developmental Psychology, 42,* 1089–102.

Crawley, R., & Eacott, M. (1999). Memory for early life events: Consistency of retrieval of memories over a one-year interval. *Memory, 7,* 439–60.

Crawley, R., & Eacott, M. (2006). Memories of early childhood: Qualities of the experience of recollection. Memory *& Cognition, 34,* 287–94.

Crovitz, H. & Quina-Holland, K. (1976). Proportion of episodic memories from early childhood by years of age. *Bulletin of the Psychonomic Society, 7,* 61–2.

Crovitz, H., & Schiffman, H. (1974). Frequency of episodic memories as a function of their age. *Bulletin of the Psychonomic Society, 4,* 517–8.

Crystal, J. (2009). Elements of episodic-like memory in animal models. *Behavioural Processes, 80,* 269–77.

Cuevas, K., Rovee-Collier, C., & Learmonth, A. (2006). Infants form associations between memory representations of stimuli that are absent. *Psychological Science, 176,* 543–9.

De Kort, S., Dickinson, A., & Clayton, N. (2005). Retrospective cognition by food-caching western scrub-jays. *Learning and Motivation, 36,* 159–76.

DeLoache, J., & Brown, A. (1984). Where do I go next? Intelligent searching by very young children. *Developmental Psychology, 20,* 37–44.

Drummey, A., & Newcombe, N. (1995). Remembering versus knowing the past: Children's explicit and implicit memories for pictures. *Journal of Experimental Child Psychology, 59,* 549–65.

Drummey, A., & Newcombe, N. (2002). Developmental changes in source memory. *Developmental Science, 5,* 502–13.

Eacott, M., & Crawley, R. (1998). The offset of childhood amnesia: Memory for events that occurred before age 3. *Journal of Experimental Psychology: General, 127,* 22–33.

Eacott, M., & Crawley, R (1999). Childhood amnesia: On answering questions about very early life events. *Memory, 7,* 279–92.

Eacott, M., & Norman, G. (2004). Integrated memory for object, place, and context in rats: A possible model of episodic-like memory? *Journal of Neuroscience, 24,* 1948–53.

Eacott, M., Easton, A., & Zinkivskay, A. (2005). Recollection in an episodic-like memory task in the rat. *Learning and Memory, 12,* 221–3.

Ecker, U. K. H., Zimmer, H. D., & Groh-Bordin, C. (2007). Color and context: An ERP study on intrinsic and extrinsic feature binding in episodic memory. *Memory & Cognition, 35,* 1483–501.

Eichenbaum, H. (2007). Comparative cognition, hippocampal function, and recollection. *Comparative Cognition & Behavior Reviews, 2,* 47–66.

Fiser, J., Scholl, B., & Aslin, R. (2007). Perceived object trajectories during occlusion constrain visual statistical learning. *Psychonomic Bulletin & Review, 14,* 173–8.

Fiske, K., & Pillemer, D. (2006). Adult recollections of earliest childhood dreams: A cross-cultural study. *Memory, 14,* 57–67.

Flavell, J., Beach, D., & Chinksy, J. (1966). Spontaneous verbal rehearsal in a memory task as a function of age. *Child Development, 37,* 283–99.

Gallo, D. A. (2004). Using recall to reduce false recognition: Diagnostic and disqualifying monitoring. *Journal of Experimental Psychology: Learning, Memory, & Cognition, 30,* 120–8.

Garcia, J., & Koelling, R. (1966). Relation of cue to consequence in avoidance learning. *Psychonomic Science, 4,* 123–4.

Garson, J. (2001). (Dis)solving the binding problem. *Philosophical Psychology, 14,* 381–92.

Ghetti, S., & Angelini, L. (2008). The development of recollection and familiarity in childhood and adolescence: Evidence from the dual-process signal detection model. *Child Development, 79,* 339–58.

Giedd, J. N., Blumenthal, J., Jeffries, N. O., Rajapaske, J. C., Vaituzis, A. C., Liu, H., . . . Castellanos, F. X. (1999). Development of the human corpus callosum during childhood and adolescence: A longitudinal MRI study. *Progress in Neuro-Psychopharmacology & Biological Psychiatry, 23,* 571–88.

Hassabis, D., & Maguire, E. (2007). Deconstructing episodic memory with construction. *Trends in Cognitive Sciences, 11,* 299–306.

Hassabis, D., Kumaran, V., Vann, S., & Maguire, E. (2007). Patients with hippocampal amnesia cannot imagine new experiences. *PNAS Proceedings of the National Academy of Sciences of the United States of America, 104,* 1726–31.

Hayne, H. (2007). Infant memory development. In L. Oakes & P. Bauer, (Eds.), *Short and long-term memory in infancy and early childhood* (pp. 209–39). New York: Oxford University Press.

Hayne, H., Boniface, J. & Barr, R. (2000). The development of declarative memory in human infants: Age-related changes in deferred imitation. *Behavioral Neuroscience, 11,* 77–83.

Hayne, H., MacDonald, S., & Barr, R. (1997). Developmental changes in the specificity of memory over the second year of life. *Infant Behavior & Development, 20,* 233–45.

Herbert, J., Gross, J., & Hayne, H. (2007). Crawling is associated with more flexible memory retrieval by 9-month-old infants. *Developmental Science, 10,* 183–9.

Howe, M., & Courage, M. (1997). The emergence and early development of autobiographical memory. *Psychological Review, 104,* 499–523.

Huttenlocher, P. R., & Dabholkar, A. S. (1997). Regional differences in synaptogenesis in human cerebral cortex. *Journal of Comparative Neurology, 387,* 167–78.

Jacoby, L. L., Jones, T. C., & Dolan, P. O. (1998). Two effects of repetition: Support for a two-process model of knowledge judgments and exclusion errors. *Psychonomic Bulletin & Review, 5,* 705–9.

Jennings, J. M., & Jacoby, L. L. (1993). Automatic versus intentional uses of memory: Aging, attention, and control. *Psychology & Aging, 8,* 283–93.

Jennings, J. M., & Jacoby, L. L. (1997). An opposition procedure for detecting age-related deficits in recollection: Telling effects of repetition. *Psychology & Aging, 12,* 352–61.

Johnson, A. & Redish, D. (2007). Neural ensembles in CA3 transiently encode paths forward of the animal at a decision point. *Journal of Neuroscience, 27,* 12176–89.

Johnson, M. K., Hashtroudi, S., & Lindsay, D. S. (1993). Source monitoring. *Psychological Bulletin, 114,* 3–28.

Jones, T. C. & Jacoby, L. L. (2001). Feature and conjunction errors in recognition memory: Evidence for dual-process theory. *Journal of Memory & Language, 45,* 82–102.

Jones, T. C. (2005). Study repetition and the rejection of conjunction lures. *Memory, 13,* 499–515.

Joordens, S., & Hockley, W. E. (2000). Recollection and familiarity through the looking glass: When old does not mirror new. *Journal of Experimental Psychology: Learning, Memory, and Cognition, 26,* 1534–55.

Kart-Teke, E., De Souza Silva, M., Huston, J. & Dere, E. (2006). Wistar rats show episodic-like memory for unique experiences. *Neurobiology of Learning and Memory, 85,* 173–82.

Kersten, A.W., Earles, J. L., Curtayne, E. S., &. Lane, J. C. (2008). Adult age differences in binding actors and actions in memory for events. *Memory & Cognition, 36,* 119–31.

Kihlstrom, J., & Harackiewicz, J., (1982). The earliest recollection: A new survey. *Journal of Personality, 50,* 134–48.

Klein, S. B., German, T. P., Cosmides, L., & Gabriel, R. (2004). A theory of autobiographical memory: Necessary components and disorders resulting from their loss. *Social Cognition, 22,* 460–90.

Klossek, U., Russell, J., & Dickinson, A. (2008). The control of instrumental action following outcome devaluation in young children aged between 1 and 4 years. *Journal of Experimental Psychology: General, 137,* 39–51.

Kovacs, S., & Newcombe, N. (2006). Developments in source monitoring: The role of thinking of others. *Journal of Experimental Child Psychology, 9,* 25–44.

Kramer, J., Mungas, D., Reed, B., Wetzel, M., Burnett, M., Miller, B., . . . Chui, H. (2007). Longitudinal MRI and cognitive change in healthy elderly. *Neuropsychology, 21,* 412–8.

Kuhl, P., Stevens, E., Hayashi, A., Deguchi, T., Kiritani, S., & Iverson, P. (2006). Infants show a facilitation effect for native language phonetic perception between 6 and 12 months. *Developmental Science, 9,* F13–21.

Lavenex, P., Lavenex, P. B., & Amaral, D. G. (2006). Postnatal development of the primate hippocampal formation. *Developmental Neuroscience, 29,* 179–92.

Lewis, M. L. & Carmody, D. P. (2008). Self-representation and brain development. *Developmental Psychology, 44,* 1329–34.

Lloyd, M. E. (2007). Metamemorial influences in recognition memory: Pictorial encoding reduces conjunction errors. *Memory & Cognition, 35,* 1067–73.

Lloyd, M. E., Doydum, A. O., & Newcombe, N. S. (2009). Memory binding in early childhood: Evidence for a retrieval deficit. *Child Development, 80,* 1321–8.

Lorsbach, T. C., & Reimer, J. F. (2005). Feature binding in children and young adults. *Journal of Genetic Psychology, 166,* 313–27.

Luck, S. J. (2008). Visual short-term memory. In S. J. Luck & A. Hollingworth (Eds.), *Visual Memory* (pp. 43–85). New York: Oxford University Press.

Luck, S., & Vogel, E. (1997). The capacity of visual working memory for features and conjunctions. *Nature, 390,* 279–81.

MacDonald, S., Uesiliana, K., & Hayne, H. (2000). Cross-cultural and gender differences in childhood amnesia. *Memory, 8,* 365–76.

Matsumoto, A., & Stanny, C. (2006). Language-dependent access to autobiographical memory in Japanese-English bilinguals and US monolinguals. *Memory, 14*, 378–90.

Meiser, T., Sattler, C., & Weisser, K. (2008). Binding of multidimensional context information as a distinctive characteristic of remember judgments. *Journal of Experimental Psychology: Learning, Memory, and Cognition, 34*, 32–49.

Mistry, J., Rogoff, B., & Herman, H. (2001). What is the meaning of meaningful purpose in children's remembering? Istomina revisited. *Mind, Culture, and Activity, 8*, 28–41.

Mitchell, K. J., Johnson, M. K., Raye, C. L., Mather, M., & D'Esposito, M. (2000). Aging and reflective processes of working memory: Binding and test load deficits. *Psychology and Aging, 15*(3), 527–41.

Mitchell, K. J., Johnson, M. K., Raye, C. L., & D'Esposito, M. (2000). fMRI evidence of age-related hippocampal dysfunction in feature binding in working memory. *Cognitive Brain Research, 10*, 197–206.

Mitchell, K. J., Johnson, M. K., Raye, C. L., & Greene, E. J. (2004). Prefrontal cortex activity associated with source monitoring in a working memory task. *Journal of Cognitive Neuroscience, 16*, 921–34.

Mitchell, K. J., Johnson, M. K., Raye, C. L., Mather, M. M., & D'Esposito, M. D. (2000). Aging and reflective processes of working memory: Binding and test load deficits. *Psychology and Aging, 15*, 527–41.

Mitroff, S. R., & Alvarez, G. A. (2007). Space and time, not surface features, guide object persistence. *Psychonomic Bulletin & Review, 14*, 1199–204.

Mullen, M. (1994). Earliest recollections of childhood: A demographic analysis. *Cognition, 52*, 55–79.

Multhaup, K., Johnson, M., & Tetirick, J. (2005). The wane of childhood amnesia for autobiographical and public event memories. *Memory, 13*, 161–173.

Naqshbandi, M., Feeney, M., McKenzie, T., & Roberts, W. (2007). Testing for episodic-like memory in rats in the absence of time of day cues: Replication of Babb and Crystal. *Behavioural Processes, 74*, 217–25.

Naveh-Benjamin, M. (2000). Adult age differences in memory performance: Tests of an associative deficit hypothesis. *Journal of Experimental Psychology: Learning, Memory and Cognition, 26*, 1170–87.

Naveh-Benjamin, M., Guez, J., & Marom, M. (2003). The effects of divided attention at encoding on item and associative memory. *Memory & Cognition, 31*, 1021–35.

Naveh-Benjamin, M., Guez, J., Kilb, A., & Reedy, S. (2004). The associative deficit of older adults: Further support using face–name associations. *Psychology and Aging, 19*, 541–6.

Naveh-Benjamin, M., Hussain, Z., Guez, J., & Bar-On, M. (2003). Adult age differences in episodic memory: Further support for an associative deficit hypothesis. *Journal of Experimental Psychology: Learning, Memory, and Cognition, 29*, 826–37.

Nelson, K. (2007). Becoming a language user: Entering a symbolic world. In C. Brownell & C. Kopp (Eds.), *Socioemotional development in the toddler years: Transitions and transformations* (pp. 221–40). New York: Guildford Press.

Nemati F., & Whishaw, I. (2007). The point of entry contributes to the organization of exploratory behavior of rats on an open field: An example of spontaneous episodic memory. *Behavioural Brain Research, 182*, 119–28.

Newcombe, N. S., Rogoff, B, & Kagan, J. (1977). Developmental changes in recognition memory for pictures of objects and scenes. *Developmental Psychology, 13*, 337–41.

Newcombe, N. S., Lloyd, M. E., & Ratliff, K. R. (2007). Development of episodic and autobiographical memory: A cognitive neuroscience perspective. In R. V. Kail (Ed.), *Advances in child development and behavior* (Vol. 35, pp. 37–85). San Diego, CA: Elsevier.

News Staff, The. (2007). Breakthroughs of the year: The runners up. *Science, 318,* 1844–49.

Oakes L. M., & Bauer, P. (2007). *Short and long-term memory in infancy and early childhood Taking the first steps toward remembering.* New York: Oxford University Press.

Oakes, L. M, Ross-Sheehy, S., & Luck, S. (2006). Rapid development of feature binding in visual short-term memory. *Psychological Science, 17,* 781–7.

Odegard, T. N., & Lampinen, J. M. (2004). Memory conjunction errors for autobiographical events: More than just familiarity. *Memory, 12,* 288–300.

Perner, J., Kloo, D., & Gornik, E. (2007). Episodic memory development: Theory of mind is part of re-experiencing experienced events. *Infant and Child Development, 16,* 471–90.

Perner, J., & Ruffman, T. (1995). Episodic memory an autonoetic consciousness: Developmental evidence and a theory of childhood amnesia. *Journal of Experimental Child Psychology, 59,* 516–48.

Peterson, C., Grant, V., & Boland, L. (2005). Childhood amnesia in children and adolescents: Their earliest memories. *Memory, 13,* 622–37.

Pierce, B. H., Sullivan, A. L., Schacter, D. L., & Budson, A. E. (2005). Comparing source-based and gist-based false recognition in aging and Alzheimer's disease. *Neuropsychology, 19,* 411–9.

Rakison, D., (2005). A secret agent? How infants learn about the identity of objects in a causal scene. *Journal of Experimental Child Psychology, 91,* 271–96.

Reder, L. M., Nhouyvanisvong, A., Schunn, C. D., Ayers, M. S., Angstadt, P., & Hiraki, K. (2000). A mechanistic account of the mirror effect for word frequency: A computational model of remember-know judgments in a continuous recognition paradigm. *Journal of Experimental Psychology: Learning, Memory, and Cognition, 26,* 294–320.

Reinitz, M. T., Lammers, W. J., & Cochran, B. P. (1992). Memory-conjunction errors: Miscombination of stored stimulus features can produce illusions of memory. *Memory & Cognition, 20,* 1–11.

Roberston, L, & Treisman, A. (2006). Attending to space within and between objects: Implications from a patient with Balint's syndrome. *Cognitive Neuropsychology, 23,* 448–62.

Rogers, W., & Fisk, A. (2000). Human factors, applied cognition, and aging. In F. Craik, & T. Salthouse (Eds.), *The handbook of aging and cognition* (2nd ed., pp. 559–91). Mahwah, NJ: Lawrence Erlbaum Associates.

Rogoff, B., Newcombe, N., & Kagan, J. (1974). Planfulness and recognition memory. *Child Development, 45,* 972–7.

Rosenbaum, R., Stuss, D., Levine, B., & Tulving, E. (2007). Theory of mind is independent of episodic memory. *Science, 318,* 1257.

Roskies, A. (1999). The binding problem. *Neuron, 24,* 7–9.

Rubin, D. (2000). The distribution of early childhood memories. *Memory, 8,* 265–9.

Schacter, D., Addis, D., & Buckner, R. (2007). Remembering the past to imagine the future: The prospective brain. *Nature Reviews Neuroscience, 8,* 657–61.

Schneider, W. (1999). The development of metamemory in children. In D. Gopher Koriat (Eds.), *Attention and performance XVII: Cognitive regulation of performance: Interaction of theory and application* (pp. 487–514). Cambridge, MA: MIT Press.

Schneider, W., & Bjorklund, D. (1998). Memory. In W. Damon (Ed.), *Handbook of child psychology* (Vol. 2, pp. 467–521). Hoboken, NJ: John Wiley & Sons, Inc.

Schneider, W., Kron, V., Hunnerkopf, M., & Krajewski, K. (2004). The development of young children's memory strategies: First findings from the Würzburg Longitudinal Memory Study. *Journal of Experimental Child Psychology, 88*, 193–209.

Shapiro, M., Kennedy, P., & Ferbinteanu, J. (2006). Representing episodes in the mammalian brain. *Current Opinion in Neurobiology, 16*, 701–9.

Sheingold, K. & Tenney, Y.J. (1982). Memory for a salient childhood event. In U. Neisser (Ed.), *Memory observed: Remembering in natural contexts* (pp. 201–12). San Francisco: Freeman.

Shing, Y., Werkle-Bergner, M., Li, S., & Lindenberger, U. (2008). Associative and strategic components of episodic memory: A life-span dissociation. *Journal of Experimental Psychology: General, 137*, 495–513.

Singer, R., & Zentall, T. (2007). Pigeons learn to answer the question "where did you just peck?" and can report peck location when unexpectedly asked. *Learning and Behavior, 35*(3), 184–9.

Skov-Rackette, S., Miller, N, & Shettleworth, S. (2006). What-where-when memory in pigeons. *Journal of Experimental Pscyhology: Animal Behavior Processes, 32*, 345–58.

Sluzenski, J., Newcombe, N., & Kovacs, S. L. (2006). Binding, relational memory, and recall of naturalistic events: A developmental perspective. *Journal of Experimental Psychology: Learning, Memory, & Cognition, 32*, 89–100.

Sluzenski, J., Newcombe, N., & Ottinger, W. (2004). Changes in reality monitoring and episodic memory in early childhood. *Developmental Science, 7*, 225–45.

Sluzenski, J., Newcombe, N., & Satlow, E. (2004). Knowing where things are in the second year of life: Implications for hippocampal development. *Journal of Cognitive Neuroscience, 16*, 1443–51.

Smirnov, A., Istomina, Z., Mal'tseva, K., & Samokhvalova, V. (1969). The formation of methods of logical remembering in preschool children and children in the lower grades. *Voprosy Psychologii, 15*, 90–101.

Sowell, E. R., Delis, D., Stiles, J., & Jernigan, T. L. (2001). Improved memory functioning and frontal lobe maturation between children and adolescents: A structural MRI study. *Journal of the International Neuropsychological Society, 7*, 312–22.

Spreng, R. N., Mar, R. A., & Kim, A. S. N. (2009). The common neural basis of autobiographical memory, prospection, navigation, theory of mind, and the default mode: A quantitative meta-analysis. *Journal of Cognitive Neuroscience, 21*, 489–510.

Suddendorf, T., & Busby J. (2003a). Like it or not? The mental time travel debate: Reply to Clayton et al. *Trends in Cognitive Sciences, 7*, 437–8.

Suddendorf, T., & Busby, J. (2003b). Mental time travel in animals? *Trends in Cognitive Sciences, 17*, 391–6.

Treisman, A. (1996). The binding problem. *Current Opinion in Neurobiology, 6*, 171–8.

Treisman, A. (1998). The perception of features and objects. In R. Wright (Ed.), *Visual attention* (pp. 26–54). New York: Oxford University Press.

Treisman, A., & Gelade, G. (1980). A feature-integration theory of attention. *Cognitive Psychology, 12*, 97–136.

Treisman, A., & Zhang, W. (2006). Location and binding in visual working memory. *Memory and Cognition, 34*, 1704–19.

Tulving, E. (1972). Episodic and semantic memory. In E. Tulving & W. Donaldson (Eds.), *Organization of memory* (pp. 381–403). New York: Academic Press.

Tulving, E. (1993). What is episodic memory? *Current Directions in Psychological Science, 2*, 67–70.

Tulving, E., (1999). On the uniqueness of episodic memory. In L. G. Nilsson & A. Markowitsch (Eds.), *Cognitive neuroscience of memory* (pp. 11–42). Ashland, OH: Hogrefe & Huber Publishers.

Underwood, B. J. & Zimmerman, J. (1973). The syllable as a source of error in multisyllable word recognition. *Journal of Verbal Learning and Verbal Behavior, 12*, 338–44.

Usher, J. N., & Neisser, U. (1993). Childhood amnesia and the beginnings of memory for four early life events. *Journal of Experimental Psychology: General, 122*, 155–165.

Waldfogel, S. (1948). The frequency and affective character of childhood memories. *Psychological Monographs, 62*, 39.

Wang, Q. (2001). Culture effects on adults' earliest childhood recollection and self-description: Implications for the relation between memory and the self. *Journal of Personality and Social Psychology, 81*, 220–33.

Werker, J. & Tees, R. (1984). Cross-language speech perception: Evidence for perceptual reorganization during the first year of life. *Infant Behavior & Development, 7*, 49–63.

Werner, J. S., & Perlmutter, M. (1979). Development of visual recognition memory infants. *Advances in Child Development and Behavior, 14*, 1–56.

Wetzler, S., & Sweeney, J. (1986). Childhood amnesia: A conceptualization in cognitive-psychological terms. *Journal of the American Psychoanalytic Association, 34*, 663–85.

Wheeler, M. A., Stuss, D. T., & Tulving, E. (1995). Frontal lobe damage produces episodic memory impairment. *Journal of the International Neuropsychological Society, 1*, 525–36.

Wilcox, T., Woods, R., & Chapa, C., McCurry, S. (2007). Multisensory exploration and object individuation in infancy. *Developmental Psychology, 43*, 479–95.

Winograd, E., & Killinger, W. (1983). Relating age at encoding in early childhood to adult recall: Development of flashbulb memories. *Journal of Experimental Psychology: General, 112*, 413–22.

Xu, F., & Carey, S. (1996). Infants' metaphysics: The case of numerical identity. *Cognitive Psychology, 30*, 111–53.

Yonelinas, A. (2002). The nature of recollection and familiarity: A review of 30 years of research. *Journal of Memory and Language, 46*, 441–517.

5

Development of Recollection

A Fuzzy-Trace Theory Perspective

CHARLES J. BRAINERD, VALERIE F. REYNA,
AND ROBYN E. HOLLIDAY

In this chapter, we discuss fuzzy-trace theory's (FTT) approach to the development of recollection, the procedures and mathematical models that it uses to measure recollection, and the developmental findings that have accumulated to date from those techniques. This chapter deals with the *how* of recollection, in the sense of measurement procedures, more than with the *what*, in the sense of process models of recollection. Although the distinctions that constitute FTT's process model of recollection and familiarity are discussed and figure throughout, the lion's share of the presentation deals with procedures for measuring those distinctions and to the findings that have accumulated. That emphasis grows out of the fact that until recently, with the exception of a few articles (e.g., Drummey & Newcombe, 1995), the recollection/familiarity distinction has had no appreciable influence on the study of memory development. The chapters in the present section, along with some other recent papers (Ghetti & Angelini, 2008; Ghetti & Castelli, 2006), suggest that the situation is changing. The change is long overdue, considering how prominent the recollection/familiarity distinction has been in adult research for more than a quarter-century (e.g., Atkinson & Juola, 1973; Jacoby, 1991; Kurilla & Westerman, 2010; Mandler, 1980; Yonelinas, 2002) and considering that this and other dual-process ideas dominate the science of false memory (Brainerd & Reyna, 2005).

The explanation for the dearth of developmental research on this topic, as noted elsewhere (e.g., Brainerd & Reyna, 2010; Brainerd, Reyna, & Howe, 2009), is methodological. The paradigm that is most commonly used to separate and quantify the influences of dual-memory processes in adults makes high cognitive demands. Owing to such demands, it is of dubious reliability with children, particularly young children, as well as with patients with certain types of cognitive impairments. The paradigm in question is the remember-know procedure (Tulving, 1985). Although there are other techniques for separating recollection and familiarity in adults (for a review, see Yonelinas, 2002), this simple, compelling procedure is the gold standard because the experimentation that has been conducted with it dwarfs that for all other techniques combined. Further, Rotello, Macmillan, and Reeder (2004) showed that if the procedure is enriched with confidence ratings, the machinery of signal detection theory can be brought to bear to extract precise numerical estimates of recollection and familiarity from remember-know data. All of that is on the positive side, but on the negative side, the validity of such data turns on the assumption that subjects can comprehend and implement the instructions that they must follow to make remember-know judgments and that instructions do not change the qualities of recognition performance (see Mulligan, Besken, & Peterson, 2010).

An example of those instructions appears in Table 5.1, for the standard type of experiment, in which subjects study a list of words and then read these instructions before responding to an old/new recognition test. As can be seen, the instructions are rather complex. They revolve around the idea that different recognition probes provoke different phenomenologies and the idea that subjects can introspect on those mental experiences to make reliable meta-cognitive judgments about recognition probes. With children, these instructions raise concerns

Table 5.1. INSTRUCTIONS FOR REMEMBER AND KNOW JUDGMENTS

Judgment Instructions

Remember — If your recognition of the item is accompanied by a conscious recollection of its prior occurrence in the study list, then write *R*. *Remember* is the ability to become consciously aware of some aspect or aspects of what happened or what was experienced at the time the word was presented (e.g., aspects of the physical appearance of the word, or something that happened in the room, or what you were thinking or doing at the time). In other words, the "remembered" word should bring back to mind a particular association, image, or something more personal from the time of study or something about its appearance or position (e.g., what came before or after that word).

Know — *Know* responses should be made when you recognize that the word was in the study list, but you cannot consciously recollect anything about its actual occurrence, or what happened, or what was experienced at the time of its occurrence. In other words, write *K* (for know) when you are certain of recognizing the words, but these words fail to evoke any specific recollection from the study list.

about both comprehension and the reliability of metacognitive judgment (Ghetti & Angelini, 2008). Concerning comprehension, the instructions require high school levels of reading comprehension (Brainerd, Stein, & Reyna, 1998). Although it is possible to mitigate this problem by reading the instructions to children, that does not ensure comprehension, and worse, it creates a new problem: memory load (i.e., children will make reliable judgments only to the extent that they can remember what was read to them). The other concern is that even if remember-know instructions are understood and remembered, children must use them to make *metacognitive* judgments. There is a large literature on the ontogenesis of metacognition (for a review, see Bjorklund, 2004), some salient results of which are that metacognitive abilities emerge at a rather leisurely pace during childhood and that it is not until middle adolescence that they begin to approximate their adult levels. The denouement is that even if children can understand and remember instructions such as those in Table 5.1, it is hazardous to imagine that the resulting metacognitive judgments have the same meaning as those that adults make, or even that such judgments are reliable.

Our response to this challenge has been to adopt more developmentally appropriate techniques that are grounded in FTT's approach to recollection and familiarity. That work is the focus of this chapter. As FTT's approach differs in certain respects from traditional perspectives and from perspectives represented in other chapters in this volume, we sketch some of its distinguishing features in the Advance Organizers section. This brief treatment is intended mainly to provide readers with a working framework, within which the more detailed material in the second and third sections will fit. Those sections form the core of this chapter. In the Specifics of FTT's Approach section, we discuss the theoretical distinctions that comprise FTT's analysis of recollection and familiarity, describe the experimental paradigm that implements those distinctions, and explain the mathematical model whose parameters provide estimates of recollection-driven and familiarity-driven remembering. In the Developmental Trends in Recollection and Similarity section, we summarize the patterns that have been obtained in developmental studies with this paradigm. In the Conclusions and Future Directions section, we consider key empirical questions about development for which such studies have yet to produce clear answers.

ADVANCE ORGANIZERS: FIVE ASPECTS OF FTT'S APPROACH TO RECOLLECTION AND FAMILIARITY

As we just said, FTT's approach to recollection and familiarity differs somewhat from other perspectives, with which readers may be more closely acquainted. Therefore, before getting into the details of experimental paradigms, mathematical models, and developmental findings, it is useful to explore a few distinguishing features of FTT's approach. Our aim here is merely to provide readers with some material that makes connections to more familiar ideas, so that it will be easier to situate the work in the next two sections within the larger enterprise of experimentation on recollection and familiarity.

False-Memory Experiments

Mainstream adult experimentation has focused on recollection and familiarity in memory for presented targets—on true memory, in other words. The same is true of the neuroscience literature on these processes. Recent review articles by Yonelinas (2002), Wixted (2007), and Parks and Yonelinas (2007) exemplify this point. However, it has long been recognized (Brainerd, Reyna, & Kneer, 1995; Hintzman & Curran, 1994) that recollection and familiarity have important implications for false memory. Crucially, although these processes reinforce each other in true memory (they both support hits), they oppose each other in false memory (one process supports false alarms whereas the other supports correct rejections). This leads to a number of interesting predictions about dissociations between true and false memory (cf. Brainerd & Reyna, 2005), which provide incisive tests of current theories of recollection and familiarity. Theory aside, the role of recollection and familiarity in false memory is of special significance in developmental research, for applied reasons. Those reasons are rooted in concerns about the reliability of the memory reports of child witnesses (Ceci & Bruck, 1995; Ceci, Ross, & Toglia, 1987), concerns that have spawned a vast literature on false memory in children (Brainerd, Reyna, & Ceci, 2008).

For reasons such as these, FTT's approach to recollection and familiarity deals simultaneously with the contributions of these processes to true and false memory. Consequently, in the next two sections, the methodologies, models, and findings that are described revolve around securing evidence of developmental trends that encompass false as well as true memory.

Representational Commitments

The earliest theoretical work on recollection and familiarity involved representational commitments, by which we mean that these processes were assumed to operate on qualitatively different types of memory representations (see Atkinson & Juola, 1973; Mandler, 1980). Nowadays, however, the modal conception eschews strong representational commitments, a trend that began with Jacoby's (1991) influential paper and has continued in his work (see especially, Jacoby, 1996) and that of other leading theorists (e.g., cf. Yonelinas, 2002). Essentially, recollection and familiarity are assumed to be distinct retrieval operations that access distinct distributions of memory information about targets. The differences between those distributions are more a matter of differences in their behavioral consequences than in the *types of information* that they code (e.g., surface versus semantic features).

In contrast, FTT's approach involves strong representational commitments. There is a large amount of literature, dating back to the early 1990s, that converges on the conclusion that in both reasoning tasks and memory tasks, subjects stored dissociated episodic traces of the surface form of targets and of various meanings, relations, and patterns that they instantiate (for reviews, see Brainerd & Reyna, 1993; Reyna, 1996, 2008; Reyna & Brainerd, 1995; Reyna, Nelson, Han, & Dieckmann, 2009). They are called *verbatim* and *gist traces* in FTT, and because semantic content is of central importance in memory research, gist traces of those particular aspects of experience are emphasized. Because the distinction between verbatim and gist traces seems to be fundamental, a good deal of attention is devoted to defining these ideas and relating them to other dual-trace theories of episodic memory in the second section of this chapter. For now, we simply note that it does not involve much of a leap to assume that this distinction has ramifications for recollection and familiarity. In that connection, we assume that on memory tests, processing verbatim traces leads to particular forms of recollective experience, whereas processing gist traces leads to particular forms of familiarity experience. Thus, a useful way to relate FTT's approach to more traditional perspectives is to think of FTT as focusing on certain subtypes of recollection and familiarity that arise from processing verbatim and gist traces.

Two further points about verbatim and gist traces need to be made before passing on, both of which respond to common misconceptions in the literature about FTT's use of these concepts. First, having or processing gist memories does not mean an absence of verbatim memories for the same material. On the contrary, FTT evolved, in part, in response to repeated demonstrations of independence between gist and verbatim memory (e.g., Brainerd & Reyna, 1993; Reyna & Kiernan, 1994), which means that gist memory can be present along with verbatim memory, or gist memory can be present without verbatim memory, or verbatim memory can be present without gist memory, or neither can be present. This independence notion is a departure from the classical concept of gist in psycholinguistics, which assumes dependence (Reyna & Brainerd, 1995). Second, gist memory does not refer only to the extraction of commonalities among a series of items or to inferences about the general theme of presented information. On the contrary, it has long been assumed that gist memories follow what have been called *hierarchies of gist*, which include the gist of single items (a single word, a single sentence, a single number, a single picture) and the relations among these single items (the gist of a list of words, the gist of inferences that integrate sentences, the gist of a series of pictures that tell a story).

Varieties of Recollection and Familiarity

Multiple forms of recollection and familiarity are considered in FTT, owing to the fact these processes are studied simultaneously for true and false memory and to the fact that strong gist memories are able to generate an ersatz form of recollection in false memory. In all, there are three types of recollection and two types of familiarity. In Table 5.2, each of these processes is defined in the context of a standard false memory experiment. In the second section of this chapter, considerable attention is devoted to (a) the problem of how to create experimental procedures that provide sufficient degrees of freedom to separate all of these processes in such experiments and (b) the problem of how to formulate mathematical models whose parameters will deliver independent measurements of these processes. In the third section, developmental findings on recollection and familiarity take the form of numerical values of such parameters.

Table 5.2. VARIETIES OF RECOLLECTION AND FAMILIARITY THAT
ARE MEASURED IN FTT'S APPROACH

Process Definition
True memory
Identity judgment: A type of recollection in which subjects perceive *target* probes to be
identical to previously presented items because they retrieve verbatim traces of
those presentations.
Similarity judgment: A type of familiarity in which subjects perceive *target* probes to be
very similar in meaning to previously presented items because they retrieve gist
traces of those presentations.
False memory
Recollection rejection: A type of recollection in which subjects perceive *distractor*
probes to be different than previously presented items, though similar in meaning,
because they retrieve verbatim traces of those presentations.
Similarity judgment: A type of familiarity in which subjects perceive *distractor* probes
to be very similar in meaning to previously presented items because they retrieve
gist traces of those presentations.
Phantom recollection: A type of illusory recollection in which subjects perceive *distractor*
probes to be *identical* to previously presented items because they retrieve very strong
gist traces that overlap almost completely with distractors' semantic content.

Neurological Bases for Varieties of Recollection and Familiarity

As multiple types of recollection and familiarity are studied in FTT, evidence of
their separability is emphasized, such evidence being of two basic types: behavioral, which was just mentioned, and neurological. Concerning the latter, neuroscience studies have supplied evidence that each of these processes is associated
with different regions of brain activation. There is a large amount of neuroscience
literature on recollection and familiarity in *true* memory. As Yonelinas (2002;
Chapter 1, this volume) has pointed out in reviews of that literature, brain-imaging
studies, electrophysiological studies, and studies of patients with selective brain
damage converge on the conclusion that the hippocampus is particularly important in recollection, whereas the region surrounding the hippocampus is particularly important in familiarity. Again, these patterns are for the types of recollection
and familiarity that are provoked by recognizing studied targets.

There is a robust and rapidly expanding literature, consisting chiefly of brain-imaging
work and patient studies, that bears on the false-memory processes in Table 5.2
(e.g., Cabeza, Rao, Wagner, Mayer, & Schacter, 2001; Dennis, Kim, & Cabeza, 2007;
Kim & Cabeza, 2007; Schacter & Slotnick, 2004). As Schacter and Slotnick pointed
out in a literature review, there are multiple studies that support the conclusions
that (a) the medial temporal lobes are important in the meaning-based familiarity that foments semantic false memories and (b) regions of the prefrontal cortex
are important in recollection-driven suppression of such false memories. In contrast, little evidence is available on the brain regions that are associated with

phantom recollection, an illusory form of meaning-based recollection that foments realistic false memories. Recently, however, Kim and Cabeza (2007) reported that increased frontoparietal activity was the brain signature of high-confidence false memories, a type of error that is usually accompanied by phantom recollection (Brainerd & Reyna, 2005). In short, there is support in the neuroscience literature for different patterns of brain activation that map with each of the processes in Table 5.2 (see also, Budson, Todman, & Schacter, 2006; Koutstaal, Verfaellie, & Schacter, 2001; Verfaellie, Page, Orlando, & Schacter, 2005).

Conjoint-Recognition Data

Experimentally, the hallmark of FTT's approach to recollection and familiarity is that it involves the production and interpretation of conjoint-recognition data. Conjoint recognition is a paradigm with two main characteristics, one methodological and the other quantitative. The methodological characteristic is that the paradigm consists of a standard false-memory design that has been expanded to include three different types of recognition tests. The quantitative characteristic is that a mathematical model is defined over this paradigm whose parameters deliver independent measurements of recollection and familiarity, for both true and false memory. In the third section this chapter, all of our developmental findings on these processes will be reported as values of the parameters of this model. Consequently, in the second section, the conjoint-recognition paradigm, the model is defined over it, and the specific processes that are measured by its parameters are all explicated in some detail.

THE SPECIFICS OF FTT'S APPROACH

As we just saw, FTT's approach to recollection and familiarity has some distinguishing features, relative to the larger literature on these processes. Perhaps the key one is that FTT is concerned with representationally driven varieties of recollection and familiarity—specifically, with verbatim traces of the surface form of experience as bases for recollection and with gist traces of the meaning of experience as bases for familiarity. Our research program has focused on how to disentangle these processes and quantify their respective contributions to recognition performance in subjects of different ages, who are attempting to remember meaningful target materials. To do that, we use a procedure called *conjoint recognition*, which requires subjects to classify probes using three different response rules. That procedure is explained in this section. First, however, we describe the basic structure of false-memory experiments and the representational distinctions that motivate the conjoint-recognition paradigm.

False-Memory Experiments

The hallmark of conjoint recognition is that it measures recollection and familiarity simultaneously for true and false memory; so it is necessary to say something about false-memory experiments. There is nothing exotic about them. They are merely episodic memory studies in which errors, as well as correct responses, are treated as providing substantive information about how memory works, rather than being regarded as noise. As usual, a subject's task is merely to remember information that was presented in a specific exposure context, with interest attaching to whether unpresented information is also reported that resembles presented information in particular respects (which are specified by the experimenter). For the sake of concreteness, we will refer to a prototypical example of such an experiment in which subjects are exposed to a collection of memory targets (words, pictures, sentences, narratives, video images), and they respond to a series of recognition probes that consists of targets, distractors that preserve salient aspects of targets (most often, their meanings), and further distractors that are nominally unrelated to the targets.

With the exception of occasional studies using nonsense materials, targets, related distractors, and unrelated distractors are instances of well-defined memory items, where memory items are representations of packets of information that subjects have encountered many times in the past. Traditionally, in memory theories, such representations are conceptualized as collections of features, with a basic distinction being drawn between storing episodic traces of surface and semantic features in FTT (Reyna & Brainerd, 1995). Similar distinctions can be found in other recent dual-trace theories, such as the processing implicit and explicit representations model of Nelson and associates (Nelson, Schreiber, & McEvoy, 1992), and the retrieving efficiently from memory model of Shiffrin and associates (e.g., Shiffrin, 2003; Shiffrin & Steyvers, 1997).

When probes are presented on recognition tests, they may be thought of as *picking out* (identifying, selecting) the corresponding memory items. Whether the memory items that are picked out by recognition probes are "true" or "false" is a purely episodic question whose answer depends on the arbitrary fact of whether an exemplar of that item was encountered in the designated context. It does *not* refer to the deeper question of subjects' understanding or knowledge. To see why, suppose that subjects study a list of sentences and that on the recognition test, two of the test probes are "Cornell is in Kansas" and "pizza is an Italian food." If the first probe were part of the study list, it would be a "true," notwithstanding that it is factually false, and if the second probe were not part of the study list, it would be a "false," notwithstanding that it is factually true. Thus, it is the contextual cues in connection with which an item is experienced that are determinative of true and false memory, in the canonical design. In theories such as FTT, processing implicit and explicit representations, and retrieving efficiently from memory, such contextual information is stored in episodic traces—where, generally speaking, episodic traces consist of samples (or subsets) of an item's features that were tagged with contextual cues when exemplars of that item were previously encountered. In FTT, a verbatim trace is a sample of an item's surface features plus contextual cues, whereas a gist trace is a sample of an item's semantic features plus contextual cues (e.g., Brainerd & Reyna, 2010).

In the canonical false-memory experiment, the test instructions that subjects receive serve two functions. First, they identify the episodic context that determines which of the items that are picked out by test probes are false and which are true (normally, the study phase). Second, and of great interest theoretically, test instructions state a *response rule* for the memory items that probes pick out. A response rule specifies a small and exhaustive set of episodic categories with which items are allowed to map and directs subjects to respond by using retrieved information to collapse items onto only those categories. In the canonical design, there are three episodic categories: (a) a probe is an exemplar of an item or of a collection of items (if it is a complex stimulus, such as a sentence or picture) that occurred in the designated context (target, true, presented); (b) a probe is an exemplar of an item or a collection of items that did not occur in the designated context, but it resembles one or more presented exemplars in specified ways (related distractor, false-but-related, unpresented-but-similar); or (c) a probe is an exemplar of an item or a collection of items that did not occur in the designated context and does not resemble any of the presented exemplars in the specified ways (unrelated distractor, false-and-unrelated, unpresented-and-dissimilar).

Conjoint Recognition: Response Rules

A conjoint-recognition experiment is just a canonical false-memory study that has been enriched with further response rules. In standard old/new recognition, the response rule says that targets are to be accepted, whereas any and all distractors are to be rejected. This rule produces the standard false-memory effect, which is that distractor acceptances (false alarms) are higher for related than for unrelated distractors (e.g., Underwood, 1965). With respect to hits, FTT assumes that retrieval of either verbatim or gist traces supports acceptances of the corresponding targets, with verbatim retrieval provoking the realistic, item-specific phenomenologies that are collectively referred to as *recollection* and gist retrieval usually provoking the more generic phenomenologies that are referred to as *familiarity*. However, gist retrieval is more specific than the inchoate I-just-know-it-was-on-the-list-but-I-don't-why feelings that are often used to characterize familiarity (e.g., Tulving, 1985). Gist retrieval carries with it the possibility of awareness of particular meaning relations, as when *dog* provokes awareness that there were animals on the study list or *table* provokes awareness that there were articles of furniture on the study list. Throughout this chapter, we will acknowledge that this more specific form of familiarity is being studied by replacing the term *familiarity* with the term *similarity*. Although this usage seems to encompass the most common experimental demonstrations of familiarity, it goes without saying that it does not rule out the possibility of other varieties of familiarity that do not fit the similarity notion. That caveat notwithstanding, there is no theoretical progress without process specificity.

In contrast to targets, FTT says that verbatim and gist retrieval support *opposite responses* to related distractors under the standard old/new response rule. On the one hand, the realistic mental reinstatement of targets' prior presentations that accompanies verbatim retrieval supports positive, principled rejections of the corresponding related distractors ("No, I didn't hear *collie* on the list. I clearly remember hearing *poodle*, instead."), which is called recollection rejection in Table 5.2. On the other hand, gist retrieval supports false acceptance of related distractors, for one of two reasons. Gist traces can make the meaning features of distractors seem so similar to those of targets that subjects decide that it is very likely that they were presented, which is referred to as a similarity judgment in Table 5.2. The prototypical false-memory effect is interpreted as showing that (a) the rate of similarity judgment is greater than the rate of recollection rejection because (b) related distractors are usually better retrieval cues for targets' gist traces than for their verbatim traces (e.g., Brainerd, Reyna, & Mojardin, 1999; Brainerd, Wright, Reyna, Mojardin, 2001). A surprising corollary of this interpretation is that it should be possible to reverse the false-memory effect—to obtain *lower* false-alarm rates for related than for unrelated distractors—under conditions that make it particularly easy for related distractors to access verbatim traces. That finding, which is called false-recognition reversal, has been reported by Stahl and Klauer (2008, 2009) and by ourselves (Brainerd et al., 1995).[1]

In addition to the traditional old/new rule, Brainerd and Reyna (1998, 2002) pointed out that there are other response rules in which distractor acceptances are hits, rather than false alarms (see also, Holliday & Haynes, 2000, 2002). When two such additional rules are combined with the traditional rule, one can separate the influences of recollection and similarity on true and false memory. One of them, which was studied by Brainerd et al. (1998), is the complement of the traditional rule: The only probes that are to be accepted are related distractors. To avoid confusing the two, the traditional one is referred to as the *verbatim (or V) rule*, whereas its complement is referred to as the *gist (or G) rule.* The remaining rule, which was studied by Reyna and Kiernan (1994, 1995), is simply a combination of the first two (i.e., both targets and related distractors are to be accepted), and is referred to as the *verbatim + gist (or VG) rule.* Conjoint recognition (Brainerd et al., 1999)

---

1. Reyna, Mills, Estrada, and Brainerd (2007) made a series of points about the phenomenon of suppressing false memories via target recollection that should be mentioned here. In the false memory literature, various phrases have been used to describe this phenomenon: verbatim-based rejection (e.g., Reyna & Kiernan, 1994), negative dependency (e.g., Reyna & Kiernan, 1995), nonidentity judgments (e.g., Brainerd et al., 1999), recollection rejection (e.g., Brainerd & Reyna, 2002), false-recognition reversal (Brainerd et al., 1995), and recall-to-reject (e.g., Gallo, 2004; Rotello, Macmillan, & Van Tassel, 2000). The last phrase, recall-to-reject, resembles the others in that it involves retrieval of memories for experienced events, but it assumes that the suppression process involves *recall* (which is more a description of a task than of an underlying process) and that recall is a unitary process (i.e., that distinguishing between verbatim and gist traces is unnecessary). The other phrases, however, all refer to FTT's notion of retrieving a *verbatim* memory for experienced events in order to reject related items. Because this process involves verbatim memories, the properties of which are well known, we can predict the factors that will facilitate rejection of false memories, such as pictorial encoding of targets (Brainerd & Reyna, 1993). Although this picture-encoding manipulation also figures in research by Schacter and associates (e.g., Schacter et al., 1999), Schacter et al.'s notion of a distinctiveness heuristic, which they use to explain the manipulation's effects, should not be confused with recollection rejection. The latter involves the retrieval of verbatim traces, whereas the former is a metacognitive strategy.

is a procedure that uses all three of these rules. That is, on recognition tests, some subjects respond under the V rule, others respond under the G rule, and still others respond under the VG rule. (Or, in within-subjects designs, some probes are accompanied by V questions, others are accompanied by G questions, and still others are accompanied by VG questions.) This factorial crossing of three response rules with the three types of items of false-memory experiments (targets, related distractors, unrelated distractors) results in the response space that is exhibited in Table 5.3. A point to note in Table 5.3 is that for targets and related distractors, the types of responses that are hits, misses, false alarms, and correct rejections *vary as a function of which response rule is operative*. In the two subsections that follow, we consider how the response space in Table 5.3 leads to a mathematical model that measures recollection and similarity processes for both true and false memory.

Measuring Recollection and Similarity in False Memory

In the canonical false-memory experiment, which implements the V rule, we have just seen how different episodic traces support opposite responses to false-memory items (related distractors). The basic proposal is that processing verbatim traces of targets supports confident rejections of related distractors (recollection rejections), whereas processing gist traces of targets supports false alarms (similarity judgments; the familiarity scenario). Ostensibly, the tendency for the second influence to predominate over the first is responsible for the prototypical false-memory effect of higher false-alarm rates for related than for unrelated distractors. However, there is a third factor that needs to be taken into account that also supports false alarms to related distractors: response bias.

These distinctions have been imbedded in simple multinomial models (e.g., Reyna, Holliday, & Marche, 2002) that are descendants of Mandler's (1980) early dual-process equation for target recognition under the V response rule:

$$p(H) = R + F - RF \qquad \text{NE (1)}$$

Table 5.3. Response Patterns in Conjoint Recognition

Type of probe
Rule/probe response

	Target	Related distractor	Unrelated distractor
V			
accept	hit	false alarm	false alarm
reject	miss	correct rejection	correct rejection
G			
accept	false alarm	hit	false alarm
reject	correct rejection	miss	correct rejection
VG			
accept	hit	hit	false alarm
reject	miss	miss	correct rejection

R is the probability that subjects recollect a probe's prior presentation. F is the probability that although the probe's presentation cannot be recollected, it seems so familiar that subjects are sure that it must have been presented. Jacoby (1991) rewrote this equation as

$$p(H) = R + (1-R)F, \qquad\qquad \text{NE (2)}$$

which stresses that recollection trumps familiarity as a basis for target recognition (e.g., on remember-know tasks; for reviews, see Donaldson, 1996; Gardiner & Java, 1991). Some years later, we introduced the equation

$$p_V(RD) = (1 - N_{RD})S_{RD} + (1 - N_{RD})(1 - S_{RD})\beta_V, \qquad\qquad \text{NE (3)}$$

to express the probability of false alarms to related distractors in the canonical false-memory design (Brainerd et al., 1999). N_{RD} is the probability of retrieving verbatim traces of distractors equalling corresponding targets and performing recollection rejections ("*Collie* was not on the list because I remember seeing *poodle* instead."), and S_{RD} is the probability that subjects retrieve gist traces of distractors equalling corresponding targets, resulting in false alarms. Importantly, the quantity $(1 - N_{RD})S_{RD}$ is the proportion of related-distractor items that occupy the state of episodic indeterminacy that is associated with semantic similarity. Under the V rule, those items are classified as targets and accepted. Last, β_V is a two-high threshold response-bias parameter (see Snodgrass & Corwin, 1988) that measures the tendency to accept recognition probes on the basis of guessing and other forms of response bias.

The same assumptions about the subjective consequences of retrieving different types of episodic traces lead to parallel expressions for the probabilities of accepting related distractors under the G and VG rules. The expression for accepting related distractors under the G rule is

$$p_G(RD) = N_{RD} + (1 - N_{RD})S_{RD} + (1 - N_{RD})(1 - S_{RD})\beta_G, \qquad\qquad \text{NE (4)}$$

where N_{RD} and S_{RD} have the same meanings as in Equation 3, but β_G is the bias parameter for the G rule. Equation 4 says that retrieving verbatim traces of distractors' corresponding targets produces the same reaction as before (i.e., confident false-but-related classifications, such as "*collie* was not on the list because I clearly remember seeing *poodle* instead"), but it supports acceptances under the G rule. The quantity $(1 - N_{RD})S_{RD}$ is still the proportion of related distractor items that are in a state of episodic indeterminacy. Owing to that indeterminacy, these items are now classified as related distractors, rather than as targets, and so they are once again accepted. The parallel expression for the VG rule is

$$p_{VG}(RD) = N_{RD} + (1 - N_{RD})S_{RD} + (1 - N_{RD})(1 - S_{RD})\beta_V, \qquad\qquad \text{NE (5)}$$

which has the same form as Equation 4, except for the bias parameter β_{VG}, whose value may be different than that of β_G. $(1 - N_{RD})S_{RD}$ is still the proportion of related-distractor items that are in a state of episodic indeterminacy, but subjects are not forced to classify them as being either targets or related distractors because the VG rule says that both types of items are to be accepted.

Before moving on to true memory, Equations 3 to 5 must be expanded to include the other false-memory process in Table 5.2, *phantom recollection*. Brainerd et al. (2001) noted that the memory items that are picked out by some related distractors are perceived to occupy the target state, as definitely as targets themselves are; their "presentations" flash in the mind's eye and echo in the mind's ear. Although most false-memory responses are not accompanied by such realistic, item-specific phenomenology (Conway, Collins, Gathercole, & Anderson, 1996; Heaps & Nash, 2001; Reyna & Lloyd, 1997), some related distractors provoke such illusory vivid experiences. This could happen, for instance, if there is very strong overlap between the semantic features that are sampled for distractor items and the features that are stored in gist traces of their corresponding targets. Brainerd et al. (2001) also pointed out that there are data that support such an interpretation. Specifically, if subjects study several different targets, which have certain semantic features in common (e.g., *nurse, sick, hospital, ill*), most of the semantic features that can be sampled for a related distractor that shares these common features (*doctor*) will be stored in gist traces, and thus, featural overlap will be high. Consistent with this line of reasoning, phantom recollection has been found to increase when the meanings of related distractors have been exemplified by many different targets (e.g., Dewhurst, 2001; Dewhurst & Farrand, 2004; Koutstaal, & Schacter, 1997).

The conjoint-recognition model includes phantom recollection by adjusting Equations 3 to 5 as follows:

$$p_V(RD) = (1 - N_{RD})P_{RD} + (1 - N_{RD})(1 - P_{RD})S_{RD}$$
$$+ (1 - N_{RD})(1 - P_{RD})(1 - S_{RD})\beta_V, \qquad \text{NE (6)}$$

$$p_G(RD) = N_{RD} + (1 - N_{RD})(1 - P_{RD})S_{RD}$$
$$+ (1 - N_{RD})(1 - P_{RD})(1 - S_{RD})\beta_G, \qquad \text{NE (7)}$$

and

$$p_{VG}(RD) = N_{RD} + (1 - N_{RD})P_{RD} + 1(1 - N_{RD})(1 - P_{RD})S_{RD}$$
$$+ (1 - N_{RD})(1 - P_{RD})(1 - S_{RD})\beta_{VG}, \qquad \text{NE (8)}$$

The parameters in these expressions have the same meanings as in Equations 3 to 5, except for P_{RD}, which is the probability that related distractors provoke phantom recollection of their "presentations." Equation 6 says that in standard old/new recognition, related distractors are falsely accepted (as targets) for one of three reasons: (a) they do not provoke retrieval of verbatim traces of their corresponding targets but they do provoke retrieval of gist traces that cause phantom recollection; (b) they do not provoke retrieval of verbatim traces of their corresponding targets or gist traces that cause phantom recollection, but they do provoke retrieval of gist traces that support similarity judgments; and (c) they do not provoke retrieval of verbatim traces of their corresponding targets or gist traces that cause phantom recollection or that support similarity judgments, but response bias produces acceptance.

Measuring Recollection and Similarity in True Memory

In the canonical false-memory experiment, different episodic traces support acceptance of targets under the V rule. The basic proposal is that processing verbatim traces of targets supports recollection-based acceptances, whereas processing gist traces of targets supports similarity-based acceptances. These distinctions produce equations for true memory that parallel those for false memory.

The expression for the V rule is

$$p_V(T) = I_T + (1 - I_T)S_T + (1 - I_T)(1 - S_T)\beta_V, \qquad \text{NE (9)}$$

where I_T is the probability that subjects retrieve targets' verbatim traces, leading to recollection of their presentation and the judgment that recognition probes are *identical* to targets, and S_T is the probability that subjects retrieve gist traces of targets, leading to similarity judgments. Importantly, the quantity $(1 - I_T)S_T$ is the proportion of targets that occupy the state of episodic indeterminacy that is associated with semantic similarity. Under the V rule, those items are classified as targets and accepted. Last, β_V is the same response-bias parameter as before.

The same assumptions about the subjective consequences of retrieving verbatim and gist traces lead to the expressions for the probabilities of accepting targets under the G and VG rules. The expression for acceptance under the G rule is

$$p_G(T) = (1 - I_T)S_T + (1 - I_T)(1 - S_T)\beta_G, \qquad \text{NE (10)}$$

where I_T and S_T have the same meanings as in Equation 9, and β_G is the same bias parameter as before under the G rule. Equation 10 says that retrieving verbatim traces of targets produces confident rejections under the G rule (i.e., "*poodle* can't be a distractor because I clearly remember it being on the list"), but similarity judgment supports acceptances. The quantity $(1 - I_T)S_T$ is still the proportion of targets that are in the state of episodic indeterminacy that is associated with semantic similarity, with that indeterminacy being responsible for the fact that these items are now classified as related distractors (whereas they were classified as targets under the V rule).

The parallel expression for the VG rule is

$$P_{VG}(T) = I_T + (1 - I_T)S_T + (1 - I_T)(1 - S_T)\beta_{VG}, \qquad \text{NE (11)}$$

where I_T and S_T have the same meanings as in Equation 9, and β_{VG} is the same bias parameter as before under the VG rule. $(1 - I_T)S_T$ is still the proportion of targets that are in a state of episodic indeterminacy, but subjects are not forced into classify them as being either targets or related distractors because the VG rule says that both types of items are to be accepted.

Statistical Methods

It is a simple matter to apply the model in Equations 6 to 11 to the data of conjoint-recognition experiments. That is because Equations 6 to 11 specify a member of the general class of multinomial cognitive models, for which the underlying statistical theory has been developed by Riefer and Batchelder (1988). The key mathematical step, which allows the theory of maximum likelihood to be used to estimate parameters, evaluate fit, and test hypotheses about parameters, is to implement these equations in a likelihood function (cf. Brainerd et al., 2001). To perform these operations on data, the likelihood function can be entered in modeling programs, such as General Processing Tree (Hu, 1998).

DEVELOPMENTAL TRENDS IN RECOLLECTION AND SIMILARITY

In this section, we come to the empirical meat. We review developmental findings on recollection and similarity that have been produced by conjoint-recognition experiments; that is, by experiments in which some or all of the processes in Table 5.2 are measured in false-memory designs. As another advance organizer, it is quite possible that the trends might be different for true and false memory, if for no other reason than that, by the principle of encoding variability (e.g., Tulving & Thompson, 1971), targets should be better cues for their episodic memory traces than related distractors are. Then, there is the additional consideration that recollection and similarity reinforce each other when subjects are responding to standard old/new recognition probes for targets, but they oppose each other when subjects are responding to such probes for related distractors. We shall see that, in the main, the developmental trends for true and false memory are analogous, but there are some quantitative differences.

We have conducted two types of developmental conjoint recognition studies, the findings of which are summarized in separate sections—namely, studies that implemented partial designs and studies that implemented complete designs. A complete design is merely one that includes the full 3 (type of memory test: V, G, VG) × 3 (type of item: target, related distractor, unrelated distractor) factorial structure, which allows all of the processes in Table 5.2 to be measured. There are two types of partial designs: a 2 (memory test: V or G) × 3 (item: target, related distractor, unrelated distractor) factorial structure and a 2 (memory test: V or VG) × 3 (item: target, related distractor, unrelated distractor) factorial structure. It transpires that the first of these simplified structures allows all of the processes in Table 5.2, *except phantom recollection*, to be measured, whereas the second allows recollection and similarity to be measured for false (but not true) memory. We summarize developmental findings from studies that implemented partial conjoint-recognition designs first, paying particular attention to global developmental trends in recollection and similarity. Then, we move on to findings from studies that implemented complete designs, again paying particular attention to global developmental trends.

Findings from Partial Designs

THE V AND G DESIGN

Brainerd et al. (1998) reported a conjoint-recognition study that used the 2 (memory test: V or G) × 3 (item: target, related distractor, unrelated distractor) design in a false-memory study. The participants were 100 elementary schoolers (50 7-year-olds and 50 10-year-olds). A continuous recognition task, modeled after Underwood's (1965) early study, was used. Half of the children at each age level were assigned to a V testing condition, whereas the other half were assigned to a G testing condition. The children were told that they would be listening to a list of vocabulary words that would consist of two types of words—namely, familiar everyday words (e.g., *friend, picture*) and nonsense words (e.g., *wux, zaffel*). The children were also told that after they had heard the first few words, most of the subsequent words that they would hear would continue to be entirely new, but others would either be (a) old words that were exactly the same as ones that they had already heard (e.g., *friend, wux*) or (b) new words that rhymed with words that they had already heard (e.g., *trend, rux*). To ensure comprehension, children were pretrained on a series of examples. Following these instructions, children listened to an audio recording of the complete vocabulary list, which consisted of 120 familiar concrete nouns and 80 nonsense words, and made recognition decisions about these words as they were presented. Specifically, children in the V condition were instructed to respond *yes* whenever they heard an old word (i.e., one that was exactly the same as one that had been previously heard), whereas children in the G condition were instructed to respond *yes* to any new word that rhymed with a word that they had previously heard. The list was constructed in such a way that (a) 10 to 15 words intervened between consecutive presentations of repeated targets and (b) 10 to 15 words intervened between presentation of a target and presentation of a rhyming distractor.

Referring to Equations 3 to 8, Brainerd et al.'s design provides four of the six empirical quantities in those expressions—namely, $p_V(T)$, $p_V(RD)$, $p_G(T)$, and $p_G(RD)$. If we assume that the task that was just described does not induce significant levels of phantom recollection, an assumption that is based on the finding that phantom recollection is most commonly associated with designs in which meanings (e.g., animal, fruit) are exemplified by several targets, the conjoint-recognition model's expressions for these quantities are

$$P_V(T) = I_T + (1-I_T)S_T + (1-I_T)(1-S_T)\beta_V \text{ (cf. Equation 9),}$$

$$p_v(RD) = (1-N_{RD})S_{RD} + (1-N_{RD})(1-S_{RD})\beta_V \text{ (cf. Equation 3),}$$

$$P_G(T) = (1-I_T)S_T + (1-I_T)(1-S_T)\beta_G, \text{ (cf. Equation 10), and}$$

$$p_v(RD) = N_{RD} + (1-N_{RD})S_{RD} + (1-N_{RD})(1-S_{RD})\beta_G \text{ (cf. Equation 4)}$$

In short, although it is not possible to measure developmental changes in phantom recollection with this design, it is possible to measure developmental changes in recollection and similarity for both true and false memory, which is a considerable advance over traditional designs.

The main qualitative findings were that (a) children were very good at recognizing previously presented words (the hit rates in the V condition were 0.90 and 0.94, respectively, for younger and older children), (b) children were reasonably good at recognizing distractors that were rhymes of previously presented words (the hit rates in the G condition were 0.48 and 0.54, respectively, for younger and older children), and (c) although both age increases were small, both were reliable. The more important findings appear in Table 5.4, where estimates of the conjoint-recognition parameters appear by age level. Concerning recollection, note that the recollection parameter for true memory (I_T) is much larger than the recollection parameter for false memory (N_{RD}) at both age levels—indeed, the former was nearly twice the latter. This is sensible because, as mentioned earlier, a target (e.g., *friend, wux*) will be a better retrieval cue for its own verbatim trace than a related distractor (e.g., *trend, rux*) will be. Next, note that the two parameters both increase with age (i.e., it becomes easier to recollect a word's prior presentation), but that N_{RD} increases more than I_T. Again, this makes sense: Age increases in recollection ought to be more marked when retrieval cues make it more difficult to access verbatim traces.

Turning to similarity, note first that, as would be expected in continuous recognition, when verbatim traces are highly accessible by virtue of the fact that targets were first presented less than a minute earlier, children did not tend to accept targets predominately because their phonology was familiar: The mean value of S_T is only 0.15. Likewise, children did not tend to accept related distractors predominantely because their phonology was familiar: The mean value of S_{RD} was only 0.10. In short, estimates of the model's parameters indicated that continuous recognition is a task that is dominated by verbatim processing. Because such dominance is expected on theoretical grounds, these results provide a validity test of the assumptions that underlie the conjoint-recognition model.

Summing up, correct acceptances of targets (V condition) and related distractors (G condition), as well as correct rejections of targets (G condition) and related distractors (V condition), were all dominated by recollection of targets' prior presentations. According to FTT, this is because verbatim traces of targets are highly accessible in a continuous recognition experiment, owing to the fact that they were presented less than a minute earlier. With respect to developmental variability in recollection and similarity, the data exhibited a pattern that will be seen in much of the other data that are reviewed herein: that recollection developed more than similarity. Specifically, both I_T and N_{RD} displayed reliable increases between the ages of 7 and 10, but neither S_T and S_{RD} increased reliably.

THE V AND VG DESIGN

We now consider three studies that made use of the other partial design, 2 (memory test: V or VG) × 3 (item: target, related distractor, unrelated distractor). All of these

Table 5.4. DEVELOPMENTAL TRENDS IN RECOLLECTIVE AND FAMILIARITY PROCESSES WITH PARTIAL CONJOINT-RECOGNITION DESIGNS

Parameter Groups/conditions

		I_T	S_T	N_{RD}	S_{RD}	β_V	β_G	βv_G
Brainerd, Stein, and Reyna (1998)								
7-year-olds		0.71	0.10	0.39	0.10	0.06	0.02	
10-year-olds		0.76	0.19	0.47	0.10	0.03	0.02	
Reyna and Kiernan (1994)								
6-year-olds								
	Immediate		0.15	0.24	0.37	0.49		
	Delayed		0.06	0.17	0.38	0.50		
9-year-olds								
	Immediate		0.39	0.31	0.22	0.52		
	Delayed		0.06	0.17	0.38	0.50		
Kiernan (1993)								
Disabled		0.26	0.27	0.44	0.48			
Nondisabled		0.54	0.39	0.44	0.44			
Immediate								
	Spatial		0.39	0.40	0.29	0.41		
	Linear		0.46	0.33	0.30	0.46		
Delayed								
	Spatial		0.35	0.39	0.40	0.47		
	Linear		0.14	0.56	0.52	0.71		
Reyna and Kiernan (1995)								
6-year-olds								
	Immediate							
	TLIT		0.08	0.13	0.05	0.29		
	TPER		0.01	0.06	0.09	0.37		
	TPSY		0.15	0.02	0.02	0.12		
	Delayed							
	TLIT		0.00	0.23	0.14	0.20		
	TPER		0.00	0.07	0.30	0.18		
	TPSY		0.07	0.10	0.50	0.29		
9-year-olds								
	Immediate							
	TLIT		0.52	0.16	0.09	0.37		
	TPER		0.39	0.02	0.02	0.12		
	TPSY		0.44	0.00	0.04	0.04		
	Delayed							
	TLIT		0.00	0.25	0.30	0.04		
	TPER		0.00	0.03	0.30	0.07		
	TPSY		0.07	0.25	0.50	0.10		

Note. FLIT = false literal paraphrases of the meanings of metaphorical targets; FPER = false perceptual descriptions of features of metaphorical targets; FPSY = false psychological interpretations of metaphorical targets; TLIT = true literal paraphrases of the meanings of metaphorical targets; TPER = true perceptual descriptions of features of metaphorical targets; TPSY = true psychological interpretations of metaphorical targets.

studies used a narrative memory procedure that was introduced by Reyna and Kiernan (1994). Reyna and Kiernan's methodology is shown in Table 5.5. Their subjects (6- and 9-year-old children) listened to a series of three-sentence narratives, two examples of which are shown at the top of Table 5.5. Each narrative revolved around either a magnitude relation (e.g., hot/cold in one of the examples in Table 5.5) or a spatial relation (e.g., on/under in the other example). Children responded to yes/no recognition tests about these narratives, which consisted of probes like those shown in Table 5.5. Note that the target probes were the three sentences that the children had just heard, the related distractors were sentences that they had not heard but that were true statements about the narrative, and the unrelated distractors were sentences that they had not heard and that were not true of the narrative. Half of the children responded to these probes under V instructions, and the other half responded under VG instructions. The children received instructions and examples to ensure that they understood the distinction between the three types of probes, and the instructions included practice narratives and

Table 5.5. MATERIALS USED BY REYNA AND KIERNAN (*1994*) TO MEASURE FALSE MEMORY FOR NARRATIVE STATEMENTS

Item type

	Linear	Spatial
Narrative/target probes		
	The coffee is hotter than the tea.	The flowers are on the table.
	The tea is hotter than the cocoa.	The table is under the light.
	The cocoa is very sweet.	The flowers are in a green pot.
True probes (related distractors)		
TPN	The tea is cooler than the coffee.	The light is above the table.
TIO	The coffee is hotter than the cocoa.	The flowers are under the light.
TIN	The cocoa is cooler than the coffee.	The light is above the flowers.
False probes (unrelated distractors)		
FPN	The coffee is cooler than the tea.	The table is above the light.
FIO	The cocoa is hotter than the coffee.	The light is under the flowers.
FIN	The coffee is cooler that the cocoa.	The flowers are above the light.

Note. FIN = false inference with new words; FIO = false inference with old words; FPO = false premise with old words; TIN = true inference with novel word; TIO = true inference with old words; TPO = true premise with old words

practice probes. The recognition test for each narrative (V or VG) was administered twice to each subject. The first test occurred immediately after the narrative
was presented, and the second occurred a week later.

Referring to Equations 3 to 8, this design provides four of the six empirical
quantities in those expressions—namely, $p_V(T)$, $p_V(RD)$, $p_G(T)$, and $p_{VG}(RD)$. If, as
before, we assume that the task in Table 5.5 does not induce significant levels of
phantom recollection, estimates of recollection and similarity can be obtained for
false memory but not for true memory. The conjoint-recognition expressions
from which those estimates are obtained are Equations 3 and 5. Therefore, in this
particular design, although it is still not possible to measure phantom recollection, the development of recollection and similarity processes can be tracked for
the data of related distractors. Estimates of these processes for Reyna and Kiernan's
(1994) data are reported in Table 5.4, along with estimates of bias parameters.

Taking the immediate test first, inspection of Table 5.4 reveals three findings of
primary interest. First, although the age difference between younger and older children was only three years, there was a substantial increase in recollection of narrative sentences, with the value of N_{RD} more than doubling. Second, the semantic
similarity of narrative sentences also increased with age, but the increase in S_{RD}
(from 0.24 to 0.31), though reliable, was less than one-third of the increase in N_{RD}.
Third, levels of response bias were much higher than those in Brainerd et al's (1998)
continuous recognition study and bias was noticeably higher under VG instructions
than under V instructions. Both of the latter findings are more consistent with what
has typically been found in complete conjoint-recognition designs with adults (for a
review, see Brainerd & Reyna, 2008; see also, Brainerd, Reyna, & Aydin, 2010).

Turning to the delayed test data in Table 5.4, a final important pattern is apparent from comparisons of the levels of recollection and similarity on the 1-week
versus the immediate test. A standard finding about forgetting curves for recollection and familiarity that has often been detected with remember-know judgments
(see Gardiner & Java, 1991) is that over time, recollection levels fall more rapidly
than familiarity levels. It can be seen that N_{RD} and S_{RD} displayed an analogous pattern. Among older children, who showed reasonably high levels of recollection
rejection on the immediate test, the decline in the recollection rejection parameter
was more marked than the decline in the similarity parameter.

Reyna and Kiernan's (1994) basic design was repeated in a dissertation by
Kiernan (1993). The novel feature of Kiernan's research is that she focused on an
ability-based index of development, rather than the usual chronological age index.
In this connection, it has long been known that although the psychometric intelligence of learning-disabled children is, by definition, within the normal range,
such children display deficits in both verbatim and gist memory (cf. Swanson,
1991). Kiernan administered Reyna and Kiernan's task to a sample of children
who had been diagnosed with a specific learning disability that involved language
acquisition and to a sample of matched control children. The results of principal
interest are shown in Table 5.4.

Using this ability-based definition of development, note that, as before, there
was a dramatic change in the recollection measure. The value of N_{RD} was more

than twice as large for nondisabled children than for disabled children. Also as before, there was a reliable change in the similarity measure, but the change in S_{RD} (from 0.27 to 0.39) was less than half the change in N_{RD}. As in Reyna and Kiernan's (1994) research, response bias levels for narrative sentences were much higher than in Brainerd et al.'s (1998) continuous recognition study. A final finding of interest concerns differences between recollection and similarity for magnitude narratives (left side of Table 5.5) versus spatial narratives (right side of Table 5.5). Following various comparisons of children's performance on the two types of narratives, Reyna and Kiernan concluded that verbatim memory for sentences was better for magnitude narratives than for spatial narratives, but that gist memory for the meaning content of sentences was worse for magnitude narratives. We estimated recollection and similarity parameters separately for the two types of narratives to evaluate this hypothesis with Kiernan's data. As can be seen in Table 5.4, the results were consistent with the hypothesis. On the one hand, the mean value of N_{RD} was larger for magnitude than for spatial narratives (0.39 vs. 0.46), but on the other hand, the mean value of S_{RD} was larger for spatial than for magnitude narratives (0.40 vs. 0.33). Another finding that is consistent with the same hypothesis is that declines in N_{RD} between the immediate and delayed test were greater for magnitude than for spatial narratives. As in Reyna and Kiernan's data, there was support for the notion that gist memories are more stable than verbatim memories because the mean value of N_{RD} declined more than the mean value of S_{RD} between the immediate and delayed test.

The final study, by Reyna and Kiernan (1995), repeated Reyna and Kiernan's basic design but used new narrative materials. Once again, the subjects were 6- and 9-year-old children who listened to short narratives and responded to immediate and delayed (1-week) sentence recognition tests under V or VG instructions. The narratives were neither spatial nor magnitude, however, and consisted, instead, of metaphorical statements about familiar objects and events. As can be seen in Table 5.6, the first two sentences in each narrative were literal ones (The woman was shopping in the grocery store. The woman saw the lost boy near the door.). The last sentence, however, was metaphorical (The woman was an aspirin, kneeling by the lost boy.) The probes on the recognition test again consisted of targets, related distractors, and unrelated distractors. However, there were three types of related distractors, which are designated as TLIT, TPER, and TPSY in Table 5.6, and there were three matched unrelated distractors, which are designated as FLIT, FPER, and FPSY in Table 5.6. The definitions of these distractors were as follows: TLIT = true literal paraphrases of the meanings of metaphorical targets; TPER = true perceptual descriptions of features of metaphorical targets; TPSY = true psychological interpretations of metaphorical targets; FLIT = false literal paraphrases of the meanings of metaphorical targets; FPER = false perceptual descriptions of features of metaphorical targets; and FPSY = false psychological interpretations of metaphorical targets.

Analysis of Reyna and Kiernan's (1995) data with the partial conjoint-recognition model produced the results at the bottom of Table 5.3. Taking the data of the immediate test first, note that there is still more evidence of dramatic improvement in

Table 5.6. MATERIALS USED BY REYNA AND KIERNAN (1995) TO
MEASURE FALSE MEMORY FOR METAPHORICAL STATEMENTS

Item type	Example
Targets	The woman was shopping in the grocery store. The woman saw the lost boy near the door. The woman was an aspirin, kneeling by the lost boy.

True Distractors

	TLIT	The woman was medicine, kneeling by the lost boy.
	TPER	The woman was white round, kneeling by the lost boy.
	TPSY	The woman made him feel better, kneeling by the lost boy.

False distractors

	FLIT	The woman was a nurse, kneeling by the lost.
	FPER	The woman had red cheeks, kneeling by the lost boy.
	FPSY	The woman was proud, kneeling by the lost boy.

Note. FLIT = a false paraphrase of the metaphorical target (i.e., aspirin .a nurse); FPER = a false perceptual interpretation of a feature of the metaphorical target (i.e., the woman did not have red cheeks); FPSY = a false psychological interpretation of the metaphorical target (i.e., the woman did not feel proud); TLIT = a true paraphrase of the metaphorical target (i.e., aspirin = medicine); TPER = a true perceptual interpretation of a feature of the metaphorical target (i.e., aspirin = white and round); TPSY = a true psychological interpretation of the metaphorical target (i.e., the woman would make the boy feel better).

recollection across this relatively narrow age range. Averaging across the three types of related distractors (TLIT, TPER, TPSY), the mean value of N_{RD} was 0.08 for 6-year-olds and 0.45 for 9-year-olds. In sharp contrast, the similarity index did not vary with age. A second finding that echoes earlier results (and conjoint-recognition studies of adults) is that levels of response bias were higher under VG instructions than under V instructions. Finally, consider the results for the 1-week delayed test. Consistent with earlier findings and with theoretical expectations, between the immediate and delayed test the recollection measure declined much more than the similarity measure. Indeed, as can be seen in Table 5.3, at both age levels, N_{RD} had declined to near-floor levels after 1 week, but there was no average decline in S_{RD}.

SUMMARY OF RESULTS FROM PARTIAL DESIGNS
In studies that have used partial conjoint-recognition designs, three patterns have emerged for which there is convergent support. First, notwithstanding that relatively narrow age ranges were studied, the recollection parameters for true and

false memory both increased with age. This was especially true for the three experiments that involved study-test designs (Kiernan, 1993; Reyna & Kiernan, 1994, 1995), rather than continuous recognition. In the former designs, age increases in the recollection parameter for false memory were quite dramatic. Second, there was only limited evidence that similarity parameters increase with age. Sometimes age increases were unreliable, and when they were reliable, increases were much smaller than the corresponding ones for recollection parameters. Thus, during the mid-elementary school years at least, processes that support recollection seem to be developing at a faster pace than processes that support similarity. The third pattern is in the nature of another validity result for the assumptions that underlie the conjoint recognition model. Because much prior research suggests that verbatim memories become inaccessible more rapidly than gist, immediate-to-delayed declines ought to be more marked for recollection parameters than for similarity parameters. That result is present in the data of all three of the experiments that implemented Reyna and Kiernan's (1994) sentence recognition paradigm.

Findings from Complete Designs

We now explore the results of three developmental experiments in which complete conjoint-recognitions designs were implemented. These experiments have three key advantages, relative to the partial-design studies that were just reviewed. First and perhaps most important, recollection and similarity can now be simultaneously measured, for the same materials, for both true and false memory. Because most of the partial design studies implemented the V and VG procedures, recollection and similarity could only be measured for *false* memory. Second, phantom recollection can now be measured. As we saw, partial designs provide no information on this theoretically important process. Third, as will be seen in the sequel, complete-design experiments have included somewhat broader age ranges.

DEVELOPMENTAL TRENDS IN RECOLLECTION
AND SIMILARITY FOR DRM LISTS

In this experiment, which was reported by Brainerd, Holliday, and Reyna (2004), we measured developmental trends in recollection and similarity simultaneously for true and false memory. Because phantom recollection could now be measured, the target materials were ones that are known to induce high levels of phantom recollection in adults—namely, Deese/Roediger/McDermott (DRM; Deese, 1959; Roediger & McDermott, 1995) lists. DRM lists are constructed by selecting a familiar stimulus word, such as *window*, and then selecting the first 15 associates of that word (*door, glass, pane, shade, ledge, ...*) from available word-association norms (e.g., Nelson, McEvoy, & Schreiber, 1999). The associates, *but not the generating word*, are then presented to participants as a study list. After several such lists have been presented, a standard yes/no recognition test is administered, which consists of targets, the generating words for the lists (usually called "critical distractors" or "critical lures"), and unrelated distractors. On such tests, adults falsely recognize critical distractors at extremely high levels, usually above 70%. Moreover, when subjects are asked to make remember-know judgments, false alarms to critical distractors stimulate high levels of remember judgments (i.e., phantom recollection), with more than 45% of false alarms stimulating such judgments.

This experiment was a developmental version of a standard adult DRM experiment (Toglia, Neuschatz, & Goodwin, 1999), with the main exception that a complete conjoint-recognition design was used. The subjects were 296 children and adolescents, divided into equal samples of 7-, 11-, and 14-year-olds. One-third of the subjects at each age level were randomly assigned to the three conjoint-recognition conditions (V, G, and VG). The study and test lists were drawn from a pool of DRM lists that were normed by Stadler, Roediger, and McDermott (1999), who ranked 36 DRM lists according to their levels of false recognition and false recall of critical distractors. The top 9 lists were selected for this experiment, the first 11 words from each list being presented as targets during the study phase. On the subsequent recognition test, three words from each list were tested (e.g., *glass, shade, sill*), the critical distractor (*window*) was tested, and another related distractor from among the unpresented words at the end of the list was tested (e.g., *screen*). These two types of related distractors were included as a validity test of FTT's assumption that the similarity and phantom recollection parameters measure gist memories of targets' meaning content. By virtue of the way DRM lists are constructed, critical distractors are better retrieval cues for such memories than other related distractors, and hence, if the assumption is correct, they ought to produce larger values of these parameters than related distractors produce. Several unrelated distractors were also tested, which were selected from unpresented lists on Stadler et al.'s norms. The overall procedure for the experiment involved four steps. First, children received instructions and pretraining examples, along the lines of Reyna and Kiernan's (1994) methodology. Second, subjects listened to three of the nine DRM lists (i.e., a total of 33 targets), followed by a recognition test for those three lists using V, G, or VG questions. Third, subjects listened to three more of the lists, followed by a V, G, or VG recognition test. Fourth, subjects listened to the remaining three lists, followed by a V, G, or VG recognition test.

The results for recollection, similarity, phantom recollection, and bias parameters appear at the top of Table 5.7. We sketch developmental patterns for recollection, similarity, and phantom recollection first, followed by other types of findings. With respect to recollection, both the recollection parameter for targets (I_T) and for related distractors (N_{RD}) increased substantially between early childhood and middle adolescence. Target recollection increased slightly but not reliably between the ages of 5 and 11 years, but then it nearly doubled between the ages of 11 and 14 years, for a net age increase of more than 100%. The developmental trend for recollection rejection was similar: N_{RD} did not change reliably between 5 and 11 years, but then it more than tripled between the ages of 11 and 15 years. In short, recollection exhibited dramatic improvement during this age range, with the improvement being concentrated during adolescence rather than childhood. A final datum recapitulates a point about recollection that follows from the principle of encoding variability. As mentioned earlier, target probes should be more

Table 5.7. DEVELOPMENTAL TRENDS IN RECOLLECTION, SIMILARITY, AND PHANTOM RECOLLECTION
WITH COMPLETE CONJOINT RECOGNITION

Designs Parameter Groups/conditions I_T	S_T	N_{RD}	P_{RD}	S_{RD}	β_V	β_G	βv_G	
Experiment 1: Brainerd, Holliday, and Reyna (2004)								
7 years								
Critical distractors	0.25	0.53	0.16	0.13	0.50	0.10	0.14	0.13
Related distractors	0.25	0.53	0.13	0.10	0.07	0.10	0.14	0.13
11 years								
Critical distractors	0.29	0.56	0.02	0.31	0.59	0.04	0.17	0.09
Related distractors	0.29	0.56	0.23	0.00	0.59	0.04	0.17	0.09
14 years								
Critical distractors	0.57	0.48	0.45	0.38	0.47	0.01	0.13	0.09
Related distractors	0.57	0.48	0.45	0.00	0.30	0.01	0.13	0.09
Experiment 2: Brainerd, Holliday, and Reyna (2004)								
5 years								
No cues	0.17	0.29	0.23	0.20	0.28	0.14	0.22	0.21
Category cues	0.19	0.50	0.04	0.24	0.48	0.14	0.28	0.25
11 years								
No cues	0.43	0.52	0.38	0.05	0.45	0.05	0.13	0.16
Category cues	0.40	0.57	0.21	0.15	0.54	0.10	0.15	0.20

(Continued)

Designs
Parameter Groups/conditions

Table 5.7. CONTINUED

I_T	S_T	N_{RD}	P_{RD}	S_{RD}	β_V	β_G	βv_G
Experiment 3: Holiday, Brainerd, and Reyna (2007)							
7 years							
Pictures							
Familiar distractors	0.16	0.70	0.02	0.04	0.29	0.08	0.09
Unfamiliar distractors	0.16	0.70	0.10	0.00	0.13	0.08	0.09
Fragments							
Familiar distractors	0.14	0.67	0.00	0.00	0.24	0.08	0.10
Unfamiliar distractors	0.14	0.67	0.00	0.02	0.18	0.08	0.10
Control							
Familiar distractors	0.17	0.67	0.02	0.00	0.34	0.07	0.09
Unfamiliar distractors	0.17	0.67	0.15	0.19	0.04	0.07	0.09
10 years							
Pictures							
Familiar distractors	0.22	0.72	0.02	0.00	0.33	0.06	0.09
Unfamiliar distractors	0.22	0.72	0.09	0.01	0.17	0.06	0.09

Note: the βv_G column values are 0.12 for all 7-years rows and 0.10 for the 10-years rows.

Fragments								
Familiar distractors	0.21	0.67	0.04	0.00	0.27	0.09	0.09	0.11
Unfamiliar distractors	0.21	0.67	0.00	0.00	0.26	0.09	0.09	0.11
Control								
Familiar distractors	0.17	0.68	0.04	0.00	0.37	0.07	0.08	0.11
Unfamiliar distractors	0.17	0.68	0.13	0.14	0.13	0.07	0.08	0.11
13 years								
Pictures								
Familiar distractors	0.30	0.73	0.04	0.00	0.37	0.04	0.09	0.10
Unfamiliar distractors	0.30	0.73	0.22	0.05	0.06	0.04	0.09	0.10
Fragments								
Familiar distractors	0.26	0.68	0.01	0.00	0.27	0.06	0.08	0.11
Unfamiliar distractors	0.26	0.68	0.02	0.00	0.17	0.06	0.08	0.11
Control								
Familiar distractors	0.26	0.69	0.15	0.00	0.41	0.06	0.07	0.12
Unfamiliar distractors	0.26	0.69	0.07	0.13	0.38	0.06	0.07	0.12

likely to provoke recollection, as measured by I_T, than related distractors, as measured by N_{RD}, because targets are better retrieval cues for their own verbatim traces. This prediction was borne out because the relation $I_T > N_{RD}$ holds for all possible comparisons of these parameters in Table 5.7.

Turning to similarity and phantom recollection, these parameters also displayed age increases, but consistent with earlier results, the increases for similarity were far smaller than those for recollection. The similarity parameter for targets, S_T, did not increase between the ages of 5 and 11 years, and neither did the similarity parameter for related distractors, S_{RD}, when it was estimated for critical distractors. However, there was an increase between 5 and 11 years in S_{RD} when it was estimated for other related distractors, though there was then a reliable *decline* between the ages of 11 and 14 years. Despite that nonmonotonic pattern of age change, the net increase in S_{RD} between the ages of 5 and 14 years (from 0.07 to 0.30) was substantial for other related distractors. Recall, in this connection, that it is more difficult to retrieve gist traces with these distractors than with critical distractors.

Turning to phantom recollection, the mean value of P_{RD} was significantly above zero at all three age levels, so DRM lists provoke phantom recollection in children as well as in adults, but the means for the three age levels (0.12, 0.16, and 0.19) did not differ reliably. This seems to show that phantom recollection develops little or not all. This is a mistaken impression, however, because developmental trends for phantom recollection, like those for similarity, depended strongly on the nature of the retrieval cue. Specifically, for critical distractors, there was a large and reliable increase in P_{RD}, with the parameter's value nearly tripling between the ages of 5 and 14 years. For related distractors, on the other hand, the parameter's value did not increase with age, and indeed, it was zero among 11- and 14-year-olds. Thus, developmental trends in similarity and phantom recollection were both found to depend on nature of the retrieval cue, with poorer retrieval cues for gist traces producing reliable age increases in similarity and better retrieval cues for gist traces producing reliable age increases for phantom recollection.

Another developmental pattern that is worthy of note because it provides a validity check on conjoint-recognition methodology concerns response bias. A common result in development studies that use standard old/new recognition tests is that response bias is greater in children than it is in adolescents or adults; that is, the liberality of the decision criterion decreases with age (Brainerd, Holliday, Reyna, Yang, & Toglia, 2010; Brainerd & Mojardin, 1998; Brainerd & Reyna, 1998; Brainerd et al., 1995). β_V is the conjoint-recognition parameter that measures bias for old/new recognition. Note that as in standard recognition designs, this parameter decreased steadily with age—from 0.10 to 0.04 to 0.01. Another validity result concerns different levels of bias for V tests versus G and VG tests, which are measured by β_V, β_G, and β_{VG}, respectively. Across many experiments with adults, the modal ordering of these parameters has been found to be that β_V is smaller than β_{VG} or β_G (Brainerd & Reyna, 2008; Brainerd, Reyna, & Aydin, 2010). Note that the average values of the three bias parameters for this experiment ($\beta_V = 0.05$, $\beta_{VG} = 0.10$, and $\beta_G = 0.15$) followed this modal ordering.

DEVELOPMENTAL TRENDS IN RECOLLECTION AND FAMILIARITY
FOR AUDITORY CATEGORIZED LISTS

This experiment was also reported by Brainerd et al. (2004). It followed the basic design of Experiment 1, except for two key changes. First, in an attempt to generalize the results of the initial experiment to other types of materials, subjects studied and responded to recognition tests for categorized lists rather than DRM lists. Categorized lists also induce phantom recollection in adults, although not generally at levels as high as those that are generated by DRM lists (e.g., Dewhurst, 2001). A key result whose generality we were particularly interested in is the finding that developmental variability in the recollection parameters outstrips that for the similarity parameters, with most comparisons showing that only the former displayed reliable age increases. Another result of interest is that another process (phantom recollection) that, like similarity, taps gist memory, exhibited more substantial age increases than similarity did. Second, in an attempt to generalize the earlier results to younger age levels, we included a sample of 5-year-olds in this experiment and restricted developmental comparisons to the 5-to-11-year age range. Here, we hoped to clarify the finding that the developmental variability in recollection parameters occurs during adolescence but not during childhood. For any number of reasons, including previously reported results from partial designs, it seemed unlikely that improvements in recollection are restricted to the adolescent years. We thought that evidence of such improvements during childhood might emerge if a younger sample of children were compared to a sample of young adolescents.

Third, we included another manipulation (gist cuing) that, like the critical versus related distractor manipulation in Experiment 1, ought to affect the similarity and phantom recollection parameters and not the recollection or recollection rejection parameters, if the former measure gist processing and the latter measure verbatim processing. We thought it was necessary to obtain further information on this point because it bears on a fundamental theoretical question: Are recollection and similarity truly distinct processes—arising, for instance, from the processing of verbatim traces versus gist traces? Although the conjoint-recognition model assumes that the answer is yes, it has often been argued in the adult literature (e.g., Donaldson, 1996) that recollection is just strong familiarity. The usual approach to deciding between these alternatives is to determine whether there are experimental manipulations that dissociate performance on measures of the two processes, because if recollection and familiarity are truly distinct, there must be manipulations that affect one but not the other or that drive them in opposite directions. The type-of-distractor manipulation in Experiment 1 (critical vs. other related) is an example. This manipulation should affect the distractor similarity parameter and the other parameter that measures gist processing (phantom recollection), but not the two parameters that measure recollection of target presentations. That pattern was confirmed (cf. Table 5.7). To generate additional data, we included a manipulation, gist cuing, that should produce the same pattern by selectively strengthening the meaning relations between list words. Gist cuing involves once again exposing subjects to short lists of words on which individual words are all related to each other in meaning. During the study phase, children in a control condition simply listen to each list as it is presented. However, children in a gist-cuing phase are given advance information about semantic relations that connect the words on a list just before it is presented (e.g., "Here's the next list of words. All of the words are the names of animals."). The theoretical prediction was that this cuing procedure should increase some or all of the parameters that supposedly tap gist memories of meaning content without affecting either of the parameters that tap verbatim memories of target presentations.

The subjects ($N = 288$) were equally divided between a sample of 5-year-olds and a sample of 11-year-olds. One-third of the subjects at each age level were randomly assigned to each of the conjoint-recognition conditions (V, G, and VG), and within each of the three conditions, one-half of the subjects were randomly assigned to the gist-cuing condition and one-half were randomly assigned to the control condition. The study materials were categorized lists that had been selected from Battig and Montague's (1969) norms for common taxonomic categories. We selected several very familiar categories (e.g., animals, clothing, fruit), and for each category, we used the norms to select its 13 most frequently mentioned exemplars.

At the beginning of the study phase, the subjects were told that they would be listening to a few vocabulary lists, after which their memory for the words would be tested. Except for the types of lists that were used, the remainder of the procedure resembled that of Experiment 1. Each subject first listened to three of the categorized lists, with each list consisting of 10 of the 13 exemplars that had been selected from the norms. For subjects in the cuing condition, this manipulation was executed just before each list, and it consisted of alerting subjects to the specific taxonomic category to which all of the upcoming words would belong. After the first three categorized lists had been presented, subjects responded to whichever recognition test was appropriate to their condition (V, G, VG). This test consisted of 30 probes, 15 targets (5 from each list), 9 semantically related distractors (the 3 unpresented exemplars from each of the presented lists), and 6 unrelated distractors. As in Experiment 1, after the first recognition test was completed, subjects participated in two more cycles, each of which consisted of the presentation of three new categorized lists followed by whichever recognition test was appropriate to the subjects' condition.

The results for the recollection, similarity, phantom recollection, and bias parameters appear in the middle of Table 5.7. As before, we summarize developmental patterns for recollection, similarity, and phantom recollection, followed by other types of findings. With respect to recollection, in contrast with the results of Experiment 1, now there was evidence of marked improvement in recollection during childhood. Both the target recollection parameter (I_T) and the corresponding parameter for related distractors (N_{RD}) displayed large age increases in both the cuing and control conditions. The average age increase for the pooled data of these parameters was greater than 100%, and all four of the possible age comparisons for these parameters (2 parameters × 2 cuing conditions) were statistically reliable. Consistent with all previous experiments, the prediction that target probes should be more likely to provoke recollection, as measured by I_T, than related distractors, as measured by N_{RD}, was confirmed. Pooling across age levels and cuing conditions, the mean value of I_T was 0.30, whereas the mean value of N_{RD} was 0.22.

With respect to similarity, this process continued its pattern of exhibiting more limited developmental improvement than recollection did. Pooling across the similarity parameters for targets (S_T) and distractors (S_{RD}) and across the two cuing conditions, the mean values were 0.39 and 0.52 for 5- and 11-year-olds, respectively. This is an average age increase of roughly one-third, as compared to an increase of greater than 100% for recollection. Further, although age increases in both parameters were reliable in the control condition, they were not reliable in the gist-cuing condition.

Turning to phantom recollection, P_{RD} was significantly above zero at both age levels, so that categorized lists, such as the DRM lists in Experiment 1, were able to provoke realistic but illusory memories of distractors' prior "presentation." Unlike Experiment 1, when the mean values of this parameter were considered, it appeared that phantom recollection declined with age because the value for 5-year-olds (0.22) was more than twice the value for 11-year-olds (0.10). The decline was reliable in both the cuing and control conditions.

What about the effects of the gist-cuing manipulation? They were as expected for targets. At both age levels, cuing did not produce a reliable difference in I_T at either age level, but the value of S_T was higher in the cuing condition at both age levels. For related distractors, however, the results were only partly as expected. On the one hand, it was expected that gist cuing would increase the values of S_{RD} and P_{RD} because both parameters ostensibly measure gist processing. It can be seen in Table 5.7 that this pattern was obtained, although one of the four age comparisons (for P_{RD} in 5-year-olds) was not reliable. On the other hand, contrary to prediction, gist cuing decreased the recollection rejection parameter at both age levels, and both effects were reliable. At this point, there is no obvious explanation of this anomalous result.

Finally, we consider results for the bias parameters because, as mentioned earlier, they provide validity checks on developmental applications of conjoint-recognition methodology. Note, first, that the average values of β_V, which is the conjoint-recognition parameter that measures bias for old/new recognition, exhibits the familiar pattern of age decline: $\beta_V = 0.25$ for 5-year-olds and 0.14 for 11-year-olds. The other validity result concerns the respective levels of bias for V versus G and VG tests, for which the modal ordering in adults is that β_V is less than β_{VG} or β_G. In this experiment, average values of the bias parameters followed this ordering because the value of β_V was only about one-half the size of the corresponding values of β_{VG} and β_G.

DEVELOPMENTAL TRENDS IN RECOLLECTION AND FAMILIARITY
FOR VISUAL CATEGORIZED LISTS

In this experiment, which was reported by Holliday, Brainerd, and Reyna (2007), we continued to measure developmental trends in recollection and similarity simultaneously for true and false memory, using categorized lists like those in

Experiment 2. In an attempt to generalize these trends still further, we switched to a very different presentation and testing procedure. Specifically, study words were presented visually and tested visually, a method that tends to amplify verbatim processing, relative to the oral methodologies that were used in the Experiments 1 and 2 (Brainerd & Reyna, 2005). We were still interested in the generality of the finding that developmental improvement in the recollection parameters swamps improvement in the similarity parameters. Also, there is an obvious need for additional findings on phantom recollection, which displayed opposite age trends in Experiments 1 and 2. It may be that DRM lists and categorized lists produce contrasting age trends, and if so, categorized lists should again produce age declines in phantom recollection.

Within the context of visual presentation, again for purposes of generality, we implemented three different presentation methods. In one condition, which we will call the word condition, categorized lists were simply presented as printed words. In a second condition, which we will call the picture condition, categorized lists were presented as printed words followed by line drawings of the objects that each word named (e.g., Schacter, Israel, & Racine, 1999). In a third condition, which we will call the stem condition, categorized lists were presented as printed words followed by printed stems in which a letter of each word was missing (e.g., Jacoby, Toth, & Yonelinas, 1993). A final methodological wrinkle is that we repeated the technique of administering two types of related distractors that presumably differ in their ability to tap gist memories of the semantic content of categorized lists.

The factorial structure of the experiment was 3 (age: 7, 10, 13 years) × 3 (presentation method: words, pictures, word stems) × 3 (conjoint recognition condition: V, G, VG), with repeated measures on the last factor. The subject sample ($N = 238$) included approximately equal numbers of 7-, 10-, and 13-year-olds, with approximately one-third of the subjects at each age level being randomly assigned to each presentation condition. Although visual rather than oral presentation and testing were used, the overall procedure resembled that of the first two experiments inasmuch as the subjects participated in three cycles of list presentation plus recognition testing. Nine lists of 10 category exemplars apiece served as the study materials. These lists, unlike those in Experiment 2, were constructed from child category norms (Cycowicz, Friedman, Rothstein, & Snodgrass, 1997; Price & Connelly, 2006). Black and white line drawings of all category exemplars were available from Cycowicz et al.'s norms, drawings that have been rated for name agreement, familiarity, and visual complexity by 5- and 6-year-old children.

As noted, there were three study-test cycles. During the study phase of each cycle, three of the nine lists of category exemplars were visually presented, on a computer screen. Each word of each list was presented as follows. First, the word (e.g., *dress*) appeared in the center of the computer screen, for 2 s. Then, the word disappeared and was immediately re-presented in one of three ways, depending on the subjects' presentation condition. For subjects in the *word* condition, the word itself reappeared for 4 s. For subjects in the *picture* condition, the line drawing for the word appeared on the computer screen for 4 s. For subjects in the *stem* condition, a stem in which the word's last letter had been omitted appeared on the screen (e.g., *dres__*), and the subject was required to fill in the missing letter by pressing the appropriate letter on the computer keyboard. During the test phase of each cycle, subjects responded to a 24-item recognition test. There were four types of items on the test: 12 targets (4 from each of the three lists), 3 familiar related distractors (1 for each list), 3 unfamiliar related distractors (1 for each list), and 6 unrelated distractors. For each type of item, the recognition question was V for one-third, G for one-third, and VG for one-third. Concerning the related distractors, with familiar taxonomic categories, such as birds or clothing, some exemplars are given by subjects with high frequency on category production norms (e.g., *robin, dress*), whereas others are given with lower frequency (e.g., *penguin, vest*). In the experiment, the familiar related distractors were high-frequency exemplars of their categories, and the unfamiliar exemplars were low-frequency exemplars. Our assumption, based on prior research (e.g., Brainerd et al., 1999), is that familiar related distractors would be better retrieval cues for the semantic content of categorized lists, and hence, would produce higher values of the distractor similarity parameter.

The results for recollection, similarity, phantom recollection, and response bias appear at the bottom of Table 5.7. The developmental patterns for recollection and similarity, which are plotted in Figure 5.1, were different for targets versus related distractors, so we consider them separately. Taking targets first, as can be seen in Figure 5.1, the recollection parameter (I_T) and the similarity parameter (S_T) continued to exhibit the pattern of greater developmental change in recollection. I_T nearly doubled between the ages of 7 and 13 years, but the change in S_T was not reliable. For related distractors, however, it can be seen that the pattern was the opposite—improvement in S_{RD} but not N_{RD}. However, the distractor data are subject to two important qualifications. First, there were floor effects for recollection

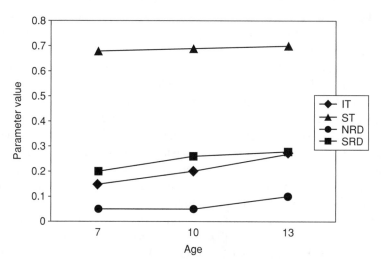

Figure 5.1. Developmental trends in target recollection (I_T), target similarity (S_T), distractor recollection rejection (N_{RD}), and distractor similarity (S_{RD}) in Experiment 3.

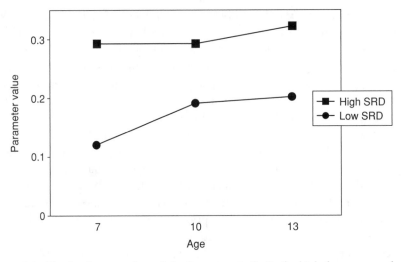

Figure 5.2. The developmental trends in distractor similarity for high-frequency and low-frequency related distractors in Experiment 2.

rejection—more than one-half of the values of N_{RD} are zero—so there was simply not sufficient variability to detect developmental trends. Second, the developmental increase in distractor similarity was confined to one type of related distractor and one age comparison. The latter qualification is illustrated in Figure 5.2, where it can be seen that the age increase in S_{RD} is restricted to unfamiliar category exemplars and is confined to comparisons of 7- versus 10-year-olds. As in previous experiments, note that the value of the target recollection parameter ($M = 0.21$, averaging across conditions and age levels) is noticeably larger than the value of the distractor recollection parameter ($M = 0.07$). Once again, this is consistent with the notion that targets are better retrieval cues for their verbatim traces than related distractors are. On the whole, then, the overall picture for developmental change in recollection versus similarity coheres with the one that has emerged in earlier experiments.

Concerning phantom recollection, unlike previous experiments, the mean value of P_{RD} was not sufficiently above zero to treat phantom recollection as an important contributor to performance in this paradigm, particularly among 5- and 10-year-olds (where the mean value of P_{RD} was only 0.05). Given the similarity of the study and test lists to those of Experiment 2, a conclusion that suggests itself is that it is more difficult for strong gist memories to generate illusory mental reinstatement of distractors' "presentations" when list presentations are visual rather than auditory. That would mean, in concrete terms, that it is harder to generate an illusory visual image of a word than an illusory auditory image.

Turning to response bias, if the values in the last three columns are compared to the corresponding values for Experiments 1 and 2, it is clear that bias levels were very low in this experiment. For instance, the mean value of β_v, the conjoint-recognition parameter that measures bias for standard old/new recognition, was only 0.07. Nevertheless, both of the validity results for the bias parameters that figure in earlier experiments were present here. First, there was once again an age decline in β_V, from 0.08 at age 5 to 0.05 at age 13, and the decline was statistically reliable because the number of data points at each age level was so large (476) that even a 0.03 difference in false alarm rates was reliable. Second, the modal ordering of the response bias parameters again followed the modal ordering for adult experiments. The mean value of β_V, pooling across age levels and presentation conditions, was 0.07, whereas the corresponding grand mean for β_G and β_{VG} was 0.10. Again, owing to the large numbers of data points for unrelated distractors, this 0.03 difference was reliable.

SUMMARY OF RESULTS FROM COMPLETE DESIGNS

Studies that used complete conjoint-recognition designs have produced further support for two of the three patterns that emerged from studies that used partial designs. First, across the child-to-adolescent age range, the recollection parameters for true and false memory both increased with age. There was only one exception to this rule—namely, the recollection parameter for false memory in Experiment 3, which exhibited floor effects. Second, across the child-to-adolescent age range, there was only slight evidence of developmental improvements in similarity parameters. There was virtually no evidence for such improvements for the target similarity parameter. For the distractor similarity parameter, there were reliable developmental improvements, but they only occurred in certain conditions, and they were usually smaller than the corresponding improvements in recollection parameters. The third pattern, that recollection parameters declined more steeply over time than similarity parameters did, was not evaluated in complete designs because delayed memory tests were not administered.

Other important patterns that were repeatedly detected were concerned with the two recollection parameters, I_T and N_{RD}, and the three bias parameters, β_V, β_G, and β_{VG}. If I_T and N_{RD} both measure retrieval of targets' verbatim traces, the relation $I_T > N_{RD}$ should hold because, by the principle of encoding variability, targets are better retrieval cues for their own verbatim traces than distractors are. That relation held for all comparisons. With respect to bias parameters, β_V was consistently found to decline age, which is congruent with much prior work in which response bias has been measured in traditional old/new recognition designs. Another finding for bias parameters, which is congruent with conjoint-recognition studies with adults, is that response bias for V questions was always lower than for G or VG questions.

CONCLUSIONS AND FUTURE DIRECTIONS

On the one hand, some converging evidence on developmental trends in recollection and similarity and on the validity of FTT's assumptions about the conjoint-recognition paradigm has been secured from developmental studies that have implemented partial or complete designs. On the other hand, such research is still in its infancy, so that important targets for future research to aim at, using conjoint-recognition methodology or other child-appropriate techniques, are thick on the ground. We comment on both of these themes in closing.

New Knowledge

As luck would have it, the strongest evidence to have emerged from these studies bears on the most fundamental question of all: What are the relative contributions of age variability in recollection and similarity to memory development? Regardless of whether the target materials were nonsense words, or familiar-but-unrelated words, or narratives or semantically related words, the answer was the same. Developmental improvement in recollection parameters outstripped improvement in similarity parameters by a wide margin. The pattern was the same for true and false memory. With true memory, the experiments could not be said to have produced any credible evidence of improvement in similarity. With false memory, there was credible evidence of improvement, but it was restricted to certain types of distractors and confined to narrow age bands. In contrast, developmental improvements for recollection encompassed a remarkably broad span of years, with some studies detecting substantial changes between early and late childhood and others detecting substantial changes between early and middle adolescence.

There were also some solid validity results bearing on four assumptions. First, in line with the encoding variability principle, FTT assumes that targets are better retrieval cues for their verbatim traces than related distractors are. If the recollection parameters measure the processing of such traces, it follows that the target parameter should be larger than the corresponding parameter for related distractors. That prediction was confirmed in all datasets in which tests were possible (i.e., in full conjoint-recognition designs). Second, also in line with the encoding variability principle, FTT assumes that certain types of related distractors (e.g., critical distractors for DRM lists, familiar exemplars for categorized lists) are better retrieval cues for targets' gist traces than other types of related distractors (e.g., noncritical related distractors for DRM lists, unfamiliar exemplars for categorized lists). If so, the similarity parameter for false memory should be larger for distractors of the former sort. That prediction, too, was confirmed. Third, if recollection parameters measure verbatim processing and similarity parameters measure gist processing, the recollection parameters should decline more steeply than similarity parameters over long-term retention intervals. That prediction was confirmed in three studies with narrative materials, though it has yet to be investigated with word lists. Fourth, FTT expects that bias levels will be higher when unpresented items have to be accepted (G or VG questions) than when only presented items are to be accepted (V question). That pattern was testable with the datasets of both partial and complete designs, and in every instance, it was confirmed.

Some Targets for Future Research

There are two fundamental questions about memory processes and a fundamental question about brain development that are entirely open at the moment and, hence, are obvious candidates for experimentation. The first question about memory processes is: Why does similarity develop more for false than for true memory, or does it? The data in Tables 5.3 and 5.7 offer tantalizing hints that, for these types of materials at least, if similarity develops at all, it only does so for false memory. That this could happen is certainly possible on theoretical grounds. Related distractors might be more sensitive than targets are to changes in gist memory because distractors are poorer retrieval cues, so that they could be more strongly affected by small age changes in the strengths of gist traces. However, the data on this possibility are weak. As we said, in individual experiments, those data were confined to certain types of related distractors and certain age ranges.

The other question about memory processes is: What are the developmental trends in phantom recollection? As we have observed elsewhere (Brainerd et al., 2001), of the three false-memory processes in Table 5.2, phantom recollection is the most intriguing to most investigators. One reason for that is that phantom recollection generates false memories that are so realistic that it is difficult to convince subjects that their memories are erroneous (Lampinen, Neuschatz, & Payne, 1998). Another reason is that phantom recollections are hallucinatory experiences. Subjects are quite literally "hearing things" and "seeing things," which means that phantom recollections are "normal" analogues of the hallucinations that characterize certain psychoses and brain diseases. Hence, phantom recollections might provide experimental procedures for acquiring scientific information about hallucinatory experiences under controlled laboratory conditions. In light of the potential importance of phantom recollection, it goes without saying that researchers would like to establish whether it displays general developmental trends. Those trends could have considerable theoretical payoff because, as we have discussed elsewhere (Brainerd, Reyna, & Forrest, 2002), some theoretical principles imply that illusory vivid phenomenology ought to decline with age whereas others imply that it should increase with age.

A single, consistent developmental trend did not emerge from the three experiments in which phantom recollection could be measured. However, that may be due to differences in procedure and to the possibility that trends are different for DRM materials than for categorized materials. On the positive side, the developmental trend that was observed with the DRM illusion—namely, a substantial age increase in phantom recollection—was consistent with what would be expected from the fact that this illusion increases with age (Brainerd et al., 2008), together with the fact that adult performance is dominated by phantom recollection (Brainerd et al., 2001). On the negative side, a clear developmental trend was not detected for categorized materials, but there were floor effects for phantom recollection with visual presentation and testing. Clearly, more and better data are needed.

Finally, we draw attention to the paucity of developmental neuroscience data on the questions that have concerned us in this chapter. The brain regions that are implicated in recollection and familiarity in *true* memory have been topics of vigorous and long-standing investigation in the adult literature. Many articles have appeared in which brain imaging (e.g., functional magnetic resonance imaging), electrophysiological techniques (e.g., electroencephalogram), and the performance of patients with selective brain damage have been used to triangulate on the brain regions that are differentially activated during recollection versus familiarity.

As mentioned, that work has converged on particular brain regions. More recently, the brain regions that are implicated in recollection and familiarity in *false* memory have also become topics of vigorous investigation in the adult literature, with brain imaging studies, electrophysiological studies, and patient studies all having been reported. That work, too, has converged on particular brain regions.

Owing to such research, it is possible to formulate hypotheses about developmental changes in activation patterns within specific brain regions. Surely the most obvious one is that developmental changes in activation patterns ought to be marked for the regions that, in adult work, have been identified with recollection. Moreover, evidence for this hypothesis ought to be forthcoming for brain regions that have been associated with recollective suppression of false memories, as well as for brain regions that have been associated with recollection in true memory. An equally obvious hypothesis is that developmental changes in brain activation will be far weaker in brain regions that, in adult work, have been associated with familiarity, and further, that such changes may only be detectable in brain regions that are associated with familiarity-driven false memory. A number of other, more fine-grained predictions about developmental changes in brain activation are possible, based on adult neuroscience studies of recollection and familiarity. Although data on such predictions remains limited, a great deal of research that may yield answers is now under way (e.g., see chapters in this volume by: Diana and Ranganath [Chapter 7]; Friedman [Chapter 10]; Riggins [Chapter 3]; St. Jacques and Cabeza [Chapter 8]; and Thomas and Jorgenson [Chapter 9]).

REFERENCES

Atkinson, R. C., & Juola, J. F. (1973). Factors influencing speed and accuracy in word recognition. In S. Kornblum (Ed.), *Attention and performance IV*. New York: Academic Press.

Battig, W. F., & Montague, W. E. (1969). Category norms for verbal items in 56 categories: A replication and extension of the Connecticut category norms. *Journal of Experimental Psychology Monograph, 80*(3, Pt. 2).

Bjorklund, D. F. (2004). *Children's thinking: Cognitive development and individual differences*. Belmont, CA: Wadsworth.

Brainerd, C. J., Holliday, R. E., & Reyna, V. F. (2004). Behavioral measurement of remembering phenomenologies: So simple a child can do it. *Child Development, 75*, 505–22.

Brainerd, C. J., Holliday, R. E., Reyna, V. F., Yang, Y., & Toglia, M. P. (2010). Developmental reversals in false memory: Effects of emotional valence and arousal. *Journal of Experimental Child Psychology, 107*, 137–54.

Brainerd, C. J., & Mojardin, A. H. (1998). Children's spontaneous false memories for narrative statements: Long-term persistence and mere-testing effects. *Child Development, 69*, 1361–77.

Brainerd. C. J., & Reyna, V. F. (1993). Memory independence and memory interference in cognitive development. *Psychological Review, 100*, 42–67.

Brainerd, C. J., & Reyna, V. F. (1998). Fuzzy-trace theory and children's false memories. *Journal of Experimental Child Psychology, 71*, 81–129.

Brainerd, C. J., & Reyna, V. F. (2002). Recollection rejection: How children edit their false memories. *Developmental Psychology, 38,* 156–72.

Brainerd, C. J., & Reyna, V. F. (2005). *The science false memory.* New York: Oxford University Press.

Brainerd, C. J., & Reyna, V. F. (2008). Episodic over-distribution: A signature effect of familiarity without recollection. *Journal of Memory and Language, 58,* 765–86.

Brainerd, C. J., & Reyna, V. F. (2010). Recollective and nonrecollective recall. *Journal of Memory and Language, 63,* 425–45.

Brainerd, C. J., Reyna, V. F., & Aydin, C. (2010). Remembering in contradictory minds: Disjunction fallacies in episodic memory. *Journal of Experimental Psychology: Learning, Memory, and Cognition, 36,* 711–35.

Brainerd, C. J., Reyna, V. F., & Ceci, S. J. (2008). Developmental reversals in false memory: A review of data and theory. *Psychological Bulletin, 134,* 343–82.

Brained, C. J., Reyna, V. F., & Forrest, T. J. (2002). Are young children susceptible to the false-memory illusion? *Child Development, 73,* 1363–77.

Brainerd, C. J., Reyna, V. F., & Howe, M. L. (2009). Trichotomous processes in early memory Development, aging, and neurocognitive impairment: A unified theory. *Psychological Review, 116,* 783–832.

Brainerd, C. J., Reyna, V. F., & Kneer, R. (1995). False-recognition reversal: When similarity is distinctive. *Journal of Memory and Language, 34,* 157–85.

Brainerd, C. J., Reyna, V. F., & Mojardin, A. H. (1999). Conjoint recognition. *Psychological Review, 106,* 160–79.

Brainerd, C. J., Stein, L., & Reyna, V. F. (1998). On the development of conscious and unconscious memory. *Developmental Psychology, 34,* 342–57.

Brainerd, C. J., Wright, R., Reyna, V. F., & Mojardin, A. H. (2001). Conjoint recognition and phantom recollection. *Journal of Experimental Psychology: Learning, Memory, and Cognition, 27,* 307–27.

Budson, A. E., Todman, R. W., & Schacter, D. L. (2006). Gist memory in Alzheimer's disease: Evidence from categorized pictures. *Neuropsychology, 20,* 113–22.

Cabeza, R., Rao, S. M., Wagner, A. D., Mayer, A. R., & Schacter, D. L. (2001). Can medial temporal lobe regions distinguish true from false? An event-related functional MRI study of veridical and illusory memory. *Proceedings of the National Academy of Sciences, 98,* 4805–10.

Ceci, S. J., & Bruck, M. (1995). *Jeopardy in the courtroom.* Washington, DC: American Psychological Association.

Ceci, S. J., Ross, D. F., & Toglia, M. P. (1987). Suggestibility in children's memory: Psycholegal implications. *Journal of Experimental Psychology: General, 116,* 38–49.

Conway, M. A., Collins, A. F., Gathercole, S. E., & Anderson, S. J. (1996). Recollections of true and false autobiographical memories. *Journal of Experimental Psychology: General, 125,* 69–95.

Cycowicz, Y. M., Friedman, D., Rothstein, M., & Snodgrass, J. G. (1997). Picture naming by young children: Norms for name agreement, familiarity, and visual complexity. *Journal of Experimental Child Psychology, 65,* 171–237.

Deese, J. (1959). On the prediction of occurrence of certain verbal intrusions in free recall. *Journal of Experimental Psychology, 58,* 17–22.

Dennis, N. A., Kim, H., & Cabeza, R. (2007). Effects of aging on true and false memory formation: An fMRI study. *Neuropsychologia, 45,* 3157–66.

Dewhurst, S. A. (2001). Category repetition and false recognition: Effects of instance frequency and category size. *Journal of Memory and Language, 44,* 153–67.

Dewhurst, S. A., & Farrand, P. (2004). Investigating the phenomenological characteristics of false recognition for categorized words. *European Journal of Cognitive Psychology, 16,* 403–16.

Diana, R. A., & Ranganath, C. (2011). Neural basis of recollection: Evidence from neuroimaging and electrophysiological research. In S. Ghetti & P. J. Bauer (Eds.), *Origins and development of recollection: Perspectives from psychology and neuroscience* (pp. 168–87). New York: Oxford University Press.

Donaldson, W. (1996). The role of decision processes in remembering and knowing. *Memory & Cognition, 24,* 523–33.

Drummey, A. B., & Newcombe, N. (1995). Remembering versus knowing the past: Children's explicit and implicit memory for pictures. *Journal of Experimental Child Psychology, 59,* 549–65.

Friedman, D. (2011). The development of episodic memory: An event-related brain potential (ERP) vantage point. In S. Ghetti & P. J. Bauer (Eds.), *Origins and development of recollection: Perspectives from psychology and neuroscience* (pp. 242–64). New York: Oxford University Press.

Gallo, D. A. (2004). Using recall to reduce false recognition. *Journal of Experimental Psychology: Learning, Memory, and Cognition, 30,* 120–8.

Gardiner, J. M., & Java, R. I. (1991). Forgetting in recognition memory with and without recollective experience. *Memory & Cognition, 18,* 617–23.

Ghetti, S., & Angelini, L. (2008). The development of recollection and familiarity in childhood and adolescence: Evidence from the dual-process signal detection model. *Child Development, 79,* 339–58.

Ghetti, S., & Castelli, P. (2006). Developmental differences in false-event rejection: Effects of memorability-based warnings. *Memory, 14,* 762–76.

Heaps, C. M., & Nash, M. (2001). Comparing recollective experience in true and false autobiographical memories. *Journal of Experimental Psychology: Learning, Memory, and Cognition, 27,* 920–30.

Hintzman, D. L., & Curran, T. (1994). Retrieval dynamics of recognition and frequency judgments: Evidence for separate processes of familiarity and recall. *Journal of Memory and Language, 33,* 1–18.

Holliday, R. E., Brainerd, C. J., & Reyna, V. F. (2007, November). *Recognition of details never experienced: The effects of encoding and age.* Paper presented at Psychonomic Society, Long Beach, CA.

Holliday, R. E., & Hayes, B. K. (2000). Dissociating automatic and intention processes in children's eyewitness memory. *Journal of Experimental Child Psychology, 75,* 1–4.

Holliday, R. E., & Hayes, B. K. (2002). Automatic and intentional processes in children's recognition memory. *Applied Cognitive Psychology, 16,* 617–36.

Hu, X. (1998). General processing tree. [Computer software]. Memphis, TN: University of Memphis.

Jacoby, L. L. (1991). A process dissociation framework: Separating automatic from intentional uses of memory. *Journal of Memory and Language, 30,* 513–41.

Jacoby, L. L. (1996). Dissociating automatic and consciously controlled effects of study/test compatibility. *Journal of Memory and Language, 35,* 32–52.

Jacoby, L. L., Toth, J. P., & Yonelinas, A. P. (1993). Separating conscious and unconscious influences of memory: Measuring recollection. *Journal of Experimental Psychology: General, 122,* 139–54.

Kiernan, B. J. (1993). *Verbatim memory and gist extraction in elementary-school children with impaired language skills.* (Unpublished doctoral dissertation,). University of Arizona, Tucson, AZ.

Kim, H., & Cabeza, R. (2007). Trusting our memories: Dissociating the neural correlates of confidence in veridical versus illusory memories. *Journal of Neuroscience, 27,* 12190–7.

Koutstaal, W., & Schacter, D. L. (1997). Gist-based false recognition of pictures in older and younger adults. *Journal of Memory and Language, 37,* 555–83.

Koutstaal, W., Verfaellie, M., & Schacter, D. L. (2001). Recognizing identical versus similar categorically related common objects: Further evidence for degraded gist representations in amnesia. *Neuropsychology, 15,* 268–89.

Kurilla, B. P., & Westerman, D. L. (2010). Source memory for unidentified stimuli. *Journal of Experimental Psychology: Learning, Memory, and Cognition, 36,* 398–410.

Lampinen, J. M., Neuschatz, & Payne, D. G. (1998). Memory illusions and consciousness: Examining the phenomenology of true and false memories. *Current Psychology: Development, Learning, Personality, Social, 16,* 181–224.

Mandler, G. (1980). Recognizing: The judgment of previous occurrence. *Psychological Review, 87,* 252–71.

Mulligan, N. W., Besken, M., & Peterson, D. (2010). Remember-know and source memory instructions can qualitatively change old-new recognition accuracy: The modality-match effect in recognition memory. *Journal of Experimental Psychology: Learning, Memory, and Cognition, 36,* 552–7.

Nelson, D. L., McEvoy, C. L., & Schreiber, T. A. (1999). *The University of South Florida word association, rhyme, and word fragment norms.* Unpublished manuscript, University of South Florida, Tampa.

Nelson, D. L., Schreiber, T. A., & McEvoy, C. L. (1992). Processing implicit and explicit representations. *Psychological Review, 99,* 32248.

Parks, C. M., & Yonelinas, A. P. (2007). Moving beyond pure signal detection models: Comment on Wixted (2007). *Psychological Review, 114,* 188–202.

Price, H. L., & Connolly, D. A. (2006). BATMON II: Children's knowledge of category exemplars. *Behavior Research Methods, 38,* 229–31.

Reyna, V. F. (1996). Conceptions of memory development, with implications for reasoning and decision making. *Annals of Child Development, 12,* 87–118.

Reyna, V. F. (2008). A theory of medical decision making and health: Fuzzy-trace theory. *Medical Decision Making, 28,* 850–65.

Reyna, V. F., & Brainerd, C. J. (1995). Fuzzy-trace theory: An interim synthesis. *Learning and Individual Differences, 7,* 1–75.

Reyna, V. F., Holliday, R., & Marche, T. (2002). Explaining the development of false memories. *Developmental Review, 22,* 436–89.

Reyna, V. F., & Kiernan, B. (1994). The development of gist versus verbatim memory in sentence recognition: Effects of lexical familiarity, semantic content, encoding instructions, and retention interval. *Developmental Psychology, 30,* 178–91.

Reyna, V. F., & Kiernan, B. (1995). Children's memory and interpretation of psychological metaphors. *Metaphor and Symbolic Activity, 10,* 309–31.

Reyna, V. F., & Lloyd, F. (1997). Theories of false memory in children and adults. *Learning and Individual Differences, 9,* 95–123.

Reyna, V. F., Mills, B., Estrada, S., & Brainerd, C. J. (2007). False memory in children: Data, theory, and legal implications. In M. P. Toglia, J. D. Read, D. F. Ross, & R. C. L. Lindsay (Eds.), *Handbook of eyewitness psychology* (pp. 479–508). Mahwah, NJ: Erlbaum.

Reyna, V. F., Nelson, W. L., Han, P. K., & Dieckmann, N. F. (2009). How numeracy influences risk comprehension and medical decision making. *Psychological Bulletin, 135,* 943–73.

Riefer, D. M., & Batchelder, W. H. (1988). Multinomial modeling and the measurement of cognitive processes. *Psychological Review, 95,* 318–39.

Riggins, T. (2011). Building blocks of recollection. In S. Ghetti & P. J. Bauer (Eds.), *Origins and development of recollection: Perspectives from psychology and neuroscience* (pp. 42–72). New York: Oxford University Press.

Roediger, H. L., III, & McDermott, K. B. (1995). Creating false memories: Remembering words not presented on lists. *Journal of Experimental Psychology: Learning, Memory, and Cognition, 21,* 803–14.

Rotello, C. M., Macmillan, N. A., & Reeder, J. A. (2004). Sum-difference theory of remembering and knowing: A two-dimensional signal-detection model. *Psychological Review, 111,* 588–616.

Rotello, C. M., Macmillan, N. A., & Van Tassel, G. (2000). Recall-to-reject in recognition: Evidence from ROC curves. *Journal of Memory and Language, 43,* 67–88.

Schacter, D. L., Israel, L., & Racine, C. (1999). Suppressing false recognition in younger and older adults: The distinctiveness heuristic. *Journal of Memory and Language, 40,* 1–24.

Schacter, D. L., & Slotnick, S. D. (2004). The cognitive neuroscience of memory distortion. *Neuron, 44,* 149–60.

Shiffrin, R. M. (2003). Modeling memory and perception. *Cognitive Science, 27,* 341–78.

Shiffrin, R. M., & Steyvers, M. (1997). Model for recognition memory: REM: Retrieving effectively from memory. *Psychonomic Bulletin & Review, 4,* 145–66.

Snodgrass, J. G., & Corwin, J. (1988). Pragmatics of measuring recognition memory: Applications to dementia and amnesia. *Journal of Experimental Psychology: General, 117,* 34–50.

Stadler, M. A., Roediger, H. L., & McDermott, K. B. (1999). Norms for words that create false memories. *Memory & Cognition, 27,* 494–500.

Stahl, C., & Klauer, C. K. (2008). Validation of a simplified conjoint recognition paradigm for the measurement of gist and verbatim memory. *Journal of Experimental Psychology: Learning, Memory, and Cognition, 34,* 570–88.

Stahl, C., & Klauer, C. K. (2009). Measuring phantom recollection in the simplified conjoint recognition paradigm. *Journal of Memory and Language, 60,* 180–93.

St. Jacques, P. L., & Cabeza, R. (2011). Neural basis of autobiographical memory. In S. Ghetti & P. J. Bauer (Eds.), *Origins and development of recollection: Perspectives from psychology and neuroscience* (pp. 188–218). New York: Oxford University Press.

Swanson, H. L. (1991). Learning disabilities, distinctive encoding, and hemispheric resources: An information-processing perspective. In J. E. Obrzut & G. W. Hynd (Eds.), *Neuropsychological foundations of learning disabilities* (pp. 241–80). San Diego, CA: Academic Press.

Toglia, M. P., Neuschatz, J. S., & Goodwin, K. A. (1999). Recall accuracy and illusory memories: When more is less. *Memory, 7,* 233–56.

Thomas, K. M., & Jorgensson, L. A. (2011). Development of remembering: Brain development and neuroimaging evidence. In S. Ghetti & P. J. Bauer (Eds.), *Origins and development of recollection: Perspectives from psychology and neuroscience* (pp. 219–41). New York: Oxford University Press.

Tulving, E. (1985). Memory and consciousness. *Canadian Psychologist, 26,* 1–12.

Tulving, E., & Thomson, D. M. (1971). Retrieval processes in recognition memory: Effects of associative context. *Journal of Experimental Psychology, 87,* 116–24.

Underwood, B. J. (1965). False recognition produced by implicit verbal responses. *Journal of Experimental Psychology, 70,* 122–9.

Verfaellie, M., Page, K., Orlando, F., & Schacter, D. L. (2005). Impaired implicit memory for gist information in amnesia. *Neuropsychology, 19,* 760–9.

Wixted, J. T. (2007). Dual-process theory and signal-detection theory of recognition memory. *Psychological Review, 114,* 152–76.

Yonelinas, A. P. (2002). The nature of recollection and familiarity: A review of 30 years of research. *Journal of Memory and Language, 46,* 441–518.

Yonelinas, A. P. (2011). Remembering:Thoughts on its definition, measurement, and functional nature. In S. Ghetti & P. J. Bauer (Eds.), *Origins and development of recollection: Perspectives from psychology and neuroscience* (pp. 3–20). New York: Oxford University Press.

6

The Development of Episodic Memory

Binding Processes, Controlled Processes, and Introspection on Memory States

SIMONA GHETTI, KRISTEN E. LYONS, AND DANA DeMASTER

"I remember growing up as a child in the city. We used to play in the summer time with the smell of food in the air and the Spanish music that you could hear blocks away. People were laughing and playing dominoes, kids were running around playing red light/green light . . ."

This quote is one of the thousands that can be readily uncovered upon searching the expression "I remember" on Google. This quote, in which an unknown Internet user reminisces about growing up in New York City, captures the defining features of episodic memory, that is, the capacity to remember specific events along with contextual details, giving rise to a sense of subjective vividness of things past.

Episodic memory is a fundamental faculty that supports mundane yet essential acts such as finding one's keys or one's way home, as well as more complex functions such as the development of autobiographical memory (Nelson, Chapter 2, this volume; Nelson & Fivush, 2004) and continuity in one's sense of self over time (Buckner & Carroll, 2007), including projection to the future (Addis, Wong, & Schacter, 2007). Given the centrality of episodic memory for the human experience, it is not surprising that scientists and philosophers have long been fascinated with questions about the processes that support the formation, retention, and retrieval of rich and enduring memories.

Researchers have also begun to address these questions with regard to development during childhood. One might assume that by the time children reach school age, the functioning of their episodic memory is essentially analogous to that of adults.

Children not only seem to remember a great deal about salient events, such as family vacations or receiving their first pet, but they also constantly surprise their parents with recollections of minute details about their daily lives. However, substantial change occurs during childhood in episodic memory, as reflected in robust age-related differences in performance on behavioral measures (Brainerd, Reyna, & Holliday, Chapter 5, this volume; Ghetti & Angelini, 2008; Ghetti, Mirandola, Angelini, Cornoldi, & Ciaramelli, in 2011; Newcombe, Lloyd, & Balcomb, Chapter 4, this volume; Riggins, Chapter 3, this volume) as well as in the relevant neural substrates (De Haan, Chapter 11, this volume; Friedman, Chapter 10, this volume; Ghetti, DeMaster, Yonelinas, & Bunge, 2010; Ofen, et al., 2007; Paz-Alonso, Ghetti, Donohue, Goodman, & Bunge, 2008; Thomas & Jorgensson, Chapter 9, this volume).

What psychological mechanisms might underlie these changes? There is now agreement that there are at least two classes of processes that underlie the capacity to remember specific episodes. First, binding processes allow us to create, store, and later reinstate representations (bound representations) that integrate information about an event with the constellation of contextual features surrounding it (Eichenbaum & Cohen, 2001; Eichenbaum, Yonelinas, & Ranganath, 2007). Second, controlled processes allow us to initiate operations, such as strategies and assessments of current memory states (e.g., Bjorklund, Dukes, & Brown, 2009; Eskritt & Lee, 2002, Hanten & Levin, Chapter 12, this volume; Schwenck, Bjorklund, & Schneider, 2009), that guide the formation and retrieval of bound representations. In the first part of the chapter, we briefly review the contribution of these processes to the development of episodic memory (see other chapters in this volume for more extensive discussions of these processes; Friedman, Chapter 10, this volume; Newcombe et al., Chapter 4, this volume; Riggins, Chapter 3, this volume; Thomas and Jorgensson, Chapter 9, this volume).

Episodic Memory is typically associated with a compelling feeling of vividness. However, to date, little research has focused on the development of the capacity to reflect and report on episodic memory. This capacity can be reasonably conceived within the category of controlled processes defined herein. Although the experience of vivid recollection may be triggered in "uncontrolled" ways, the appreciation of the vividness of memories and the capacity to report on this experience seem to require control. The capacity to reflect and report on episodic memories is such a central part of our memory experiences that, in the second part of the chapter, we focus on the development of the ability to introspect on memory states as an integral aspect of episodic memory.

THE DEVELOPMENT OF EPISODIC MEMORY: THE ROLE OF BINDING AND CONTROLLED PROCESSES

Episodic memory entails the capacity to encode, store, and retrieve memory representations that include information about an event as well as information about the spatiotemporal context in which the event occurred (e.g., "I went swimming in the Adriatic Sea with Alec, last summer"). Extant models of memory have demonstrated that episodic memory can be differentiated functionally and neurologically from other forms of explicit memory (Diana & Ranganath, Chapter 7, this volume; Eichenbaum et al., 2007; Yonelinas, Chapter 1, this volume). For example, episodic memory is different from a sense of familiarity, which enables us to quickly experience an event as being part of our past in the absence of memory for contextual features (e.g., "I was here before, but I cannot remember when or with whom").

In the past several years, a handful of researchers have begun to adapt experimental methods originally designed to study adult function to differentiate the developmental course of episodic memory from other forms of explicit memory. For example, we (and others) employed formal models for quantifying the contribution of recollection, the retrieval process resulting in episodic remembering, and distinguishing it from the familiarity process (e.g., Ghetti & Angelini, 2008; see also Brainerd, Holliday, & Reyna, 2004; Brainerd et al., Chapter 5, this volume). Overall, these behavioral results suggest that the process of recollection improves throughout childhood and adolescence, whereas the process supporting the global sense of familiarity stabilizes around 7 or 8 years of age.

Thus, memory development beyond middle childhood predominantly involves increasingly skilled retention of complex event representations encompassing multiple features (as opposed to, for example, quick recognition of past events based on familiarity). The implications of this development extend beyond remembering personal past episodes. For example, we recently demonstrated that recollection is preferentially involved in reading comprehension because it supports the ability to integrate text ideas during retrieval (Mirandola, Del Prete, Ghetti, & Cornoldi, 2011); this result suggests that recollection may fundamentally support learning of facts. Although this claim may seem at odds with the classical distinction between episodic and semantic memory grounded on early evidence that amnesic patients could still acquire semantic knowledge, more recent evidence shows that with damaged neurological substrates of recollection (i.e., hippocampal regions), semantic learning occurs more slowly and may not reach the level of typically developing individuals (Gardiner, Brandt, Baddeley, Vargha-Khadem, & Mishkin, 2008; Martins, Guillery-Girard, Jambaqué, Dulac, & Eustache, 2006; see DeHaan, Chapter 11, this volume).

At this time, there is a general consensus that episodic memory depends on at least two classes of processes. One class of processes is responsible for forming and reinstating memory representations that integrate the multiple features of an event and its context; here, we refer to this class as *binding processes* and the integrated representations that they generate as *bound representations*. The other class of processes is responsible for guiding the formation and monitoring the retrieval of bound representations; here we refer to this class as *controlled processes*. Despite the general consensus about their existence, the relative contribution of these processes during the course of childhood is not clearly understood.

Developmental Trajectories of Binding and Controlled Processes: Behavioral and Neural Evidence

Binding and controlled processes likely exhibit distinct developmental trajectories. Binding processes are thought to develop substantially in infancy and early childhood (e.g., Bauer, 2009; Riggins, Chapter 3, this volume) with the maturation of the hippocampus, which is the brain structure subserving the formation, retention, and reinstatement of bound representations (Davachi, 2006; Konkel & Cohen, 2009; Moscovitch, 2008). Indeed a number of studies have documented the emergence of the capacity to form arbitrary associations at the end of the first year (Bauer, 2007; Richmond & Nelson, 2009; Riggins, Chapter 3, this volume), with robust development occurring during the second year of life. Consistent with this trajectory, animal models have provided evidence of early development of the hippocampal formation: In a human time frame, the hippocampus has been shown to reach adultlike dimensions by approximately the second half of the first year of life (e.g., Seress & Ribak, 1995), with the exception of the dentate gyrus, which would do so during early childhood (Seress, 2007).

During middle childhood, age-related behavioral improvements in episodic memory are consistently observed when demand for controlled processes, such as strategic encoding or retrieval are present, but improvements are reduced or absent when this component is removed. For example, Ghetti and Angelini (2008) showed that improvements in recollection during childhood and adolescence were only observed when participants encoded content semantically; recollection did not improve during this period when participants encoded content perceptually. Furthermore, a recent behavioral study compared age-related differences in memory for arbitrary animal-backgrounds associations in a short-term version versus a long-term version of the task (Lloyd, Doydum, & Newcombe, 2009). Lloyd and colleagues showed that 6-year-olds, compared to 4-year-olds, exhibited better memory for arbitrary animal-backgrounds combinations (despite no age differences for memory for individual animals or scenes) after a delay of several minutes, but not after 20 s. Given the absence of age differences in performance on the short-delay task, which reduced demands for controlled processes involved in retrieval, the investigators argued that the development of long-term memory for arbitrary associations during middle childhood is fundamentally driven by controlled processes, rather than binding processes.

Evidence of substantial early behavioral and neural development related to binding processes in conjunction with behavioral data showing that removing the controlled demands from episodic memory tasks diminishes or eliminates age differences in performance has contributed to the dominant view in the field that the development of controlled processes, not the development of binding processes, drives episodic memory development during middle childhood. However, there is now evidence that this view may underestimate the developmental course of binding processes (Ghetti et al., 2010; Thomas & Jorgensson, Chapter 9, this volume).

We provided critical new evidence of protracted development of the hippocampus with functional magnetic resonance imaging (Ghetti et al., 2010; Paz-Alonso et al., 2008), suggesting protracted development of binding processes. For example, in Ghetti et al. (2010), functional magnetic resonance imaging data were collected during an incidental encoding task from 8-year-olds, 10- to 11-year-olds, 14-year-olds, and young adults. Line drawings were presented in green or red ink, while participants performed a semantic encoding task that differed based on the color of the drawing. Encoding was followed by a recognition test (performed outside the scanner) in which old and new drawings were presented. During the recognition test, participants reported whether or not they had encoded each drawing and, if they responded affirmatively, they were asked to report in what color of ink it was shown. Given previous evidence showing selective hippocampal activation during encoding for items that are subsequently recollected along with specific details (as opposed to items that are recognized without the recollection of specific details; Davachi, Mitchell, & Wagner, 2003; Ranganath et al., 2004), age-related differences in the activation profiles of the hippocampus were predicted. Results were consistent with prediction (Figure 6.1): Whereas 14-year-olds and adults engaged regions of the left hippocampus selectively for trials that were subsequently recollected with encoding details,

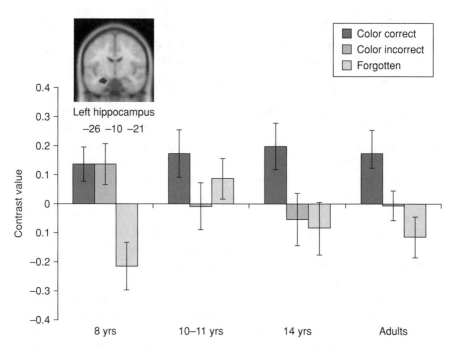

Figure 6.1. Age-related differences in patters of hippocampal activation during encoding as a function of subsequent memory performance. Adapted from Ghetti, S., DeMaster, D. M., Yonelinas, A. P., & Bunge, S.A. (2010). Developmental differences in the contribution of medial temporal lobes to memory formation. *Journal of Neuroscience, 30,* 9548–56, with permission.

8-and 10- to 11-year-olds did not. In 8-year-olds, these regions were recruited indiscriminately (i.e., for all items that were subsequently recognized, regardless of whether or not their encoding context was accurately recollected), and in 10-to 11-year-olds, activation in these regions did not consistently predict subsequent memory.

Of interest, age-related differences were also found in the activation profile of the posterior parahippocampal gyrus, another region in the medial temporal lobes that has been previously associated with subsequent detail recollection (Diana & Ranganath, Chapter 7, this volume; Ranganath et al. (2004). These results suggest changes in the functional organization of the hippocampus and posterior parahippocampal gyrus such that these regions may become increasingly specialized for episodic recollection.

These results are consistent with recent anatomical evidence indicating subtle but potentially important hippocampal development. Gogtay et al. (2006) provided evidence that the hippocampus and surrounding cortex may continue to mature into middle childhood. In their longitudinal magnetic resonance imaging investigation, they found no age-related change in total volume of the hippocampus in children aged 8 to 16 years. In contrast, volume increase was observed bilaterally in the posterior third of the hippocampus and, in the anterior third of the hippocampus volume decreased bilaterally. Although Gogtay et al. (2006) suggest that developmental change in the structure of the hippocampus may be linked to developmental changes in its function, this relation has not been tested empirically. Together, these results suggest that counter to prevailing opinion, age-related differences in hippocampal structure and function may contribute to developmental changes in binding processes beyond early childhood.

These findings do not detract from the robust evidence indicating substantial development of controlled processes, as indicated by more frequent and efficient use of *strategies* based on semantic organization during middle childhood (e.g., Bjorklund et al., 2009; Ornstein et al., 2006), as well as increased sophistication of processes involved in monitoring and regulation of memory accuracy (Ghetti, 2008; Ghetti, Lyons, Lazzarin, & Cornoldi, 2008; Koriat, Goldsmith, Schneider, & Nakash-Dura, 2001; Plude, Nelson, & Scholnick, 1998; Roebers, 2002; Roebers, von der Linden, Schneider, & Howie, 2007; Schneider & Lockl, 2002). Controlled processes have been found to mediate developmental improvements in episodic remembering, as well as developmental improvements in the ability to suppress retrieval; development of inhibitory processes during late childhood has been found to underlie an increased ability to intentionally forget previously recollected events (Paz-Alonso, Ghetti, Matlen, Anderson, & Bunge, 2009). Overall, mounting evidence indicates that the development of controlled processes plays a fundamental role in encoding and retrieval of memory episodes.

Neuroscience research lends convergent support for the protracted development of controlled processes over childhood and adolescence. Functional activation in the ventrolateral and dorsolateral prefrontal cortices, which support strategic encoding (Blumenfeld & Ranganath, 2007; Ranganath, Johnson & D'Espesotio, 2003), become increasingly associated with episodic memory with age (Ofen et al., 2007). Similarly, with age, activity in these regions exhibits increasingly differentiated patterns of activation during retrieval, and these differences likely reflect development of decision operations (dorsolateral prefrontal cortex) and cue specification (ventrolateral prefrontal cortex) (Paz-Alonso, et al., 2008). Finally, cortical thinning in PFC is correlated with episodic memory in cross-sectional samples (e.g., Sowell, Delis, Stiles, & Jerningan, 2001). Overall, it is clear that changes in controlled processes fundamentally support improvements in episodic encoding and retrieval. In sum, there is mounting evidence that both binding and controlled processes undergo development during childhood. Nevertheless, several questions are open to investigation. Some of these questions are raised in the next section.

Unraveling Change in the Contribution of Binding and Controlled Processes during Development

The initial evidence that binding mechanisms may exhibit protracted change throughout childhood along with the substantial body of work confirming robust changes in controlled processes motivate several intriguing questions about future research. Two of them are outlined here.

First, future research should further probe the nature of the developmental trajectory of memory binding processes. For example, binding trajectories might differ based on the nature of the contextual attribute to be remembered. Increasing evidence suggests that event spatial and temporal attributes recruit distinct regions of the hippocampus (e.g., Ekstrom & Bookheimer, 2007), and animal research has shown that remembering temporal attributes is more challenging than remembering spatial attributes (e.g., Bird, Roberts, Abroms, Kit, & Crupi, 2003). Developmental research indicates that children experience difficulty in memory for temporal attributes (Carelli, Forman, & Mäntylä, 2008), but it remains unknown whether this difficulty can be attributed to the development of binding processes. Differences in the rate of the development of binding processes may not only constrain children's ability to bind individual contextual details about an event (e.g., time versus spatial information about an event). These constraints may also influence children's ability to encode and retrieve more complex representations requiring binding of multiple elements of an episode.

A second question to be addressed in future research concerns changes in the interaction between binding and controlled processes. Episodic memory is an emerging property of the interaction between these two classes of processes and neuroscience research has begun to show age-related differences in anatomical and functional connectivity between hippocampal and prefrontal regions (Fair et al., 2007; Mabbott, Rovet, Noseworthy, Smith, & Rockel, 2009; Menon, Boyett-Anderson, Reiss, 2005). Future research should investigate the implications of these changes in connectivity, on both regional changes in structure and function, as well as performance on behavioral measures of episodic memory.

THE DEVELOPMENT OF THE SUBJECTIVE EXPERIENCE
OF EPISODIC MEMORY

In the previous section, we discussed binding and controlled processes as the basic classes of processes contributing to episodic memory. However, episodic memory does not only involve the capacity to form and retrieve complex memories about past events, but also the capacity to re-experience past events in a way that is subjectively vivid and compelling (e.g., Gardiner, 1988; James, 1890; Tulving, 1985; Yonelinas, 1999). The quote with which we opened this chapter captures this quality.

The phenomenological experience of *remembering* has long been considered an integral component of episodic memory. William James (1890) described memory, as involving the retrieval of mental images of past events with "warmth and intimacy" (p. 650), and with the recognition that these images correspond to personally experienced past events. More recently, the phenomenological experience of remembering has played a central role in Tulving's distinction between episodic and semantic memory (Tulving, 1985, 2005). In this framework, the autonoetic quality of episodic memory allows for mental time travel, so that individuals subjectively experience episodic memories as "remembered" rather than simply "known" (Gardiner, 1988; Tulving, 1985; Yonelinas, 1999).

Despite this longstanding tradition, researchers have only recently begun to examine the development of subjective remembering. Investigations on the topic can broadly be classified as following one of two approaches. The first approach entails examining the conceptual prerequisites that provide the foundation for children's capacity to appreciate the nature of the subjective experience of episodic memory (e.g., Naito, 2003; Perner, Kloo, & Gornik,; Perner, Kloo, & Stottinger,; Perner & Ruffman, 1995). In this vein, empirical research, rooted in theory of mind (Perner & Ruffman, 1995) or metacognitive traditions (Flavell, 1979) have examined associations between children's understanding of relevant mental states and episodic memory.

The second approach, rooted in the field of procedural metamemory (e.g., Nelson & Narens, 1990), involves the examination of children's ability to introspect upon and assess their memorial experiences (e.g., Ghetti, et al., 2008; Roebers, 2002). Research using this approach has largely focused on developments in middle childhood relating to improvements in children's ability to access and evaluate the quality of their remembering experience (e.g., Roebers & Schneider, 2005). Research from both approaches has provided evidence that age-related improvements in children's ability to subjectively *remember* past events are a critical component of memory development from early childhood to adolescence. This evidence is discussed in the next sections.

The Role of Understanding of Mental States in the Development of the Subjective Experience of Episodic Memory

The subjective experience of episodic memory (i.e., referred to as "subjective recollection" for brevity purposes) has been thought to be a property of memory representations being brought back to mind, with the recognition that these past events were previously experienced by the self (Tulving, 1985). Perner and colleagues (e.g., Perner & Ruffman, 1995; Perner, Kloo, & Stottinger,2007) have contended that in order to reexperience the past in this manner, at least two conceptual prerequisites are necessary: (a) the understanding that memories are mental images of a past reality, and (b) the understanding that memorial images were generated by one's own past experiences.

In the first studies testing for an association between these conceptual achievements and episodic remembering, episodic memory was assessed by comparing memory performance on free-recall versus cued-recall tasks (the former being assumed to rely more on episodic memory and the latter being assumed to rely more on semantic memory; e.g., Perner & Ruffman, 1995). Using this approach, Perner and Ruffman (1995) found an association between 3- to 6-year-olds' performance on free-recall tests and their awareness of the origins of their own knowledge, as assessed by see-know tests (assessing children's understanding that seeing leads to knowing and not seeing leads to not knowing), know-guess tests (assessing whether children can correctly identify that, regardless of whether their answer to a question is correct or not, that they can only *know* the answer when they had access to it and they have to *guess* the answer when they do not have access to it), and aspectuality tests (assessing children's knowledge that information about specific qualities of objects is gained through different senses, such as the knowledge that sight informs us about an object's color, whereas lifting an object tells us about the object's weight). These results were observed controlling for both cued-recall (i.e., semantic memory) ability and verbal intelligence (Perner & Ruffman, 1995), leading to the conclusion that developments in children's understanding of the origins of their own knowledge are related to their ability to episodically remember past events. In a later study, some confirmation of these relations was found: 6-year-olds' performance on a source memory task (assessing when a fact was learned—a measure of episodic memory) was related to their performance on representational change theory of mind tasks assessing children's understanding that when an individual (or oneself) is ignorant about the true nature of an object (e.g., the contents of a candy box), he or she will not know the true nature of an object (e.g., that pencils are really inside the box) (Naito, 2003).

Finally, more recently Perner and colleagues (Perner, Kloo, & Gornik, 2007) confirmed a relation between episodic memory and understanding of origins of knowledge in 3- to 6-year-olds with a cleverly designed procedure. Based on the consideration that the reexperiencing of an event is a defining feature of episodic remembering, they experimentally manipulated whether or not individuals could reexperience past events. In the direct condition, participants placed pictures of objects in a box, whereas in the indirect condition, participants put pictures in a box while blindfolded and later learned what was on these pictures by watching a video of these pictures. During the test, participants in both conditions were asked to recall what pictures they had placed in the box. Perner and colleagues found that levels of understanding of origins of knowledge was associated with memory performance in the direct but not the indirect condition; this result suggests that the conceptual understanding of the origins of knowledge is specifically relevant for episodic memory (when memories can be retrieved by reinstating the encoding experience, interpreted as representing the personal past). As a result of such investigations of children's understanding of the origin of their own memories, Perner and colleagues (Perner & Ruffman, 1995; Perner, Kloo, & Stottinger, 2007; see also Naito, 2003) concluded that self-referential representation develops critically between 3 and 6 years of age and that this ability is a strong predictor of free recall, particularly when the events are directly experienced (Perner, Kloo, & Gornik, 2007). Overall, this body of research provides interesting evidence that conceptual understanding about memory states is critically related to subjective recollection.

Additional evidence in support of this notion comes from research investigating the relation between episodic memory and metamemory development. Specifically, the ability to appreciate differences between subjective recollection and other memory experiences (such as familiarity) presumes a conceptual understanding of the difference between the two states. During the course of childhood, knowledge about memory functioning (i.e., declarative metamemory) develops substantially. Although research has shown that even young children exhibit declarative metamemory in some domains (e.g., most 4-year-olds appear to have a general understanding that to remember or forget, one must have first acquired a memory; Lyon & Flavell, 1993, 1994; Kreutzer, Leonard, & Flavell, 1975; Wellman & Johnson, 1979; even 5-year-olds recognize that salient events are more memorable than non-salient events; Ghetti & Alexander, 2004), most of children's notions become apparent later in childhood (e.g., Caponi & Cornoldi, 1989; Kreutzer et al., 1975). Indeed, several pioneering studies have documented important differences between 6- to 7-year-olds' and 9- to 10-year-olds' declarative metamemory in a number of domains (e.g., effects of the nature of the stimulus on retention, effects of time on memory loss; Kreutzer et al., 1975; Pressley, Levin, Ghatala, & Ahmad, 1987; Worden & Sladewski-Awig, 1982). Of interest, there is some indirect evidence that notions that are relevant to subjective recollection appear to be achieved even later in childhood. For example, in a study of temporal metamemory (i.e., knowledge about how individuals remember the time of a past event), Friedman (2007) found that only sixth graders and college students, but not kindergartners, second graders, and fourth graders, appreciated that the vividness of a memory could be a useful indicator of the recency of that memory, suggesting that subjective experiences about memory quality are not commonly factored in notions about memory in earlier years. Together, this work highlights that important development of understanding of memory functioning occurs during childhood, which might have implications for the subjective experience of episodic recollection.

A recent study examined the relation between children's understanding of episodic recollection (as it compares to a sense of familiarity for past events), and its relations with reports of actual subjective experiences of episodic remembering (Ghetti, et al., 2011). In the study, participants ages 6 to 18 years classified

30 statements depicting simple experiences of subjective recollection (e.g., "I can tell I saw this picture before because I saw it in green") or subjective familiarity (e.g., "There was definitely a cup in the list, but I can't tell why") as *remember* or *familiar* memory experiences. Age-related improvements in correct classifications were observed, though even 6-year-olds performed well above chance. Most important, across ages, greater understanding of the distinction between recollection and familiarity was associated with lower reports of subjective recollection, but not with lower levels of actual recall of accurate details. In other words, better understanding of subjective recollection did not result in higher levels of detailed memory per se, but in more cautious claiming of subjective recollection.

This result is important in that it underscores the potential role of understanding as critical for individuals' decisions to claim subjective recollection. To date, we know surprisingly little about developmental change in memorial decision processes. We will discuss possible venues of future research later in the chapter.

The lack of an association between understanding of subjective recollection and levels of accuracy about detailed recall stands in apparent contradiction with previous results showing that understanding of the origin of knowledge and memory is associated with levels of episodic recall (Perner & Ruffman, 1995; Perner, Kloo, & Gornick,2007). However, as acknowledged by the authors of this work (e.g., Perner, Kloo, & Stottinger,2007), the measures of understanding employed in previous research not only require this capacity, but also required a capacity to introspect on current states, thereby potentially conflating these constructs. Thus, a direct measure of introspection may be particularly useful. The next section discusses this critical aspect.

The Role of Introspection in the Development of the Subjective Experience of Episodic Memory

Another defining feature of subjective recollection is the ability to introspect on one's own memories. We argue that although conceptual understanding of the origin of one's knowledge or understanding of the distinction among memory states may support the developing ability to subjectively experience recollection, this understanding may not be the only critical factor. Subjective recollection might be an emerging property of memory function that reflects the ability to directly access memory representations and report on their content and quality. From this perspective, the development of metamemory monitoring and control (i.e., procedural memory; Schneider & Pressley, 1997) of memory processes is fundamental.

Previous research has shown that children as young as 5 can monitor varying degrees of memories strength as indicated by confidence ratings (e.g., Ghetti, Qin, & Goodman, 2002; Roebers, Gelhaar, & Schneider, 2004). For example, 5-year-olds express more confidence in recognized words that had been previously heard while seeing a picture representing the word compared to words that had been heard alone (Ghetti et al., 2002). Furthermore, even 5-year-olds appear to differentiate among their experiences of the quality of remote autobiographical memories (in their subjective ratings of memory detail and clarity). Specifically, we recently reanalyzed archival data from a previously published study (Ghetti & Castelli, 2006). In this study, 5-, 7-, and 9-year-olds were interviewed about true and false autobiographical events, which, based on parental reports, differed on how salient they were in children's lives. All of the events were presented as true regardless of their actual veridicality because the goal of the original study was to examine how children reject false memories. However, when children endorsed the occurrence of these false events, they provided judgments about how detailed their memories were (i.e., subjective memorability). The current analysis involved the subset of participants (n = 108 of 144; 39 5-year-olds, 33 7-year-olds, and 36 9-year-olds) who endorsed the occurrence of both true and false autobiographical events and thus provided subjective judgments on both types of events. As illustrated in Figure 6.2, within each age group, children rated endorsed true events as significantly higher in subjective memorability than false events were. Thus, even though these children endorsed false events as having occurred, their subjective experience, including that of 5-year-olds, still significantly distinguished true from false memories. Furthermore, within each age group, children rated high-salience compared with low-salience true events as significantly higher in subjective memorability; this difference was not found for false events. Thus, based on these findings, we can infer that some fundamental skills are already in place at the beginning of middle childhood, which allow children to reflect and report on the quality of their memories.

Nevertheless, it is clear that relevant development in the capacity to assess memory representations occurs during middle childhood (e.g., Schneider &

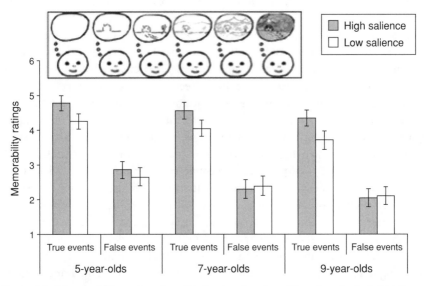

Figure 6.2. Memorability ratings (provided using the pictorial anchors included in the figure and ranging from 1 = "I don't remember anything" to 6 = "I remember very well") as a function of age, event veridicality, and event salience.

Lockl, 2002). For example, in a recent study (Ghetti et al., 2008), children were asked to attribute sources to their memories (i.e., they had to establish whether a series of actions had been previously enacted, imagined, or never encountered), 7-year-olds and 10-year-olds reported higher confidence ratings for accurate source attributions of enacted actions as compared to accurate source attributions of imagined actions. This result confirmed previously documented monitoring skills. However, only 10-year-olds provided higher confidence ratings for correct source attributions of actions imagined twice as compared to actions imagined once. Why was the evaluation of memories for imagined actions challenging for younger children? There are several possibilities. One possibility is that evaluating the quality of memory stemming from imagination presents unique challenges for younger children perhaps due to the kind of cognitive markers that might be helpful to make the appropriate assessments (e.g., mental effort; Lindsay & Johnson, 2000). Another possibility is that metacognitive monitoring of generally subtle differences in memory strength emerges late in middle childhood; indeed, the repeated imagination manipulation was a rather subtle one. Finally, another possibility is that developmental differences in monitoring abilities may differ as a function of level of memory strength alone. From this perspective, 7-year-olds' difficulties may have reflected the fact that providing confidence ratings for source attributions for actions imagined once versus twice required monitoring of overall weak memories. While future research should adjudicate among these possibilities, it is clear that some dimensions of monitoring emerge later than others, despite the presence of some early monitoring skills.

The studies reviewed thus far provide a foundation to advance predictions about the developmental trajectory of subjective recollection, though they do not examine this trajectory directly. In a recent study (Ghetti et al., 2011), we examined age-related differences in reports of subjective recollection. Participants ages 6 to 18 years semantically encoded drawings of objects presented in green or red ink. During a subsequent recognition task, participants were asked to discriminate old from new items. For items recognized as old, participants were additionally asked to rate their confidence in the recognition judgment, to report whether the item was recollected or familiar, and to describe the color and the semantic judgment performed. Results showed that children as young as 6 were significantly more likely to remember the color and the judgment they had made when they claimed to experience subjective recollection as opposed to when they claimed familiarity for the events. Furthermore, children as young as 6 years expressed higher confidence in their item recognition when they claimed subjective recollection compared with when they claimed subjective familiarity. For both rates of correct recall of specific details and confidence ratings, the extent of the differentiation increased with age, as indicated by significant age by subjective judgment interactions. Overall, and in line with the metamemory monitoring literature, these results provide both evidence of early ability and continued development during middle childhood and beyond, which might afford finer online monitoring of the quality of memory representations.

In some ways consistent with our proposal that introspection is a key capacity for episodic memory, Perner and colleagues (Perner, Kloo, & Stottinger, 2007) recently observed that the conceptual understanding of the origin of one's knowledge may not capture the essential components of true episodic memory, whereas the ability to introspect might be more centrally situated. As an initial investigation of this hypothesis, these investigators assessed introspection by examining children's ability to use imagery to solve mental rotation problems (Estes, 1998). Introspection is necessary to perform such tasks because one must form a mental representation of the target item, mentally rotate it, and finally reflect and report on the results of this mental activity. Results indicated that the ability to perform mental rotation was significantly correlated with remembering personally experienced events between 5 and 6 years of age. Thus, Perner and colleagues found a relation between episodic memory and an independent measure of introspection for mental activity that was not directly related to memory, thereby raising the question of whether and the extent to which general introspective skills, in addition to memory-specific introspection skills, are related to the development of episodic memory.

The Origins and Consequences of the Subjective Experience of Episodic Memory during Child Development

Research on the development of the subjective experience of episodic memory (i.e., subjective recollection) has only recently begun and numerous questions remain unanswered. The most important ones, we believe, pertain to our understanding of the origins and consequences of subjective recollection. Here we discuss several critical next steps, without which this investigation cannot come to full fruition.

The first step concerns the examination of the emergence of subjective recollection. Most research has investigated development of metacognitive monitoring during middle childhood, under the assumption that (a) methods currently available are not appropriate for investigations with younger children, and (b) the psychological prerequisites for subjective recollection may emerge during middle childhood (e.g., Perner, Kloo, & Stottinger, 2007). However, recent research has provided new evidence that even preschoolers as young as 3 years of age can introspect on the accuracy of their mental representations (Lyons & Ghetti, 2011) raising new questions about whether methods can be devised to investigate early development of subjective recollection at this young age. Although emergence of introspection on subjective recollection may occur earlier than previously thought, it is still the case that middle childhood is perhaps the period of most interesting change; the next steps for future investigation concerns this developmental period.

The second step concerns the assessment of developmental change in the informational origin of subjective recollection, that is, whether there exists developmental differences in the type of information that, when retrieved, provides more subjectively compelling evidence of episodic memory. In the study discussed previously (Ghetti et al., 2011), it was found that 6- to 7-year-olds were more likely to associate subjective recollection with accurate memory for item color compared with memory for type of semantic judgments, whereas the opposite was true for 17- to 18-year-olds (Figure 6.3). This result could not be accounted for by differences in accuracy for the two types of contextual details (i.e., younger children's memory for color is not more accurate than their memory for type of semantic judgment) or by understanding of the distinction between *remember* and *familiar* (i.e., children who understand the distinction exhibit even a stronger connection between memory for color and subjective recollection). This finding therefore suggests that there may be an actual change on the basis of the subjective experience of episodic memory during childhood. It is possible that younger children may be more inclined to track their memory for color over memory for semantic judgments because its visual vividness is higher than that of a semantic judgment.

The importance of visual vividness in relation to the development of introspective abilities has been raised in previous discussions (Flavell, Green, & Flavell, 1995; Harris, 1995). For example, Harris (1995) argued that mental representations that are more visually vivid are more likely to be noticed, evaluated, and reported on than mental representations that are less visually vivid. If this is the case, the relatively late emergence of semantic information as providing compelling evidence of subjective recollection may not be specific to semantics, but perhaps extend to any form of judgment that does not include salient perceptual features. On the other hand, semantic processing may provide more compelling evidence of subjective recollection as individuals become more aware of the role of deep elaboration on long-term retention. If this is the case, this result

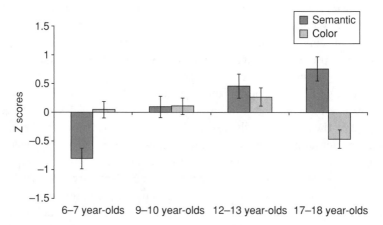

Figure 6.3. Rates of accurate memory for semantic and color (in *z* scores) associated with *remember* judgments as a function of age. Reprinted from Ghetti, S., Mirandola, C., Angelini, L., Cornoldi, C. & *Ciaramelli, E. (2011). Development of subjective remembering: Understanding of and introspection on memory states. *Child Development*, with permission from Wiley-Blackwell.

should extend to other dimensions that facilitate detailed recollection and whose effect on retention becomes more clearly understood metacognitively during development. These dimensions might include event personal salience, distinctiveness, and temporal proximity. Overall, to fully account for developmental change in the ability to introspect, research needs to account for age-related changes in what one is more inclined or able to introspect on.

Nevertheless, it is clear that the ability to access and report on memory states changes considerably during childhood. From this perspective, it is crucial to account for developmental changes in decision processes. In Ghetti et al. (2011), a relationship was found between claiming subjective recollection and conservative recognition bias in children 8 years and older and adults, but not in younger children showing that those with more conservative bias were less likely to claim to experience recollection. To date, very little is known about the nature of these changes in such memorial decision processes. Most research examining potential response biases has occurred within the child eyewitness memory field (e.g., Brady, Poole, Warren, & Jones, 1999) with the scope of examining the potential risks of asking young children yes/no recognition questions in forensic contexts (e.g., Lamb et al., 2003). Other studies focusing on middle childhood have examined how responses, including confidence ratings, change as a function of whether or not the questions are answerable (Howie & Roebers, 2007) or repeated (Howie, Sheehan, Mojarrad, & Wrzesiska, 2004). Overall, this research has provided some insight on the conditions that might interfere with memorial decision processes, but to date there is surprisingly little knowledge about functional developmental changes of these processes. For example, very little research has systematically examined normative developmental change in response bias, and factors underlying these developmental changes (see Berch, 1977, for an early example). Most of the work reporting data on response bias along with measures of accuracy has focused on the latter rather than the former (e.g., Ghetti et al., 2002).

The third step concerns the functional consequences of the subjective episodic memory. Tulving (2005) argued that one of the functions of the subjective experience of episodic memory is to provide a basis for action. That is, individuals should be more likely to act on the basis of these subjectively compelling memories. Furthermore, this capacity should allow individuals to better navigate situations in that they must integrate information about their personal past to project themselves into future states. From this perspective, the functional consequences of age-related changes in subjective recollection would not simply depend on the capacity to retrieve detailed memories; rather, the quality of the individual's subjective experience of episodic memory would be the primary factor. In other words, action would be a consequence of the subjective feeling of episodic memory, not necessarily the reality of accurate recollection.

One challenge in testing this idea is that the capacity to remember specific details is strongly and positively related to the subjective sense of recollection, making it difficult to assess the independent contribution of these factors. For example, when one insists to look for an object in a certain location, is it her accurate memory for the location that drives her action or is its subjective vividness of the memory? It would also be challenging to test the idea that the capacity to experience subjective recollection is related the ability to preexperience a future episode (e.g., envisioning one's finger poked by rose thorns), with direct implications for decision making (e.g., remembering to put band-aids in one's purse before going to pick roses), independent of other knowledge states.

To address these questions, it is critical to devise experimental paradigms that dissociate true subjective recollection and future projection from the objective capacity to retrieve detailed memories. In adult research on metacognition, such dissociations have been documented and their implications for action studied. For example, Metcalfe and Finn (2008) demonstrated that metacognitive assessments about learning, not actual learning, caused study choices. They first had participants study word pairs, some of which were presented five times in the list and some of which were only presented once. On a second study trial, the pairs that had been studied five times on the first trial were studied once (i.e., 5-1 condition), and those studied only once were studied five times (i.e., 1-5 condition). The comparison between the 5-1 condition and 1-5 condition was enlightening. The proportion of accurate recall was the same in the two conditions. However, people's judgments of learning after studying on the second trial were higher for the 5-1 pairs compared with the 1-5 pairs. This difference in people's metacognitive judgment, which was not based on a real difference in learning, produced differences in participants' study choices. In the 5-1 condition, when participants mistakenly thought they knew the items better, they declined the option to study the pairs more frequently relative to the 1-5 condition, when they thought they knew them less well. In another study, Finn and Metcalfe (2008) asked people to judge whether they would remember or forget an answer. Participants' memory in these two conditions was comparable, but when remember framing was used, the participants tended to decline the option to study the items again. In contrast, when forget framing was used, they were more likely to engage in further study. Together, these studies show that individuals' subjective states play a causal role in predicting choices that are relevant for learning. In a similar manner, experimental conditions designed to equate participants' objective episodic memory (e.g., the number of contextual details recalled), while manipulating participants' subjective feelings of recollection could prove enlightening in elucidating age-related changes in the functional consequences of subjective recollection for learning and decision making.

One final venue for future investigation involves the examination of the neural substrates of subjective recollection. Functional neuroimaging research with adults thus far has identified a network of regions within the prefrontal and parietal cortex that are critically involved in metacognitive monitoring as indicated by confidence judgments (e.g., Chua, Schacter, Rand-Giovanetti, & Sperling, 2006; Chua, Schacter, & Sperling, 2009; Kim & Cabeza, 2009). Furthermore, recent findings indicate that in adults, individual differences in anterior prefrontal gray matter volume and connectivity are correlated with individual differences in metacognitive insight (i.e., the ability to provide confidence ratings that discriminate between accurate and inaccurate responses; Fleming, Weil, Nagy, Dolan, & Rees, 2010). These results converge with those of research with adult and child patient populations (Del Cul, Dehaene, Reyes, Bravo, Slachevsky, 2009; Hogan, Vargha-Khadem, Saunders, Kirkham, & Baldeweg, 2006) and transcranial magnetic stimulation studies indicating that damage in prefrontal cortex impairs monitoring ability. Given that prefrontal and parietal cortices undergo substantial developmental change during early childhood (e.g., Gogtay et al., 2004; Sowell et al., 2001), critical improvements in subjective awareness of memory states ought to be observed during this period. Age-related maturation of prefrontal and parietal structure and connectivity supporting the development of self-monitoring operations may thus play a critical role in the development of subjective recollection, providing children with fundamental skills for reflecting on their mental representations of past events.

CONCLUSIONS

In recent years, developmental researchers have become increasingly interested in the processes allowing for successful retrieval of specific details about past episodes (e.g., Brainerd et al., 2004; Ghetti & Angelini, 2008; Holiday, 2003; Sluzenski, Newcombe, & Kovacs, 2006) and their neural underpinning (e.g., Friedman, Chapter 10, this volume; Ghetti et al., 2010; Ofen et al., 2007; Thomas & Jorgenson, Chapter 9, this volume). The investigation of the developmental trajectories of binding and controlled processes will surely continue to provide important new insights on developmental changes in the capacity to remember.

However, little research has examined the development of the subjective experience associated with episodic memory, which is an integral component of episodic memory development. We contend that a metacognitive framework can guide new investigations on this topic, by elucidating age-related changes in children's understanding of and introspection on episodic memories. We have found the examination of conceptual understanding and use of remember and familiar classifications of memory states to be a promising approach in this regard. The examination of conceptual understanding of remember and familiar states has begun to provide insight into potential limits in the ability to represent the distinction between episodic remembering and other memory experiences (e.g., familiarity) and has begun to elucidate developmental differences in reliance of different types of information to substantiate recollective states. Thus, the use of the remember/familiar paradigm holds promise to gain new insight on age-related changes in what subjectively counts as recollection and familiarity, affording a window into the general development of monitoring and control processes involved in memory retrieval. By integrating our understanding of age-related changes in measures of the capacity to remember specific details about past events with our understanding of age-related changes in the subjective experience of episodic recollection, the field may achieve a comprehensive understanding of the development of episodic memory.

REFERENCES

Addis, D. R., Wong, A. T., & Schacter, D. L. (2007). Remembering the past and imagining the future: Common and distinct neural substrates during event construction and elaboration. *Neuropsychologia, 45*, 1363–77.

Bauer, P. J. (2007). Recall in infancy: A neurodevelopmental account. *Current Directions in Psychological Science, 16*, 142–6.

Bauer, P. J. (2009). The cognitive neuroscience of the development of memory. In M. Courage, & N. Cowen (Eds.), *The development of memory in infancy and childhood* (2nd ed., pp. 115–44). New York: Psychology Press.

Berch, D. B. (1977). Effects of stimulus probability and information feedback on response biases in childrens recognition memory. *Bulletin of the Psychonomic Society, 10*, 328–30.

Bird, L. R., Roberts, W. A., Abroms, B., Kit, K. A., & Crupi, C. (2003). Spatial memory for food hidden by rats (Rattus norvegicus) on the radial maze: Studies of memory for where, what, and when. *Journal of Comparative Psychology, 117*, 176–87.

Bjorklund, D. F., Dukes, C., & Brown, R. D. (2009). The development of memory strategies. In M. Courage, & N. Cowen (Eds.), *The development of memory in infancy and childhood* (2nd ed., pp. 145–75). New York: Psychology Press.

Blumenfeld, R. S., & Ranganath, C. (2007). Dorsolateral prefrontal cortex promotes long-term memory formation through its role in working memory organization. *Journal of Neuroscience, 26*, 916–25.

Brady, M. S., Poole, D. A., Warren, A. R., & Jones, H. R. (1999). Young children's responses to yes-no questions: Patterns and problems. *Applied Developmental Science, 3*, 47–58.

Brainerd, C. J., Holliday, R. E., & Reyna, V. F. (2004). Behavioral measurement of remembering phenomenologies: So simple a child can do it. *Child Development, 75*, 505–22.

Brainerd, C. J., Reyna, V. F., & Holliday, R. E. (2011). Development of recollection: A fuzzy-trace theory perspective. In S. Ghetti & P. J. Bauer (Eds.), *Origins and development of recollection: Perspectives from psychology and neuroscience* (pp. 101–43). New York: Oxford University Press.

Buckner, R. L., & Carroll, D. C. (2007). Self-projection and the brain. *Trends Cognitive Science, 11*, 49–57.

Caponi, B., & Cornoldi, C. (1989). Metamemoria, strategicità e ricordo in bambini della scuola elementare. *Etá Evolutiva, 34*, 5–15.

Carelli, M. G., Forman, H., & Mäntylä, T. (2008). Sense of time and executive functioning in children and adults. *Child Neuropsychology, 14*, 372–86.

Chua, E. F., Schacter, D. L., Rand-Giovannetti, E., & Sperling, R. A. (2006). Understanding metamemory: Neural correlates of the cognitive process and subjective level of confidence in recognition memory. *Neuroimage, 29*, 1150–60.

Chua, E. F., Schacter, D. L., & Sperling, R. A. (2009). Neural correlates of metamemory: A comparison of feeling-of-knowing and retrospective confidence judgments. *Journal of Cognitive Neuroscience, 21*, 1751–65.

Davachi, L. (2006). Item, context and relational episodic encoding in humans. *Current Opinion Neurobiology, 16*, 693–700.

Davachi, L., Mitchell, J. P., & Wagner, A. D. (2003). Multiple routes to memory: Distinct medial temporal lobe processes build item and source memories. *Proceedings of the National Academy of Sciences of the United States of America, 100*, 2157–62.

De Haan, M. (2011). Memory development following early medial temporal lobe injury. In S. Ghetti & P. J. Bauer (Eds.), *Origins and development of recollection: Perspectives from psychology and neuroscience* (pp. 265–85). New York: Oxford University Press.

Del Cul, A., Dehaene, S., Reyes, P., Bravo, E., & Slachevsky, A. (2009). Causal role of prefrontal cortex in the threshold for access to consciousness. *Brain, 132,* 2531–40.

Diana, R., & Ranganath, C. (2011). Neural basis of recollection: Evidence from neuroimaging and electrophysiological research. In S. Ghetti & P. J. Bauer (Eds.), *Origins and development of recollection: Perspectives from psychology and neuroscience* (pp. 168–87). New York: Oxford University Press.

Eichenbaum, H., & Cohen, N. J. (2001). From conditioning to conscious recollection: Memory systems of the brain. New York: Oxford University Press.

Eichenbaum, H., Yonelinas, A. P., & Ranganath, C. (2007). The medial temporal lobe and recognition memory. *Annual Review of Neuroscience, 30,* 123–52.

Ekstrom, A. D., & Bookheimer, S. Y. (2007). Spatial and temporal episodic memory retrieval recruit dissociable functional networks in the human brain. *Learning & Memory, 14,* 645–54.

Eskritt, M., & Lee, K. (2002). "Remember where you last saw that card": Children's production of external symbols as a memory aid. *Developmental Psychology, 38,* 254–66.

Estes, D. (1998). Young children's awareness of their mental activity: The case of mental rotation. *Child Development, 69,* 1345–60.

Fair, D. A., Dosenbach, N. U., Church, J. A., Cohen, A. L., Brahmbhatt, S., Miezin, F. M., . . . Schlaggar, B. L. (2007). Development of distinct control networks through segregation and integration. *Proceedings of the National Academy of Sciences USA, 33,* 13507–12.

Finn, B., & Metcalfe, J. (2008). Judgments of learning are influenced by memory for past test. *Journal of Memory and Language, 58,* 19–34.

Flavell, J. H. (1979). Metacognition and cognitive monitoring: A new area of cognitive–developmental inquiry. *American Psychologist, 34,* 906–11.

Flavell, J. H., Green, F. L., & Flavell, E. R. (1995). Young children's knowledge about thinking. *Monographs of the Society for Research in Child Development, 60,* 1–96; discussion 97–114.

Fleming, S. M., Weil, R. S., Nagy, Z., Dolan, R. J., & Rees, G. (2010). Relating introspective accuracy to individual differences in brain structure. *Science, 329,* 1541–1543.

Friedman, D. (2011). The development of episodic memory: An event-related brain potential (ERP) vantage point. In S. Ghetti & P. J. Bauer (Eds.), *Origins and development of recollection: Perspectives from psychology and neuroscience* (pp. 242–64). New York: Oxford University Press.

Friedman, W. J. (2007). The development of temporal metamemory. *Child Development, 78,* 1472–91.

Gardiner, J. M. (1988). Functional aspects of recollective experience. *Memory & Cognition, 16,* 309–13.

Gardiner, J. M., Brandt, K. R., Baddeley, A. D., Vargha-Khadem, F., & Mishkin, M. (2008). Charting the acquisition of semantic knowledge in a case of developmental amnesia. *Neuropsychologia, 46,* 2865–8.

Ghetti, S. (2008). Rejection of false events in childhood: A metamemory account. *Current Directions in Psychological Science, 17,* 16–20.

Ghetti, S., & Alexander, K. W. (2004). "If it happened, I would remember it": Strategic use of event memorability in the rejection of false autobiographical events. *Child Development, 75*, 542–61.

Ghetti, S., & Angelini, L. (2008). The development of recollection and familiarity in childhood and adolescence: Evidence from the dual-process signal detection model. *Child Development, 79*, 339–58.

Ghetti, S., & Castelli, P. (2006). Developmental differences in false-event rejection: Effects of memorability-based warnings. *Memory, 14*, 762–76.

Ghetti, S., DeMaster, D. M., Yonelinas, A. P., & Bunge, S. A. (2010). Developmental differences in medial temporal lobe function during memory encoding. *Journal of Neuroscience, 30*, 9548–56.

Ghetti, S., Lyons, K. E., Lazzarin, F., & Cornoldi, C. (2008). The development of metamemory monitoring during retrieval: The case of memory strength and memory absence. *Journal of Experimental Child Psychology, 99*, 157–81.

Ghetti, S., Mirandola, C., Angelini, L., Cornoldi, C., & Ciaramelli, E. (2011). Development of subjective remembering: Understanding of and introspection on memory states. *Child Development.* doi:10.1111/j.1467-8624.2011.01645.x

Ghetti, S., Qin, J., & Goodman, G. S. (2002). False memories in children and adults: Age, distinctiveness, and subjective experience. *Developmental Psychology, 38*, 705–18.

Gogtay, N., Giedd, J. N., Lusk, L., Hayashi, K. M., Greenstein, D., Vaituzis, A. C., . . . Thompson, P. M. (2004). Dynamic mapping of human cortical development during childhood through early adulthood. *Proceedings of the National Academy of Sciences USA, 101*, 8174–9.

Gogtay, N., Nugent III, T. F., Herman, D. H., Ordonez, A., Greenstein, D., Hayashi, K. M., . . . Thompson, P. M. (2006). Dynamic mapping of normal human hippocampal development. *Hippocampus, 16*, 664–72.

Hanten, G., & Levin, H. S. (2011). Memory development and frontal lobe insult. In S. Ghetti & P. J. Bauer (Eds.), *Origins and development of recollection: Perspectives from psychology and neuroscience* (pp. 286–208). New York: Oxford University Press.

Harris, P. L. (1995). The rise of introspection. *Monographs of the Society for Research in Child Development, 60*, 1, 97–103.

Hogan, A. M., Vargha-Khadem, F., Saunders, D. E., Kirkham, F. J., & Baldeweg, T. (2006). Impact of frontal white matter lesions on performance monitoring: ERP evidence for cortical disconnection. *Brain, 129*, 2177–88.

Holliday, R. E. (2003). Reducing misinformation effects in children with cognitive interviews: Dissociating recollection and familiarity. *Child Development, 74*, 728–51.

Howie, P., & Roebers, C. M. (2007). Developmental progression in the confidence-accuracy relationship in event recall: Insights provided by a calibration perspective. *Applied Cognitive Psychology, 21*, 871–93.

Howie, P., Sheehan, M., Mojarrad, T., & Wrzesinska, M. (2004). "Undesirable" and "desirable" shifts in children's responses to repeated questions: Age differences in the effect of providing a rationale for repetition. *Applied Cognitive Psychology, 18*, 1161–80.

James, W. (1890). *Principles of psychology.* Cambridge, MA.: Harvard University Press.

Kim, H., & Cabeza, R. (2009). Common and specific brain regions in high- versus low-confidence recognition memory. *Brain Research, 1282*, 103–13.

Konkel, A., & Cohen, N. J. (2009). Relational memory and the hippocampus: Representations and methods. *Frontiers Neuroscience, 3*, 166–74.

Koriat, A., Goldsmith, M., Schneider, W., & Nakash-Dura, M. (2001). The credibility of children's testimony: Can children control the accuracy of their memory reports? *J Exp Child Psychol, 79*(4), 405–37.

Kreutzer, M. A., Leonard, C., & Flavell, J. H. (1975). An interview study of children's knowledge about memory. *Monographs of the Society for Research in Child Development, 40*, 1–60.

Lamb, M. E., Sternberg, K. J., Orbach, Y., Esplin, P. W., Stewart, H. L., & Mitchell, S. (2003). Age differences in young children's responses to open-ended invitations in the course of forensic interviews. *Journal of Consulting & Clinical Psychology, 71*, 926–34.

Lindsay, D. S., & Johnson, M. K. (2000). False memories and the source monitoring framework: A reply to Reyna and Lloyd (1997). *Learning & Individual Differences, 12*, 145–61.

Lloyd, M. E., Doydum, A. O., & Newcombe, N. S. (2009). Memory binding in early childhood: Evidence for a retrieval deficit. *Child Development, 80*, 1321–8.

Lyon, T. D., & Flavell, J. H. (1993). Young children's understanding of forgetting over time. *Child Development, 64*, 789–800.

Lyon, T. D., & Flavell, J. H. (1994). Young children's understanding of "remember" and "forget." *Child Development, 65*, 1357–71.

Lyons, K., & Ghetti, S. (2011). The development of uncertainty monitoring in early childhood. *Child Development.* doi:10.1111/j.1467-8624.2011.01649.x

Mabbott, D. J., Rovet, J., Noseworthy, M. D., Smith, M. L., & Rockel, C. (2009). The relations between white matter and declarative memory in older children and adolescents. *Brain Research, 1294*, 80–90.

Martins, S., Guillery-Girard, B., Jambaque, I., Dulac, O., & Eustache, F. (2006). How children suffering severe amnesic syndrome acquire new concepts? *Neuropsychologia, 44*, 2792–805.

Menon, V., Boyett-Anderson, J. M., & Reiss, A. L. (2005). Maturation of medial temporal lobe response and connectivity during memory encoding. *Cognitive Brain Research, 25*, 379–85.

Metcalfe, J., & Finn, B. (2008). Familiarity and retrieval processes in delayed judgments of learning. *Journal of Experimental Psychology: Learning, Memory, and Cognition, 34*, 1084–97.

Mirandola, C., Del Prete, F., Ghetti, S. & Cornoldi, C. (2011). Recollection, but not familiarity, differentiates memory for text in students with and without learning difficulties. *Learning and Individual Differences, 21*,206–9.

Moscovitch, M. (2008). The hippocampus as a "stupid," domain-specific module: Implications for theories of recent and remote memory, and of imagination. *Canadian Journal of Experimental Psychology, 62*, 62–79.

Naito, M. (2003). The relationship between theory of mind and episodic memory: Evidence for the development of autonoetic consciousness. *Journal of Experimental Child Psychology, 85*, 312–36.

Nelson, K. (2011). Development of meaning-conserving memory. In S. Ghetti & P. J. Bauer (Eds.), *Origins and development of recollection: Perspectives from psychology and neuroscience* (pp. 21–41). New York: Oxford University Press.

Nelson, K., & Fivush, R. (2004). The emergence of autobiographical memory: A social cultural developmental theory. *Psychological Review, 111*, 486–511.

Nelson, T., & Narens, L (1990). Metamemory: A theoretical framework and new findings. In G. H. Bower (Ed.) *The psychology of learning and motivation: Advances in research and theory* (pp. 125–69). New York: Academic Press.

Newcombe, N. S., Lloyd, M. E., & Balcomb, F. (2011). Contextualizing the development of recollection: Episodic memory and binding in young children. In S. Ghetti &
P. J. Bauer (Eds.), *Origins and development of recollection: Perspectives from psychology
and neuroscience* (pp. 73–100). New York: Oxford University Press.

Ofen, N., Kao, Y., Sokol-Hessner, P., Kim, H., Whitfield-Gabrieli, S., & Gabrieli, J.
(2007). Development of the declarative memory system in the human brain. *Nature
Neuroscience, 10,* 1198–1205.

Ornstein, P. A., Baker-Ward, L., Gordon, B. N., Pelphrey, K. A., Tyler, C. S., & Gramzow, E.
(2006). The influence of prior knowledge and repeated questioning on children's long-
term retention of the details of a pediatric examination. *Devopmental Psychology, 42,*
332–44.

Paz-Alonso, P. M., Ghetti, S., Donohue, S. E., Goodman, G. S., & Bunge, S. A. (2008). Neurodevelopmental correlates of true and false recognition. *Cerebral Cortex, 18,* 2208–16.

Paz-Alonso, P. M., Ghetti, S., Matlen, B. J., Anderson, M. C., & Bunge, S. A. (2009).
Memory suppression is an active process that improves over childhood. *Frontiers
Human Neuroscience, 3,* 1–6.

Perner, J., Kloo, D., & Gornik, E. (2007). Episodic memory development: Theory of
mind is part of re-experiencing experienced events. *Infant & Child Development, 16,*
471–90.

Perner, J., Kloo, D., & Stottinger, E. (2007). Introspection and remembering. *Synthese,
159,* 253–70.

Perner, J., & Ruffman, T. (1995). Episodic memory and autonoetic consciousness:
Developmental evidence and a theory of childhood amnesia. *Journal of Experimental
Child Psychology, 59,* 516–48.

Plude, D. J., Nelson, T. O., & Scholnick, E. K. (1998). Analytical research on developmental aspects of metamemory. *Journal of Psychology of Education, 13,* 29–42.

Pressley, M., Levin, J., Ghatala, E., & Ahmad, M. (1987). Test monitoring in young grade
school children. *Journal of Experimental Child Psychology, 43,* 96–111.

Ranganath, C., Johnson, M. K., & D'Esposito, M. (2003). Prefrontal activity associated with
working memory and episodic long-term memory. *Neuropsychologia, 41,* 378–89.

Ranganath, C., Yonelinas, A. P., Cohen, M. X., Dy, C. J., Tom, S. M., & D'Esposito, M.
(2004). Dissociable correlates of recollection and familiarity within the medial temporal lobes. *Neuropsychologia, 42,* 2–13.

Richmond, J., & Nelson, C. A. (2009). Relational memory during infancy: Evidence
from eye tracking. *Developmental Science, 12,* 549–56.

Riggins, T. (2011). Building blocks of recollection. In S. Ghetti & P. J. Bauer (Eds.),
Origins and development of recollection: Perspectives from psychology and neuroscience
(pp. 42–72). New York: Oxford University Press.

Roebers, C. M. (2002). Confidence judgments in children's and adults' event recall and
suggestibility. *Developmental Psychology, 38,* 1052–67.

Roebers, C. M., Gelhaar, T., & Schneider, W. (2004). "It's magic!" The effects of presentation modality on children's event memory, suggestibility, and confidence judgments.
Journal of Experimental Child Psychology, 87, 320–35.

Roebers, C. M., & Schneider, W. (2005). The strategic regulation of children's memory
performance and suggestibility. *Journal of Experimental Child Psychology, 91,* 24–44.

Roebers, C. M., von der Linden, N., Schneider, W., & Howie, P. (2007). Children's
metamemorial judgments in an event recall task. *Journal of Experimental Child
Psychology, 97,* 117–37.

Schneider, W., & Lockl, K. (2002). The development of metacognitive knowledge in children and adolescents. In T. Perfect & B. Schwartz (Eds.), *Applied metacognition* (pp. 224–57). New York: Cambridge University Press.

Schneider, W., & Pressley, M. (1997). Metamemory. In. *Introduction to memory: Development during childhood and adolescence* (pp. 91–108). Mahwah, NJ: Lawrence Erlbaum Associates Publishers.

Schwenck, C., Bjorklund, D. F., & Schneider, W. (2009). Developmental and individual differences in young children's use and maintenance of a selective memory strategy. *Developmental Psychology, 45*, 1034–50.

Seress, L. (2007). Comparative anatomy of the hippocampal dentate gyrus in adult and developing rodents, non-human primates and humans. *Progress in Brain Research, 163*, 23–41.

Seress, L., & Ribak, C. E. (1995). Postnatal development and synaptic connections of hilar mossy cells in the hippocampal dentate gyrus of rhesus monkeys. *Journal of Comparative Neurology, 355*, 93–110.

Sluzenski, J., Newcombe, N, & Kovacs, S. L. (2006). Binding, relational memory, and recall of naturalistic events: A developmental perspective. *Journal of Experimental Psychology: Learning, Memory, and Cognition, 32*, 89–100.

Sowell, E. R., Delis, D., Stiles, J., & Jernigan, T. L. (2001). Improved memory functioning and frontal lobe maturation between childhood and adolescence: A structural MRI study. *Journal of the International Neuropsychological Society, 7*, 312–22.

Thomas, K. M., & Jorgensson, L. A. (2011). Development of remembering: Brain development and neuroimaging evidence. In S. Ghetti & P. J. Bauer (Eds.), *Origins and development of recollection: Perspectives from psychology and neuroscience* (pp. 219–41). New York: Oxford University Press.

Tulving. (1985). Memory and consciousness. *Canadian Psychology, 26*, 1–12.

Tulving, E. (2005). Episodic memory and autonoesis: Uniquely human?. In H. S. Terrace & J. Metcalfe (Eds.), *The missing link in cognition: Origins of self-reflective consciousness* (pp. 3–56). New York: Oxford University Press.

Wellman, H. M., & Johnson, C. N. (1979). Understanding of mental processes: A developmental study of "remember" and "forget." *Child Development, 50*, 79–88.

Worden, P. E., & Sladewski-Awig, L. J. (1982). Children's awareness of memorability. *Journal of Educational Psychology, 74*, 341–50.

Yonelinas, A. P. (1999). The contribution of recollection and familiarity to recognition and source-memory judgments: A formal dual-process model and an analysis of receiver operating characteristics. *Journal of Experimental Psychology, Learning, Memory, and Cognition, 25*, 1415–34.

Yonelinas, A. P. (2011). Remembering: Thoughts on its definition, measurement, and functional nature. In S. Ghetti & P. J. Bauer (Eds.), *Origins and development of recollection: Perspectives from psychology and neuroscience* (pp. 3–20). New York: Oxford University Press.

7

Neural Basis of Recollection

Evidence from Neuroimaging and Electrophysiological Research

RACHEL A. DIANA AND CHARAN RANGANATH

No mind is much employed upon the present: recollection and anticipation fill up almost all our moments

—SAMUEL JOHNSON

What is recollection? Although this concept has been and remains central to the study of memory, defining and specifying the processes that give rise to recollection has proven to be a difficult challenge. Evidence from cognitive neuroscience approaches to the study of episodic memory supports the claim that recollection is based on processes that differ qualitatively from those that support familiarity, and recent research is shedding light on the brain regions that might contribute to recollective experience.

DISTINCTIONS BETWEEN RECOLLECTION AND FAMILIARITY

Early research on the neural mechanisms of memory focused on distinguishing between memory systems that support conscious access to memories for past events (i.e., *declarative* or *explicit* memory) and those that support the unconscious expression of past learning (i.e., *nondeclarative* or *implicit* memory). More recent event-related potential (ERP) and functional magnetic resonance imaging (fMRI) studies have suggested that declarative/explicit memory may be further subdivided. One distinction that has received widespread support is that between recollection and familiarity. Many models suggest that recollection and familiarity differ in terms of the type of information that is retrieved, but that in typical situations, both of these processes support item recognition memory.

In general, *familiarity* is thought to be the process of recognizing an item based on its perceived memory strength but without any specific details being retrieved about the study episode, whereas *recollection* is thought to be based on the retrieval of specific contextual details that were previously associated with the item. This operational definition allows for a priori predictions regarding the extent to which recollection or familiarity will support performance on a particular memory task or phenomenological judgment. Recollection and familiarity have also been defined in terms of the degree of conscious awareness of the memory (with recollection involving greater conscious awareness), the amount of cognitive control required to achieve recognition (with recollection requiring more cognitive control), and the confidence with which memory is asserted (with recollection generally being more confident). We believe that all of these factors are related to the type of information that is retrieved. More specifically, retrieval of contextual information (recollection) is likely to require controlled processing and to give rise to the conscious experience of recollection and, consequently, high confidence responses. This is because recollection requires a specific search for contextual details, whereas familiarity requires assessment of the test item without a specific search, and because the retrieval of contextual details tends to increase confidence as a confirmation of memory. However, we do not claim that these three characteristics of recollection are sufficient to define the process. Familiarity processes may also be highly conscious, controlled, and confident in certain situations. However, when contextual information is not retrieved, the memory is based on familiarity.

Before proceeding, we must emphasize that no behavioral measure or memory test is expected to be completely process-pure. That is, recollection and familiarity may be thought of as latent variables, and although a given memory test or response type may be more sensitive to one process than the other, all empirical measures are subject to error. Accordingly, it is only by seeking convergence across multiple measures that we can clarify the functional organization and neural substrates of recollection and familiarity.

One final point that must be considered is that, although recollection occurs during retrieval, it must be based on successful encoding of episodic information. Encoding may affect recollection processes both in terms of the type of information that is successfully encoded and the way that information is represented. Recollection at may also be affected by variables such as the information being tested and the lures that are used (if any) at retrieval. Therefore, any account of recollection must address both encoding and retrieval. We will consider the information and processing at encoding and retrieval for imaging studies of recollection, both ERP studies and fMRI studies.

ERP STUDIES OF RECOLLECTION

ERPs represent field potentials that emerge primarily from neocortical activity (Luck, 2005). These methods are ideally suited therefore to reveal network-related activity patterns that correspond to the implementation of specific cognitive processes in real time. If two measures or tasks are associated with different cognitive processes, such differences will be manifest as differences in spatiotemporal patterns of cortical activity that are measured by the amplitude and spatial topography of averaged ERPs. In memory research, ERP studies have revealed significant functional differences between recollection and familiarity processes.

Most ERP studies of recognition memory have focused on activity during retrieval (i.e., at test). Results from these studies have typically revealed differences between the processing of studied items that were correctly recognized as old and new items that were correctly rejected. In general, ERPs are more positive for old words than for new words, with differences emerging as early as 300 ms after stimulus presentation and lasting for 400 to 500 ms (Paller, Kutas, & Mayes, 1987; Rugg & Nagy, 1989). Smith and Halgren (1989) suggested that ERP differences between old and new items (old/new effects) could be decomposed into at least two previously studied components, an early negative-going component and a slightly later positive-going component. Although Smith and Halgren concluded that the old/new effects reflect recollection processes, later studies have contradicted their view (Potter, Pickles, Roberts, & Rugg, 1992; Rugg, Cox, Doyle, & Wells, 1995). Current evidence increasingly indicates that the earlier component is related to a familiarity process, whereas the later component is related to a recollective process.

The early old/new component was dubbed the FN400 by Curran (1999) because it was more frontally distributed than the well-established N400 component.[1] The FN400 is associated with know responses in the remember-know paradigm (Duzel, Yonelinas, Mangun, Heinze, & Tulving, 1997) such that the less familiar an item, the more negative in amplitude is the FN400 component. In addition to the remember-know findings, Curran (2000) used plurality reversed lures to isolate the contribution of familiarity. This paradigm involves presenting both plural and singular words at study, with the plurality of those words sometimes being reversed at test. Therefore, acceptance of plurality-reversed lures is thought to indicate the use of familiarity, whereas acceptance of identical plurality targets and rejection of plurality-reversed lures reflects correct recollection of the study context. Curran found that the FN400 was more negative for new items than for both studied items and plurality reversed lures. Thus, the FN400 is more negative when items are less familiar but does not distinguish between studied and nonstudied items with similar familiarity. In addition, the FN400 is modulated by confidence, indicating that the component is sensitive to memory strength gradations (Finnigan, Humphreys, Dennis, & Geffen, 2002; Woodruff, Hayama, & Rugg, 2006).

The parietal old/new effect is correlated with phenomenological judgments of recollection (specifically remember responses), associated with various types of source memory, and affected by variables that likewise influence recollection more than familiarity. Duzel et al. (1997) demonstrated that the parietal old/new

---

1. It should be noted that this effect has also been interpreted as a correlate of conceptual priming rather than familiarity (for a review, see Paller, Voss, & Boehm, 2007).

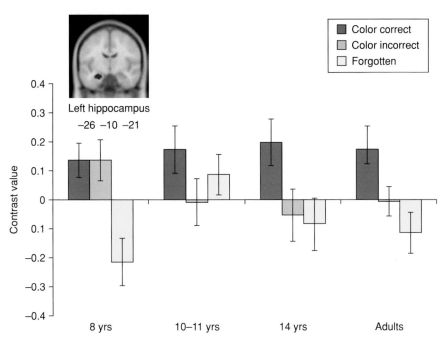

Figure 6.1. Age-related differences in patters of hippocampal activation during encoding as a function of subsequent memory performance. Adapted from Ghetti, S., DeMaster, D. M., Yonelinas, A. P, & Bunge, S.A. (2010). Developmental differences in the contribution of medial temporal lobes to memory formation. *Journal of Neuroscience, 30,* 9548–56, with permission.

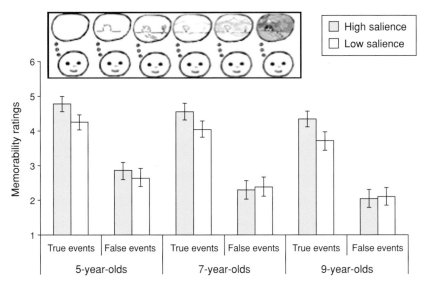

Figure 6.2. Memorability ratings (provided using the pictorial anchors included in the figure and ranging from 1 = "I don't remember anything" to 6 = "I remember very well") as a function of age, event veridicality, and event salience.

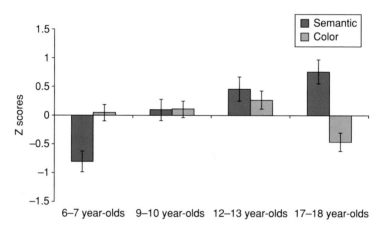

Figure 6.3. Rates of accurate memory for semantic and color (in *z* scores) associated with *remember* judgments as a function of age. Reprinted from Ghetti, S., Mirandola, C., Angelini, L., Cornoldi, C. & *Ciaramelli, E. (in press). Development of subjective remembering: Understanding of and introspection on memory states. *Child Development*, with permission from Wiley-Blackwell.

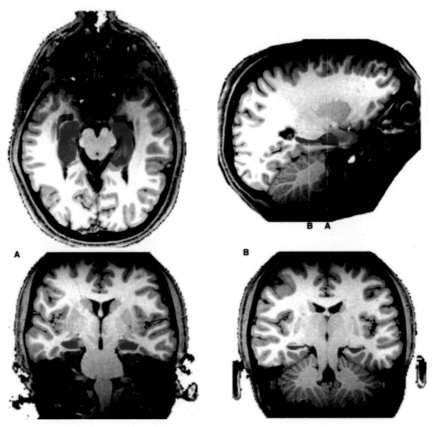

Figure 7.1. Anatomy of the MTL region. The approximate locations of the hippocampus (red), perirhinal cortex (blue), and parahippocampal cortex (green) are shown on T¹-weighted MR images. Reprinted from Diana, R. A., Yonelinas, A. P., & Ranganath, C. (2010). Imaging recollection and familiarity in the middle temporal lobe: A three component model. *Trends in Cognitive Science, 11*, 379–86, with permission of Elsevier.

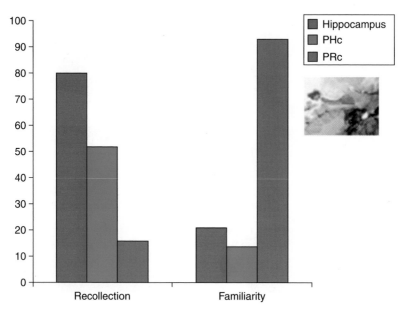

Figure 7.2. Results of contrasts from a review of all fMRI studies of recollection and familiarity through May 2008. The percentage of contrasts that revealed significant activation foci in recollection and familiarity-related contrasts are reported separately for each subregion. Reprinted from Diana, R. A., Yonelinas, A. P., & Ranganath, C. (2010). Imaging recollection and familiarity in the middle temporal lobe: A three component model. *Trends in Cognitive Science, 11*, 379–86, with permission of Elsevier.

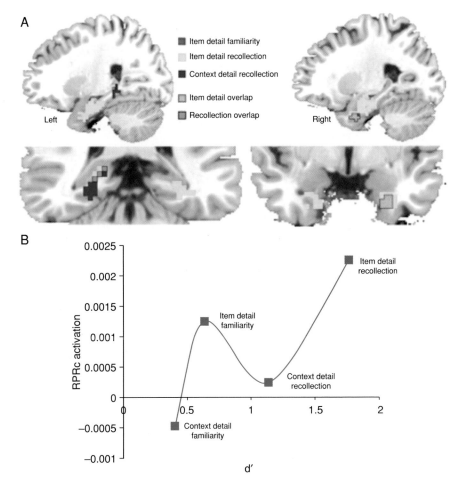

Figure 7.3. Results from Diana, Yonelinas, & Ranganath (2010). (A) Activation in MTL subregions according to encoding condition (item detail or context detail) and retrieval process (recollection or familiarity). Common areas of activation for item-detail encoding (regardless of retrieval process) occurred in PRc (plotted in orange). Common areas of activation for recollection (regardless of encoding condition) occurred in the hippocampus (plotted in green). (B) Parameter estimates extracted from the common area of activation in PRc (seen in part A in orange) plotted versus d' (a measure of memory strength) indicated a nonmonotonic relationship between PRc activation and memory strength.

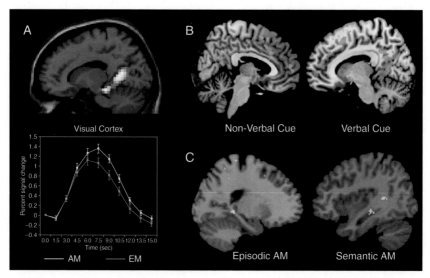

Figure 8.2. Comparing the unique and common neural correlates of autobiographical memory, episodic memory, and semantic memory. (A) Visual cortex activity was greater for autobiographical memory compared with episodic memory, when visuospatial imagery was not controlled in the prospective method (Cabeza et al., 2004). (B) Autobiographical memory conditions elicited greater activity in the medial prefrontal cortex (PFC) compared with semantic memory for both nonverbal and verbal cues (Denkova et al., 2006b). (C) The amount of contextual details modulated activity in the hippocampus for both episodic autobiographical memory and semantic autobiographical memories (Addis, Moscovitch, et al., 2004).

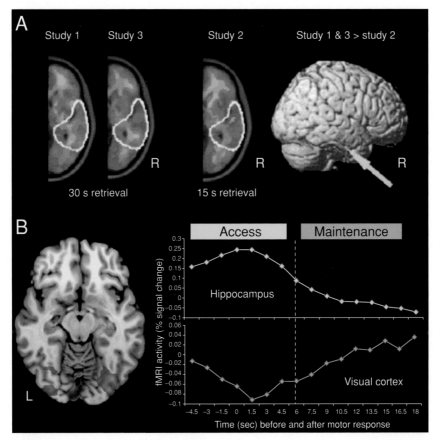

Figure 8.4. Autobiographical memory involves a protracted retrieval length. (A) Longer retrieval times recruited a more right lateralized activity in the middle temporal cortices and led to increased retrieval of episodic autobiographical memories (Graham et al., 2003). Red shading indicates greater activation in the right hemisphere (Studies 1 and 3), and blue shading indicates greater activation in the left hemisphere (Study 2). The temporal lobe is outlined in white. (B) Activity in the hippocampus related to memory access occurs early, whereas visual cortex activity related to maintenance and additional elaboration of memory occurs late (Daselaar et al., 2008).

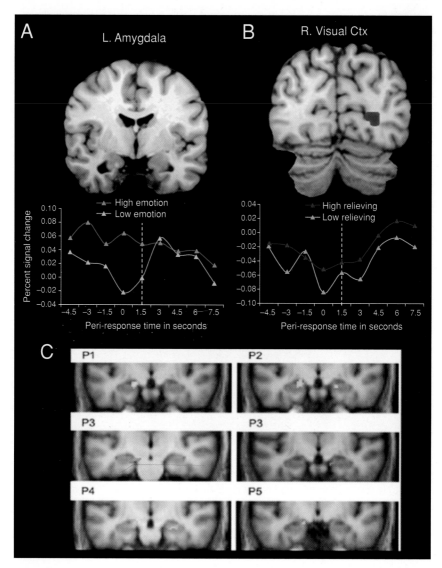

Figure 8.5. Properties that modulate recollection during autobiographical memory retrieval. (A) *Emotion*. Emotional intensity influences amygdala activity during the initial search for an autobiographical memory (Daselaar et al., 2008). (B) *Vividness*. Activity in the visual cortex was positively correlated with subjective ratings of reliving following the formation of an autobiographical memory (Daselaar et al., 2008). (C) *Remoteness*. The hippocampus continues to remain involved in vivid autobiographical memories recruited from recent to remote time periods (Viard et al., 2007). P1 = 0–17 years; P2 = 18–30 years; P3 = >31 years, except for the past 5 years; P4 = past 5 years, except the past 12 months; P5 = past 12 months.

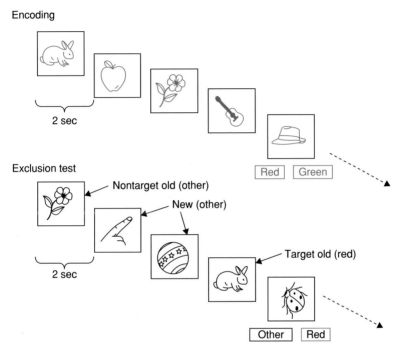

Figure 10.5. A schematic depiction of an encoding series (top) and the exclusion-memory test phase (bottom). During the former, participants made speeded and accurate red/green, choice RT decisions. During the latter, participants made speeded and accurate target old/other judgments. In the case illustrated here, participants pressed the target old button to any previously studied picture that they thought had been outlined in red during the encoding phase and pressed the "other" button to pictures that had been presented in green or were new

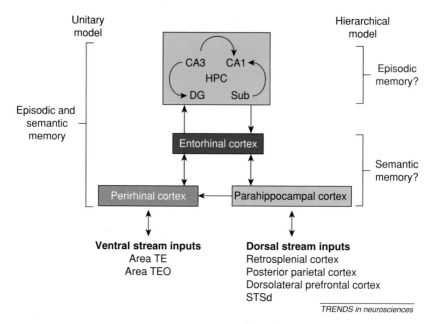

Figure 11.1. The hierarchical and unitary models provide different accounts for the neural basis of the semantic and episodic components of cognitive memory. According to the hierarchical model, information from the *what* (ventral) and *where* (dorsal) visual streams first enters the perirhinal and parahippocampal cortices, respectively, and then can pass via the entorhinal cortex to the hippocampus. In this model, semantic memory is mediated by the perirhinal, entorhinal, and posterior parahippocampal regions, whereas episodic memory relies on the hippocampus; thus, information is first encoded in semantic memory before it can pass on in the hierarchy to be encoded in episodic memory. Therefore, this model predicts that selective damage to the hippocampus can result in impaired episodic memory but that semantic memory can remain intact, whereas damage to the surrounding cortical regions would impair both types of memory. In the unitary model, both semantic and episodic memory rely on the hippocampus and the surrounding cortices. Thus, damage to any of these components should affect both semantic and episodic memory. Reprinted from de Haan, M., Mishkin, M., Baldeweg, T., & Vargha-Khadem, F. (2006). Human memory development and its dysfunction after early hippocampal injury. *Trends in Neurosciences, 29*, 374–81, with permission from Elsevier. Area TE and Area TEO = regions of the inferior temporal cortex; DG = dentate gyrus; HPC = hippocampal complex; STSd = dorsal superior temporal sulcus; Sub = subiculum

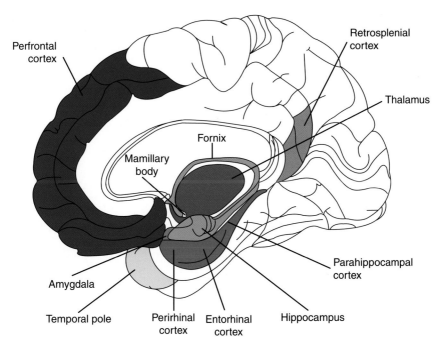

Figure 11.2. A sketch showing the approximate locations of MTL and extra-MTL regions involved in cognitive memory

effect is of greatest magnitude in the remember-know paradigm when a remember response is made.[2] Also, Curran's (2000) reversed plurality experiment showed a more positive parietal old/new effect for studied words than for either reversed plurality lures or new items, with lures and new items evoking highly similar waveforms.

The parietal old/new effect's association with recollection is also demonstrated in source memory experiments, which examine memory for study context. If the encoding process is successful, information about the study context of the item should be available in episodic memory at the time of retrieval. Wilding, Doyle, and Rugg (1995) demonstrated that the parietal old/new effect was indeed not evoked by stimuli that were not correctly identified with their study modality, and further that ERPs to misses and false alarms did not differ from those to correct rejections. These findings indicate that simply making an old response is not sufficient to produce a parietal old/new effect. A correct source judgment is necessary. Similarly, when an exclusion task is used (Jacoby, 1991) such that participants must respond old to only those items that occurred in a particular study modality while excluding items from another modality, both target and nontarget items that were correctly identified are associated with the parietal old/new effect.

There are a number of variables that are thought to influence recollection more strongly than familiarity. These variables should influence a recollection-based ERP component, if such a component exists. Normal participants show a larger parietal old/new effect when their memory performance is better. However, hippocampal amnesic participants, who presumably have impaired recollection, do not show this difference in the parietal old/new effect (Olichney et al., 2000). In addition, high-frequency words have been shown to evoke a weaker parietal effect than low frequency words (Rugg & Nagy, 1989), consistent with the view that high-frequency words are less likely to be recognized based on a recollection process than low-frequency words are (Reder et al., 2000).

RECOGNITION MEMORY IN AMNESIA

Studies of amnesic patients have prompted researchers to focus on the role of the medial temporal lobes (MTL) in different memory processes. Early studies of patients with MTL damage, most famously HM, indicated pervasive amnesia (Scoville & Milner, 1957). Initially researchers thought that the MTL was important for recollection-based memory, whereas cortical regions outside of the MTL were important for familiarity-based memory (Huppert & Piercy, 1978; Wickelgren, 1979). An alternative view is that the MTL more generally supports declarative memory (i.e., both recollection and familiarity;) Squire, 1994; Squire & Zola, 1998). Findings from more recent amnesia research using techniques that

2. This finding was based on two-step remember-know judgments, such that latency for the initial old response was not significantly different for items that were later judged as remember or know. This provides some evidence that the finding was not due to latency jitter as has been previously argued (Spencer, Abad, & Donchin, 2000).

differentiate recollection and familiarity (including remember-know, processing dissociation, and receiver operating characteristic [ROC] studies) have clarified that the MTL is important for both recollection and familiarity, but that recollection is more harmed by MTL damage than is familiarity (Yonelinas, Kroll, Dobbins, Lazzara, & Knight, 1998).

As seen in Figure 7.1, anatomical distinctions can be made between three regions in the MTL—the hippocampus, parahippocampal cortex (PHc), and perirhinal cortex (PRc)—and several theories have proposed that these areas might differentially support recollection and familiarity. Eichenbaum, Otto, & Cohen (1994) proposed that the hippocampus is involved in recollection, whereas the parahippocampal region (including both PRc and PHc) is involved in familiarity processing. This view states that the hippocampus is required for memory tasks that require associations, whereas the parahippocampal region (including

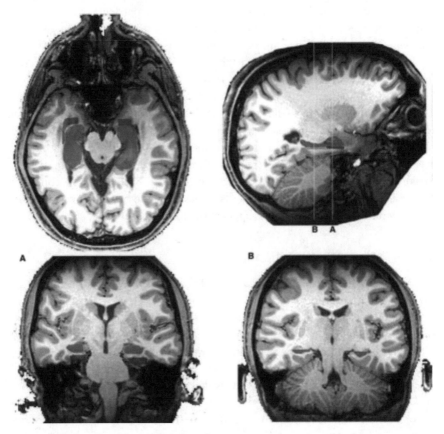

Figure 7.1. Anatomy of the MTL region. The approximate locations of the hippocampus (red, see color inserts), perirhinal cortex (blue), and parahippocampal cortex (green) are shown on T_1-weighted MR images. Reprinted from Diana, R. A., Yonelinas, A. P., & Ranganath, C. (2010). Imaging recollection and familiarity in the middle temporal lobe: A three component model. *Trends in Cognitive Science, 11*, 379–86, with permission of Elsevier.

PHc and PRc) is required for familiarity-based judgments. Aggleton and Brown (Aggleton & Brown, 2006; Brown & Aggleton, 2001) also proposed that the hippocampus is important for recollection but clarified that PRc in particular supports familiarity judgments. This model is similar to the Eichenbaum model except that it specifies PRc as the area responsible for familiarity-based functions and does not give a specific role to PHc. The Eichenbaum et al. and Aggleton and Brown models have gained support from studies that have shown that selective damage to the hippocampus disrupts recollection, while leaving familiarity relatively unaffected, whereas both recollection and familiarity are impaired when damage extends into the surrounding MTL regions (for a review, see Aggleton & Brown, 2006). Furthermore, patients with hippocampal dysfunction due to fornix and mamillary body lesions also show impaired recollection and intact familiarity-based recognition (Tsivilis et al., 2008; Vann et al., 2009).

Converging evidence has come from studies showing that rats with hippocampal lesions have impaired recollection, but generally intact familiarity-based recognition, as measured by modeling of ROC curves (Fortin, Wright, & Eichenbaum, 2004; Sauvage, Fortin, Owens, Yonelinas, & Eichenbaum, 2008). ROC curves are constructed by measuring hit and false alarm rates at varying levels of response bias. Typically the ROCs are asymmetrical and curvilinear, which has been taken as evidence for contributions of recollection and familiarity, respectively (Yonelinas, 1994). Interestingly, ROCs from healthy rats are asymmetrical and curvilinear, whereas ROCs from rats with selective damage to the hippocampus are curvilinear but symmetric. These findings, like those from human amnesics, indicate that hippocampal damage specifically affects the recollection component of recognition and suggest that familiarity may be supported by extrahippocampal regions (Fortin et al., 2004).

In general, data from lesion and amnesia studies have not revealed detailed information about the roles of PRc and PHc in recognition because it is exceptionally rare to find a patient with localized damage to one of these areas. It is notable, however, that there is one report of a patient with a relatively focal lesion to the left PRc (Bowles et al., 2007). Interestingly, this patient shows relatively intact recollection but grossly reduced familiarity, which is the opposite of what has been reported in patients with hippocampal damage. Although the results of this study should be viewed with caution as they come from a single patient, they converge with results from functional imaging studies implicating PRc in familiarity-based recognition.

FUNCTIONAL MRI STUDIES OF RECOLLECTION AND FAMILIARITY: INVOLVEMENT OF MTL SUBREGIONS

Several fMRI studies have investigated the neural correlates of recollection and familiarity, and these studies have revealed a great deal of information regarding the way in which different regions within the MTL (i.e., the hippocampus, PRC and PHc) contribute to recognition memory. Figure 7.2 presents the findings from a review of all event-related fMRI studies of recognition memory that reported neural correlates of recollection and familiarity in the MTL (as of May 2008). These include experiments in which subjects studied individual items and were then given recognition tests that either required remember-know, source memory, or recognition-confidence responses. Regions identified in the recollection contrasts were those that produced greater activity for remember than know responses, source correct compared with source incorrect responses, and the highest confidence compared with lower confidence responses. Familiarity contrasts were those that showed activity differences between recognized, nonrecollected items, as compared with nonrecognized items (misses) or regions where activity increased or decreased monotonically with increasing recognition confidence.

As shown in Figure 7.2, hippocampal activity is reliably increased for items that are recollected, as compared with recognized items that are not recollected, whereas hippocampal activity is not sensitive to differences in the familiarity of an item. This effect has been found both during encoding and retrieval. A similar, but less robust pattern of results (greater activity for recollected items than for nonrecollected items but no sensitivity to familiarity) is apparent for regions corresponding to PHc during both encoding and retrieval. Three techniques have been used to identify the neural correlates of recollection: remember-know judgments, source recognition, and confidence ratings.

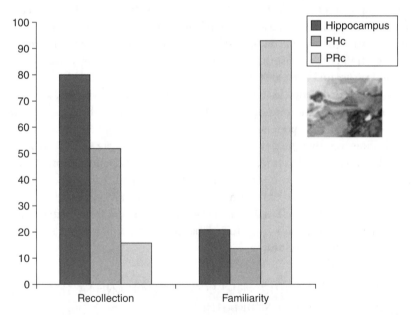

Figure 7.2. Results of contrasts from a review of all fMRI studies of recollection and familiarity through May 2008. The percentage of contrasts that revealed significant activation foci in recollection and familiarity-related contrasts are reported separately for each subregion. Reprinted from Diana, R. A., Yonelinas, A. P., & Ranganath, C. (2010). Imaging recollection and familiarity in the middle temporal lobe: A three component model. *Trends in Cognitive Science, 11,* 379–86, with permission of Elsevier.

Participants are remarkably accurate at determining whether their recognition of an item is based on recollection of contextual details or item familiarity alone. Both hippocampal and PHc activation are consistently found to correlate with remember responses but not know responses. Some studies have found only hippocampal activation (Montaldi, Spencer, Roberts, & Mayes, 2006; Otten, 2007; Suchan, Gayk, Schmid, Köster, & Daum, 2008; Uncapher & Rugg, 2005; Wheeler & Buckner, 2004) and others have found only PHc activation (Johnson & Rugg, 2007; Murray & Ranganath, 2007; Sharot, Delgado, & Phelps, 2004). However, a number of studies have found both regions to be associated with remember responses (Dolcos, LaBar, & Cabeza, 2005; Eldridge, Knowlton, Furmanski, Bookheimer, & Engel, 2000; Vilberg & Rugg, 2007, 2008; Woodruff, Johnson, Uncapher, & Rugg, 2005). These results are independent of study or test stimulus type and occur for words (Eldridge et al., 2000), neutral pictures (Dolcos et al., 2005; Sharot et al., 2004), emotional pictures (Dolcos et al., 2005), and pictures tested as words (Woodruff et al., 2005).

Source recognition tests assess recollection because memory for a contextual detail is required. However, it should be noted that source tests may underestimate the contribution of recollection because retrieval of context details that are not the target of the source test still qualifies as recollection but would not be labeled recollection by the source test. Thus, source tests provide a conservative estimate of the neural correlates of recollection and are consistent with the results provided by remember-know tests. Some studies find hippocampal activation alone is associated with retrieval of source information (Dougal, Phelps, & Davachi, 2007; Staresina & Davachi, 2008; Uncapher, Otten, & Rugg, 2006; Weis et al., 2004), but many studies find both hippocampal and parahippocampal activation is correlated with memory for source (Cansino, Maquet, Dolan, & Rugg, 2002; Davachi, Mitchell, & Wagner, 2003; Dobbins, Rice, Wagner, & Schacter, 2003; Kensinger & Schacter, 2006; Ranganath et al., 2003). Source information has been defined in a number of ways, suggesting that these brain regions are involved in encoding and retrieval of context in general rather than a specific type of context information. For example, font color (Dougal et al., 2007; Ranganath et al., 2003; Staresina & Davachi, 2008; Uncapher et al., 2006), artificial picture coloration (Weis et al., 2004), encoding task (Davachi et al., 2003; Kahn, Davachi, & Wagner, 2004; Kensinger & Schacter, 2006; Staresina & Davachi, 2008), and screen position at encoding (Cansino et al., 2002; Uncapher et al., 2006) have all been successfully used as the target of source retrieval tasks. Finally, successful encoding of two available sources (word color and location) has been found to produce greater hippocampal activation than successful encoding of one source or a lack of source encoding (Uncapher et al., 2006).

Another method to assess the contribution of recollection is the use of confidence scales. As noted earlier, it is often assumed that recollection supports high confidence decisions, so fMRI studies have identified neural correlates of recollection by contrasting high and low confidence hits. Using this technique, two studies have found hippocampal activation to be disproportionately associated with the highest confidence bin (Daselaar, Fleck, & Cabeza, 2006; Daselaar, Fleck,

Dobbins, Madden, & Cabeza, 2006), and one study has found both hippocampal and PHc activation to be disproportionately associated with high confidence (Yonelinas, Otten, Shaw, & Rugg, 2005).

Unlike activity in the hippocampus and PHc, activity in regions corresponding to PRc is consistently correlated with familiarity. In contrast, PRc activity is rarely observed in contrasts examining recollection of items. PRc effects associated with familiarity have been found using remember-know judgments, source recognition, and confidence ratings. The association between PRc and familiarity is highly replicable, with only one study not finding a familiarity effect in this region (Yonelinas et al., 2005).

Remember-know studies have found MTL activation associated with familiarity (Suchan et al., 2008; Uncapher & Rugg, 2005), although remember-know judgments may provide an underestimate of familiarity. That is, remembered items may also be familiar, but participants are instructed to report familiarity only when recollection does not occur. Source recognition tests can also provide a measure of familiarity; however, this measure is similar to that provided by remember-know judgments. Contrasts of correctly recognized items for which source was incorrectly recognized are typically considered to be familiarity-based. PRc activation has been associated with item but not source memory in a number of experiments (Davachi et al., 2003; Dougal et al., 2007; Kensinger & Schacter, 2006; Uncapher et al., 2006; Weis et al., 2004). This measure may also underestimate the contribution of familiarity to recognition because a portion of items with correctly recognized sources may be correctly guessed sources and therefore are actually familiarity-based trials that are excluded from the familiarity analysis.

Confidence ratings are a more effective measure of familiarity in imaging studies. The expected pattern of familiarity-based responses over a confidence scale is a graded, monotonic change in activity from the least confident response to the most confident response. This monotonic function has often been found to correlate with PRc activation and typically increases with confidence at encoding (Ranganath et al., 2003) and decreases with confidence at retrieval (Daselaar, Fleck, & Cabeza, 2006; Daselaar, Fleck, Dobbins, et al., 2006; Montaldi et al., 2006).

The results summarized in Figure 7.2 overwhelmingly support the claim that activity patterns in hippocampus and PHc can be distinguished from those in PRc. Furthermore, three studies have reported within-study double dissociations, linking activity in the hippocampus and PHc to recollection and activation in PRc to familiarity (Davachi et al., 2003; Kensinger & Schacter, 2006; Ranganath et al., 2003).

Findings from the fMRI studies reviewed and summarized in Figure 7.2 have several implications for models of the neural correlates of recollection. First, the data are not consistent with models that fail to differentiate between MTL subregions. If the hippocampus, PRc, and PHc equally contribute to both recollection and familiarity, then one would expect to see similar patterns of MTL activation for both types of responses. This was clearly not the case. Similarly, if these regions specifically contributed to recollection, one would expect to see MTL activation for recollection but not for familiarity, which was also not the case. The data are more consistent with the models proposed by Eichenbaum et al. (1994) and Brown and Aggleton (2001), because these models link the hippocampus with recollection and PRc with familiarity. These models, however, do not explain the dissociation between PHc and PRc that is evident in the literature. Accordingly, these models cannot fully explain the complete pattern of results in the imaging literature without some modification. In the next section, we will describe an anatomically guided model of MTL function that can account for the imaging results and describe specific predictions that the model makes for future imaging research.

THE BIC MODEL OF MTL FUNCTION

In order to understand the role MTL subregions in memory, it is helpful to consider the anatomical organization of the MTL. In general, information from all over the cerebral cortex is conveyed to neocortical regions that surround the hippocampus, and these projections are not homogenous. Specifically, the PRc predominantly receives input from neocortical areas that process information about qualities of objects (i.e., "what"), whereas the PHc additionally receives input from areas that process polymodal spatial information (i.e., "where"). PRc and PHc project to the entorhinal cortex and the "what" and "where" information converges mainly within the hippocampus (see Eichenbaum, Yonelinas, & Ranganath, 2007, for review). Based on differences in neuroanatomical connectivity between PRc, PHc, and the hippocampus, it is reasonable to suggest that each of these regions contribute to recognition memory in different ways. More specifically, PRc receives detailed information about specific items that are to be remembered, whereas PHc receives detailed information about spatial and nonspatial contextual information associated with each item. These areas provide input to the hippocampus, where item information from PRc and context information from PHc can be bound. These same regions are assumed to be involved in retrieval as well, and together they support recollection and familiarity. In the following text, we elaborate on this three-component model, originally proposed by Eichenbaum et al. (2007), which we will refer to as the binding of items and contexts (BIC) model (Diana, Yonelinas, & Ranganath, 2007).

Like previous models, the BIC model assumes that item representations in PRc support familiarity because no specific contextual information is necessary to make a familiarity judgment. In contrast, recollection additionally involves the hippocampus because it plays a critical role in linking item information to other aspects of the study event such as the study context or some other studied item. The BIC model suggests that PHc, in addition to the hippocampus, is important for recollection because it represents contextual information. That is, when an item cue is presented, activation of relevant item representations in PRc can elicit a familiarity signal that is sufficient to support recognition. Additionally, input to the hippocampus may trigger completion of the activity pattern that occurred during the learning event. This hippocampal activity would in turn lead to reactivation of the associated contextual information in PHc networks, thereby leading to recollection.

The BIC account of recollection and familiarity provides an anatomically based explanation of existing fMRI studies of item recognition. In addition, further consideration of the model generates new insights into how these regions might behave under other conditions. For example, tests of associative recognition in which pairs of items are studied and memory is then tested for the specific item pairings may involve brain areas that are somewhat different from those seen in tests of single item recognition. As is the case for item recognition, recollection of interitem associations should elicit hippocampal activation because hippocampal representations are required to link one item to the other or to the study context. In addition, if the study context is retrieved, PHc activation should be observed, and if presentation of one item leads to pattern completion of the other item, then PRc activity might be observed.

Another expectation derived from the model is that PRc may be able to support associative recognition based on familiarity, if the associated items are encoded as single units (i.e., unitized). That is, the distinction between items and associations is determined by the manner in which the stimuli are processed (e.g., BIC can be processed either as three separate letters, or as a single word). Consequently, if two paired items are encoded as a single unit (e.g., a word), then PRc-mediated familiarity signals should become useful in discriminating between studied pairings and pairs that consist of familiar items for which the pairings have been rearranged. Unitization may explain why PRc activation is sometimes correlated with successful associative memory (Staresina & Davachi, 2006). Imaging studies have demonstrated that unitization of item pairs produces PRc activation during encoding (Haskins, Yonelinas, Quamme, & Ranganath, 2008).

Perhaps the most novel aspect of the BIC model is that it predicts that item and context representations are encoded by PRc and by PHc, respectively, and that these types of information can be distinguished from item-context bindings, which are encoded by the hippocampus. This theory was directly tested in a recent fMRI study (Diana, Yonelinas, & Ranganath, 2010) that compared the brain regions involved in retrieving source information (in this case, background color). The critical manipulation in this study was that participants were encouraged to either encode the color information as a detail of a particular item or as a contextual detail. In the item-detail task, participants were asked to imagine the study item being the same color as the background and to explain why that might be the case, whereas in the context-detail task, participants were asked to imagine the study item interacting with a stop sign or dollar bill (depending on the background color) and to explain why that might occur. Consistent with our previous research (Diana, Yonelinas, & Ranganath, 2008), behavioral results showed that source memory for words encoded in the context detail condition was supported primarily by recollection, but source memory for words encoded in the item detail condition was supported by familiarity and recollection The fMRI findings (see Figure 7.3) indicated that PRc activation was associated with successful retrieval of item detail, showing more activation when the source information was encoded using the item-detail task. However, activation in the hippocampus and PHc was associated with recollection-based source retrieval.

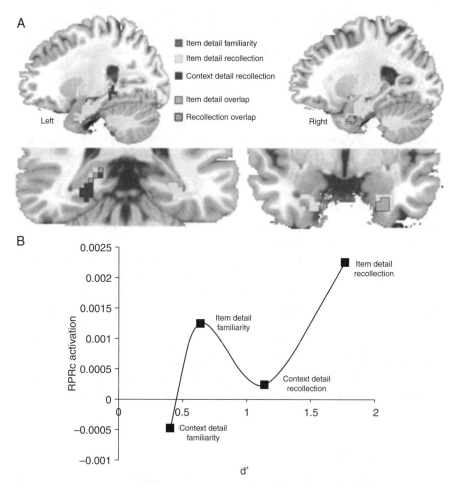

Figure 7.3. Results from Diana, Yonelinas, & Ranganath (2010). (A) Activation in MTL subregions according to encoding condition (item detail or context detail) and retrieval process (recollection or familiarity). Common areas of activation for item-detail encoding (regardless of retrieval process) occurred in PRc (plotted in orange , see color inserts). Common areas of activation for recollection (regardless of encoding condition) occurred in the hippocampus (plotted in green). (B) Parameter estimates extracted from the common area of activation in PRc (seen in part A in orange) plotted versus d' (a measure of memory strength) indicated a nonmonotonic relationship between PRc activation and memory strength.

This was true regardless of the encoding condition, indicating that retrieval of context information (as indicated by recollection responses) involves the hippocampus and PHc.

In addition to supporting the BIC model, these findings (Diana et al., 2010) refute the idea that MTL subregions collectively support declarative memory in a graded manner, such that activity in particular subregions are simply sensitive to overall memory strength. Memory strength theory requires that activation in MTL subregions should have a monotonic relationship with memory strength but our findings demonstrated that PRc activation had a nonmonotonic relationship with memory strength (see Figure 7.3).

Given the complimentary nature of PRc and PHc, one may expect to see some parallels in activation patterns across these two regions. For example, during encoding, PRc exhibits decreases in activity with repeated presentations of an item, and PHc should exhibit similar decreases in activity with repeated presentations of contextual information. Although this prediction has not been directly tested, some imaging studies have reported results that are broadly consistent. For example, activation in the posterior hippocampus and PHc is increased during processing of new arrangements of familiar items in a grid, whereas the anterior hippocampus and PRc activate when unique objects are added to the grid but the spatial arrangement is unchanged.

The model also makes clear predictions for retrieval. That is, retrieval of item information should be associated with PRc activity, whereas retrieval of context information should be associated with PHc activity. In addition, given adequate temporal and spatial resolution, it should be possible to observe dissociations in the time course of brain activation observed in PHc, PRc, and the hippocampus during recollection. The model predicts that presentation of a studied context should activate PHc, followed by the association of item and context in the hippocampus and completion of the pattern with item information in PRc. However, presentation of an item should activate PRc, followed by the hippocampus and completion of the pattern in PHc.

PREFRONTAL CORTEX

The frontal lobes are thought to be involved in executive function, such as decision making, strategizing, inhibition of inappropriate behaviors, and organization of information. Results from patient studies have been inconclusive with regard to the role of the frontal lobes in recollection and familiarity. Studies have found either disproportionate impairments for recall and source recognition, suggesting a recollection deficit (Janowsky, Risch, Irwin, & Schuckit, 1989; Janowsky, Shimamura, Kritchevsky, & Squire, 1989; Jetter, Poser, Freeman, & Markowitsch, 1986; Johnson, O'Connor, & Cantor, 1997; Simons et al., 2002) or impairments of item recognition, which may be attributable to recollection or familiarity (Alexander, Stuss, & Fansabedian, 2003; Stuss et al., 1994; Wheeler, Stuss, & Tulving, 1995). A recent patient study that was designed to assess familiarity and recollection in frontal lobe patients found that both familiarity-based item recognition and recollection-based source recognition were impaired (Duarte, Ranganath, & Knight, 2005). One reason for the inconsistent results in this area may be that these memory impairments are due to difficulty with executive function rather than memory storage (Ranganath & Knight, 2002). Thus, patient deficits would be expected to correlate with the degree of executive function required by a task rather than the contribution from recollection or familiarity. This account is supported by the finding that patients with frontal lobe damage fail to use the strategies used by healthy participants. However, when forced to use those strategies, memory performance improved (Hirst & Volpe, 1988).

Imaging studies of the prefrontal cortex have also produced somewhat inconsistent findings. In general, a number of regions of prefrontal cortex are active during memory encoding and retrieval. It appears that some regions are more active for recollection than familiarity and other regions are equally active for both processes. However, the locations of the recollection-sensitive regions have varied. Although left anterior prefrontal cortex is sometimes more active for source recognition (Ranganath, Johnson, & D'Esposito, 2000) and remember responses (Henson, Rugg, Shallice, Josephs, & Dolan, 1999), it is also sometimes insensitive to source versus item memory (Rugg, Henson, & Robb, 2003). A right dorsolateral prefrontal region has also been identified as being sensitive to source information (Rugg et al., 2003); however, this region was not sensitive to such information in other studies (Ranganath et al., 2000). Once again, these findings suggest that the frontal lobes may be involved in strategic encoding and retrieval processes that promote recollection, but may not be necessary for recollection to occur.

PARIETAL CORTEX

The parietal cortex is also increasingly implicated as being involved in long-term memory processing and dissociations between parietal regions for recollection and familiarity have been suggested. Both medial and inferior lateral parietal cortices have consistently demonstrated recollection-sensitive activation based on remember-know and source recognition (see Vilberg & Rugg, 2008; Wagner, Shannon, Kahn, & Buckner, 2005, for reviews). However, lesions of parietal cortex do not consistently produce episodic memory deficits. This may indicate that the contribution of parietal cortex to memory is not critical but for recollection but is correlated with recollection.

Several hypotheses have been proposed to explain the contribution of parietal cortex to recollection (Vilberg & Rugg, 2008; Wagner et al., 2005). Parietal regions may control attention to the information retrieved from the MTL (e.g. Ciaramelli, Grady, & Moscovitch, 2008). Alternatively, parietal regions may be involved in the accumulation of mnemonic evidence and, thus, contribute to memory-based decision making. A third possibility is that parietal regions act as an "episodic buffer" (Baddeley, 2000), supporting the maintenance or representation of information retrieved through recollection (Vilberg & Rugg, 2008). Finally, parietal cortex may be critical for the subjective experience that accompanies recollection but not for recollection of context information itself (Ally, Simons, McKeever, Peers, & Budson, 2008; Simons et al., 2008).

Although these three theories of parietal function indicate importance in memory decision making and representation of retrieved information, they do not indicate a role for parietal cortex in the encoding or direct retrieval of information. Based on our definition of recollection and familiarity (which relies on the information encoded and retrieved), the parietal cortex does not seem to be critical for these processes. Clearly, strategic and decision-making processes are important for memory tasks; however, the core of memory processing is based on the information encoded and retrieved.

GENERAL CONCLUSIONS

The studies demonstrate the remarkable progress that has been made in understanding the neural processes that support recollection. The results of imaging and neuropsychological studies converge in demonstrating that recollection can be functionally and neurally dissociated from familiarity. Furthermore, the results suggest that these dissociations may reflect the different kinds of information that support recollection and familiarity processes. That is, PRc may encode item representations that subsequently support the assessment of item familiarity, and PHc and hippocampus may encode context information and item-context bindings, respectively, that should support recollection. Prefrontal areas may additionally support executive control processes that often support recollection, but are not necessary for recollection to occur. Finally, parietal cortical areas clearly show activity that is correlated with recollection, although further work needs to be done to delineate the precise functions of these areas. It is clear that a complex ability such as recollection likely depends on other brain areas as well. Accordingly, an important challenge for future research will be to identify these areas and understand the way they interact to give rise to recollection.

REFERENCES

Aggleton, J. P., & Brown, M. W. (2006). Interleaving brain systems for episodic and recognition memory. *Trends in Cognitive Sciences, 10,* 455–63.

Alexander, M. P., Stuss, D. T., & Fansabedian, N. (2003). California Verbal Learning Test: Performance by patients with focal frontal and non-frontal lesions. *Brain: A Journal of Neurology, 126,* 1493–503.

Ally, B. A., Simons, J. S., McKeever, J. D., Peers, P. V., & Budson, A. E. (2008). Parietal contributions to recollection: Electrophysiological evidence from aging and patients with parietal lesions. *Neuropsychologia, 46,* 1800–12.

Baddeley. (2000). The episodic buffer: A new component of working memory? *Trends in Cognitive Sciences, 4,* 417–23.

Bowles, B., Crupi, C., Mirsattari, S. M., Pigott, S. E., Parrent, A. G., Pruessner, J. C., . . . Köhler, S. (2007). Impaired familiarity with preserved recollection after anterior temporal-lobe resection that spares the hippocampus. *Proceedings of the National Academy of Sciences, 104,* 16382–7.

Brown, M. W., & Aggleton, J. P. (2001). Recognition memory: What are the roles of the perirhinal cortex and hippocampus? *Nature Reviews Neuroscience, 2,* 51–61.

Cansino, S., Maquet, P., Dolan, R. J., & Rugg, M. D. (2002). Brain activity underlying encoding and retrieval of source memory. *Cerebral Cortex, 12,* 1047–56.

Ciaramelli, E., Grady, C. L., & Moscovitch, M. (2008). Top-down and bottom-up attention to memory: A hypothesis (AtoM) on the role of the posterior parietal cortex in memory retrieval. *Neuropsychologia, 46,* 1828–51.

Curran, T. (1999). The electrophysiology of incidental and intentional retrieval: ERP old/new effects in lexical decision and recognition memory. *Neuropsychologia, 37,* 771–85.

Curran, T. (2000). Brain potentials of recollection and familiarity. *Memory & Cognition, 28,* 923–38.

Daselaar, S. M., Fleck, M. S., & Cabeza, R. (2006). Triple dissociation in the medial temporal lobes: Recollection, familiarity, and novelty. *Journal of Neurophysiology, 96,* 1902–11.

Daselaar, S. M., Fleck, M. S., Dobbins, I. G., Madden, D. J., & Cabeza, R. (2006). Effects of healthy aging on hippocampal and rhinal memory functions: An event-related fMRI study. *Cerebral Cortex, 16,* 1771–82.

Davachi, L., Mitchell, J. P., & Wagner, A. D. (2003). Multiple routes to memory: Distinct medial temporal lobe processes build item and source memories. *Proceedings of the National Academy of Sciences, 100,* 2157–62.

Diana, R. A., Yonelinas, A. P., & Ranganath, C. (2007). Imaging recollection and familiarity in the medial temporal lobe: A three-component model. *Trends in Cognitive Sciences, 11,* 379–86.

Diana, R. A., Yonelinas, A. P., & Ranganath, C. (2008). The effects of unitization on familiarity-based source memory: Testing a behavioral prediction derived from neuroimaging data. *Journal of Experimental Psychology. Learning, Memory, and Cognition, 34,* 730–40.

Diana, R. A., Yonelinas, A. P., & Ranganath, C. (2010). Medial temporal lobe activity during source retrieval reflects information type, not memory strength. *Journal of Cognitive Neuroscience, 22,* 1808–18.

Dobbins, I. G., Rice, H. J., Wagner, A. D., & Schacter, D. L. (2003). Memory orientation and success: Separable neurocognitive components underlying episodic recognition. *Neuropsychologia, 41,* 318–33.

Dolcos, F., LaBar, K. S., & Cabeza, R. (2005). Remembering one year later: Role of the amygdala and the medial temporal lobe memory system in retrieving emotional memories. *Proceedings of the National Academy of Sciences, 102,* 2626–31.

Dougal, S., Phelps, E. A., & Davachi, L. (2007). The role of medial temporal lobe in item recognition and source recollection of emotional stimuli. *Cognitive, Affective & Behavioral Neuroscience, 7,* 233–42.

Duarte, A., Ranganath, C., & Knight, R. T. (2005). Effects of unilateral prefrontal lesions on familiarity, recollection, and source memory. *The Journal of Neuroscience: The Official Journal of the Society for Neuroscience, 25,* 8333–7.

Duzel, E., Yonelinas, A. P., Mangun, G. R., Heinze, H. J., & Tulving, E. (1997). Event-related brain potential correlates of two states of conscious awareness in memory. *Proceedings of the National Academy of Sciences, 94,* 5973–8.

Eichenbaum, H., Otto, T., & Cohen, N. J. (1994). Two functional components of the hippocampal memory system. *Behavioral and Brain Sciences, 17,* 449–517.

Eichenbaum, H., Yonelinas, A. P., & Ranganath, C. (2007). The medial temporal lobe and recognition memory. *Annual Review of Neuroscience, 30,* 123–52.

Eldridge, L. L., Knowlton, B. J., Furmanski, C. S., Bookheimer, S. Y., & Engel, S. A. (2000). Remembering episodes: A selective role for the hippocampus during retrieval. *Nature Neuroscience, 3,* 1149–52.

Finnigan, S., Humphreys, M. S., Dennis, S., & Geffen, G. (2002). ERP "old/new" effects: Memory strength and decisional factor(s). *Neuropsychologia, 40,* 2288–304.

Fortin, N. J., Wright, S. P., & Eichenbaum, H. (2004). Recollection-like memory retrieval in rats is dependent on the hippocampus. *Nature, 431*, 188–91.

Haskins, A. L., Yonelinas, A. P., Quamme, J. R., & Ranganath, C. (2008). Perirhinal cortex supports encoding and familiarity-based recognition of novel associations. *Neuron, 59*, 554–60.

Henson, R. N., Rugg, M. D., Shallice, T., Josephs, O., & Dolan, R. J. (1999). Recollection and familiarity in recognition memory: An event-related functional magnetic resonance imaging study. *The Journal of Neuroscience: The Official Journal of the Society for Neuroscience, 19*, 3962–72.

Hirst, W., & Volpe, B. T. (1988). Memory strategies with brain damage. *Brain and Cognition, 8*, 379–408.

Huppert, F. A., & Piercy, M. (1978). The role of trace strength in recency and frequency judgments by amnesic and control subjects. *Quarterly Journal of Experimental Psychology, 30*, 347–54.

Jacoby, L. L. (1991). A process dissociation framework: Separating automatic from intentional uses of memory. *Journal of Memory and Language, 30*, 513–41.

Janowsky, D. S., Risch, S. C., Irwin, M., & Schuckit, M. A. (1989). Behavioral hyperactivity to physostigmine in detoxified primary alcoholics. *The American Journal of Psychiatry, 146*, 538–9.

Janowsky, J. S., Shimamura, A. P., Kritchevsky, M., & Squire, L. R. (1989). Cognitive impairment following frontal lobe damage and its relevance to human amnesia. *Behavioral Neuroscience, 103*, 548–60.

Jetter, W., Poser, U., Freeman, R. B., & Markowitsch, H. J. (1986). A verbal long term memory deficit in frontal lobe damaged patients. *Cortex: A Journal Devoted to the Study of the Nervous System and Behavior, 22*, 229–42.

Johnson, J. D., & Rugg, M. D. (2007). Recollection and the reinstatement of encoding-related cortical activity. *Cerebral Cortex, 17*, 2507–15.

Johnson, M. K., O'Connor, M., & Cantor, J. (1997). Confabulation, memory deficits, and frontal dysfunction. *Brain and Cognition, 34*, 189–206.

Kahn, I., Davachi, L., & Wagner, A. D. (2004). Functional-neuroanatomic correlates of recollection: Implications for models of recognition memory. *The Journal of Neuroscience, 24*, 4172–80.

Kensinger, E. A., & Schacter, D. L. (2006). Amygdala activity is associated with successful encoding of item, but not source, information for positive and negative stimuli. *The Journal of Neuroscience, 26*, 2564–70.

Luck, S. J. (2005). *An introduction to the event-related potential technique.* Cambridge, MA: MIT Press.

Montaldi, D., Spencer, T. J., Roberts, N., & Mayes, A. R. (2006). The neural system that mediates familarity memory. *Hippocampus, 16*, 504–20.

Murray, L., & Ranganath, C. (2007). The dorsolateral prefrontal cortex contributes to successful relational memory encoding. *Journal of Neuroscience, 27*, 5515–22.

Olichney, J. M., van Petten, C., Paller, K. A., Salmon, D. P., Iragui, V. J., & Kutas, M. (2000). Word repetition in amnesia: Electrophysiological measures of impaired and spared memory. *Brain, 123*, 1948–63.

Otten, L. J. (2007). Fragments of a larger whole: Retrieval cues constrain observed neural correlates of memory encoding. *Cerebral Cortex, 17*, 2030–8.

Paller, K. A., Kutas, M., & Mayes, A. R. (1987). Neural correlates of encoding in an incidental learning paradigm. *Electroencephalography and Clinical Neurophysiology*, *67*, 360–71.

Paller, K. A., Voss, J. L., & Boehm, S. G. (2007). Validating neural correlates of familiarity. *Trends in Cognitive Sciences*, *11*, 243–50.

Potter, D. D., Pickles, C. D., Roberts, R. C., & Rugg, M. D. (1992). The effects of scopolamine on event-related potentials in a continuous recognition memory task. *Psychophysiology*, *29*, 29–37.

Ranganath, C., Johnson, M. K., & D'Esposito, M. (2000). Left anterior prefrontal activation increases with demands to recall specific perceptual information. *The Journal of Neuroscience: The Official Journal of the Society for Neuroscience*, *20*, RC108.

Ranganath, C., & Knight, R. T. (2002). Prefrontal cortex and episodic memory: Integrating findings from neuropsychology and functional brain imaging. In A. Parker, E. L. Wilding, & T. J. Bussey (Eds.), *The cognitive neuroscience of memory: Encoding and retrieval* (pp. 83–99). New York: Psychology Press.

Ranganath, C., Yonelinas, A. P., Cohen, M. X., Dy, C. J., Tom, S. M., & D'Esposito, M. (2003). Dissociable correlates of recollection and familiarity within the medial temporal lobes. *Neuropsychologia*, *42*, 2–13.

Reder, L. M., Nhouyvanisvong, A., Schunn, C. D., Ayers, M. S., Angstadt, P., & Hiraki, K. (2000). A mechanistic account of the mirror effect for word frequency: A computational model of remember/know judgments in a continuous recognition paradigm. *Journal of Experimental Psychology: Learning, Memory, & Cognition*, *26*, 294–320.

Rugg, M. D., Cox, C. J., Doyle, M. C., & Wells, T. (1995). Event-related potentials and the recollection of low and high frequency words. *Neuropsychologia*, *33*, 471–84.

Rugg, M. D., Henson, R. N. A., & Robb, W. G. K. (2003). Neural correlates of retrieval processing in the prefrontal cortex during recognition and exclusion tasks. *Neuropsychologia*, *41*, 40–52.

Rugg, M. D., & Nagy, M. E. (1989). Event-related potentials and recognition memory for words. *Electroencephalography and Clinical Neurophysiology*, *72*, 395–406.

Sauvage, M. M., Fortin, N. J., Owens, C. B., Yonelinas, A. P., & Eichenbaum, H. (2008). Recognition memory: Opposite effects of hippocampal damage on recollection and familiarity. *Nature Neuroscience*, *11*, 16–8.

Scoville, W. B., & Milner, B. (1957). Loss of recent memory after bilateral hippocampal lesions. *Journal of Neurology, Neurosurgery, and Psychiatry*, *20*, 11–21.

Sharot, T., Delgado, M. R., & Phelps, E. A. (2004). How emotion enhances the feeling of remembering. *Nature Neuroscience*, *7*, 1376–80.

Simons, J. S., Peers, P. V., Hwang, D. Y., Ally, B. A., Fletcher, P. C., & Budson, A. E. (2008). Is the parietal lobe necessary for recollection in humans? *Neuropsychologia*, *46*, 1185–91.

Simons, J. S., Verfaellie, M., Galton, C. J., Miller, B. L., Hodges, J. R., & Graham, K. S. (2002). Recollection-based memory in frontotemporal dementia: Implications for theories of long-term memory. *Brain: A Journal of Neurology*, *125*, 2523–36.

Smith, M. E., & Halgren, E. (1989). Dissociation of recognition memory components following temporal lobe lesions. *Journal of Experimental Psychology: Learning, Memory, and Cognition*, *15*, 50–60.

Spencer, K. M., Abad, E. V., & Donchin, E. (2000). On the search for the neurophysiological manifestation of recollective experience. *Psychophysiology*, *37*, 494–506.

Squire, L. R. (1994). Declarative and nondeclarative memory: Multiple brain systems
supporting learning and memory. In D. L. Schacter & E. Tulving (Eds.), *Memory
Systems*. Cambridge, MA: MIT Press.

Squire, L. R., & Zola, S. (1998). Episodic memory, semantic memory, and amnesia.
Hippocampus, *8*, 205–11.

Staresina, B. P., & Davachi, L. (2006). Differential encoding mechanisms for subsequent
associative recognition and free recall. *Journal of Neuroscience*, *26*, 9162–72.

Staresina, B. P., & Davachi, L. (2008). Selective and shared contributions of the hippocampus and perirhinal cortex to episodic item and associative encoding. *Journal of
Cognitive Neuroscience*, 20, 1478–89.

Stuss, D. T., Alexander, M. P., Palumbo, C. L., Buckle, L., Sayer, L., & Pogue, J. (1994).
Organizational strategies of patients with unilateral or bilateral frontal lobe injury in
word list learning tasks. *Neuropsychology*, *8*, 355–73.

Suchan, B., Gayk, A. E., Schmid, G., Köster, O., & Daum, I. (2008). Hippocampal
involvement in recollection but not familiarity across time: A prospective study.
Hippocampus, *18*, 92–8.

Tsivilis, D., Vann, S. D., Denby, C., Roberts, N., Mayes, A. R., Montaldi, D., & Aggleton, J.
(2008). A disproportionate role for the fornix and mammillary bodies in recall versus
recognition memory. *Nature Neuroscience*, *11*, 834–42. doi: 10.1038/nn.2149.

Uncapher, M. R., Otten, L. J., & Rugg, M. D. (2006). Episodic encoding is more than the
sum of its parts: An fMRI investigation of multifeatural contextual encoding. *Neuron*,
52, 547–56.

Uncapher, M. R., & Rugg, M. D. (2005). Encoding and the durability of episodic memory:
A functional magnetic resonance imaging study. *The Journal of Neuroscience*, *25*,
7260–7.

Vann, S. D., Tsivilis, D., Denby, C. E., Quamme, J. R., Yonelinas, A. P., Aggleton, J. P., . . .
Mayes, A. R. (2009). Impaired recollection but spared familiarity in patients with
extended hippocampal system damage revealed by 3 convergent methods. *Proceedings
of the National Academy of Sciences of the United States of America*, *106*, 5442–7.

Vilberg, K. L., & Rugg, M. D. (2007). Dissociation of the neural correlates of recognition
memory according to familiarity, recollection, and amount of recollected information. *Neuropsychologia*, *45*, 2216–25.

Vilberg, K. L., & Rugg, M. D. (2008). Memory retrieval and the parietal cortex: A review
of evidence from a dual-process perspective. *Neuropsychologia*, *46*, 1787–99.

Wagner, A. D., Shannon, B. J., Kahn, I., & Buckner, R. L. (2005). Parietal lobe contributions to episodic memory retrieval. *Trends in Cognitive Sciences*, *9*, 445–53.

Weis, S., Specht, K., Klaver, P., Tendolkar, I., Willmes, K., Ruhlmann, J., . . . Fernández, G.
(2004). Process dissociation between contextual retrieval and item recognition.
NeuroReport, *15*, 2729–33.

Wheeler, M. E., & Buckner, R. L. (2004). Functional-anatomic correlates of remembering and knowing. *NeuroImage*, *21*, 1337–49.

Wheeler, M. A., Stuss, D. T., & Tulving, E. (1995). Frontal lobe damage produces episodic memory impairment. *Journal of the International Neuropsychological Society*,
1, 525–36.

Wickelgren, W. A. (1979). Chunking and consolidation: A theoretical synthesis of semantic networks, configuring in conditions, S-R versus cognitive learning, normal forgetting, the amnesic syndrome, and the hippocampal arousal system. *Psychological Review*, *86*, 52–61.

Wilding, E. L., Doyle, M. C., & Rugg, M. D. (1995). Recognition memory with and without retrieval of context: An event-related potential study. *Neuropsychologia, 33*, 743–67.

Woodruff, C. C., Hayama, H. R., & Rugg, M. D. (2006). Electrophysiological dissociation of the neural correlates of recollection and familiarity. *Brain Research*, 1100, 125–35.

Woodruff, C. C., Johnson, J. D., Uncapher, M. R., & Rugg, M. D. (2005). Content-specificity of the neural correlates of recollection. *Neuropsychologia, 43*, 1022–32.

Yonelinas, A. P. (1994). Receiver-operating characteristics in recognition memory: Evidence for a dual-process model. *Journal of Experimental Psychology: Learning, Memory, & Cognition, 206*, 1341–54.

Yonelinas, A. P., Kroll, N. E. A., Dobbins, I., Lazzara, M., & Knight, R. T. (1998). Recollection and familiarity deficits in amnesia: Convergence of remember-know, process dissociation, and receiver operating characteristic data. *Neuropsychology, 12*, 323–39.

Yonelinas, A. P., Otten, L. J., Shaw, K. N., & Rugg, M. D. (2005). Separating the brain regions involved in recollection and familiarity in recognition memory. *The Journal of Neuroscience, 25*, 3002–8.

8

Neural Basis of Autobiographical Memory

PEGGY L. ST. JACQUES AND ROBERTO CABEZA

Autobiographical memory refers to memory for events from our own life. Compared with retrieval associated with *laboratory memory*, or memory for simple stimuli encoded in the controlled environment of the laboratory (e.g., word lists), retrieval of memories from our own life provides a greater range of the many factors that affect *recollection*, or the recovery of contextual details and the associated sense of reexperiencing. Thus, the results of functional neuroimaging studies of autobiographical memory can inform our understanding of the neural correlates of recollection in several ways. First, autobiographical memory typically involves an integration of episodic and semantic memories, and thus, the extent of recollection during autobiographical memory retrieval varies depending on the relative contribution of these two forms of memory. Second, autobiographical memory construction involves a protracted retrieval time that allows the examination of the multiple retrieval processes mediating recollection. Third, properties that might modulate recollection processes, such as emotion, vividness, and remoteness are more easily examined at the upper boundary in autobiographical memory. The present review focuses on these three domains where functional neuroimaging studies of autobiographical memory can make unique contributions to our understanding of the complex nature of recollection. Before turning to these domains, we first review the main functional neuroimaging methods for investigating autobiographical memory, which differ primarily in their ability to elicit recollection.

FUNCTIONAL NEUROIMAGING METHODS FOR INVESTIGATING AUTOBIOGRAPHICAL MEMORY

Although there are several methodological challenges in functional neuroimaging studies of autobiographical memory (for review, see Maguire, 2001; also see Svoboda, McKinnon, & Levine, 2006), the modification of existing techniques and the advance of new methodologies has resulted in an explosion in the number of functional neuroimaging studies of autobiographical memory in recent years. Four main methods have been used to investigate autobiographical memory using functional neuroimaging (see Table 8.1; for review, see Cabeza & St. Jacques, 2007). First, in the *generic cues method*, autobiographical memories are generated from novel retrieval cues (e.g., *table*; Crovitz & Schiffman, 1974). Although the memories elicited by generic cues are not necessarily emotional or significant, they tend to be "fresh," unrehearsed memories. Thus, online ratings of *reliving*, the sense of reexperiencing, and other phenomenological properties associated with memory retrieval during scanning are more consistent with the ongoing experience. Also, because retrieval in the scanner is protracted and is not contaminated by recent retrieval attempts, memory search processes can be investigated more easily (e.g., Daselaar et al., 2008; St. Jacques, Rubin, & Cabeza, 2010; St. Jacques, Botzung, Miles, & Rubin, 2011).

Table 8.1. MAIN METHODS OF ELICITING AUTOBIOGRAPHICAL MEMORY IN FUNCTIONAL NEUROIMAGE

Method	Advantage	Disadvantage
Generic cues	Retrieval during scanning is not contaminated by recent retrieval episodes	Less control over the age and content of the memory
	Memory search processes can be investigated	Memory search requires longer retrieval times
	Typically unpracticed "fresh" memories	Difficult to access memory accuracy
Prescan interview	More control over the age and content of the memory	Retrieval during scanning is contaminated by the prescan session
	Shorter trials can be used	Memory search processes cannot be investigated
		Difficult to access memory accuracy
Independent sources	Retrieval during scanning is not contaminated by recent retrieval episodes	Variability in ability to remember the events selected
	More control over the age and content of the memory	Difficult to access memory accuracy
Prospective method	Retrieval during scanning is not contaminated by recent retrieval episode	Impractical to investigate remote memories
	Greater control over the age and content of the memory	Some methods interfere with the natural encoding of events
	Retrieval accuracy can be accessed	

Second, in the *prescan interview method*, autobiographical memories are elicited by cues that refer to specific events (e.g., *visiting the London Eye*) collected prior to the scanning session (e.g., Maguire, Henson, Mummery, & Frith, 2001). The memories retrieved in the scanner can be controlled using prescan ratings (e.g., age of the memory, emotion, vividness), and trials are often shorter because retrieval cues identify particular memories. The main disadvantage with this method is that the additional retrieval practice may alter the original phenomenological properties of the memories, but this problem might be attenuated by interposing a substantial time interval between prescan and scanning sessions (e.g., Maguire & Mummery, 1999).

Third, in the *independent sources method*, autobiographical memory cues are generated by relatives or friends (e.g., Gilboa, Winocur, Grady, Hevenor, & Moscovitch, 2004). This method combines the advantages of the foregoing two methods, in that it tends to elicit unrehearsed memories and additional information provided by the sources can constrain the types of memories recalled during scanning. One disadvantage is that participants might have trouble remembering the event provided by the sources; however, this can also be seen as an advantage by providing greater variability in the amount of memory details and the phenomenological properties under investigation (e.g., vividness, reliving).

Finally, in the *prospective method*, participants are asked to keep a record of events in their lives to be used as retrieval cues in the scanner (e.g., Cabeza et al., 2004). The main advantage of the prospective method is that it allows accuracy assessment, which is important given that brain activity in medial temporal and other regions tends to vary as a function of retrieval accuracy (e.g., Buckner & Wheeler, 2001). However, until recently, the main disadvantage of the prospective method is that it might interfere with the natural encoding of autobiographical memories. Using innovative camera technologies that employ sensors and timers to automatically capture hundreds of photographs when worn (e.g., SenseCam, ViconRevue), it is now possible to prospectively generate idiosyncratic and visually rich retrieval cues that may be more effective in eliciting autobiographical memories in the laboratory (e.g., St. Jacques, Conway, Lowder, & Cabeza, 2011; St. Jacques, Conway, & Cabeza, 2010). An additional advantage of these sensor-based camera technologies is that they are easier to implement in special populations (e.g., children, patients; see Berry et al., 2007) because they require minimal input from the user. A remaining disadvantage, however, is that the prospective methods do not easily allow the study of remote memories (i.e., decades old).

In sum, each of these four methods has advantages and disadvantages that can influence the richness of recollection during retrieval. We discuss these advantages and disadvantages in more detail as they relate to each of the following sections.

AUTOBIOGRAPHICAL MEMORY IS AN INTEGRATION OF EPISODIC MEMORY AND SEMANTIC MEMORY

There is much controversy regarding the components and nature of autobiographical memory (e.g., Brewer, 1986, 1995; Larsen, 1992). On the one hand, autobiographical memory can be viewed as a distinct memory system, although there is no consensus regarding which new terms should be used (Brewer, 1995; Conway, 2005; Conway & Pleydell-Pearce, 2000). On the other hand, autobiographical memory is closely related to both *episodic memory*, which refers to memory for events with specific spatiotemporal coordinates and their associated contextual details, and *semantic memory*, which refers to factual information not tied to a specific place or time (Tulving, 1972, 1983). Thus, autobiographical memory can be conceptualized as part of a continuum between episodic memory and semantic memory (Barsalou, 1988; also see Moscovitch et al., 2005). Like episodic memory, autobiographical memories comprise spatiotemporally unique memories that are associated with *autonoetic consciousness*, or the sense of mental time travel to when the event occurred, but similar to semantic memory, autobiographical memories also entail generic personal facts and knowledge typically associated with *noetic consciousness*, or simply knowing that events occurred (Tulving, 1985). Thus, autobiographical memories are composed of *episodic autobiographical memories*, specific to time and place, and *semantic autobiographical memories*, memories not located in time (see Figure 8.1). Semantic autobiographical memories can also be divided into two further categories: (a) *autobiographical facts*, concerning idiosyncratic and shared cultural knowledge, and (b) *repeated events*, involving event-related generic and schematic knowledge (e.g., Bartlett, 1932). Further complicating these distinctions, a single episodic autobiographical memory can involve a mixture of episodic autobiographical memories, semantic autobiographical memories, and general semantic knowledge (e.g., Levine, Svoboda, Hay, Winocur, & Moscovitch, 2002). For example, the episodic autobiographical memory for a poster session might include a vivid image of a poster board toppling to the ground (episodic) intermixed with details about one's general enjoyment in disseminating research (fact), details about the many poster

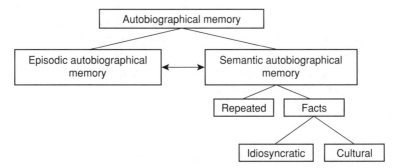

Figure 8.1. Organization of autobiographical memory. Autobiographical memory is an integration of *episodic autobiographical memory*, specific to time and place, and *semantic autobiographical memory*, memories not located in time. Semantic autobiographical memories can also be divided into *autobiographical facts*, concerning idiosyncratic and shared cultural knowledge, and *repeated events*, involving event-related generic and schematic knowledge.

sessions attended (repeated events), and the standard sequence of events of a poster session (general semantic knowledge). In fact, episodic autobiographical memories and semantic autobiographical memories interact in several ways during the construction of autobiographical memory in both patients (e.g., Snowden, Griffiths, & Neary, 1994, 1995, 1996) and healthy individuals (e.g., Berntsen & Rubin, 2004; Conway & Pleydell-Pearce, 2000; Westmacott, Leach, Freedman, & Moscovitch, 2001). Thus, autobiographical memory is neither purely episodic nor purely semantic, but is an integration of both memory types (also see Cabeza & St. Jacques, 2007; Levine, 2004).

Common and Unique Neural Activations in Autobiographical, Episodic, and Semantic Memory

Consistent with the idea that autobiographical memory has both shared properties with episodic memory and semantic memory and unique properties, functional neuroimaging studies have revealed both common and distinctive activations when comparing autobiographical memory retrieval to episodic memory and to semantic memory (e.g., Burianova & Grady, 2007; Burianova, McIntosh, & Grady, 2010; Gilboa, 2004; Maguire & Mummery, 1999; for meta-analyses, see Gilboa, 2004; McDermott, Szpunar, & Christ, 2009; Svoboda et al., 2006). Both autobiographical memory and episodic memory studies often report activations in prefrontal cortex (PFC), lateral parietal, posterior midline (posterior cingulate, precuneus), and medial temporal lobe (MTL) regions, whereas both autobiographical memory and semantic memory often report activations in lateral temporal cortices (for a meta-analysis of episodic memory and semantic memory imaging studies, see Cabeza & Nyberg, 2000). However, differences in the frequencies of autobiographical memory and episodic memory or semantic memory activations *across studies* are difficult to interpret unless the several factors that tend to differ between these tasks are taken into account (for some of these factors see Table 8.2). A meta-analysis (Gilboa, 2004), which controlled several critical factors (e.g., test type), concluded that autobiographical memory and episodic memory recruited similar preretrieval regions involved in search processes, but led to distinct activations in subregions of the PFC during postretrieval monitoring and verification. Whereas autobiographical memory tasks typically activate the ventromedial PFC, which is involved in the quick intuitive "felt rightness" (e.g., Moscovitch & Winocur, 2002), episodic memory recruited activity in the dorsolateral PFC, which is involved in more elaborate monitoring. Thus, recollection process in autobiographical memory might differ in important ways from episodic memory.

Very few studies have directly contrasted autobiographical memory and episodic memory within the same study and most of them did not control for many of the confounding factors. For example, in most of these studies autobiographical memories were likely older than the episodic memories (e.g., Conway et al., 1999; Fink et al., 1996; Greenberg et al., 2005; Maguire et al., 2001). One way of exerting greater control over the factors that differ between autobiographical memory and episodic memory is to use the prospective method to elicit

Table 8.2. Factors That Tend to Differ Between Typical Autobiographical Memory and Episodic or Semantic Memory Studies

Factors	Autobiographical Memory	Episodic Memory	Semantic Memory	Regions That Might Be Affected
1. Test type	Usually recall	Usually recognition	Usually recall	Left vs. right PFC
2. Emotional content	More	Less	Less	Amygdala, medial PFC, cortex
3. Visual/ spatial imagery	More	Less	Less	Visual cortex, parahippocampal cortex, precuneus
4. Age of memories	Recent to remote	Recent	N/A	Hippocampus
5. Retieval success	Unknown	Measured	Measured	MTL, PFC, parietal cortex, etc.
6. Semantic memory content	More	Less	More	Left PFC, parietal cortex, etc.
7. Episodic memory content	More	More	Less	Hippocampus
8. Internal structure	Complex, connected events	Simple, disconnected	N/A	PFC, parietal cortex,
9. Self-referential processing	More	Less	None	Medial PFC
10. Context (time. space)	More	Less	Less	MTL, parietal cortex
11. Rehearsal	More	Less	More	Hippocampus

MTL = medial temporal lobe; N/A = not applicable; PFC = prefrontal cortex.

memories (Cabeza et al., 2004; Levine et al., 2004). For example, in a study using the photo paradigm (Cabeza et al., 2004), participants took photographs in different campus locations and were scanned with functional magnetic resonance imaging (fMRI) while recognizing the photographs they took (autobiographical memory condition) and similar photographs viewed previously in the laboratory (episodic memory condition). This method controlled for differences in type of test (recognition in both), emotional content (minimal in both), memories' age (recent in both), retrieval success (measured and similar in both), semantic memory (similar in both), and internal structure (simple, disconnected events in both). With these six factors controlled, autobiographical memory and episodic memory yielded very similar activations in several brain regions, including right

dorsolateral PFC. It is possible that when accuracy is assessed, retrieving autobiographical memories involves the same kind of "elaborate monitoring" (e.g. Gilboa,
2004) usually engaged by episodic memory. The two factors that were not controlled, visuospatial imagery and self-referential processing, can account for
greater activity for autobiographical memory than for episodic memory in visual
cortex and medial PFC, respectively (see Figure 8.2A). Autobiographical memory
also elicited greater activity in the hippocampus, possibly reflecting richer recollection than in the episodic memory condition. In this study, greater recollection
for autobiographical memory than for episodic memory probably reflected the
fact that autobiographical memories were encoded in the rich multisensory environment of the real world with the participant controlling the picture-taking
event, whereas episodic memories were encoded in the impoverished environment of a computer screen with little self-involvement. Thus, these results do not
necessarily mean that recollection is always greater for autobiographical memory
than for episodic memory, and it is not difficult to imagine situations in which the
opposite could be the case.

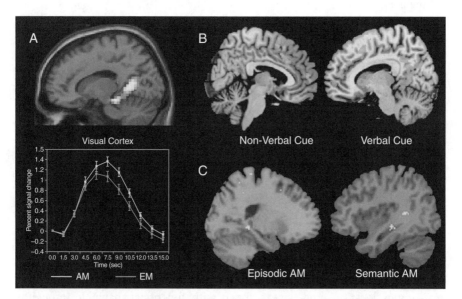

Figure 8.2. Comparing the unique and common neural correlates of autobiographical
memory, episodic memory, and semantic memory. (A) Visual cortex activity was
greater for autobiographical memory compared with episodic memory, when
visuospatial imagery was not controlled in the prospective method (Cabeza et al., 2004).
(B) Autobiographical memory conditions elicited greater activity in the medial
prefrontal cortex (PFC) compared with semantic memory for both nonverbal and
verbal cues (Denkova et al., 2006b). (C) The amount of contextual details modulated
activity in the hippocampus for both episodic autobiographical memory and semantic
autobiographical memories (Addis, Moscovitch, et al., 2004).

Even fewer functional neuroimaging studies have directly compared autobiographical memory and semantic memory (Denkova, Botzung, Scheiber, & Manning, 2006b; Graham, Lee, Brett, & Patterson, 2003; Ryan et al., 2001). One consistent difference is that autobiographical memory retrieval is associated with greater medial PFC activity than semantic memory retrieval. For example, in two parallel studies, Denkova et al. (2006b) found that autobiographical memories triggered by nonverbal and verbal cues elicited greater activity in medial PFC (see Figure 8.2B), when compared with control conditions involving a semantic relatedness task or identification of famous people, respectively. The medial PFC is frequently associated with self-referential processing (e.g., Craik et al., 1999; Kelley et al., 2002; Macrae, Moran, Heatherton, Banfield, & Kelley, 2004) including self-related judgments versus semantic decisions (e.g., Johnson et al., 2002), inference of mental states to self versus other (for review see Gallagher & Frith, 2003), and autobiographical memory retrieval (for meta-analysis, see Svoboda et al., 2006). The greater involvement of medial PFC in autobiographical memory compared with semantic memory is consistent with the importance of the self as a defining feature of autobiographical memory (Conway & Pleydell-Pearce, 2000), and as a critical component in the development of autobiographical memory (for review, see Howe, 2003). Alternative theories of medial PFC suggest that this region is involved in internal representation of thoughts and feelings (e.g., Simons, Owen, Fletcher, & Burgess, 2005), which is likely to be recruited more during autobiographical memory compared to semantic memory retrieval.

Common and Unique Neural Activations in Episodic Autobiographical Memory and Semantic Autobiographical Memory

Few functional neuroimaging studies have directly compared episodic autobiographical memory and semantic autobiographical memory, including autobiographical facts and repeated events (Addis, Moscovitch, Crawley, & McAndrews, 2004; Levine et al., 2004; Maguire & Mummery, 1999). The results of these studies suggest that there is substantial overlap in the regions recruited by episodic autobiographical memory and semantic autobiographical memory (for meta-analysis, see Svoboda et al., 2006), but potential differences in the involvement of typical recollection regions including subregions of the MTL (for review see Diana, Yonelinas, & Ranganath, 2007), posterior cingulate/retrosplenial and posterior parietal cortices (for review see Cabeza, Ciaramelli, Olson, & Moscovitch, 2008; Wagner, Shannon, Kahn, & Buckner, 2005), and frontal cortices (for review, see Rugg & Yonelinas, 2003).

Some studies have found that episodic autobiographical memories recruited (a) greater activity in the hippocampus than semantic autobiographical memory (facts) and semantic memory (Maguire & Mummery, 1999) and (b) greater activity in the parahippocampal cortex (Levine et al., 2004) than semantic autobiographical memories (repeated events) and semantic memory. These results are consistent with evidence from patients with retrograde amnesia, which suggest that the hippocampus is necessary for retrieving episodic autobiographical memories but less important for semantic autobiographical memories (although see Bayley, Gold, Hopkins, & Squire, 2005; for reviews, see Nadel & Moscovitch, 1997). On the other hand, it might not be the type of memory per se that is critical in the engagement of MTL (Ryan, Cox, Hayes, & Nadel, 2008), but rather the vividness associated with retrieval (although see Bayley, Hopkins, & Squire, 2003; e.g., Steinvorth, Levine, & Corkin, 2005). Indeed, it seems possible to vividly recollect both a unique, episodic autobiographical memory of last year's Christmas Eve, as well as a more general semantic autobiographical memory of repeated Christmas Eves spent at home. Consistent with this idea, Addis, Moscovitch, et al. (2004) found that the level of detail, but not the type of memory retrieved (i.e., episodic autobiographical memory or semantic autobiographical memory), modulated activity in the hippocampus (see Figure 8.2C). However, retrieving many contextual details for a semantic autobiographical memory might not be equivalent to reliving a unique episodic autobiographical memory. Future research is needed to directly examine the contribution of recollection in episodic autobiographical memories and semantic autobiographical memories that are composed of both repeated and autobiographical facts, as well as to understand the contribution of episodic and semantic components in these memories.

Episodic autobiographical memories were also found to recruit greater activity in the posterior cingulate/retrosplenial cortex, which has direct anatomical connections to the hippocampus (Kobayashi & Amaral, 2003) and is an area where lesions can result in amnesia (e.g., Valenstein et al., 1987). For example, Addis, Moscovitch, et al. (2004) found that episodic autobiographical memories recruited greater activity in left posterior cingulate, albeit at a slightly lower threshold, and were also given higher subjective ratings on the amount of detail, compared with semantic autobiographical memories (repeated events). Similarly, Levine et al. (2004) found that episodic autobiographical memories, compared with repeated events and semantic memory, relied more on posterior cingulate/retrosplenial cortices and tended to have higher subjective ratings of vividness. Furthermore, activity in posterior cingulate cortices has also been found to be sensitive to the amount of reliving associated with autobiographical memory retrieval (Daselaar et al., 2008). Thus, greater activity here for episodic autobiographical memories, compared with semantic autobiographical memories, likely contributes to greater recollection.

Another region that has been found to show greater activity for episodic than semantic autobiographical memory is the angular gyrus (roughly Brodmann area 39). Although this region is activated in most autobiographical memory conditions (for a meta-analysis, see Svoboda et al., 2006), there is evidence that the right angular gyrus is more activated for episodic autobiographical memory than semantic autobiographical memory (Levine et al., 2004). Together with the supramarginal gyrus (roughly Brodmann area 40), the angular gyrus is part of the ventral parietal cortex, whereas intraparietal sulcus and the superior parietal lobule (roughly Brodmann area 7) constitute the dorsal parietal cortex. Although parietal lesions are not associated with severe autobiographical memory deficits, recent studies have found that ventral parietal cortex regions can produce significant autobiographical memory deficits (Berryhill, Phuong, Picasso, Cabeza, & Olson, 2007; Davidson et al., 2008). For example, Berryhill et al. (2007) examined verbal recall of autobiographical memories in patients with bilateral damage to ventral parietal cortices using the autobiographical interview (e.g., Levine et al., 2002), which distinguishes episodic and semantic components in autobiographical memory while varying retrieval support. Compared with control subjects, they found that the parietal patients were unable to spontaneously recover details, although they could retrieve this information when provided with specific retrieval prompts. These results are consistent with the attention to memory model (Cabeza, 2008; Cabeza et al., 2008; Ciaramelli, Grady, & Moscovitch, 2008), which postulates that during episodic retrieval, ventral parietal cortex mediates bottom-up attentional processes captured by the retrieval output, whereas dorsal parietal cortex mediates top-down attentional processes that control the retrieval search. Thus, the greater involvement of parietal cortices in episodic autobiographical memories could reflect increased attention to details recovered during retrieval and lead to the enhanced specificity and richness associated with these events.

Finally, there is some evidence suggesting that episodic autobiographical memories might recruit greater activity in medial PFC, a region associated with self-referential processes and mental time travel (for reviews, see Buckner & Carroll, 2007; Schacter, Addis, & Buckner, 2007; Wheeler, Stuss, & Tulving, 1997). For example, Levine et al. (2004) found that both episodic autobiographical memories and semantic autobiographical memories (repeated events) were associated with activity in the medial PFC, but episodic autobiographical memories recruited greater activity in this region (also see Maguire & Mummery, 1999). Levine et al. (2004) interpreted this finding by suggesting that episodic autobiographical memories might involve a greater sense of the self in subjective time or autonoetic awareness. These results fit well with current definitions of episodic memory that focus on the importance of autonoetic consciousness and the role of the frontal lobes in fulfilling this capacity (Wheeler et al., 1997). Indeed, patients with degenerative damage to the frontal lobes resulting from frontotemporal dementia were shown to be impaired on autonoetic consciousness (Piolino et al., 2003) and focal lesion studies have suggested that the sense of remembering (i.e., subjective reporting of recollection) is supported by frontopolar regions that overlap with medial PFC (Duarte, Ranganath, & Knight, 2005; Wheeler & Stuss, 2003).

Summary of the Integration of Episodic and Semantic Memory in Autobiographical Memory

Functional neuroimaging studies are consistent with the idea that autobiographical memory is an integration of episodic memory and semantic memory, with substantial overlap in the pattern of activation across these memory types. Potential differences between autobiographical memory and episodic memory depend on which factors (i.e., Table 8.2) are controlled, such that autobiographical memory tasks might not necessarily involve greater recollection than episodic memory tasks. Compared with semantic memory, autobiographical memory tends to recruit greater activity in medial PFC involved in greater internal and self-referential processing. Despite the substantial overlap in the pattern of activation between episodic autobiographical memory and semantic autobiographical memory, there are also differences here in the typical recollection regions (i.e., MTL subregions, parietal, and frontal cortices), which suggest the involvement of greater recollection for episodic autobiographical memories compared with semantic autobiographical memories. In sum, autobiographical memory is not synonymous with recollection, but can vary according to the nature of the comparison condition as well as the type of autobiographical memory elicited.

AUTOBIOGRAPHICAL MEMORY CONSTRUCTION INVOLVES A PROTRACTED RETRIEVAL LENGTH

Compared with laboratory memory, autobiographical memory retrieval typically requires a protracted retrieval length possibly because of the complex organization of autobiographical memories and the ways in which episodic autobiographical memory and semantic autobiographical memory interact during voluntary retrieval. It is generally agreed that autobiographical memories are organized within a nested, hierarchical structure (Barsalou, 1988; Conway, 1990; Conway & Pleydell-Pearce, 2000; Linton, 1986; Schooler & Herrmann, 1992). The lowest level of the hierarchy might be an episodic event (e.g., *visit to the London Eye*), nested in a more intermediate level that could involve repeated (e.g., *attending conferences*) or extended events (e.g., *two week vacation*), which are part of a higher-level hierarchy involving a longer period of time (e.g., *when I was in graduate school*; see Figure 8.3). Thus, episodic autobiographical memories are at the lowest level of this hierarchy, with extended and repeated semantic autobiographical memories at higher levels. Within this framework, higher levels provide access to lower levels in a top-down fashion, such that providing participants with cues from higher levels facilitates retrieval of episodic autobiographical memories (e.g., Conway & Bekerian, 1987), and providing temporal structure (e.g., morning versus afternoon) can lead to more accurate temporal ordering of episodic autobiographical memories (e.g., St. Jacques, Rubin, Labar, & Cabeza, 2008). A single episodic autobiographical memory, which represents the lowest or most specific level of the hierarchy, is typically what we think of as autobiographical memory; however, there is substantial evidence suggesting that semantic autobiographical memories are the preferred level of recall (Barsalou, 1988; Burt, Kemp, & Conway, 2003; Conway & Pleydell-Pearce, 2000). Conway and colleagues (Conway, 2005; Conway & Pleydell-Pearce, 2000) suggest that this generic knowledge is the basic level or entry point to autobiographical memories and that episodic autobiographical memories are only accessed via additional generative or direct retrieval processes. *Generative retrieval* is effortful and requires longer retrieval times, whereas *direct retrieval* is effortless and requires shorter retrieval times. In contrast to voluntary retrieval, episodic autobiographical memories can also be retrieved *involuntarily*, where there is no conscious attempt at retrieval (for review,

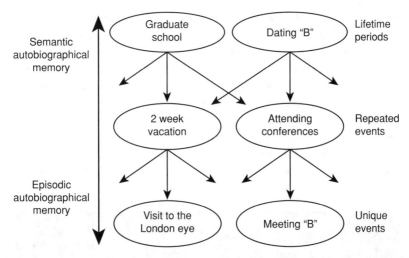

Figure 8.3. Autobiographical memories are organized in a hierarchical, nested structure, ranging from more semantic (general) to more episodic (specific) and including lifetime periods, which represent general knowledge characteristics of an extended duration of time; repeated events, involving generic episodes that represent the preferred level of access to autobiographical memory; and specific events, which are unique episodic memories. Thus, the retrieval of an autobiographical memory can encompass a more general or specific event.

see Berntsen, 2007). Functional neuroimaging studies have generally focused on voluntary, generative retrieval.

In sum, construction of autobiographical memory involves the interaction of semantic memory and episodic memory, which guide and support particular episodic components to create a coherent, richly recollected narrative. Thus, the protracted retrieval of episodic autobiographical memories is not surprising. The length of autobiographical memory construction is an advantage in functional neuroimaging studies, because it allows the segregation of the time courses of brain regions involved during different stages of retrieval, which is more difficult to examine in laboratory memory.

Variability in the Length of Autobiographical Memory Retrieval

Functional neuroimaging studies of autobiographical memory have used retrieval lengths that have varied from a few seconds to minutes long (for a meta-analysis, see Svoboda et al., 2006), but only a few have directly examined activation differences related to differences in the length of retrieval (Addis, McIntosh, Moscovitch, Crawley, & McAndrews, 2004; Graham et al., 2003). For example, using positron emission tomography (PET) imaging, Graham et al. (2003) varied the length of time allotted to autobiographical memory retrieval during PET scanning from 15 s (Study 2) to 30 s (Studies 1 and 3), and found a greater proportion of specific autobiographical memories retrieved in the longer retrieval time. Furthermore, they found that activity in the middle temporal cortices, a region involved in semantic knowledge, was initially engaged in the left hemisphere for shorter retrieval lengths and was more right lateralized for longer retrieval lengths (see Figure 8.4A). Similarly, a recent meta-analysis (Svoboda et al., 2006) found that autobiographical memory studies using shorter retrieval lengths (< 10 s) often found activity in left middle temporal cortices, whereas, studies using longer retrieval lengths (> 20 s) tended to find activity in the right temporal cortex. Thus, allocating more time for autobiographical memory retrieval should increase the amount and specificity of the semantic information retrieved via the increasing involvement of middle temporal cortices, which subsequently supports the retrieval of episodic

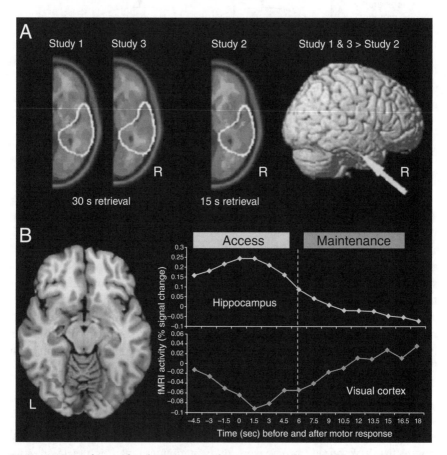

Figure 8.4. Autobiographical memory involves a protracted retrieval length. (A) Longer retrieval times recruited a more right lateralized activity in the middle temporal cortices and led to increased retrieval of episodic autobiographical memories (Graham et al., 2003). Red shading indicates greater activation in the right hemisphere (Studies 1 and 3), and blue shading indicates greater activation in the left hemisphere (Study 2). The temporal lobe is outlined in white. (B) Activity in the hippocampus related to memory access occurs early, whereas visual cortex activity related to maintenance and additional elaboration of memory occurs late (Daselaar et al., 2008).

autobiographical memories. In an fMRI study, Addis, McIntosh et al. (2004) directly examined differences in the time course of activity between generic (repeated auto-biographical memories) and unique (episodic autobiographical memories) events collected in a prescan interview. They found that there were differences in the peak of the time lags, with regions associated with generic autobiographical memories peaking much earlier (2 to 4 s) following the cue to elicit a memory, whereas regions involved in unique autobiographical memories peaked later (6 to 8 s). Thus, generic autobiographical memories were accessed more quickly than unique autobio-graphical memories were. The results of these studies are consistent with theories of autobiographical memory that suggest that semantic autobiographical memory is the preferred level of access during retrieval (e.g., Conway & Pleydell-Pearce, 2000), and that with increasing effort and subsequently longer retrieval times, the retrieval of more specific information leading to an episodic autobiographical memory and richer recollection is more likely (see Figure 8.3). However, there are two important caveats to the assumption that longer retrieval lengths elicit episodic autobiographical memories: (a) Retrieval of episodic autobiographical memories can fail (Barsalou, 1988; Conway, 2005); in which case, longer retrieval lengths would not reliably elicit episodic autobiographical memories. And (b) retrieval of episodic autobiographical memories can occur directly; in which case, a shorter retrieval length would be sufficient.

Whether generative or direct retrieval occurs likely depends on the method used to elicit autobiographical memories (e.g., Table 8.1; for reviews, see Cabeza & St. Jacques, 2007; Maguire, 2001). The generic cue method, which typically requires long trials, likely involves more generative retrieval, whereas other methods, such as the prospective method, which involves more recent memories, or the prescan interview, where memories are initially retrieved prior to scanning, might involve more direct retrieval. For example, in a recent meta-analysis, Svoboda et al. (2006) found that fMRI studies using the prospective method (e.g., Cabeza et al., 2004; Levine et al., 2004) failed to find activity in lateral temporal cortices involved in semantic memory, which they interpreted as evidence for greater direct retrieval processes. In order to precisely examine brain regions that are recruited during successful generative versus direct retrieval it might be necessary to acquire reac-tion time data.

Phases of Autobiographical Memory Retrieval

Several functional neuroimaging studies have sought to segregate the brain regions involved during different phases of autobiographical memory retrieval by using a *self-paced design*, in which participants indicate when a memory is retrieved and then maintain or further elaborate on the memory. The self-paced design has been used primarily to examine generative retrieval. For example, using slow cortical potentials, Conway, Pleydell-Pearce, and Whitecross (2001) found that left PFC regions came online early as participants searched for a cue, whereas posterior temporal and occipital regions came online later during the formation and main-tenance of the retrieved memory (also see Conway, Pleydell-Pearce, Whitecross, &

Sharpe, 2003). Similarly, in an fMRI study, Botzung, Denkova, Ciuciu, Scheiber, and Manning (2008) showed that left PFC peaked earlier than did left MTL regions. Thus, during the initial generative search for a memory, left PFC regions supporting strategic retrieval are involved, whereas when a specific memory is formed and held in mind, posterior regions come online to support the retrieval of specific contextual details.

Although several studies have used the self-paced design (Botzung et al., 2008; Conway et al., 2001; Daselaar et al., 2008; Steinvorth, Corkin, & Halgren, 2006), none have examined the effects of response times to elicit an autobiographical memory. According to models proposed by Conway and colleagues (e.g., Conway & Pleydell-Pearce, 2000), direct retrieval should be associated with shorter retrieval times than those for generative retrieval. Although the generic cue method tends to engage generative retrieval processes, there is considerable variance in the response times necessary to elicit an autobiographical memory. Indeed, participants frequently note that sometimes the memory seemed to appear effortlessly, whereas other times retrieval was more effortful. Future research should address the impact of retrieval speed on the autobiographical memory network.

Given the iterative nature of autobiographical memory, one interesting line of research is to examine the common and unique activations involved during the initial access of an autobiographical memory and the sustained elaboration of that memory. For example, Steinvorth et al. (2006) examined fMRI activity related to search and reminiscence periods and found a common pattern of activity. However, they did not directly compare the activity between these two phases. In contrast, Daselaar et al. (2008) compared activity related to accessing an autobiographical memory to activity related to maintaining and elaborating the memory. They found that the initial access period engaged frontal regions involved in search (ventrolateral-PFC) and self-referential processes (medial PFC), and posterior regions involved in accessing the memory trace (e.g., hippocampus, retrosplenial cortex), whereas the later period recruited regions involved in the retrieval of contextual details (e.g., visual cortices, precuneus; see Figure 8.4B).

Summary of Autobiographical Memory Construction

Autobiographical memory typically involves a protracted retrieval length, especially when the generic cue method is employed, which is an advantage in fMRI studies because it allows the segregation of the time courses of brain regions involved during search, formation, and elaboration. *Search* has been linked to brain regions involved in strategic retrieval that is guided by semantic information (e.g., ventrolateral frontal and temporal cortices), *formation* to accessing the memory trace (e.g., hippocampus), and *elaboration* to posterior brain regions involved in the recovery of contextual details (e.g., precuneus and visual cortices). Furthermore, brain regions supporting the retrieval of episodic autobiographical memories peak much later than those regions supporting retrieval of semantic autobiographical memories, with longer retrieval times tending to elicit episodic autobiographical memories and shorter retrieval times eliciting semantic autobiographical memories. However, some autobiographical memories are formed more quickly via direct retrieval, and might reflect access of the memory trace. In sum, during generative retrieval, longer search periods tend to elicit greater recollection in autobiographical memory studies because episodic autobiographical memories can be accessed; however, future research is needed to examine how the time course of activity might differ in direct retrieval. In particular, dissecting the neural mechanisms underlying autobiographical memory construction may be critical for understanding developmental changes (e.g., St. Jacques, Rubin, & Cabeza, 2010).

PROPERTIES THAT MODULATE RECOLLECTION IN AUTOBIOGRAPHICAL MEMORY

In laboratory memory, recollection can be modulated by the emotion, vividness, and the remoteness associated with retrieved memories, and the same holds for autobiographical memory retrieval (e.g., Dolcos, LaBar, & Cabeza, 2005; Dudukovic & Knowlton, 2006; Wheeler & Buckner, 2004). Functional neuroimaging studies of autobiographical memory allow us to more easily investigate the extremities of each of these properties. Thus, we can examine a very traumatic, vivid memory containing many details, which is decades old. Examining these same aspects in laboratory memory would be very difficult because of ethical and practical issues.

Emotion

Emotion, which varies along the two dimensions of *valence*, from positive to negative, and *arousal*, from calm to excited (Bradley & Lang, 2000), is an important component of autobiographical memory that imparts meaning to the experiences in our lives and can lead to memorable—or even indelible—memories. In laboratory memory, arousal enhances memory via the modulation of memory encoding and consolidation processes in the hippocampus by the amygdala (for reviews, see LaBar & Cabeza, 2006; Phelps, 2004) and may have long-lasting effects (Ritchey, Dolcos, & Cabeza, 2008). A recent study (Botzung, LaBar, Kragel, Miles & Rubin, 2010), which examined the influence of emotion on encoding using naturalistic stimuli (i.e., a basketball game), confirms these findings and suggests that encoding of more complex stimuli involves additional recruitment of visual and social cognitive networks. There is growing evidence that emotional arousal can also influence memory during retrieval (for review, see Buchanan, 2007). For example, Dolcos, LaBar, and Cabeza (2005) found that activity in the amygdala and hippocampus was greater for emotionally arousing stimuli associated with recollection versus familiarity. They suggest that the amygdala and hippocampus involve a "synergistic mechanism in which emotion enhances recollection and recollection enhances emotion" (p. 2631). Thus, it might be difficult to tease apart the effects of emotional arousal on the *process* of retrieval versus the emotional response elicited by the *products* of retrieval (Buchanan, 2007). Emotional valence can also influence memory by increasing attention and controlled processes during encoding mediated by frontal cortices (e.g., Kensinger & Corkin, 2004), but there is less evidence about the effects of valence during retrieval in laboratory memory studies, perhaps because of difficulty in equating the arousal associated with positive and negative memories. Consistent with the influence of emotion on laboratory memory, autobiographical memories that are more arousing (Reisberg, Heuer, McLean, & O'Shaugnessy, 1988; Talarico, LaBar, & Rubin, 2004) or positively valenced (D'Argembeau, Comblain, & Van der Linden, 2003; Destun & Kuiper, 1999; Schaefer & Philippot, 2005) are also more richly recollected. Further, a recent study found that positively valenced autobiographical memories were also more accurate (Botzung, Rubin, Miles, Cabeza, & LaBar, 2010). However, very few studies have directly investigated how the effects of emotion on richly recollecting autobiographical memories are instantiated in the brain (for meta-analysis, see Svoboda et al., 2006), and none have yet to examine the contributions of discrete emotions (e.g., fear, anger, happiness).

Autobiographical memory retrieval is influenced by emotional intensity. For example, Botzung, Rubin, et al. (2010) observed modulation of amygdala and hippocampus by online ratings of emotional intensity associated with retriev-ing complex memory for a basketball game. Similarly, Addis, Moscovtich, et al. (2004) found that the emotional intensity associated with autobiographical memory retrieval modulated activity in the hippocampus, although amygdala activity was not directly observed (also see Maguire & Frith, 2003; St. Jacques, Botzung et al., 2011; Viard et al., 2007). Further, in an fMRI study, Greenberg et al. (2005) found greater amygdala-hippocampal interactions during autobiographi-cal memory compared with semantic memory. Activity in the amygdala was also correlated with activity in right ventrolateral PFC, which might suggest a possible interaction between the emotional response and memory construction. Consistent with this idea, Daselaar et al. (2008) found that emotional intensity influenced amygdala activity during the initial search for a memory, but there was less of an effect here during elaboration or after a memory was retrieved (see Fig-ure 8.5A). They suggested that activity in emotional brain regions should occur relatively early during the retrieval process, if emotions signal appropriate actions (e.g. Leventhal & Scherer, 1987) to guide construction. Emotional autobiographi-cal memories are often associated with a right lateralized or more bilateral pattern of activation compared with the typical left-lateralized pattern (e.g., Denkova, Botzung, Scheiber, & Manning, 2006a; Fink et al., 1996; Markowitsch et al., 2000; Vandekerckhove, Markowitsch, Mertens, & Woermann, 2005), and patients with damage to the right hemisphere recall less emotional autobiographical memories (Cimino, Verfaellie, Bowers, & Heilman, 1991). Furthermore, evidence from patients with damage to the amygdala also suggests that this region is necessary for the recall of emotionally arousing autobiographical memories (Buchanan, Tranel, & Adolphs, 2005, 2006).

The pattern of activity during autobiographical memory retrieval is also influ-enced by emotional valence, with positive and negative autobiographical memories leading to differential activity in subregions of the PFC (e.g., Botzung, Rubin, et al., 2010). For example, in a PET study, Markowitsch, Vandekerckhovel, Lanfermann,

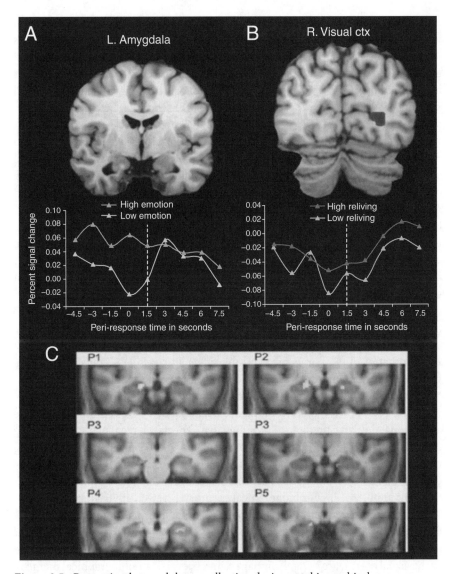

Figure 8.5. Properties that modulate recollection during autobiographical memory retrieval. (A) *Emotion.* Emotional intensity influences amygdala activity during the initial search for an autobiographical memory (Daselaar et al., 2008). (B) *Vividness.* Activity in the visual cortex was positively correlated with subjective ratings of reliving following the formation of an autobiographical memory (Daselaar et al., 2008). (C) *Remoteness.* The hippocampus continues to remain involved in vivid autobiographical memories recruited from recent to remote time periods (Viard et al., 2007). P1 = 0–17 years; P2 = 18–30 years; P3 = >31 years, except for the past 5 years; P4 = past 5 years, except the past 12 months; P5 = past 12 months.

and Russ (2003) asked participants to retrieve happy or sad autobiographical memories associated with high emotional intensity. Sad autobiographical memories led to greater bilateral activity in orbitofrontal cortex (OFC), whereas happy autobiographical memories resulted in greater medial OFC activity. Furthermore, greater left hippocampal activity was found in happy compared with sad autobiographical memories, consistent with behavioral results of greater intensity felt for the happy autobiographical memories, perhaps relying on greater recollection of these memories. Similarly, in a blocked design fMRI study, Piefke, Weiss, Zilles, Markowitsch, and Fink (2003) found that positive memories led to greater activity in medial OFC (also see Keedwell, Andrew, Williams, Brammer, & Phillips, 2005; St. Jacques, Botzung, et al., 2011). Thus, these results point to the importance of the subregions in OFC and medial PFC that are differentially involved in the retrieval of positive autobiographical memories, via medial OFC and ventromedial regions, and negative autobiographical memories, mediated by lateral OFC (e.g., Kuchinke et al., 2006). These results are consistent with the involvement of different OFC subregions in emotional evaluation of valence (for review see Kringelbach & Rolls, 2004), with medial areas involved in reward processing and lateral areas in evaluation of punishers.

Vividness

Autobiographical memories are typically richer in sensorial details or *vividness* than laboratory memories because they are composed of multisensory information (e.g., Rubin, 2006) associated with a complex, three-dimensional environment (for review, see Cabeza & St. Jacques, 2007). Subjective reports of vividness are among the best predictors of subjective reports of recollection or *reliving* (Rubin, Burt, & Fifield, 2003; Rubin & Siegler, 2004), and for distinguishing real versus imagined events (e.g., Johnson, Foley, Suengas, & Raye, 1988). Visuospatial imagery, involving both descriptive imagery and spatial imagery, is particularly important in autobiographical memory (Brewer, 1986; Rubin & Kozin, 1984) and might be a necessary component of autobiographical memory retrieval (for review, see Greenberg & Rubin, 2003). For example, patients with *visual memory-deficit amnesia*, a deficit in visual descriptive memory following damage to the visual cortex, are severely impaired in retrieval of autobiographical memory (Rubin & Greenberg, 1998). Not only are these patients impaired on retrieval of autobiographical memories via visual cues, but they also show deficits in the recall of memories cued via other modalities. Greenberg and Rubin (2003) interpreted these findings by proposing that impairment of visual memory disrupts the entire retrieval process because autobiographical memory retrieval depends upon the interconnection and activation of many separate systems (also see Rubin, 2006). Consistent with these findings, Rubin, Burt, and Fifield (2003) showed that degrading visual input in healthy individuals during the encoding of staged laboratory events, by asking participants to wear blindfolds, impaired some phenomenological aspects of later memory recall.

Turning to spatial imagery, the ability to construct a spatial scene is an essential component of autobiographical memory (e.g., Hassabis & Maguire, 2007), just as the ability to link a memory to a specific spatial location is an integral feature of episodic memory (e.g., Tulving, 1983). Allocentric spatial representations stored in memory have been linked to the MTL, such that patients with damage to the hippocampus were shown to be impaired on spatial memory tasks, whereas egocentric spatial representations that allow for imageable representations are supported by posterior parietal and precuneus cortices, such that patients with lesions to parietal cortices are impaired on viewpoint-dependent spatial imagery tasks (for reviews, see Burgess, Becker, King, & O'Keefe, 2001; Moscovitch et al., 2005). The link between these impairments on spatial tasks and autobiographical memory are readily apparent in patients with damage to the MTL who have amnesia. For example, patient K.C., who has damage to the hippocampus and other MTL regions, has severe loss of both autobiographical memories and the detailed spatial representations of familiar neighborhoods (for review, see Moscovitch et al., 2005). However, there is less evidence regarding the effects of parietal lesions on autobiographical memory, suggesting that the egocentric aspects of spatial imagery in autobiographical memory might be more subtle (e.g., Berryhill et al., 2007).

Functional neuroimaging studies of autobiographical memory have linked visuospatial imagery with activity in visual cortex (cuneus), posterior midline regions (precuneus and parietal cortices), and MTL regions (for review, see Cabeza & St. Jacques, 2007; for meta-analysis, see Svoboda et al., 2006). For example, the retrieval of images from autobiographical memory (*test driving a Honda Civic*) versus specific images (*imagining a Honda Civic*) yielded greater activity in left precuneus, parahippocampal, and bilateral posterior cingulate cortices (Gardini, Cornoldi, De Beni, & Venneri, 2006). Similarly, compared with laboratory memory, autobiographical memory elicited greater activity in cuneus and parahippocampal cortices, as would be expected given the richer sensory details associated with these memories (Cabeza et al., 2004). In combination with other brain regions (e.g., MTL, frontal), visual cortex activity could initiate the vivid sense of reliving associated with remembering the personal past (e.g., Rubin & Kozin, 1984), just as the reactivation of posterior cortices in episodic memory tasks results in vivid remembering (Wheeler, Petersen, & Buckner, 2000). Consistent with this role of the visual cortex in autobiographical memory, in an fMRI study using auditory cues, Daselaar et al. (2008) found that activity in this region was positively correlated with subjective ratings of reliving following the formation of an autobiographical memory (see Figure 8.5B) when participants were maintaining and elaborating further details about the memory (also see Conway et al., 2001). Furthermore, vividness of details can modulate activity in the hippocampus (Addis, Moscovitch, et al., 2004), which is consistent with the strong association between vividness and recollection.

Remoteness

Compared with laboratory memory, there is a considerable temporal range in autobiographical memories from recent (e.g., days) to remote (e.g., decades), and the remoteness of the event might affect how vividly the memory will be recollected. The neural substrates of recent versus remote autobiographical memories have been the focus of many neuroimaging studies, especially with respect to the permanent involvement of the hippocampus (for review, see Cabeza & St. Jacques, 2007). According to the standard consolidation model (Alvarez & Squire, 1994), the hippocampus has a time-limited role in the storage and retrieval of autobiographical memories, such that memories become independent from the hippocampus and dependent on neocortical areas following consolidation. This idea is consistent with evidence from patients with focal lesions in the MTL who demonstrate autobiographical memory loss that is temporally graded in the favor of remote autobiographical memories (for review, see Squire & Bayley, 2007). For example, Bayley et al. (2003) asked patients with MTL damage and healthy control subjects to recall remote autobiographical memories (i.e., decades old) and coded these memories with respect to the number of details. They found that patients were able to retrieve detailed remote autobiographical memories that were on par with the control subjects. In contrast, multiple trace theory (MTT, Nadel & Moscovitch, 1997) posits a permanent role for the hippocampus in the retrieval of memories that are detailed and vivid. Consistent with MTT, emerging evidence from patients with hippocampal damage suggests that the impairment in the ability to reexperience autobiographical memories from across the lifespan is greater than was previously found (for review, see Moscovitch et al., 2005). For example, Steinvorth et al. (2005) asked patients with bilateral MTL to recall autobiographical memories, and they used a more sensitive coding scheme that included specific prompts to examine the full potential of retrieval. Consistent with MTT, they found no temporal gradient in the autobiographical memory impairment, although both patients performed normally on semantic memory.

Although these issues continue to be strongly debated within the neuropsychological literature, especially with respect to the locus and extent of MTL damage, neuroimaging studies of autobiographical memory provide the opportunity to examine these issues in healthy individuals. Each theory makes a clear hypothesis regarding the sensitivity of the hippocampus to the remoteness of the memory. Standard consolidation model predicts that recent memories should involve greater hippocampal activation than remote ones, whereas MTT predicts no differences in hippocampal activation between recent and remote memories that are detailed and vivid. In this respect, several of the neuroimaging studies of autobiographical memory are more consistent with MTT (Addis, Moscovitch, et al., 2004; Conway et al., 1999; Gilboa et al., 2004; Maguire & Frith, 2003; Maguire et al., 2001; Piefke et al., 2003; Piolino et al., 2004; Rekkas & Constable, 2005; Ryan et al., 2001; Steinvorth et al., 2006; Tsukiura et al., 2002; but see Niki & Luo, 2002; Piefke et al., 2003). For example, Viard et al. (2007) asked older adults to recall episodic autobiographical memories from across the entire lifespan, which did not differ on objective ratings of detail. They found that the left hippocampus was recruited for all time periods (see Figure 8.5C), with additional right hippocampus activity coming online to support some time periods where autobiographical memories received higher subjective ratings (i.e., mental imagery). Consistent with MTT,

Viard et al. (2007) suggest that the left hippocampus is always necessary to retrieve vividly recollected autobiographical memories, and once some threshold of recollection is reached, variability in the richness of memories could recruit additional activity in the right hippocampus. However, functional neuroimaging studies cannot determine the necessity of the hippocampus in autobiographical memory retrieval for remote memories. Furthermore, hippocampal activation is affected by the method used to elicit an autobiographical memory as well as other memory dimensions (e.g., vividness), and these factors are not always controlled (for review, see Cabeza & St. Jacques, 2007).

In addition to the hippocampus, other core regions in the autobiographical memory network are sensitive to the remoteness of the memory. The most consistent finding is greater activation in the retrosplenial cortex for recent versus remote autobiographical memories (for review, see Moscovitch et al., 2005). Retrosplenial cortex has dense reciprocal connections with the hippocampus, which might interface with dorsolateral PFC (e.g., Kobayashi & Amaral, 2003), and damage to this region can cause "retrosplenial amnesia" (e.g., Valenstein et al., 1987), but the function of retrosplenial cortex in memory is not clear. The role of retrosplenial cortex in more recent autobiographical memories has been linked to several factors including the construction of generic visual representations and retrieval of personally familiar information (Gilboa et al., 2004), emotional processing (Piefke et al., 2003), and vividness (although see Gilboa et al., 2004; Steinvorth et al., 2006). Greater activity in retrosplenial cortex for recent autobiographical memories could also reflect increased recollection, consistent with some laboratory memory studies (e.g., Daselaar, Fleck, & Cabeza, 2006). PFC regions were also found to be sensitive to the age of autobiographical memories. However, results here have been more variable, with some studies showing greater PFC activity for recent autobiographical memories (Maguire et al., 2001; Piolino et al., 2004), and other studies showing greater PFC activity for remote autobiographical memories (Steinvorth et al., 2006). Moreover, there is evidence that different PFC regions are activated depending on the age of the autobiographical memories (Niki & Luo, 2002; Rekkas & Constable, 2005). Inconsistency in PFC activity could reflect variability in the ease of autobiographical memory retrieval, as activity here would be expected to increase for more difficult retrieval conditions or, alternatively, greater integration between the memory trace and cue specification (e.g., Maguire et al., 2001).

Summary of Properties that Modulate Recollection in Autobiographical Memory

Autobiographical memories are ideal for investigating the contribution of properties that modulate the neural correlates of recollection because they often involve rich emotional content and vivid sensory details. Furthermore, one strength of autobiographical memory is that it enables the study of the neural correlates of remote memories, which cannot be created in the laboratory, versus recent memories, which is a crucial issue for current models of memory consolidation. Emotional autobiographical memories are associated with activity in the amygdala and subregions of the OFC, whereas vividness is associated with visual cortex activity. Although functional neuroimaging evidence is missing, autobiographical memories that involve strong auditory, tactile, or taste sensations should also involve activity in the corresponding sensory regions. Emotion and vividness have also been associated with increased activity in the hippocampus, a region that might continue to be involved in the recollection of remote autobiographical memories.

CONCLUSIONS

The results of functional neuroimaging studies of autobiographical memory provide us with the opportunity to consider how recollection of our personal past compares with recollection of simple laboratory memory stimuli. First, the integration of episodic and semantic memory in autobiographical memory suggests that autobiographical memory retrieval is not synonymous with recollection, but can vary according to the type of autobiographical memory elicited. Furthermore, the rich recollection associated with some autobiographical memories challenges us to consider how current retrieval models can account for more or less recollection. Second, the construction of autobiographical memories typically involves a protracted length that allows the examination of the multiple retrieval components involved in recollection. Generative retrieval of autobiographical memories requires longer retrieval times to recover the contextual details associated with recollection, but whether this is also true for direct retrieval of autobiographical memories has yet to be examined. Third, several of the properties that modulate recollection, such as emotion, vividness, and remoteness, occur at their extremities in autobiographical memory. The results of these studies suggest that the hippocampus has a critical role in mediating the recovery of a richly recollected past. Current studies have established that functional neuroimaging of autobiographical memory can answer important questions regarding the neural correlates of recollection. The challenge for future studies will be to develop new techniques for examining autobiographical memories in the scanner that can answer multifaceted questions concerning where these components interact.

ACKNOWLEDGMENT

This research was supported by a National Institute on Aging grants AG023123 and AG23770 awarded to R.C.

REFERENCES

Addis, D. R., McIntosh, A. R., Moscovitch, M., Crawley, A. P., & McAndrews, M. P. (2004). Characterizing spatial and temporal features of autobiographical memory retrieval networks: A partial least squares approach. *Neuroimage, 23*, 1460–71.

Addis, D. R., Moscovitch, M., Crawley, A. P., & McAndrews, M. P. (2004). Recollective qualities modulate hippocampal activation during autobiographical memory retrieval. *Hippocampus, 14,* 752–62.

Alvarez, P., & Squire, L. R. (1994). Memory consolidation and the medial temporal lobe: A simple network model. *Proceedings of the National Academy of Sciences of the United States of America, 91,* 7041–45.

Barsalou, L. W. (1988). The content and organization of autobiographical memories. In U. Neisser & E. Winograd (Eds.), *Remembering reconsidered: Ecological and traditional approaches to memory* (pp. 193–243). Cambridge: Cambridge University Press.

Bartlett, F. C. (1932). *Remembering.* Cambridge: Cambridge University Press.

Bayley, P. J., Gold, J. J., Hopkins, R. O., & Squire, L. R. (2005). The neuroanatomy of remote memory. *Neuron, 46,* 799–810.

Bayley, P. J., Hopkins, R. O., & Squire, L. R. (2003). Successful recollection of remote autobiographical memories by amnesic patients with medial temporal lobe lesions. *Neuron, 38,* 135–44.

Berntsen, D. (2007). Involuntary autobiographical memories: Speculations, findings and an attempt to integrate them. In J. Mace (Ed.), *Involuntary memory* (pp. 20–49). Malden, MA: Blackwell.

Berntsen, D., & Rubin, D. C. (2004). Cultural life scripts structure recall from autobiographical memory. *Memory & Cognition, 32,* 427–42.

Berry, E., Kapur, N., Williams, L., Hodges, S., Watson, P., Smyth, G., . . . Wood. K. (2007). The use of a wearable camera, SenseCam, as a pictorial diary to improve autobiographical memory in a patient with limbic encephalitis: A preliminary report. *Neuropsychological Rehabilitation, 17,* 582–601.

Berryhill, M. E., Phuong, L., Picasso, L., Cabeza, R., & Olson, I. R. (2007). Parietal lobe and episodic memory: Bilateral damage causes impaired free recall of autobiographical memory. *Journal of Neuroscience, 27,* 14415–23.

Botzung, A., Denkova, E., Ciuciu, P., Scheiber, C., & Manning, L. (2008). The neural bases of the constructive nature of autobiographical memories studied with a self-paced fMRI design. *Memory, 16,* 351–63.

Botzung, A., Rubin, D. C., Miles, A., Cabeza, R., & Labar, K. S. (2010). Mental hoop diaries: Emotional memories of a college basketball game in rival fans. *Journal of Neuroscience, 30,* 2130–37.

Botzung, A., Labar, K. S., Kragel, P., Miles, A., & Rubin, D. C. (2010). Component neural systems for the creation of emotional memories during free viewing of a complex, real-world event. *Frontiers in Human Neuroscience, 4,* Article 34, 1–10.

Bradley, M. M., & Lang, P. J. (2000). Measuring emotion: Behavior, feeling, and physiology. In R. Lane & L. Nadel (Eds.), *Cognitive neuroscience of emotion* (pp. 242–76). New York: Oxford University Press.

Brewer, W. F. (1986). What is autobiographical memory? In D. C. Rubin (Ed.), *Autobiographical memory* (pp. 25–49). New York: Cambridge University Press.

Brewer, W. F. (1995). What is recollective memory? In D. C. Rubin (Ed.), *Remembering our past: Studies in autobiographical memory* (pp. 19–66). New York: Cambridge University Press.

Buchanan, T. W. (2007). Retrieval of emotional memories. *Psychological Bullettin, 133,* 761–79.

Buchanan, T. W., Tranel, D., & Adolphs, R. (2005). Emotional autobiographical memories in amnesic patients with medial temporal lobe damage. *Journal of Neuroscience*, 25, 3151–60.

Buchanan, T. W., Tranel, D., & Adolphs, R. (2006). Memories for emotional autobiographical events following unilateral damage to medial temporal lobe. *Brain, 129*, 115–27.

Buckner, R. L., & Carroll, D. C. (2007). Self-projection and the brain. *Trends in Cognitive Science, 11*, 49–57.

Buckner, R. L., & Wheeler, M. E. (2001). The cognitive neuroscience of remembering. *Nature Review Neuroscience, 2*, 624–34.

Burgess, N., Becker, S., King, J. A., & O'Keefe, J. (2001). Memory for events and their spatial context: models and experiments. *Philosophical Transactions of the Royal Society of London. Series B: Biological Sciences, 356*, 1493–503.

Burianova, H., & Grady, C. L. (2007). Common and unique neural activations in autobiographical, episodic, and semantic retrieval. *Journal of Cognitive Neuroscience, 19*, 1520–34.

Burianova, H., McIntosh, A. R., & Grady, C. L. (2010). A common functional brain network for autobiographical, episodic, and semantic memory retrieval. *Neuroimage, 49*, 865–74.

Burt, C. D., Kemp, S., & Conway, M. A. (2003). Themes, events, and episodes in autobiographical memory. *Memory and Cognition, 31*, 317–25.

Cabeza, R. (2008). Role of parietal regions in episodic memory retrieval: The dual attentional processes hypothesis. *Neuropsychologia, 46*, 1813–27.

Cabeza, R., Ciaramelli, E., Olson, I., & Moscovitch, M. (2008). The parietal cortex and episodic memory: An attentional account. *Nature Reviews Neuroscience, 9*, 613–25.

Cabeza, R., & Nyberg, L. (2000). Imaging cognition II: An empirical review of 275 PET and fMRI studies. *Journal of Cognitive Neuroscience, 12*, 1–47.

Cabeza, R., Prince, S. E., Daselaar, S. M., Greenberg, D. L., Budde, M., Dolcos, F., . . . Rubin, D. C. (2004). Brain activity during episodic retrieval of autobiographical and laboratory events: An fMRI study using a novel photo paradigm. *Journal of Cognitive Neuroscience, 16*, 1583–94.

Cabeza, R., & St. Jacques, P. (2007). Functional neuroimaging of autobiographical memory. *Trends in Cognitive Science, 11*, 219–27.

Ciaramelli, E., Grady, C. L., & Moscovitch, M. (2008). Top-down and bottom-up attention to memory: A hypothesis (AtoM) on the role of the posterior parietal cortex in memory retrieval. *Neuropsychologia, 46*, 1828–51.

Cimino, C. R., Verfaellie, M., Bowers, D., & Heilman, K. M. (1991). Autobiographical memory: Influence of right hemisphere damage on emotionality and specificity. *Brain and Cognition, 15*, 106–18.

Conway, M. A. (1990). *Autobiographical memory: An introduction*. Milton Keynes, UK: Open University Press.

Conway, M. A. (2005). Memory and the self. *Journal of Memory and Language, 53*, 594–628.

Conway, M. A., & Bekerian, D. A. (1987). Organization in autobiographical memory. *Memory and Cognition, 15*, 119–32.

Conway, M. A., & Pleydell-Pearce, C. W. (2000). The construction of autobiographical memories in the self-memory system. *Psychological Review, 107*, 261–88.

Conway, M. A., Pleydell-Pearce, C. W., & Whitecross, S. E. (2001). The neuroanatomy of autobiographical memory: A slow wave cortical potential study of autobiographical memory. *Journal of Memory & Language, 45*, 493–524.

Conway, M. A., Pleydell-Pearce, C. W., Whitecross, S. E., & Sharpe, H. (2003). Neurophysiological correlates of memory for experienced and imagined events. *Neuropsychologia, 41*, 334–40.

Conway, M. A., Turk, D. J., Miller, S. L., Logan, J., Nebes, R. D., Meltzer, C. C., & Becker, J. T. (1999). A positron emission tomography (PET) study of autobiographical memory retrieval. *Memory, 7*, 679–702.

Craik, F., Moroz, T., Moscovitch, M., Stuss, D., Winocur, G., Tulving, E., & Kapur, S. (1999). In search of self: A positron emission tomography study. *Psychological Science, 1*, 26–34.

Crovitz, H. F., & Schiffman, S. (1974). Frequency of episodic memories as a function of their age. *Bulletin of the Psychonomic Society, 4*, 517–51.

D'Argembeau, A., Comblain, C., & Van der Linden, M. (2003). Phenomenal characteristics of autobiographical memories for positive, negative, and neutral events. *Applied Cognitive Psychology, 17*, 281–94.

Daselaar, S. M., Fleck, M. S., & Cabeza, R. (2006). Triple dissociation in the medial temporal lobes: Recollection, familiarity, and novelty. *Journal of Neurophysiology, 96*, 1902–11.

Daselaar, S. M., Rice, H. J., Greenberg, D. L., Cabeza, R., LaBar, K. S., & Rubin, D. C. (2008). The spatiotemporal dynamics of autobiographical memory: Neural correlates of recall, emotional intensity, and reliving. *Cerebral Cortex, 18*, 217–29.

Davidson, P., Anaki, D., Ciaramelli, E., Cohn, M., Kim, A., Murphy, K., . . . Levine, B. (2008). Does lateral parietal cortex support episodic memory? Evidence from focal lesion patients. *Neuropsychologia, 46*, 1743–55.

Denkova, E., Botzung, A., Scheiber, C., & Manning, L. (2006a). Implicit emotion during recollection of past events: A nonverbal fMRI study. *Brain Research, 1078*, 143–50.

Denkova, E., Botzung, A., Scheiber, C., & Manning, L. (2006b). Material-independent cerebral network of re-experiencing personal events: Evidence from two parallel fMRI experiments. *Neuroscience Letters, 407*, 32–6.

Destun, L. M., & Kuiper, N. A. (1999). Phenomenal characteristics associated with real and imagined events: The effects of event valence and absorption. *Applied Cognitive Psychology, 13*, 175–86.

Diana, R. A., Yonelinas, A. P., & Ranganath, C. (2007). Imaging recollection and familiarity in the medial temporal lobe: A three-component model. *Trends in Cognitive Science, 11*, 379–86.

Dolcos, F., LaBar, K. S., & Cabeza, R. (2005). Remembering one year later: Role of the amygdala and the medial temporal lobe memory system in retrieving emotional memories. *Proceedings of the National Academy of Science U S A, 102*, 2626–31.

Duarte, A., Ranganath, C., & Knight, R. T. (2005). Effects of unilateral prefrontal lesions on familiarity, recollection, and source memory. *Journal of Neuroscience, 25*, 8333–7.

Dudukovic, N. M., & Knowlton, B. J. (2006). Remember-know judgments and retrieval of contextual details. *Acta Psychologica, 122*, 160–73.

Fink, G. R., Markowitsch, H. J., Reinkemeier, M., Bruckbauer, T., Kessler, J., & Heiss, W. D. (1996). Cerebral representation of one's own past: Neural networks involved in autobiographical memory. *Journal of Neuroscience, 16*, 4275–82.

Gallagher, H. L., & Frith, C. D. (2003). Functional imaging of "theory of mind." *Trends in Cognitive Science, 7,* 77–83.

Gardini, S., Cornoldi, C., De Beni, R., & Venneri, A. (2006). Left mediotemporal structures mediate the retrieval of episodic autobiographical mental images. *Neuroimage, 30,* 645–55.

Gilboa, A. (2004). Autobiographical and episodic memory—one and the same? Evidence from prefrontal activation in neuroimaging studies. *Neuropsychologia, 42,* 1336–49.

Gilboa, A., Winocur, G., Grady, C. L., Hevenor, S. J., & Moscovitch, M. (2004). Remembering our past: Functional neuroanatomy of recollection of recent and very remote personal events. *Cerebral Cortex, 14,* 1214–25.

Graham, K. S., Lee, A. C., Brett, M., & Patterson, K. (2003). The neural basis of autobiographical and semantic memory: New evidence from three PET studies. *Cognitive, Affective, & Behavioral Neuroscience, 3,* 234–54.

Greenberg, D. L., Rice, H. J., Cooper, J. J., Cabeza, R., Rubin, D. C., & LaBar, K. S. (2005). Co-activation of the amygdala, hippocampus and inferior frontal gyrus during autobiographical memory retrieval. *Neuropsychologia, 43,* 659–74.

Greenberg, D. L., & Rubin, D. C. (2003). The neuropsychology of autobiographical memory. *Cortex, 39,* 687–728.

Hassabis, D., & Maguire, E. A. (2007). Deconstructing episodic memory with construction. *Trends in Cognitive Science, 11,* 299–306.

Howe, M. (2003). Memories from the cradle. *Current Directions in Psychological Science, 12,* 62–65.

Johnson, M. K., Foley, M. A., Suengas, A. G., & Raye, C. L. (1988). Phenomenal characteristics of memories for perceived and imagined autobiographical events. *Journal of Experimental Psychology: General, 117,* 371–76.

Johnson, S. C., Baxter, L. C., Wilder, L. S., Pipe, J. G., Heiserman, J. E., & Prigatano, G. P. (2002). Neural correlates of self-reflection. *Brain, 125,* 1808–14.

Keedwell, P. A., Andrew, C., Williams, S. C., Brammer, M. J., & Phillips, M. L. (2005). A double dissociation of ventromedial prefrontal cortical responses to sad and happy stimuli in depressed and healthy individuals. *Biological Psychiatry, 58,* 495–503.

Kelley, W. M., Macrae, C. N., Wyland, C. L., Caglar, S., Inati, S., & Heatherton, T. F. (2002). Finding the self? An event-related fMRI study. *Journal of Cognitive Neuroscience, 14,* 785–94.

Kensinger, E. A., & Corkin, S. (2004). Two routes to emotional memory: Distinct neural processes for valence and arousal. *Proceedings of the National Academy of Sciences of the United States of America, 101,* 3310–5.

Kobayashi, Y., & Amaral, D. G. (2003). Macaque monkey retrosplenial cortex: II. Cortical afferents. *Journal of Comparative Neurology, 466,* 48–79.

Kringelbach, M. L., & Rolls, E. T. (2004). The functional neuroanatomy of the human orbitofrontal cortex: Evidence from neuroimaging and neuropsychology. *Progress in Neurobiology, 72,* 341–72.

Kuchinke, L., Jacobs, A. M., Vo, M. L., Conrad, M., Grubich, C., & Herrmann, M. (2006). Modulation of prefrontal cortex activation by emotional words in recognition memory. *Neuroreport, 17,* 1037–41.

LaBar, K. S., & Cabeza, R. (2006). Cognitive neuroscience of emotional memory. *Nature Review Neuroscience, 7,* 54–64.

Larsen, S. F. (1992). Personal context in autobiographical and narrative memories. In M. A. Conway, D. C. Rubin, H. Spinnler & W. A. Wagenaar (Eds.), *Theoretical perspectives on autobiographical memory* (pp. 53–71). Norwell, MA: Kluver Academics.

Leventhal, H., & Scherer, K. (1987). The relationship of emotion to cognition: A functional approach to a semantic controversy. *Cognition and Emotion*, 1, 3–28.

Levine, B. (2004). Autobiographical memory and the self in time: Brain lesion effects, functional neuroanatomy, and lifespan development. *Brain and Cognition*, 55, 54–68.

Levine, B., Svoboda, E., Hay, J. F., Winocur, G., & Moscovitch, M. (2002). Aging and autobiographical memory: Dissociating episodic from semantic retrieval. *Psychology and Aging*, 17, 677–89.

Levine, B., Turner, G. R., Tisserand, D., Hevenor, S. J., Graham, S. J., & McIntosh, A. R. (2004). The functional neuroanatomy of episodic and semantic autobiographical remembering: A prospective functional MRI study. *Journal of Cognitive Neuroscience*, 16, 1633–46.

Linton, M. (1986). Ways of searching and the contents of memory. In D. C. Rubin (Ed.), *Autobiographical memory* (pp. 50–67). New York: Cambridge University Press.

Macrae, C. N., Moran, J. M., Heatherton, T. F., Banfield, J. F., & Kelley, W. M. (2004). Medial prefrontal activity predicts memory for self. *Cerebral Cortex*, 14, 647–54.

Maguire, E. A. (2001). Neuroimaging studies of autobiographical event memory. *Philosophical Transactions of the Royal Society of London. Series B: Biological Sciences*, 356, 1441–51.

Maguire, E. A., & Frith, C. D. (2003). Lateral asymmetry in the hippocampal response to the remoteness of autobiographical memories. *Journal of Neuroscience*, 23, 5302–7.

Maguire, E. A., Henson, R. N., Mummery, C. J., & Frith, C. D. (2001). Activity in prefrontal cortex, not hippocampus, varies parametrically with the increasing remoteness of memories. *Neuroreport*, 12, 441–4.

Maguire, E. A., & Mummery, C. J. (1999). Differential modulation of a common memory retrieval network revealed by positron emission tomography. *Hippocampus*, 9, 54–61.

Markowitsch, H. J., Thiel, A., Reinkemeier, M., Kessler, J., Koyuncu, A., & Heiss, W. D. (2000). Right amygdalar and temporofrontal activation during autobiographic, but not during fictitious memory retrieval. *Behavioural Neurology*, 12(4), 181–90.

Markowitsch, H. J., Vandekerckhovel, M. M., Lanfermann, H., & Russ, M. O. (2003). Engagement of lateral and medial prefrontal areas in the ecphory of sad and happy autobiographical memories. *Cortex*, 39, 643–65.

McDermott, K.B., Szpunar, K.K., & Christ, S.E. (2009). Laboratory-based and autobiographical retrieval tasks differ substantially in their neural substrates. *Neuropsychologia*, 2290–98.

Moscovitch, M., Rosenbaum, R. S., Gilboa, A., Addis, D. R., Westmacott, R., Grady, C., . . . Nadel, L. (2005). Functional neuroanatomy of remote episodic, semantic and spatial memory: A unified account based on multiple trace theory. *Journal of Anatomy*, 207, 35–66.

Moscovitch, M., & Winocur, G. (2002). The frontal cortex and working with memory. In D. T. Stuss & R. T. Knight (Eds.), *Principles of frontal lobe function* (pp. 188–209). London: Oxford University Press.

Nadel, L., & Moscovitch, M. (1997). Memory consolidation, retrograde amnesia and the hippocampal complex. *Current Opinion in Neurobiology*, 7, 217–27.

Niki, K., & Luo, J. (2002). An fMRI study on the time-limited role of the medial temporal lobe in long-term topographical autobiographic memory. *Journal of Cognitive Neuroscience*, *14*, 500–7.

Phelps, E. A. (2004). Human emotion and memory: Interactions of the amygdala and hippocampal complex. *Current Opinion in Neurobiology*, *14*, 198–202.

Piefke, M., Weiss, P. H., Zilles, K., Markowitsch, H. J., & Fink, G. R. (2003). Differential remoteness and emotional tone modulate the neural correlates of autobiographical memory. *Brain*, *126*, 650–68.

Piolino, P., Desgranges, B., Belliard, S., Matuszewski, V., Lalevee, C., De la Sayette, V., & Eustache, F. (2003). Autobiographical memory and autonoetic consciousness: Triple dissociation in neurodegenerative diseases. *Brain*, *126*, 2203–19.

Piolino, P., Giffard-Quillon, G., Desgranges, B., Chetelat, G., Baron, J. C., & Eustache, F. (2004). Re-experiencing old memories via hippocampus: A PET study of autobiographical memory. *Neuroimage*, *22*, 1371–83.

Reisberg, D., Heuer, F., McLean, J., & O'Shaugnessy, M. (1988). The quantity, not the quality, of affect predicts memory vividness. *Bulletin of the Psychonomic Society*, *26*, 100–3.

Rekkas, P. V., & Constable, R. T. (2005). Evidence that autobiographic memory retrieval does not become independent of the hippocampus: An fMRI study contrasting very recent with remote events. *Journal of Cognitive Neuroscience*, *17*, 1950–61.

Ritchey, M., Dolcos, F., & Cabeza, R. (2008). Role of amygdala connectivity in the persistence of emotional memories over time: An event-related fMRI investigation. *Cerebral Cortex*, *18*, 2494–2504.

Rubin, D. C. (2006). The basic-systems model of episodic memory. *Perspectives in Psychological Science*, *1*, 277–311.

Rubin, D. C., Burt, C. D., & Fifield, S. J. (2003). Experimental manipulations of the phenomenology of memory. *Memory and Cognition*, *31*, 877–86.

Rubin, D. C., & Greenberg, D. L. (1998). Visual memory-deficit amnesia: A distinct amnesic presentation and etiology. *Proceedings of the National Academy of Science U S A*, *95*, 5413–6.

Rubin, D. C., & Kozin, M. (1984). Vivid memories. *Cognition*, *16*, 81–95.

Rubin, D. C., & Siegler, I. C. (2004). Facets of personality and the phenomenology of autobiographical memory. *Applied Cognitive Psychology*, *18*, 913–30.

Rugg, M. D., & Yonelinas, A. P. (2003). Human recognition memory: A cognitive neuroscience perspective. *Trends in Cognitive Science*, *7*, 313–9.

Ryan, L., Cox, C., Hayes, S. M., & Nadel, L. (2008). Hippocampal activation during episodic and semantic memory retrieval: Comparing category production and category cued recall. *Neuropsychologia*, *46*, 2109–21.

Ryan, L., Nadel, L., Keil, K., Putnam, K., Schnyer, D., Trouard, T., & Moscovitch, M. (2001). Hippocampal complex and retrieval of recent and very remote autobiographical memories: Evidence from functional magnetic resonance imaging in neurologically intact people. *Hippocampus*, *11*, 707–14.

Schacter, D. L., Addis, D. R., & Buckner, R. L. (2007). Remembering the past to imagine the future: The prospective brain. *Nature Review Neuroscience*, *8*, 657–61.

Schaefer, A., & Philippot, P. (2005). Selective effects of emotion on the phenomenal characteristics of autobiographical memories. *Memory*, *13*, 148–60.

Schooler, J. W., & Herrmann, D. J. (1992). There is more to episodic memory than just episodes. In M. A. Conway, D. C. Rubin, H. Spinnler, & W. A. Wagenaar (Eds.),

Theoretical perspectives on autobiographical memory (pp. 241–61). Norwell, MA: Kluver Academics.

Simons, J. S., Owen, A. M., Fletcher, P. C., & Burgess, P. W. (2005). Anterior prefrontal cortex and the recollection of contextual information. *Neuropsychologia, 43*, 1774–83.

Snowden, J. S., Griffiths, H. L., & Neary, D. (1994). Semantic dementia: Autobiographical contribution to preservation of meaning. *Cognitive Neuropsychology, 11*, 265–88.

Snowden, J. S., Griffiths, H. L., & Neary, D. (1995). Autobiographical experience and word meaning. *Memory, 3*, 225–46.

Snowden, J. S., Griffiths, H. L., & Neary, D. (1996). Semantic–episodic memory interactions in semantic dementia: Implications for retrograde memory function. *Cognitive Neuropsychology, 13*, 1101–37.

Squire, L. R., & Bayley, P. J. (2007). The neuroscience of remote memory. *Current Opinion in Neurobiology, 17*, 185–96.

St. Jacques, P. L., Botzung, A., Miles, A., & Rubin, D. C. (2011). Functional neuroimaging of emotionally intense autobiographical memories in post-traumatic stress disorder. *Journal of Psychiatric Research, 45*, 630–7.

St. Jacques, P. L., Conway M. A., Lowder M., & Cabeza R. (2011). Watching my mind unfold versus yours: An fMRI study using a novel camera technology to examine the neural correlates of self-projection of self versus other. *Journal of Cognitive Neuroscience, 23*, 1275–84.

St. Jacques, P. L., Conway, M. A., & Cabeza, R. (2010). Gender differences in autobiographical memory for everyday events: Retrieval elicited by SenseCam images versus verbal cues, *Memory*, DOI:10.1080/09658211.2010.516266.

St. Jacques, P. L., Rubin, D. C., & Cabeza R. (2010). Age-related effects on the neural correlates of autobiographical memory retrieval, *Neurobiology of Aging*, DOI:10.1016/j. neurobiolaging.2010.11.007.

St. Jacques, P. L., Rubin, D. C., Labar, K. S., & Cabeza, R. (2008). The short and long of it: Neural correlates of temporal-order memory for autobiographical events. *Journal of Cognitive Neuroscience, 20*, 1327–41.

Steinvorth, S., Corkin, S., & Halgren, E. (2006). Ecphory of autobiographical memories: An fMRI study of recent and remote memory retrieval. *Neuroimage*, 285–98.

Steinvorth, S., Levine, B., & Corkin, S. (2005). Medial temporal lobe structures are needed to re-experience remote autobiographical memories: Evidence from H.M. and W.R. *Neuropsychologia, 43*, 479–96.

Svoboda, E., McKinnon, M. C., & Levine, B. (2006). The functional neuroanatomy of autobiographical memory: A meta-analysis. *Neuropsychologia, 44*, 2189–208.

Talarico, J. M., LaBar, K. S., & Rubin, D. C. (2004). Emotional intensity predicts autobiographical memory experience. *Memory and Cognition, 32*, 1118–32.

Tsukiura, T., Fujii, T., Okuda, J., Ohtake, H., Kawashima, R., Itoh, M., . . . Yamadori, A. (2002). Time-dependent contribution of the hippocampal complex when remembering the past: A PET study. *Neuroreport, 13*, 2319–23.

Tulving, E. (1972). Episodic and semantic memory. In E. Tulving & W. Donaldson (Eds.), *Organization of memory* (pp. 381–403). New York: Academic Press.

Tulving, E. (1983). *Elements of memory*. Oxford: Clarendon Press.

Tulving, E. (1985). Memory and consciousness. *Canadian Psychology, 26*, 1–12.

Valenstein, E., Bowers, D., Verfaellie, M., Heilman, K. M., Day, A., & Watson, R. T. (1987). Retrosplenial amnesia. *Brain, 110*, 1631–46.

Vandekerckhove, M. M., Markowitsch, H. J., Mertens, M., & Woermann, F. G. (2005). Bi-hemispheric engagement in the retrieval of autobiographical episodes. *Behavioural Neurology, 16,* 203–10.

Viard, A., Piolino, P., Desgranges, B., Chetelat, G., Lebreton, K., Landeau, B., . . . Eustache, F. (2007). Hippocampal activation for autobiographical memories over the entire lifetime in healthy aged subjects: An fMRI study. *Cerebral Cortex, 17,* 2453–67.

Wagner, A. D., Shannon, B. J., Kahn, I., & Buckner, R. L. (2005). Parietal lobe contributions to episodic memory retrieval. *Trends in Cognitive Science, 9,* 445–53.

Westmacott, R., Leach, L., Freedman, M., & Moscovitch, M. (2001). Different patterns of autobiographical memory loss in semantic dementia and medial temporal lobe amnesia: A challenge to consolidation theory. *Neurocase, 7,* 37–55.

Wheeler, M. A., & Stuss, D. T. (2003). Remembering and knowing in patients with frontal lobe injuries. *Cortex, 39,* 827–46.

Wheeler, M. A., Stuss, D. T., & Tulving, E. (1997). Toward a theory of episodic memory: The frontal lobes and autonoetic consciousness. *Psychological Bulletin, 121,* 331–54.

Wheeler, M. E., & Buckner, R. L. (2004). Functional-anatomic correlates of remembering and knowing. *Neuroimage, 21,* 1337–49.

Wheeler, M. E., Petersen, S. E., & Buckner, R. L. (2000). Memory's echo: Vivid remembering reactivates sensory-specific cortex. *Proceedings of the National Academy of Sciences of the United States of America, 97,* 11125–9.

9

Development of Remembering

Brain Development and Neuroimaging Evidence

KATHLEEN M. THOMAS AND LYRIC JORGENSON

The ability to recollect past experiences and events is an essential part of human cognitive and social behavior. Memory for prior experience, whether consciously recollected or not, forms the basis for future learning, and is essential in building a personal knowledge base about the world around us. Even one's sense of self is based in part on memory for life experiences accrued at earlier ages. Previous chapters in this volume have already illuminated the many developmental changes in memory or recollection that occur from infancy and early childhood through adulthood, as well as the brain bases of recollection in adults. In this chapter, we explore the role of brain development in the development of recollection. Our discussion has three main goals. First, we review the basic neurobiology of physical brain development, including primary events in prenatal and early post-natal brain development, as well as developmental processes that continue into later childhood, adolescence, and adulthood. Second, we review animal studies and human neuroimaging studies, addressing the structural development of regions previously associated with mature memory functions. Finally, we review the relatively small but burgeoning literature using functional neuroimaging methods to examine developmental changes in the functioning of brain systems underlying memory across childhood and adolescence. It is our hope that this review will provide the reader with an overview of the existing knowledge base concerning the structural and functional development of memory systems across infancy and childhood.

THE NEUROBIOLOGY OF BRAIN DEVELOPMENT

The onset of human brain development occurs approximately 2 to 3 weeks post-conception with the processes of *neural induction* and *neurulation* (Lumsden &

Kintner, 2003). These steps comprise the transformation of undifferentiated tissue in the outer layer of the embryo (ectoderm) into nervous system tissue, and the further differentiation of brain tissue from spinal cord. Perhaps the most familiar aspect of brain development for psychologists or even the lay public is the formation of the *neural tube* beginning around gestational day 18. The ectoderm thickens, forming the *neural plate*. This plate of cells begins to cave inward forming a longitudinal groove, and the edges of this groove rise upward and inward to form a tube (Keith, 1948). The tube fuses first in the middle and then continues to fuse outward to either end (Sidman & Rakic, 1982). It is this neural tube that forms the central nervous system, with the brain forming at the rostral end, and the spinal cord at the caudal end. The birth defects resulting from disruptions at this stage in development have been well-documented, including *craniorachischisis* (complete failure of neural tube closure), *anencephaly* (failure of the rostral end to close), and most commonly, *myelomeningocele* or *spina bifida* (failure of the caudal end to close) (Volpe, 1995). These processes of neurulation are dependent on a complex cascade of gene transcription factors (e.g., Brown et al., 1998; Hol et al., 1996) and are sensitive to environmental factors such as maternal nutrition (e.g., folic acid).

Following the formation of the neural tube, the cells along the ventricular zone, the inner surface of the tube, proliferate through a process of mitosis, and new neuronal precursor cells are generated (Brown, Keynes, & Lumsden, 2001). Mitosis begins around the fifth week of gestation and peaks by 12 to 16 weeks gestation. This process of *neurogenesis* has several phases. In the early phase, each cell divides once, resulting in two cells that then continue to divide. The duration of this mitotic phase appears to determine the total number of cells in the final cerebral cortex. In a second phase, some cells begin to move outward and back from the ventricular layer to the outer portion of the neural tube to what will later become the cortex (Takahashi, Nowakowski, & Caviness, 2001, for review). The duration of the entire proliferation period differs for different groups of cells, and completion of the proliferation period appears to initiate the onset of final cell migration. The process of neurogenesis results in a gross overproduction of neurons that is balanced by a later period of programmed cell death. It has been estimated that as many as half of all generated neurons undergo programmed cell death between the sixth prenatal month and the second postnatal month (Lenroot & Giedd, 2006; Volpe, 1995).

Following neurogenesis, the newly formed neurons begin to migrate to their final destinations (peaking between 13 and 22 weeks gestation). This neuronal migration is dependent on radial glial cells that have long processes that reach to the outer surface of the developing brain (Kriegstein & Götz, 2003). Young neurons travel along these glial processes to reach their final destinations. These glial cells are present only during this developmental stage. Once all of the neurons in their region have migrated, the radial glial cells undergo a final cell division and become astrocytes. Given the vast number of individual neurons that must migrate during this stage, errors of migration might be expected. It has been estimated that approximately 3% of neurons land in the incorrect location. Most of these simply degenerate during a period of programmed cell death and cause no problems. However, serious errors of migration can occur, resulting in gross brain anomalies, such as missing portions of cortex or lack of gyri. These issues usually arise between 13 and 15 weeks gestation and all result in mental retardation (Naegele & Lombroso, 2001).

Cell differentiation begins concurrently with migration. That is, at the end of the proliferation period, cells have already differentiated into glial cells or specific types of neurons. In fact, their fate appears to be established. Cells not only migrate, but migrate to a specific destination. In general, cells generated at a similar time appear to end up in similar locations. Therefore, the time at which a cell stops proliferating appears to determine many of its ultimate characteristics. However, the cell's environment also plays a role. For example, some cells will alter their characteristics (e.g., the neurotransmitter they produce) depending on the local environment, including the other cells around them. Once neurons have reached their final destination, they attach themselves to other cells of a similar kind, creating an aggregate. These aggregates later become functional units, such as a particular layer of cortex, or a specific nucleus of the thalamus. This aggregation is accomplished by the interaction of a class of molecules on the cell surface termed *cell adhesion molecules* (Jaffe et al., 1990; Whitesides & LaMantia, 1995).

Once neurons have reached their target destinations, intrinsic and extrinsic molecular signals initiate the growth of characteristic neuronal morphology such as dendritic and axonal processes. Some of this growth appears to be genetically determined. Cells that have been experimentally moved or rotated begin growing axonal and dendritic processes initially as if they were in the original orientation. However, the subsequent growth and extension of these processes is determined by local physical and chemical cues (Condron, 2002). In axons, the leading edge of the axon (*growth cone*) sends fingerlike *filopodia* to explore the local environment. If the filopodia encounter a physical barrier or do not sense the appropriate chemical signals, they will retract and search in an alternate direction (Bixby & Harris, 1991). This developmental stage shows a great deal of early plasticity. Such plasticity appears to depend on the timed expression of specific genes. Once the genes are no longer expressed, the proteins that the axons seek may no longer be available (Evans & Bashaw, 2010).

After neuronal fate has been established and axons and dendrites have begun to form, neurons begin to build a complex network of communication by establishing synaptic connections, the communication sites between neurons and the structures that they will regulate. This process, termed *synaptogenesis*, is initiated around the fifth month of gestation in the primate (Rakic, 1974) and is detectable in human cortex by the third trimester (Huttenlocher, 1990; Huttenlocher & Dabholkar, 1997; Lenroot & Giedd, 2006). Synapses are the site of neurotransmitter release. Given the degree of cell differentiation at this point in development, it is not surprising that each type of neuron is limited to making synaptic connections with only a select range of other cell types. Synapse formation begins prenatally but peaks postnatally in humans. Synaptic density increases most rapidly following birth, but undergoes a long period of activity-dependent refinement.

Peak synaptic number is reached within the first 6 to 20 months postnatally. However, this number is approximately twice that of the adult brain (Huttenlocher, 1979, 1990). A period of refinement or *synaptic pruning* follows during which active synaptic connections are strengthened while those with weak or inconsistent activity are redirected or lost (Chechik, Meilijson & Ruppin, 1999). The excess of synapses appears to be predominantly controlled by genetics, since experiential factors such as premature birth and lack of sensory stimulation have little or no effect on this overproduction (Bourgeois, Jastreboff & Rakic, 1989). However, the pruning of synapses is dependent, at least in part, on the activity among neurons (Changeux & Danchin, 1976; Huang & Reichardt, 2001). Synaptic pruning is considered to be one of the most regionally variable processes in human brain development (Huttenlocher & Dabholkar, 1997; Rakic, Bourgeois, Eckenhoff, Zecevic, & Goldman-Rakic, 1986; Volpe, 1995). In the visual cortex, synaptic pruning is complete by early childhood (4 to 6 years of age), whereas synaptic pruning in the prefrontal cortex continues into adolescence (Huttenlocher & Dabholkar, 1997).

The most protracted stage of development in the human brain is the production of myelin, which begins during the second trimester, but occurs predominantly postnatally (Counsell et al., 2002; Inder & Huppi, 2000; Prayer et al., 2006). In the central nervous system, myelin is produced by oligodendroglial cells. This lipid-protein membrane wraps around the axon of neuronal cells, effectively insulating the axon and increasing the efficiency of communication through the fiber. Early studies examining the development of myelin relied on postmortem staining techniques and showed that myelination begins prenatally in the peripheral nervous system and the motor and sensory root ganglia. During the first postnatal year, myelination continues in the brain stem, the cerebellum, and the corpus callosum. More recent advances in neuroimaging technology have proved to be useful for examining the ontogeny of myelination in the human brain. A recent study has demonstrated generally that myelination is most rapid during the first two postnatal years (Cascio, Gerig, & Piven, 2007). However, although most fiber tracts are significantly myelinated early in development, many brain regions continue to show changes in myelination into adulthood. Like synaptic pruning, myelination shows regional variability. Regions of the visual and auditory cortex show adult levels of myelination early in childhood, whereas the prefrontal cortex shows protracted myelination into adulthood (Benes, 2001). The protracted development of myelination in certain regions is presumed to underlie at least some of the functional improvements in motor and cognitive functions observed across childhood and adolescence.

Building a human brain requires a multitude of individual events to be coordinated in both space and time. Alterations or disruptions at a single stage or level may have consequences for both anatomical and functional development of the brain. Some of these effects result in gross anatomical changes, including lack of individual structures or atypical cortical layering. These are typically, although not exclusively, associated with global cognitive deficits such as mental retardation. However, other alterations are likely more subtle and may contribute to individual differences in cognitive function within the normal range. Studies of gross injury or degeneration of the brain have aided our understanding of the contributions of these insults to typical cognitive competence. However, despite the potential for variability at every stage and level, we understand very little about the cognitive correlates of small changes in these developmental processes.

DEVELOPMENT OF MEMORY-RELATED BRAIN REGIONS

Clearly, the timing of specific developmental events varies considerably across brain regions. Given the scope of this chapter, we focus on the development of brain regions previously implicated in mature recognition/declarative memory. The most commonly identified regions involved in mediating human memory are the medial temporal lobe (MTL; including the hippocampus, perirhinal cortex, entorhinal cortex, and the parahippocampal gyrus), and prefrontal cortex.

Cellular and Molecular Brain Development

Rodent and nonhuman primate studies suggest that the timing of basic cell formation in the hippocampus can vary widely across species. In rodent models, pyramidal cells in the hippocampus are formed late in prenatal development, whereas granule cells of the dentate gyrus are formed primarily in the postnatal period (Bayer, 1980). However, in primates, hippocampal neurons are generated early in prenatal development (36 to 65 days) (Rakic & Nowakowski, 1981). By 25 weeks of gestation in humans, all of the neuronal subtypes in the hippocampal formation have been differentiated and demonstrate adult cytoarchitecture (Arnold & Trojanowski, 1996). In contrast, cells continue to proliferate in the temporal cortex adjacent to hippocampus in the postnatal period until approximately 1 year of age (Seress, Abraham, Tornoczky, & Kosztolanyi, 2001). It is unclear how many of these cells are neurons versus glia; however, the temporal cortex does appear to show a longer period of neuronal proliferation than the hippocampus (Seress et al., 2001). Interestingly, these newly born cells of the human hippocampal formation (e.g., CA1 to CA3, dentate gyrus) show a high rate of survival and a very low rate of apoptosis, in contrast to evidence of programmed cell death in the postnatal rat brain (Rakic & Nowakowski, 1981; Siman, Bozyczko-Coyne, Meyer, & Ad Bath, 1999).

Cell migration in the hippocampus continues into the first postnatal year of life, particularly for granule cells (Seress et al., 2001). This prolonged migration is accompanied by a longer period of neurochemical maturation of both excitatory and inhibitory neurons (Seress et al., 1993). For example, one class of inhibitory interneurons (parvalbumin-positive cells) shows late development. Dendritic branching and axonal growth of these cells is immature even in the 2-year-old child, though mature by age 8 years. Because no data are available between ages 2 and 8 years, precise delineation of this developmental time course is difficult (Seress & Abraham, 2008). Seress and colleagues have proposed that the long postnatal development of hippocampal neurons may be key in understanding some aspects of cognitive development in children.

Structural development of the prefrontal cortex begins early in gestation, similar to other brain regions, but continues postnatally well into adolescence and early adulthood. Neurogenesis of prefrontal neurons begins by 7 weeks of gestation (Kostovic, Skavic, & Strinovic, 1988). Laminar organization of the prefrontal cortex begins early and reaches a 6-layer form by 34 weeks of gestation. However, this organization is not equivalent to adult cortical layers or even the laminar structure of the postnatal 3-month-old. Early in development, the cortex includes additional sublayers that are not present in the postnatal brain (Glenn & Barkovich, 2006; Mrzljak, Uylings, Kostovic, & Van Eden, 1992). One consistently reported developmental trend in the prefrontal cortex is the prolonged development of dendritic spines (Mrzljak et al., 1992; Petanjek, Judas, Kostovic, & Uylings, 2007). Peak spine density and synapse formation is reached by 2.5 years of age in the human prefrontal cortex and remains high in childhood and adolescence, showing a decrease in adulthood, although estimates of the duration this peak density vary across different laboratories (e.g., Bourgeois, Goldman-Rakic, & Rakic, 1994; Huttenlocher & Dabholkar, 1997). No definitive relationship has been established between synaptogenesis and cognitive development; however, the periods of greatest synapse overproduction and turnover coincide with periods of increased brain activity in the prefrontal cortex and changes in cognitive functioning (e.g., Klingberg, Forssberg, & Westerberg, 2002; Kostovic et al., 1988; Luciana & Nelson, 1998). Neurochemical maturation in prefrontal cortex also occurs on a protracted time frame. Dopamine transmission and synthesis reaches its peak around 2 to 3 years in nonhuman primates, which is roughly equivalent to puberty or adolescence in humans (Rosenberg & Lewis, 1995). On a structural level, dopamine innervation of some layers of the prefrontal cortex occurs early and remains relatively constant across development. However, in layer III, dopamine innervation increases dramatically from infancy into puberty (Rosenberg & Lewis, 1995). Similarly, layer-specific changes are observed in the functional development of GABAergic inhibitory interneurons, with a peak change in early adolescence (Lewis, Cruz, Eggan, & Erickson, 2004).

Human Structural Brain Imaging

Structural magnetic resonance imaging (MRI) data have generally supported the histological and cytoarchitectural data presented thus far. Early studies using quantitative structural brain imaging demonstrated greater gray matter volume in children than in young adults (Jernigan & Tallal, 1990; Jernigan, Trauner, Hesselink, & Tallal, 1991). This finding is consistent with developmental changes in synaptic proliferation and pruning, as well as changes in myelination, and therefore, the ratio of white matter to gray matter volume between childhood and adulthood. Overall, gray matter volume decreases after 6 to 7 years of age and continues to decrease throughout adolescence. In contrast, white matter volume seems to increase in a linear fashion through age 20 years (Giedd et al., 1999; Gogtay et al., 2004; Sowell et al., 2003; Sowell et al., 2004). In a longitudinal analysis, Giedd and colleagues (1999) demonstrated that gray matter loss is regionally specific, similar to patterns of synaptogenesis and pruning, and is nonlinear across development. Frontal and parietal gray matter reached peak volume by early adolescence (age 12 years), whereas temporal gray matter continued to increase for several years (age 16 years) before showing decreases. More recent longitudinal data have suggested a complex pattern of cortical development that generally matches the functional maturation of various brain regions. Gogtay and colleagues (2004) examined repeated MRI scans from individual children over an 8 to 10 year period to characterize the dynamic nature of gray matter development between 4 and 21 years of age (Gogtay et al., 2004). Total gray matter volume increased until early puberty, followed by regionally specific patterns of loss. Primary sensorimotor cortices matured first, then gray matter loss spread both rostrally to the frontal cortex, and caudally and laterally over the parietal, occipital, and temporal cortices. The occipital and frontal poles, as well as the pre-and post-central gyri lost gray matter early, whereas the dorsolateral prefrontal cortex and lateral temporal lobes were among the last regions to mature, losing gray matter only during late adolescence (Gogtay et al., 2004). MTL regions associated with recollection (e.g., entorhinal cortex) matured relatively early, although multimodal association regions such as the posterior superior temporal gyrus were among the very last to mature. Similar results were found in a longitudinal study examining cortical thickness longitudinally from 5 to 11 years of age (Sowell et al., 2004). In general, phylogenetically older regions show early refinement of gray matter, whereas more recently evolved association cortices show later maturation of gray matter.

Given these findings of prolonged gray matter loss, it will be important to continue to examine cortical development into adulthood. Sowell and colleagues (2003) have begun this process by examining gray matter loss cross-sectionally in individuals 7 to 87 years of age (Sowell et al., 2003). Their data show progressive declines in gray matter density in the dorsal frontal, and parietal cortices between 7 and 60 years of age, with little or no decline beyond age 60 years. In contrast, the superior temporal gyrus shows subtle increases in gray matter density until approximately age 30 years, after which it stabilizes before dropping precipitously after 70 years of age. Clearly, gray matter continues to be shaped across the lifespan, particularly in areas such as the dorsal prefrontal cortex (Sowell et al., 2003).

Despite the large literature examining structural changes in gray and white matter in childhood and adolescence, the relationship between these structural changes and cognitive function is unknown. More recent developmental studies have begun to address aspects of cognitive development in relation to changes in gray matter density and cortical thickness. Wilke, Sohn, Byars, and Holland (2003) reported a significant correlation between gray matter density and general IQ in the cingulate gyrus (medial prefrontal cortex). Frangou, Chitins, and Williams (2004) observed a similar correlation in orbitofrontal cortex, and other groups have reported correlations between prefrontal gray matter density and IQ in adults (e.g., Haier, Jung, Yeo, Head, & Alkire, 2004). In their longitudinal study, Sowell and colleagues (2004) explored the relationship between normative developmental thinning in cortical gray matter and performance on the vocabulary subtest of the Wechsler Intelligence Scale for Children (Wechsler, 1991). Their data suggest a positive correlation between thinning in left dorsolateral frontal and left lateral parietal cortices and verbal IQ (Sowell et al., 2004). Most recently, Shaw and colleagues (2006) examined cortical thickness and IQ in a longitudinal study of 307 children and adolescents. They found only modest correlations between these measures in their whole sample, but reported differential patterns of correlation by IQ range. By splitting their sample into "average", "high", and "superior" IQ groups, these investigators were able to show that frontal cortical thickness was lower in early childhood for the superior IQ group, but higher for this group in later childhood and adolescence (Shaw et al., 2006). This effect appears to be due to a significant increase in medial prefrontal cortical thickness in the superior IQ group around 11 years of age. In contrast, the average IQ group showed gradual thinning of prefrontal cortex across the age range studied (7 to 19 years), with the high IQ group showing a pattern between these two. Despite the increase in thickness in medial prefrontal cortex, the superior IQ group showed the most rapid pattern of cortical thinning. Although a number of studies have shown significant correlations between structural changes in gray matter and general cognitive ability, few have examined more specific cognitive domains. Lu and colleagues (2007) have examined phonological processing and motor skills in relation to cortical thickness in the same longitudinal sample reported by Sowell et al. (2004). The investigators sought a double dissociation between language and motor processing and structural changes in left inferior frontal gyrus and motor cortex. Their results demonstrated a significant correlation between phonological processing and gray matter thickness in left inferior frontal cortex, but no correlation between motor processing and thickness in this region. Likewise, motor processing abilities were associated with cortical thinning in left primary motor cortex but phonological processing was not correlated with this region. To our knowledge, no large-scale anatomical studies have been conducted relating normative developmental changes in brain structure to developments in memory and recollection.

Overall, human neuroimaging and animal studies have suggested that the hippocampus and MTL cortical regions show early maturation of volume and physiological function relative to cortical association regions such as the prefrontal or parietal cortices. Therefore, cognitive correlates of temporal lobe development may be more apparent in early childhood when variability in development is higher. In contrast, alterations in prefrontal and parietal cortex extend further into adulthood and may lend themselves more easily to MRI methodologies. However, the more recent literature in anatomical MRI highlights the lifelong refinement of most cortical regions, as well as the importance of specific methodology in capturing ongoing refinement. Gogtay and colleagues (2006) note that, although the overall volume of the hippocampus remains relatively static across childhood and adolescence, more pronounced changes are observed in the spatial distribution of gray matter volume. Specifically, data from their lagged longitudinal design suggest increases in volume in the posterior hippocampus with volume decreases in the anterior hippocampus. These results were obtained by including additional measures of hippocampal morphology to capture overall changes in shape as well as spatial extent. Few studies have examined relationships between structure and cognitive functions. In the previously mentioned study (Gogtay et al., 2006), no memory assessments were available to examine correlations between hippocampal morphology and cognitive functions presumed to depend on the hippocampus. Overall, the nonhuman animal and MRI literatures provide a general portrait of regional brain development within the typical population, but few clues as to the impact of these changes on specific cognitive competencies.

FUNCTIONAL NEUROIMAGING STUDIES OF MEMORY DEVELOPMENT ACROSS CHILDHOOD

Functional neuroimaging measures of typical child development first hit the literature circa 1995 (Casey et al., 1995). These early studies tested the feasibility of applying the relatively new technique of functional magnetic resonance imaging (fMRI) to pediatric populations. This early work addressed questions regarding the hemodynamic response in the developing brain as well as the practical concerns of working with children in the MRI environment (see Casey, Giedd, & Thomas, 2000; Thomas & Casey, 1999, for review). Since then, the developmental neuroimaging literature has expanded by leaps and bounds. Whereas early work extended existing cognitive paradigms from the adult literature into the study of child development, more recent work addresses questions that are of particular interest to developmentalists, including the development of basic cognitive functions and, most commonly, the development of executive functions and the prefrontal cortex. This emphasis on executive functions could perhaps be predicted by evidence of prolonged structural development of the prefrontal cortex. However, only recently has developmental neuroimaging research addressed more basic cognitive processes, including memory and recollection.

Despite a rich history of behavioral research addressing the development of recollection, the pediatric neuroimaging literature has been slow to examine basic memory processes. Functional MRI studies of recollection in childhood have emerged only in the past 6 years in contrast to the extensive electrophysiological literature addressing the brain bases of memory development in infancy and childhood (see St. Jacques & Cabeza, Chapter 8, this volume). In the following section, we review the fMRI literature addressing the brain bases of memory encoding and retrieval in childhood. Given our focus on recollection, we will not discuss the pediatric imaging literature on working memory.

One of the first fMRI studies of episodic memory addressed the maturation of hippocampal and MTL systems involved in memory encoding in adults. Menon, Boyett-Anderson, and Reiss (2005) asked 15 children and adolescents (mean age 15.1 years, range 11 to 19 years) to study and remember 48 photographs of outdoor scenes during functional brain imaging. After a 10-min delay, participants were given a yes/no recognition memory test outside the MRI scanner with previously viewed and novel scenes. Variants of this task have been used extensively in the adult neuroimaging literature to examine brain activity related to encoding of new items into memory (e.g., Brewer, Zhao, Desmond, Glover, & Gabrieli, 1998; Menon, White, Eliez, Glover, & Reiss, 2000; Wagner et al., 1998). Given an interest in the development of memory systems, the investigators examined age-related differences in performance as well as age-related differences in brain activity. In adults, successful encoding, as tested by the post-scanning recognition test, is associated with increased activity in the MTL, including, in some cases, the hippocampus (e.g., Brewer et al., 1998). Subsequent memory effects have similarly been observed in prefrontal and parietal cortices in adult samples (Uncapher & Wagner, 2009; see Paller & Wagner, 2002 for review). Menon and colleagues found that age was positively, although not significantly, related to accuracy on the subsequent memory test, and negatively correlated with retrieval reaction time. Younger children took longer to decide whether the item was new or old and were generally less accurate than older children and adolescents (Menon et al., 2005).

Encoding-related brain activity was assessed by comparing the fMRI response acquired during encoding blocks to the fMRI response acquired during baseline blocks. These analyses revealed increased activity in striate and extrastriate regions of visual cortex, as well as in the MTL (hippocampus, entorhinal cortex, and parahippocampal gyrus) during encoding. None of these regions showed increased activity with age. However, activity in the left hippocampus and entorhinal cortex decreased significantly with age, even when encoding accuracy was included as a covariate. This result is consistent with findings in other cognitive domains that maturation may be a significant factor in functional activation over and above effects of performance (e.g., Kwon, Reiss, & Menon, 2002). However, such claims would be bolstered by event-related paradigms that allow for a comparison of activity across specific trial types (e.g., successful encoding vs. unsuccessful encoding). Results from this initial study of memory development suggest age-related changes in the recruitment of hippocampal and entorhinal regions, with greater processing resources required for younger children to encode items in memory.

Menon and colleagues (2005) went one step further to investigate whether age-related changes in functional activation were related to developmental differences in structure of the MTL and/or connections between the temporal lobe and prefrontal cortex. As discussed previously, age-related changes in gray matter have been reported in the MTL as well as prefrontal and parietal areas implicated in memory and recollection (Giedd et al., 1999; Gogtay et al., 2004; Gogtay et al., 2006; Sowell et al., 2003; Sowell et al., 2004). Gray matter density was examined in the same region of the MTL where differences in activity were observed. Age was not correlated with gray matter density in this region, eliminating the possibility that age-related differences in activity can be explained by differences in gray matter density among participants (Menon et al., 2005). Measures of effective connectivity indicated an increase in correlated activity between left dorsolateral prefrontal cortex (DLPFC) and the entorhinal cortex (but not the hippocampus) with age, despite no age-related differences in left DLPFC activity itself or in DLPFC gray matter density.

Overall, this initial study suggested that developmental changes in memory performance and recollection may be due to changes in connectivity between the

MTL and the prefrontal cortex rather than a development within the hippocampus or the entorhinal cortex. Activity in temporal lobe regions showed age-related decreases consistent with a model of increased cortical efficiency with age, over and above any age-related changes in encoding performance. However, a number of issues and new lines of research were highlighted by this initial study. First, the age range of participants was relatively wide, with a primary focus on the period of adolescence (15 years) not typically associated with large behavioral changes in memory function. Therefore, although these data address maturation of MTL activity, they do not necessarily address the development of recollection, as activity was not strongly related to performance. Similarly, the block-design approach used provided an initial starting point for thinking about memory-related brain activity, but did not allow for the examination of activity associated with individual trials. Therefore, it is unclear whether similar age-related changes in activity are observed even when only successfully encoded trials are included. Block designs also necessitate the selection of an appropriate baseline condition. In the Menon et al. (2005) study, encoding of trial-unique scenes was compared with viewing or encoding a single, repeated scene. Given the focus on encoding, the selected control task may not have provided an ideal comparison. Further studies of recollection have addressed some of these limitations.

Around the same time that Menon and colleagues were conducting their work on memory encoding, several other groups were also exploring the neural bases of memory development. In a paper symposium at the biennial meeting of the Society for Research in Child Development in 2003, four laboratories presented papers using event-related potentials and/or fMRI measures of memory in childhood. This symposium resulted in a special issue of the journal *Developmental Neuropsychology* in 2006. One of the fMRI papers in this issue addressed episodic memory encoding within the context of more general cognitive tasks. Chiu, Schmithorst, Brown, Holland, and Dunn (2006) asked 7- to 18-year-olds to perform both a verb generation task and a story comprehension task and then examined subsequent memory for specific items presented in the two tasks. Two groups of children were tested: a younger group (7- to 8-year-olds) and an older group (10- to 18-year-olds). Children completed separate experimental runs with alternating blocks of verb generation and bilateral finger tapping, or story comprehension and passive tone listening. In the verb-generation task, participants were presented with an auditory concrete noun and asked to mentally generate an associated verb. For the comparison task of bilateral finger tapping, participants were instructed to tap their fingers sequentially from pinky to thumb simultaneously for both hands whenever they heard a signal tone. Following fMRI scanning, participants were given a surprise recognition test asking them to identify the presented nouns from target–foil pairs. In the sentence-comprehension task, children were instructed to listen to a short story (9 to 11 sentences) so that they could answer questions about the stories later in the session. A comparison task of listening to random auditory tones was included as a baseline condition. Following the scanning session, children were asked to identify exact sentences from the stories in a yes/no recognition task including paraphrased and novel sentences as well as old sentences. Regions showing differential activation during the experimental task and the control task were then reduced to those showing a significant correlation with subsequent memory (Chiu et al., 2006).

Results from this study showed areas of prefrontal, temporal, and parietal cortices that showed task-related activity differences as a function of subsequent memory. MTL activity during verb generation showed no relationship to subsequent noun memory. However, memory for exact sentences was positively correlated with MTL activity during story comprehension. This activity differed for younger and older children. Older children showed subsequent memory effects for both posterior and anterior portions of the MTL, including the hippocampus itself, as well as in the inferior frontal cortex (Brodmann area [BA] 44/45). However, younger children showed memory-related activity only in the left posterior temporal lobe (Chiu et al., 2006). Given the age differences in memory performance, with older children showing better recognition of sentences, it is unclear whether the differences in hippocampal activation relate to age, performance, or both. Similar to the Menon et al. (2005) study, the block-design paradigm limits the ability to test specific performance effects on brain activity.

A second pediatric fMRI paper was also included in this special issue. Curtis, Zhuang, Townsend, Hu, and Nelson (2006) examined MTL activity during memory performance in typically developing and at-risk 12- to 15-year-olds. The at-risk group consisted of adolescents who were born prematurely and spent time in the newborn intensive care unit. The nine at-risk teens included in this study had a mean gestational age of 30 weeks and spent an average of 35 days in the newborn intensive care unit at birth. All were intrauterine growth retarded and showed respiratory distress, and six of the nine were born with very low birth weight (<1500 g). Comparison teens were born full term with no birth complications and came from families with similar income and education. Adolescents performed versions of the delayed-match-to-sample and the delayed-nonmatch-to-sample tasks during acquisition of data from a single sagittal slice through each hippocampus (left and right). Previous studies from this group had demonstrated significant hippocampal activation during delayed-match-to-sample and delayed-nonmatch-to-sample tasks in adults (Monk et al., 2002), with additional prefrontal activation for the nonmatch task. Results from this developmental sample showed no significant differences in either behavioral performance or hippocampal activity for the typical and at-risk groups. Group differences were observed in the caudate nucleus on a separate task, but were not directly related to memory performance.

Overall, this study represents a first attempt to examine memory-related functional brain activity in children and adolescents at risk due to early brain insult. MTL activity was not different between the at-risk and control groups at this age using the delayed-match-to-sample or delayed-nonmatch-to-sample tasks. However, imaging was limited to four sagittal slices, one through each hippocampus and each caudate nucleus. Therefore, it is unclear whether interactions between the MTL and other brain regions, including the prefrontal cortex, may have differed between groups.

More recent developmental imaging studies of memory have returned the focus to basic processes of recognition and recollection. Ofen and colleagues (2007) conducted an event-related fMRI study of subsequent memory effects across childhood and into adulthood. In particular, this study examined whether activity in regions engaged during successful encoding changes as a function of age. Similar to Menon et al. (2005), participants (ages 8 to 24 years) viewed photographs of indoor and outdoor scenes during fMRI scanning and were subsequently tested for encoding accuracy outside the scanner. During encoding, participants were explicitly instructed to memorize the scenes for a later memory test. A subsequent memory task required participants to identify photographs as old or new, and to indicate their degree of certainty for old items (actual memory vs. feeling of knowing or familiarity). Age-related differences were examined for both behavioral and MRI analyses, separating trials by memory category (remember, know, forgotten).

Behaviorally, memory for scenes increased with age, but only for recollection (*remember* items) and not familiarity (*know* items). MRI analyses were conducted comparing activation during remembered items versus forgotten items (remembered > forgotten), revealing subsequent memory effects in the ventral visual processing stream and MTL, as well as the dorsal visual stream (precuneus, superior parietal lobule) and prefrontal cortex (Ofen et al., 2007). Of these regions, two areas of prefrontal cortex showed changes in activity as a function of age. Memory-related activity in DLPFC (left BA 46 and right BA 9) increased significantly with age. Direct comparisons between recollection and familiarity (remember > know) revealed age-related activity differences only in left BA 9. Therefore, age-related improvements in memory for specific details are accompanied by increased activity in left DLPFC (BA 9). In contrast to the prefrontal cortex, activity in the hippocampus and other MTL regions did not vary with age, despite showing overall effects of subsequent memory (remembered > forgotten). Previous studies of subsequent memory effects in adults have suggested a correlation between activity and performance (Paller & Wagner, 2002, for review). Further analyses of these developmental data demonstrated a positive correlation between recognition accuracy and activity in multiple areas of prefrontal cortex as well as bilaterally in the parahippocampal gyrus and the hippocampus proper (Ofen et al., 2007). Overall, results from this study suggest that both MTL structures (including the hippocampus and the parahippocampal gyrus) and the prefrontal cortex are engaged during memory formation and that later recognition is associated with greater activity during encoding. However, in this sample, MTL activity was not associated with age, suggesting that the association between hippocampal activity and performance is equivalent from ages 8 to 24 years. These data suggest an earlier functional maturation in MTL and a relatively prolonged maturation of prefrontal cortex contributions to recollection (Ofen et al, 2007).

This event-related study of subsequent memory effects across childhood and adolescence provides some of the most definitive evidence of differential contributions of MTL and prefrontal cortex to the development of recollection. As the investigators caution, however, the particular task demands likely play a critical role in the degree to which medial temporal or prefrontal regions are engaged during encoding. Tasks that involve memory for relational information, such as context, source, or other specific associations may illuminate age-related changes in MTL function that are not apparent in the current paradigm. One looming question from this work is the nature of memory retrieval systems and their developmental course.

One study to address the development of memory retrieval comes from Paz-Alonso, Ghetti, Donohue, Goodman, and Bunge (2008), who examined brain activity associated with recognition processes in 8- and 12-year-old children. These investigators employed the Deese/Roediger/McDermott paradigm to examine false recognition memory in middle to late childhood. This paradigm involves presenting participants with lists of words around a specific semantic theme that is never presented in the study list. When these theme words (or critical lures) are then presented in an old/new recognition test, adult participants falsely recognize the critical lures at very high rates, labeling the items as "old" although they never appeared in the study list. In their study of false recognition in childhood, Paz-Alonso and colleagues asked participants to study and remember 23 lists of 12 words, presented 1 word at a time for 2.5 s. After each list, the participants completed a verbal interference task for 30 s (counting backward by 2 or by 6). Following study, fMRI data were collected from participants during a yes/no recognition test including studied words, critical lures, and unrelated new words.

Both true and false recognition increased with age, such that adults recognized more studied items, but also endorsed more critical lures than 8-year-olds did, with 12-year-olds performing between these two groups (Paz-Alonso et al., 2008). Performance on unrelated new words did not differ between age groups. The fMRI analyses focused on age-related differences in both true recognition and false recognition. Activity during true recognition (memory hits > correct rejections of unrelated new words) was positively correlated with age in the left hippocampus, bilateral superior parietal cortex, and bilateral prefrontal cortex (including dorsolateral and ventrolateral regions). That is, older children and adults showed greater activity during true recognition. Correlations of activity with memory performance were not significant over and above these effects of age. In contrast, false memory (false alarms to critical lures > correct rejections of unrelated new words) elicited significant age-related activity in left middle temporal gyrus, left superior parietal cortex, and both dorsal and ventral prefrontal cortex. Again, older children and adults evidenced greater activity in these regions than younger children during false recognition of critical lures. These basic results support the notion that true and false recognition engage a similar set of brain areas involving the hippocampus, parietal cortex, and prefrontal cortex, and involve age-related increases in activity (Paz-Alonso et al., 2008).

The investigators followed up their initial analyses with region of interest analyses to examine the relative activity for true and false recognition in a priori regions of interest, including hippocampus, posterior parietal cortex, and prefrontal cortex. These secondary analyses were designed to examine age differences in the response to specific trial types (hits, correct rejections of critical lures, false alarms to critical lures, correct rejections of unrelated new words). Using regions defined in the previous regression analyses, fMRI signal was extracted for each trial type for each age group. In the left hippocampus, activity was generally highest for hits compared to other trial types. However, this pattern was not observed for 8-year-olds, who showed greater hippocampal activity for novel items (correct rejection of unrelated new words). Similarly, in the posterior parietal cortex, 8-year-olds showed few differences in response across trial types, whereas 12-year-olds and adults showed large signal differences between conditions, with the largest signal values for hits, and the smallest values for correct rejections of unrelated words. Additional age group differences were observed in prefrontal cortex. Adults showed larger signal changes than both 8- and 12-year olds in ventrolateral prefrontal cortex for hits and critical lures. Adults showed significantly less signal than children in both the ventrolateral prefrontal cortex and anterior prefrontal cortex when identifying novel, unrelated lures (Paz-Alonso et al., 2008).

These data suggest developmental changes in the function of both MTL and prefrontal brain regions during middle to late childhood. Activation in the hippocampus became more item-specific with age, such that younger children activated the hippocampus for novel stimuli, whereas adults activated the hippocampus most strongly when distinguishing true from false memories (Paz-Alonso et al., 2008). This result is contrary to previous neuroimaging studies of memory development that have proposed that the hippocampus reaches functional maturation prior to middle childhood (Menon et al., 2005; Ofen et al., 2007). Earlier studies focused mainly on brain activity during encoding. It is possible that the encoding functions of the hippocampus show early development, whereas retrieval functions of hippocampus demonstrate prolonged development. However, more recent data suggest that a distinction between encoding and retrieval may not be the only factor to explain these conflicting results.

Ghetti, DeMaster, Yonelinas, and Bunge (2010) used an fMRI subsequent memory paradigm to examine incidental encoding of line drawings in children (8 years), preadolescents (10 to 11 years), early adolescents (14 years), and adults (college students). The task required semantic judgments of the objects during encoding (i.e., Found in a house? Animate?), later recognition of previously viewed objects during an unexpected memory test, and explicit recall of object color (red or green) at test. The investigators were interested in activation of MTL regions during encoding of specific item details (i.e., color) across middle childhood and adolescence. They hypothesized that activity in MTL during encoding of objects that are later recalled in detail may relate to age differences in performance on such source memory tasks. Indeed, age differences in MTL activity were observed, with the youngest children demonstrating strong hippocampal and parahippocampal activation broadly for subsequently recognized items compared with forgotten items, regardless of their success in recalling the color of the object. However, adolescents and adults showed increased MTL activity specifically for the detailed recollections and not for item recognition more generally. The preadolescent group showed no differences in MTL activity for remembered versus forgotten items, or detailed memory versus basic recognition.

These findings lead to the question of whether differential behavioral performance between age groups can account for the results. That is, would adults who
are poor at the memory task activate MTL regions in the same pattern as children
who are good at the memory task? Using a subset of their sample matched for
behavioral performance, the investigators found similar results across age groups,
suggesting that at least some of the observed age-related activation differences
reflect more general development of the MTL beyond performance on this task.

Recent data from our laboratory suggest a similar result from an explicit task
of relational memory (Güler & Thomas, 2010). Eight-year-olds and 12-year-olds
underwent fMRI scanning during encoding and retrieval of arbitrary object pairs.
Children were presented with pairs of line drawings during encoding and asked
to intentionally memorize the object pairs. During retrieval, the first member of
the object pair was presented and children were asked to explicitly recall the object
with which it had been paired. Age-related differences in MTL activity were
observed during encoding. Twelve-year-olds showed greater MTL activation for
correctly recalled items, but eight-year-olds showed no memory-related differences in MTL activity during encoding. A similar result was observed during
retrieval, with older children demonstrating greater activation of MTL regions
during successful recall of the paired object. These effects are presumed to reflect
age-related differences in encoding strategies, but may also mark basic development of MTL regions. Patterns of activity in individual participants suggest that
subsequent memory effects were observed for some but not all children in both
age groups, with a higher percentage of 12-year-olds than 8-year-olds showing
such effects. Paradigms requiring memory for detail, source, or item associations
may place a greater demand on MTL memory circuits, allowing observation of
developmental variability in recruitment of these systems. However, preliminary
evidence points to additional developmental change in this system not directly
related to memory function.

Recently researchers have investigated the link between memory development
and brain development less directly. In a series of pediatric functional imaging
studies, Golarai and colleagues (Golari et al., 2007; Golari, Liberman, Yoon, &
Grill-Spector, 2010) examined the development of object specificity in high level
visual cortex between 7 years of age and adulthood, and subsequently investigated
correlations between development of high level visual areas of the brain and
memory for specific object categories. In their initial study, Golarai et al. (2007)
used fMRI to examine the development of object-specific regions of the ventral
visual cortex in children (7 to 11 years), adolescents (12 to 16 years), and adults
(18 to 35 years). Participants viewed blocks of object stimuli, including faces,
scenes, abstract sculpture, or scrambled versions of these stimuli. On a small percentage of trials, the image was an immediate repeat of the previous stimulus and
required a button-press response. Accuracy on this task was greater than 90% in
all age groups and across all image categories and did not differ by age or category.
Category-selective regions were defined by the number of voxels showing sensitivity to faces (faces > objects), objects (objects > scrambled objects), or spatial
information (scenes > objects). Peak amplitude in these regions did not differ as a

function of age. However, the extent or number of voxels activated in the fusiform face area (FFA) and parahippocampal place area was greater in adults than in children or adolescents, suggesting age-related changes in functional selectivity for faces and spatial locations in visual cortex. No age-related changes were observed for object-sensitive regions of cortex (e.g., lateral occipital complex). The investigators then compared these patterns of activity to measures of recognition memory for faces, places, and objects in behavioral tasks completed outside the MRI scanner. Performance on the recognition task improved significantly with age for face and scene stimuli, but was equivalent across ages for abstract sculpture stimuli (objects). Recognition memory performance for face stimuli was positively correlated with age and with number of voxels in the functionally defined right FFA but not object- or place-sensitive regions of cortex. Similarly, recognition memory for scenes was positively correlated with age and with voxel extent in the left parahippocampal place area, but not in any of the other regions tested. The investigators suggest that age-related improvements in recognition memory for faces and places is related to age-related increases in the functional volume of the right FFA and left parahippocampal place area between 7 and 35 years of age. Golarai et al. (2010) replicated these findings in a second group of adolescents, demonstrating that adults showed greater functional extent of activation in face-selective cortex (FFA) than adolescents, and that this age-related change correlated significantly with recognition memory for faces. This more recent dataset showed increases in peak signal amplitude in right FFA with age, as well. Importantly, the extent of FFA activation was related to recognition memory for faces, but it was unrelated to perceptual matching of faces or to facial affect perception, suggesting that it is specific to memory processes.

Overall, fMRI studies of memory across childhood are relatively rare, leaving a critical gap in our understanding of the emergence of mature memory systems throughout the lifespan. Although early studies in this area suggested few if any developmental changes in recruitment of MTL structures including the hippocampus and parahippocampal gyrus, further exploration cautions that differences in tasks, forms of memory, and memory strategies likely complicate interpretation of the developmental literature thus far. Further development of tasks for tapping specific memory processes may advance our understanding of the development of specific components of memory.

CONCLUSIONS

A resurgence of interest in the development of basic cognitive functions has led to a growing literature examining links between recollection and brain development. A growing understanding of developmental neurobiology and brain plasticity has spurred interest in the use of in vivo brain imaging measures across development. Animal research and human postmortem studies have elucidated the importance of early experience and the timing and duration of environmental events in altering the complex and multilayered course of structural and physiological brain development. Methods such as structural MRI have expanded our ability to examine ongoing brain development in the living organism. Such methods have identified an orderly, though complex, pattern of maturation with early maturation of basic functional regions and prolonged refinement in areas supporting higher level functions. Recent structural MRI studies suggest that the prefrontal cortex is not the only region to show protracted developmental change, and that most brain regions experience ongoing developmental refinement as a function of experience and maturation.

MRI methods for studying memory development have been slower to take hold. Although the field of cognitive development has a rich history of behavioral studies addressing memory processes, functional neuroimaging studies of memory development in general, and recollection in particular, are rare. In part, this disconnect may reflect trends in the field of cognitive development, which has seen a surge in interest in higher order cognitive or executive functions in children and adolescents, with less attention to basic cognitive domains beyond infancy and early childhood. In fact, the pediatric fMRI literature is dominated by studies of higher level cognition, including inhibitory control, working memory, and cognitive conflict. One contributing factor may be a technical challenge. Current fMRI techniques require significant behavior regulation by the participant in order to acquire sufficient signal and, therefore, are rarely used in children under 6 or 7 years of age. Likewise, behavioral studies of memory development are weighted toward infancy and early childhood, periods of development that are less amenable to the use of fMRI methods. However, recent publications suggest increased interest in the use of both structural and functional MRI techniques in the study of memory and recollection in childhood. Initial studies in this domain supported developmental changes in functioning of prefrontal cortex during memory, but failed to find evidence for ongoing development of MTL structures known to be critical for memory function in adulthood. However, advances in both structural morphometry methods and functional activation tasks hold promise for the detection of more subtle but potentially critical indices of ongoing MTL development. Future work in this domain is likely to focus on refinement of activation tasks to allow for separation of unique components of memory and recollection. In addition, as in all fMRI studies of development, further consideration of performance-related changes and maturational changes will be necessary to refine our interpretations of structural and functional imaging results.

REFERENCES

Arnold, S. E., & Trojanowski, J. Q. (1996). Human fetal hippocampal development. I. Cytoarchitecture, myeloarchitecture and neuronal morphologic features. *Journal of Comparative Neurology, 367,* 274–92.

Bayer, S. A. (1980). The development of the hippocampal region in the rat. I. Neurogenesis examined with 3H-thymidine autoradiography. *Journal of Comparative Neurology, 190,* 87–114.

Benes, F. M. (2001). Development of prefrontal cortex: Maturation of neurotransmitter systems and their interactions. In C. A. Nelson & M. Luciana (Eds.), *Handbook of developmental cognitive neuroscience* (pp. 79–92). Cambridge, MA: MIT Press.

Bixby, J. L., & Harris, W. A. (1991). Molecular mechanisms of axon growth and guidance. *Annual Review of Cell Biology, 7,* 117–59.

Bourgeois, J.-P., Goldman-Rakic, P. S., & Rakic, P. (1994). Synaptogenesis in the prefrontal cortex of rhesus monkeys. *Cerebral Cortex, 4,* 78–96.

Bourgeois, J.-P., Jastreboff, P. J., & Rakic, P. (1989). Synaptogenesis in visual cortex of normal and preterm monkeys: Evidence for intrinsic regulation of synaptic overproduction. *Proceedings of the National Academy of Sciences USA, 86,* 4297–301.

Brewer, J. B., Zhao, Z., Desmond, J. E., Glover, G. H., & Gabrieli, J. D. (1998). Making memories: Brain activity that predicts how well visual experience will be remembered. *Science, 281,* 1185–7.

Brown, M., Keynes, R., & Lumsden, A. (2001). *The developing brain.* Oxford, UK: Oxford University Press.

Brown, S. A., Warburton, D., Brown, L. Y., Yu, C. Y., Roeder, E. R., Stengel-Rutkowski, S., ... Muenke, M. (1998). Holoprosencephaly due to mutations in ZIC2, a homologue of Drosophila odd-paired. *Nature Genetics, 20,* 180–3.

Cascio, C. J., Gerig, G. & Piven, J. (2007). Diffusion tensor imaging: Application to the study of the developing brain. *Journal of the American Academy of Child & Adolescent Psychiatry, 46,* 213–23.

Casey, B. J., Cohen, J. D., Jezzard, P., Turner, R., Noll, D. C., Trainor, R. J., ... Rapoport, J. L. (1995). Activation of prefrontal cortex in children during a nonspatial working memory task with functional MRI. *Neuroimage, 2,* 221–9.

Casey, B. J., Giedd, J., & Thomas, K. M. (2000). Structural and functional brain development and its relation to cognitive development. *Biological Psychology, 54,* 241–57.

Changeux, J., & Danchin, A. (1976). Selective stabilisation of developing synapses as a mechanism for the specification of neuronal networks. *Nature, 264,* 705–12.

Chechik, G. Meilijson, I., & Ruppin, E. (1999). Neuronal regulation: A mechanism for synaptic pruning during brain maturation. *Neural Computation, 11,* 2061–80.

Chiu, C.-Y. P., Schmithorst, V. J., Brown, R. D., Holland, S. K., & Dunn, S. (2006). Making memories: A cross-sectional investigation of episodic memory encoding using fMRI. *Developmental Neuropsychology, 29,* 321–40.

Condron, B. (2002). Gene expression is required for correct axon guidance. *Current Biology, 12,* 1665–9.

Counsell, S. J., Maalouf, E. F., Fletcher, A. M., Duggan, P., Battin, M., Lewis, H. J., ... Rutherford, M. A. (2002). MR imaging assessment of myelination in the very preterm brain. *American Journal of Neuroradiology, 23,* 872–81.

Curtis, W. J., Zhuang, J., Townsend, E. L., Hu, X., & Nelson, C. A. (2006). Memory in early adolescents born prematurely: A functional magnetic resonance imaging investigation. *Developmental Neuropsychology, 29,* 341–77.

Evans, T. A. & Bashaw, G. J. (2010). Functional diversity of Robo receptor immunoglobulin domains promotes distinct axon guidance decisions. *Current Biology, 20,* 567–72.

Frangou, S., Chitins, X., & Williams, S. C. (2004). Mapping IQ and gray matter density in healthy young people. *Neuroimage, 23,* 800–5.

Ghetti, S., DeMaster, D. M., Yonelinas, A. P., & Bunge, S. A. (2010). Developmental differences in medial temporal lobe function during memory encoding. *Journal of Neuroscience, 30*, 9548–56.

Giedd, J. N., Blumenthal, J., Jefferies, N. O., Castellanos, F. X., Liu, H., Zijdenbos, A., . . . Rapoport, J. L. (1999). Brain development during childhood and adolescence: A longitudinal MRI study. *Nature Neuroscience, 2*, 861–3.

Glenn, O. A. & Barkovich, A. J. (2006). Magnetic resonance imaging of fetal brain and spine: An increasingly important tool in prenatal diagnosis, part 1. *American Journal of Neuroradiology, 27*, 1604–11.

Gogtay, N., Giedd, J. N., Lusk, L., Hayashi, K. M., Greenstein, D., Vaituzis, A. C., . . . Thompson, P. M. (2004). Dynamic mapping of human cortical development during childhood through early adulthood. *Proceedings of the National Academy of Sciences USA, 101*, 8174–9.

Gogtay, N., Nugent, T. F., III, Herman, D. H., Ordonez, A., Greenstein, D., Hayashi, K. . . . Thompson, P. M. (2006). Dynamic mapping of normal human hippocampal development. *Hippocampus, 16*, 664–72.

Golarai, G., Ghahremani, D. G., Whitfield-Gabrieli, S., Reiss, A., Eberhardt, J. L., Gabrieli, J. D., & Grill-Spector, K. (2007). Differential development of high-level visual cortex correlates with category-specific recognition memory. *Nature Neuroscience, 10*, 512–22.

Golarai, G., Liberman, A., Yoon, J. M., & Grill-Spector, K. (2010). Differential development of the ventral visual cortex extends through adolescence. *Frontiers in Human Neuroscience, 22*, 3–80.

Güler, O. E., & Thomas, K. M. (2010, June). *Neural bases of the development of relational memory.* Poster session presented at the Organization for Human Brain Mapping, Barcelona, Spain.

Haier, R. J., Jung, R. E., Yeo, R. A., Head, K., & Alkire, M. T. (2004). Structural brain variation and general intelligence. *Neuroimage, 23*, 425–33.

Hol, F. A., Geurds, M. P., Chatkupt, S. Shugart, Y. Y., Balling, R., Schrander-Stumpel, C. T., . . . Mariman, E. C. (1996). PAX genes and human neural tube defects: An amino acid substitution in PAX1 in a patient with spina bifida. *Journal of Medical Genetics, 33*, 655–60.

Huang, E. J., & Reichardt, L. F. (2001). Neurotrophins: Roles in neuronal development and function. *Annual Review of Neuroscience, 24*, 677–736.

Huttenlocher, P. R. (1979). Synaptic density in human frontal cortex—developmental changes and effects of aging. *Brain Research, 163*, 195–205.

Huttenlocher, P. R. (1990). Morphometric study of human cerebral cortex development. *Neuropsychologia, 28*, 517–27.

Huttenlocher, P. R., & Dabholkar, A. S. (1997). Regional differences in synaptogenesis in human cerebral cortex. *Journal of Comparative Neurology, 387*, 167–78.

Inder, T. E., & Huppi, P. S. (2000). In vivo studies of brain development by magnetic resonance techniques. *Mental Retardation & Developmental Disabilities Research Reviews, 6*, 59–67.

Jaffe, S. H., Friedlander, D. R., Matsuzaki, F., Crosslin, K. L., Cunningham, B. A., & Edelman, G. M. (1990). Differential effects of the cytoplasmic domains of cell adhesion molecules on cell aggregation and sorting-out. *Proceedings of the National Academy of Sciences USA, 87*, 3589–93.

Jernigan, T. L., & Tallal, P. (1990). Late childhood changes in brain morphology observable with MRI. *Developmental Medicine and Child Neurology*, *32*, 379–85.

Jernigan, T. L., Trauner, D. A., Hesselink, J. R., & Tallal, P. A. (1991). Maturation of human cerebrum observed in vivo during adolescence. *Brain*, *114*, 2037–49.

Keith, A. (1948). *Human embryology and morphology*. London: Edward Arnold & Company.

Klingberg, T., Forssberg, H., & Westerberg, H. (2002). Increased brain activity in frontal and parietal cortex underlies the development of visuospatial working memory capacity during childhood. *Journal of Cognitive Neuroscience*, *14*, 1–10.

Kostovic, I., Skavic, J., & Strinovic, D. (1988). Acetylcholinesterase in the human frontal associative cortex during the period of cognitive development: Early laminar shifts and late innervation of pyramidal neurons. *Neuroscience Letters*, *90*, 107–12.

Kriegstein, A. R., & Götz, M. (2003). Radial glia diversity: A matter of cell fate. *Glia*, *43*, 37–43.

Kwon, H., Reiss, A. L., & Menon, V. (2002). Neural basis of protracted developmental changes in visuo-spatial working memory. *Proceedings of the National Academy of Sciences USA*, *99*, 13336–41.

Lenroot, R. K., & Giedd, J. N. (2006). Brain development in children and adolescents: Insights from anatomical magnetic resonance imaging. *Neuroscience & Biobehavioral Reviews*, *30*, 718–29.

Lewis, D. A., Cruz, D., Eggan, S., & Erickson, S. (2004). Postnatal development of prefrontal inhibitory circuits and the pathophysiology of cognitive dysfunction in schizophrenia. *Annals of the New York Academy of Sciences*, *1021*, 64–76.

Lu, L. H., Leonard, C. M., Thompson, P. M., Kan, E., Jolley, J., Welcome, S. E., . . . Sowell, E. R. (2007). Normal developmental changes in inferior frontal gray matter are associated with improvement in phonological processing: A longitudinal MRI analysis. *Cerebral Cortex*, *17*, 1092–9.

Luciana, M., & Nelson, C. A. (1998). The functional emergence of prefrontally-guided working memory systems in four- to eight-year-old children. *Neuropsychologia*, *36*, 273–93.

Lumsden, A., & Kintner, C. (2003). Neural induction and pattern formation. In L. R. Squire, F. E. Bloom, S. K. McConnell, J. L. Roberts, N. C. Spitzer, & M. J. Zigmond (Eds.), *Fundamental neuroscience* (2nd ed., pp. 363–90). New York: Academic Press.

Menon, V., Boyett-Anderson, J. M., & Reiss, A. L. (2005). Maturation of medial temporal lobe response and connectivity during memory encoding. *Cognitive Brain Research*, *25*, 379–85.

Menon, V., White, C. D., Eliez, S., Glover, G. H., & Reiss, A. L. (2000). Analysis of distributed neural system involved in spatial, novelty, and memory processing. *Human Brain Mapping*, *11*, 117–29.

Monk, C. S., Zhuang, J., Curtis, W. J., Ofenloch, I. T., Tottenham, N., Nelson, C. A., & Hu, X. (2002). Human hippocampal activation in the delayed matching-and non-matching-to-sample memory tasks: An event-related fMRI approach. *Behavioral Neuroscience*, *116*, 716–21.

Mrzljak, L., Uylings, H. B., Kostovic, I., & Van Eden, C. G. (1992). Prenatal development of neurons in the human prefrontal cortex. II. A quantitative Golgi study. *Journal of Comparative Neurology*, *316*, 485–96.

Naegele, J. R., & Lombroso, P. J. (2001). Genetics of central nervous system developmental disorders. *Child & Adolescent Psychiatric Clinics of North America, 10,* 225–39.

Ofen, N., Kao, Y.-C., Sokol-Hessner, P., Kim, H., Whitfield-Gabrieli, S., & Gabrieli, J. D. E. (2007). Development of the declarative memory system in the human brain. *Nature Neuroscience, 10,* 1198–205.

Paller, K., & Wagner, A. (2002). Observing the transformation of experience into memory. *Trends in Cognitive Sciences, 6,* 93–102.

Paz-Alonso, P. M., Ghetti, S., Donohue, S. E., Goodman, G. S., & Bunge, S. A. (2008). Neurodevelopmental correlates of true and false recognition. *Cerebral Cortex, 18,* 2208–16.

Petanjek, Z., Judas, M., Kostovic, I., & Uylings, H. B. M. (2007). Lifespan alterations of basal dendritic trees of pyramidal neurons in the human prefrontal cortex: A layer-specific pattern. *Cerebral Cortex, 18,* 915–29.

Prayer, D., Kasprian, G., Krampl, E., Ulm, B., Witzani, L., Prayer, L., & Brugger, P. C. (2006). MRI of normal fetal brain development. *European Journal of Radiology, 57,* 199–216.

Rakic, P. (1974). Neurons in rhesus monkey visual cortex: Systematic relation between time of origin and eventual disposition. *Science, 183,* 425–7.

Rakic, P., Bourgeois, J. P., Eckenhoff, M. F., Zecevic, N., & Goldman-Rakic, P. S. (1986). Concurrent overproduction of synapses in diverse regions of the primate cerebral cortex. *Science, 232,* 232–5.

Rakic, P. & Nowakowski, R. S. (1981). The time of origin of neurons in the hippocampal region of the rhesus monkey. *Journal of Comparative Neurology, 196,* 99–128.

Rosenberg, D., & Lewis, D. (1995). Postnatal maturation of the dopaminergic innervation of monkey prefrontal cortices: A tyrosine hydroxylase immunohistochemical analysis. *Journal of Comparative Neurology, 358,* 383–400.

Seress, L., & Abraham, H. (2008). Pre- and postnatal morphological development of the human hippocampal formation. In C. A. Nelson & M. Luciana (Eds.), *Handbook of developmental cognitive neuroscience* (2nd ed., pp. 187–212). Cambridge, MA: MIT Press.

Seress, L., Abraham, H., Tornoczky, T., & Kosztolanyi, G. (2001). Cell formation in the human hippocampal formation from mid-gestation to the late postnatal period. *Neuroscience, 105,* 831–43.

Seress, L., Gulyas, A. I., Ferrer, I., Tunon, T., Soriano, E., & Freund, T. F. (1993). Distribution, morphological feartures, and synaptic connections of parvalbumin- and calbindin D^{28k}-immunoreactive neurons in the human hippocampal formation. *Journal of Comparative Neurology, 337,* 208–30.

Shaw, P., Greenstein, D., Lerch, J., Clasen, L., Lenroot, R., Gogtay, N., . . . Giedd, J. (2006). Intellectual ability and cortical development in children and adolescents. *Nature, 440,* 676–9.

Sidman, R. L., & Rakic, P. (1982). Development of the human central nervous system. In W. Haymaker & R. D. Adams (Eds.), *Histology and histopathology of the nervous system.* Springfield, IL: Charles C. Thomas.

Siman, R., Bozyczko-Coyne, D., Meyer, S. L., & Ad Bhat, R. V. (1999). Immunolocalization of caspase proteolysis in situ: Evidence for widespread caspase-mediated apoptosis of neurons and glia in postnatal rat brain. *Neuroscience, 92,* 1425–42.

Sowell, E. R., Peterson, B. S., Thompson, P. M., Welcome, S. E., Henkenius, A. L., & Toga, A. W. (2003). Mapping cortical change across the human life span. *Nature Neuroscience*, 6, 309–15.

Sowell, E. R., Thompson, P. M, Leonard, C. M., Welcome, S. E., Kan, E., & Toga, A. W. (2004). Longitudinal mapping of cortical thickness and brain growth in normal children. *Journal of Neuroscience*, 24, 8223–31.

St. Jacques, P. L., & Cabeza, R. (2011). Neural bases of autobiographical memory. In S. Ghetti & P. J. Bauer (Eds.), *Origins and development of recollection: Perspectives from psychology and neuroscience* (pp. 188–218). New York: Oxford University Press.

Takahashi, T, Nowakowski, R. S., & Caviness, V. S. (2001). Neocortical neurogenesis: Regulation, control points, and a strategy of structural variation. In C. A. Nelson & M. Luciana (Eds.), *Handbook of developmental cognitive neuroscience* (pp. 3–22). Cambridge, MA: MIT Press.

Thomas, K. M., & Casey, B. J. (1999). Functional magnetic resonance imaging in pediatrics. In P. Bandetinni & C. Moonen (Eds.), *Medical radiology: Functional magnetic resonance imaging* (pp. 513–23). New York, NY: Springer Verlag.

Uncapher, M. R., & Wagner, A. D. (2009). Posterior parietal cortex and episodic encoding: Insights from fMRI subsequent memory effects and dual-attention theory. *Neurobiology of Learning and Memory*, 91, 139–54.

Volpe, J. J. (1995). *Neurology of the newborn* (3rd ed.). Philadelphia, PA: W.B. Saunders.

Wagner, A., Schacter, D., Rotte, M., Koutstaal, W., Maril, A., Dale, A., . . . Buckner, R. L. (1998). Building memories: Remembering and forgetting of verbal experiences as predicted by brain activity. *Science*, 281, 1188–91.

Wechsler, D. (1991). *Wechsler Intelligence Scale for Children* (3rd ed.). SanAntonio,TX: The Psychological Corporation.

Whitesides, J. G., III, & LaMantia, A. S. (1995). Distinct adhesive behaviors of neurons and neuronal precursor cells during regional differentiation in the mammalian forebrain. *Developmental Biology*, 169, 229–41.

Wilke, M., Sohn, J. H., Byars, A. W., & Holland, S. K. (2003). Bright spots: Correlations of gray matter volume with IQ in a normal pediatric population. *Neuroimage*, 20, 202–15.

10

The Development of Episodic Memory

An Event-Related Brain Potential Vantage Point

DAVID FRIEDMAN

THE DEVELOPMENT OF EPISODIC MEMORY: AN ERP VANTAGE POINT

Transforming experience into episodic representations is a critical aspect of human cognition. The ability to encode these experiences enables one to access them whenever necessary, that is, to "time travel" to the past, a ubiquitous and critical aspect of everyday functioning. In daily life, such memory traces are extremely valuable because they enable us to apply previous experience in the service of current decision making and problem solving. Nonetheless, despite the importance of episodic memory in the acquisition of skills throughout childhood and adolescence (Ornstein & Haden, 2001) and, therefore, in the maturation of the mind, developmental and lifespan investigations that take a neurocognitive perspective on encoding- and retrieval-related processes are scarce (for reviews of data published prior to 1990, see Friedman, 1991, 1992; from 1990 to 2000, see Cycowicz, 2000).

In the literature on young-adult mnemonic function (see Diana & Ranganath, Chapter 7, this volume), the various processes thought to underlie our ability to encode information into and retrieve it from long-term episodic memory have been related to several differences in event-related brain potential (ERP) activity between experimental conditions (Friedman & Johnson, 2000; Johnson, 1995; Paller, Voss, & Westerberg, 2009; Paller & Wagner, 2002; Rugg & Curran, 2007). The ERP technique is important in the search for the neurocognitive processes underlying episodic memory because, unlike the Bold Oxygenated Level Dependent (BOLD) signal, it is able to track those processes at the speed with which they unfold (i.e., milliseconds). For example, in theoretical accounts of familiarity-versus recollection-based processes, the former are thought to occur earlier in the processing stream than the latter (Yonelinas, 2002), with many ERP studies supporting this distinction (Rugg & Yonelinas, 2003). This type of temporal information would be much more difficult to infer using hemodynamic data alone.

The Development of Episodic Memory: Encoding Processes

Evidence that successful encoding processes are reflected in the brain's electrical activity has been provided by the subsequent-memory technique, first introduced by Sanquist, Rohrbaugh, Syndulko, and Lindsley (1980). These investigators averaged the ERPs elicited by to-be-remembered study items that were subsequently correctly recognized (hits) and compared them to the neural activity associated with those study items that were subsequently unrecognized (misses). The difference between these two sets of ERPs (the subsequent memory effect) provided a measure of neurocognitive activity at the time of encoding that was associated with successful recognition-memory performance. Sanquist et al. (1980) found that a late-onset, long-duration, positive-going activity focused over the frontal portion of the scalp, was associated with subsequent successful memory performance.

In follow-up of the seminal report by Sanquist et al., Paller, Kutas, and Mayes (1987) provided important evidence that deep (i.e., semantic) relative to shallow (e.g., orthographic) encoding processes (Craik, 2002; Craik & Lockhart, 1972) engendered greater ERP subsequent memory effects focused over the frontal scalp between about 400 and 800 ms in association with better recognition memory performance. Paller et al. (1987) labeled this difference *Dm* for difference in subsequent memory, and I will use this term throughout this chapter. The important contribution of Paller and colleagues was that the Dm activity they observed could have reflected the elaborative component of episodic encoding that is thought to be critical for forming richly detailed, integrated memory representations that ensure a high probability of subsequent, successful retrieval via recollection-based processes (Craik, 2002). The evidence that has accumulated since several early investigations (Friedman, 1990; Paller, McCarthy, & Woods, 1988; Paller, 1990; reviewed by Johnson, 1995) and Werkle-Bergner, Muller, Li, and Lindenberger (2006) suggests that there may be two unique aspects reflected in Dm activity, one occurring relatively early between ~300 and 800 ms focused around the centroparietal scalp, the other overlapping this early activity but with a longer duration (~1000 to 1400 ms) and a maximum over the frontal scalp. Differences in scalp distribution and latency suggest that these two components of Dm are likely to reflect distinct cognitive processes that contribute to successful episodic encoding. Significantly, the frontal focus of the late Dm component is consistent with hemodynamic data that demonstrate greater activation of the left inferior prefrontal cortex (LIPFC) to study items that are subsequently remembered versus those that are subsequently missed (Fletcher & Henson, 2001; Wagner et al., 1998). Moreover, this prefrontal region shows greater BOLD activity under deep, semantic relative to nonsemantic encoding conditions (Demb et al., 1995; Fletcher, Stephenson, Carpenter, Donovan, & Bullmorel, 2003; Kohler, Paus, Buckner, & Milner, 2004; Nessler, Johnson, Bersick, & Friedman, 2006). Furthermore, very recent developmental hemodynamic data support the increasing use throughout childhood and adolescence of semantic elaboration in concert with the increasing recruitment of LIPFC (Chiu, Schmithorst, Brown, Holland, & Dunn, 2006; McAuley, Brahmbhatt, & Barch, 2007; Ofen et al., 2007). Therefore, these data lend credence to the argument that the recruitment of LIPFC and semantic elaboration show developmental trajectories and are important neurocognitive components of initial memory formation. Although the ERP evidence is limited, it suggests that the early Dm component could reflect the transformation of sensory experience into coherent representations. In accord with its later onset, longer duration, and frontal distribution and the LIPFC activations reported in hemodynamic investigations, the later-onset Dm component may reflect the semantic elaboration of those representations (e.g., Paller & Wagner, 2002).

Children do not appear to recruit elaborative strategies spontaneously during episodic-memory encoding. In addition, the young child's episodic-memory traces appear to be more heavily weighted by sensory/perceptual than conceptual features, thereby precluding, on some percentage of trials, the formation of contextually rich engrams. Several studies have supported this idea (e.g., Cramer, 1976; Sophian & Hagen, 1978), particularly when encoding strategies are unconstrained (Chi, 1976; Emmerich & Ackerman, 1979; Ghatala, Carbonari, & Bobele, 1980; Perlmutter, 1980). Based on these findings, one would expect that, to the extent that elaborative processes are reflected in the late-onset, frontal Dm effect, this electrical activity would be reduced in children.

We set out to explore this assumption using an episodic-memory paradigm in which encoding activity was unconstrained (de Chastelaine, Friedman, Cycowicz, & Horton, 2009). Sixteen 9- to 10-year-old children, 15 13- to 14-year-old adolescents, and 18 young adults (20 to 30 years of age) studied the same 40 symbol-like objects over 4 study/test blocks. (Figure 10.1 depicts a schematic of a study and test series.) Foils were completely new to each test block. The symbol-like objects were preexperimentally unfamiliar. Participants were asked to study them in any fashion they saw fit and were instructed that their memories for the objects would be tested subsequently. During the encoding series, the symbol-like objects were presented either to the left or right of central fixation and participants made speeded and accurate choice, left/right decisions. To avoid the possibility of repetition priming effects confounding any subsequent memory effects that were observed, ERP averages were computed only for Study 1 items that were subsequently correct and subsequently incorrect in Test Block 1. This procedure was also used because of the increasing overlap across test blocks in the items that were successfully recognized (see discussion of the data averaged during the test phases). That is, Study Block 1 items would comprise the "purest" Dm effects. To the best of our knowledge, this type of lifespan assessment of episodic encoding activity does not exist (see Fabiani, Gratton, Chiarenza, & Donchin, 1990, for a study of encoding in 11-year-old children during a Von Restorff paradigm).

Figure 10.2 depicts the grand-mean ERPs for each age group recorded during the first study block and averaged as a function of subsequent Test 1 performance. The Dm effect for all age groups generally takes the form of greater positive activity for the subsequently correct relative to the subsequently incorrect waveforms.

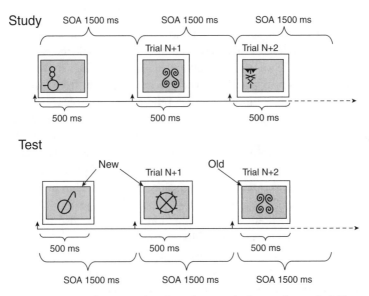

Figure 10.1. Schematic of a series of study and test trials during the symbol-like study/ test paradigm

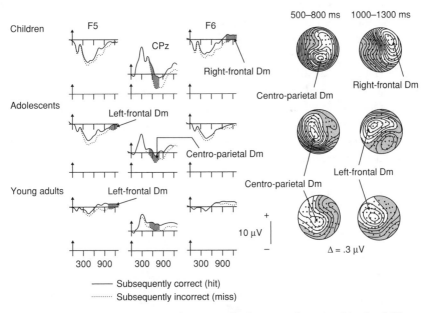

Figure 10.2. Grand-mean ERP waveforms averaged across subjects within the child, adolescent, and young adult groups to studied symbol-like items that were (solid-line ERPs) or were not (dashed-line ERPs) subsequently recognized. The data are depicted at three scalp locations where the Dm effects were largest. Time lines every 300 ms; arrows mark stimulus onset. The scalp distributions corresponding to the Dm effects in the 500 to 800 ms and 1000 to 1300 ms shaded regions are illustrated to the right of the waveforms. Small dots represent the electrode locations. Isopotential lines are separated by 0.3 μV for each age group. Negative activity is indicated by shaded areas and positive activity by unshaded areas

Between 500 and 800 ms, all age groups show centroparietal maximal Dm activity (light gray shading in Figure 10.2; first column of topographic maps). By contrast, in the late region of the waveforms (1000 to 1300 ms), children show right-frontal Dm activity, whereas young adults and adolescents show left-frontal activity (dark gray shading and right column of topographic maps). Although it is difficult to infer the intracranial generators of activity at the scalp simply via inspection of topography, the distribution and timing of this latter activity is consistent with the hemodynamic data indicating a role for the LIPFC in semantic elaboration.

Assessment of an index of memory sensitivity, Pr (Snodgrass & Corwin, 1988), lends some support to this tentative conclusion. As illustrated in Figure 10.3, children show the lowest Pr values, with adolescents showing somewhat better and young adults the best memory-discrimination scores. Because the symbol-like objects were preexperimentally unfamiliar, they were not likely to have had preexisting semantic representations, at least during the first encoding and test block. Nonetheless, participants could have attempted to encode the items semantically by attempting to associate a "name" with each object;: that is, they could have engaged in semantic or conceptual processing. To determine whether this might have occurred, a postexperiment symbol-naming task was administered. Each of the symbols was re-presented and participants stated whether or not they had attempted to associate a name with that particular symbol at any time during the series of study/test blocks. Although some individuals within the three age groups did report this type of strategy, more young adults, whose memory sensitivity was the greatest at Test 1 (Figure 10.3), also showed the greatest tendency to attach a label or name to subsequently correctly recognized versus unrecognized symbols. The adolescent naming data were in the same direction, although not as marked as for the adults. Children, by contrast, did not show this pattern of findings. Hence, because all age groups show centroparietal Dm activity (500 to 800 ms), whereas only young adults and, to some extent, adolescents show left-frontal activity (1000 to 1300 ms),

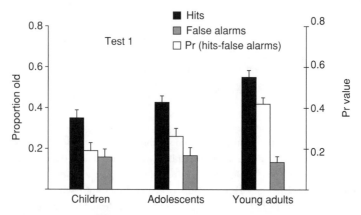

Figure 10.3. Grand-mean hits, false alarms, and Pr (memory sensitivity) during Test 1 of the symbol-recognition phase in children, adolescents, and young adults. Error bars represent the standard error of the mean

the ERP data in Figure 10.2 suggest that the increment in performance may have been supported by putatively conceptually driven processes reflected in the left-prefrontal Dm effect, a view that is broadly consistent with the results of the extant developmental hemodynamic studies (Chiu et al., 2006; McAuley et al., 2007; Ofen et al., 2007). However, at this juncture, the precise nature of those processes is a matter subject to a certain amount of speculation. I outline some possibilities herein.

Based on the available behavioral, ERP, and hemodynamic evidence, our working hypothesis is that, in showing commonality among age groups, the centroparietal Dm effect reflects the encoding and transformation of sensory experience into detailed representations. The later-onset Dm activity, which showed its greatest magnitude in the young adult data, may reflect processes responsible for elaborating those representations semantically. To the extent that the enhanced Dm activity over the prefrontal scalp reflects generators similar to those observed in hemodynamic studies, this electrical activity may reflect the control this region of the pre-frontal cortex exerts over the selection, organization, and elaboration of the to-be-remembered information. Nonetheless, different investigators make slightly different claims about the nature of these control processes and the regions of LIPFC in which their computations take place (Blumenfeld & Ranganath, 2007; Thompson-Schill, D'Esposito, Aguirre, & Farah, 1997; Wagner, Pare-Blagoev, Clark, & Poldrack, 2001), so that further work will be necessary to provide a stronger link between the left-frontal ERP activity (Figure 10.2) and the hemodynamic findings. It is more difficult to interpret the functional significance of the right-lateralized Dm activity observed only in the children. It may reflect less-efficient encoding processes that differed from those of the adolescents and young adults, consistent with the lowest memory performance in this age group. However, a better understanding of the variables that modulate this brain activity as well as the left-frontal Dm effect is clearly needed before much can be said concerning its functional significance. Thus, these encoding-related ERP data must be considered preliminary because they are the only developmental data available and, therefore, require replication. Nonetheless, though requiring interpretive caution, the data reviewed herein suggest that one aspect of the child's episodic-memory skill that is still developing is the spontaneous elaboration of to-be-remembered material, presumably in association with continued maturation of regions of the prefrontal cortex and their interactions with other brain areas (McAuley et al., 2007).

THE DEVELOPMENT OF EPISODIC MEMORY: RETRIEVAL PROCESSES

Another critical aspect of episodic memory is the retrieval of events that have been encoded recently. Events are more vividly remembered (and, not surprisingly, mnemonic performance is better) if the episodic trace contains features that had been elaborated semantically during encoding (Craik, 2002; Craik & Lockhart, 1972). This phenomenon stands in contrast to experiences that appear only to be familiar, possibly because they received shallow encoding during study via instruction (Rugg et al., 1998) or attention was diverted, thereby precluding deep encoding (Yonelinas, 2002). Based on these phenomenological experiences, episodic memories have been partitioned into source and item memories, respectively: those that do and do not contain information about the initial learning context. Retrieval of source memories requires recollection, a process that presumably necessitates effortful control (Jacoby, Bishara, Hessels, & Toth, 2005), whereas retrieval of item memories can be based on a relatively fast-acting, relatively automatic, and less effortful familiarity process (Mandler, 1980; Yonelinas, 2002). Although item as well as source memory depend critically on medial temporal lobe structures (Brown & Aggleton, 2001; Thaiss & Petrides, 2003), the prefrontal cortex plays an equally vital, though primarily supervisory, role in the retrieval of contextually detailed memories (Dobbins, Foley, Schacter, & Wagner, 2002).

A great deal of evidence with young adults as participants suggests that recollection-based processes at retrieval are reflected in a scalp-recorded old minus new parietal positivity between approximately 500 and 800 ms (Friedman & Johnson, 2000; Paller et al., 2009; Rugg & Yonelinas, 2003). This has been labeled the parietal episodic-memory (EM) effect by Friedman and Johnson (2000), and I will refer to it by this label in the remainder of this chapter. The evidence for familiarity-based processes in the electrical record is arguably more difficult to agree on (for conflicting views, see Paller, Voss, & Boehm, 2007; Rugg & Curran, 2007). Hence, I will concentrate here on the development of recollection-based processing as reflected in the parietal EM effect. Again, however, developmental data are scarce. In investigations from this (Berman & Friedman, 1993; Cycowicz, Friedman, & Duff, 2003; Friedman, de Chastelaine, Nessler, & Malcolm, 2010) and other (Czernochowski, Brinkmann, Mecklinger, & Johansson, 2004; Czernochowski, Mecklinger, Johansson, & Brinkmann, 2005; Mecklinger, Brunnemann, & Kipp, 2010) laboratories, recollection-based processes (as indexed by the parietal EM effect) have generally been reported to be similar to those of adults by 8 to 10 years of age. I should note, however, that ERP (and functional magnetic resonance imaging [fMRI]) neurodevelopmental investigations of episodic memory with children below the age of 8 are extremely rare. Because recognition-memory and, in particular, source-memory performance, continue to improve throughout childhood and adolescence (de Chastelaine, Friedman, & Cycowicz, 2007; Friedman et al., 2010; Ghetti & Angelini, 2008; Schneider, 2002), other factors aside from recollection per se, such as improvement in the control of retrieval, are likely to contribute to the documented maturational increments in episodic-memory performance.

One of the factors that influences recollection-based processing is repetition, which has powerful and advantageous effects on memory performance. Repetition has been shown, in some instances, to increment behavioral estimates of recollection- but not familiarity-based processing, although it does modulate familiarity in other instances (Yonelinas, 2002). A similar distinction exists in the results of the few ERP studies that have repeated items over more than one study phase—the putative index of familiarity-based recognition (mid-frontal EM effect) has been shown not to increase reliably in magnitude with repeated testing, whereas the sign of recollection-based processing, the parietal EM effect, has (de Chastelaine et al., 2009; Johnson, Kreiter, Russo, & Zhu, 1998; Nessler, Friedman, Johnson, & Bersick, 2007a). Hence, to determine whether repetition would enhance recollection-based processes in children and adolescents in similar fashion to young adults, the retrieval data from the multiple study–test investigation whose encoding data (at Test 1) were described earlier were assessed (Figure 10.1 shows a schematic test series).

The test phase ERP data that resulted are depicted in Figure 10.4. To enhance the signal-to-noise ratios in the individual averaged waveforms, especially for the children and adolescents, the data have been collapsed across Tests 1 and 2 and Tests 3 and 4. As shown in Table 10.1, repetition of the symbol-like objects led to increments in memory sensitivity (Pr) in all three age groups. However, as might be expected, the young adults began and ended the test series at a higher level and benefited somewhat more from repeated testing than the children and adolescents did. During the test phases, we also collected remember (recollection-based) and know (familiarity-based) judgments (Tulving, 1985; but see Brainerd, Holliday, & Reyna, 2004; Ghetti & Angelini, 2008, for arguments against using

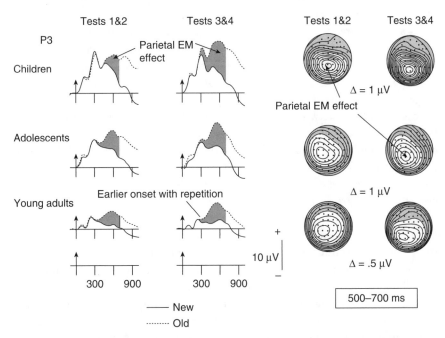

Figure 10.4. Grand-mean ERP waveforms at the P3 scalp location (left two columns) averaged across subjects within the child, adolescent, and young adult groups. The data have been collapsed across the first two and last two test phases. Dark gray shading indicates the parietal EM effect. Note that this effect onsets earlier in Tests 3 and 4 relative to Tests 1 and 2 in each of the three groups' waveforms. The old-new scalp topographies for each test phase are depicted to the right of the waveforms and are based on a measurement window between 500 and 700 ms. Small dots represent the electrode locations. Isopotential lines are separated by 1 μV for the children and adolescents and 0.5 μV for the young adults. Negative activity is indicated by shaded areas, positive activity by unshaded areas

Table 10.1. MEAN MEMORY SENSITIVITY MEASURES
(±SE; PR = HITS - FALSE ALARMS) IN THE THREE AGE
GROUPS DURING THE SYMBOL-RECOGNITION TASK

Age Group	Tests 1 and 2	Tests 3 and 4
Children	0.26 (0.04)	0.51 (0.06)
Adolescents	0.35 (0.04)	0.59 (0.05)
Young adults	0.54 (0.03)	0.83 (0.02)

these judgments with children). The percentage of remember judgments increased reliably with repetition, whereas the percentage of know judgments remained the same (both indices were corrected by the appropriate false alarm rate). The grand-averaged ERP data are illustrated at the left-parietal scalp site, P3 (Mecklinger, 2000; Rugg & Yonelinas, 2003). Paralleling the increase in memory sensitivity and remember judgments, recollection-based processing (putatively reflected by the parietal EM effect) increased with repetition. Importantly, repetition of the study items also appeared to engender an earlier onset in recollection-based processes. This was reflected by a reliably earlier divergence at the parietal scalp site between the ERPs elicited by old and new items (i.e., the parietal EM effect) in Tests 3 and 4 compared with Tests 1 and 2 (see Figure 10.4). These data provide electrophysiological evidence that repetition leads to an enhancement in recollection-based processing. Most likely, with repetition, a greater number of contextual details becomes available (e.g., creating names and/or semantic associations for the symbols, or remembering the peculiar shape of the symbol), thereby enabling increments in the use of recollection-based processes to guide retrieval (Wilding, 2000). Furthermore, the results suggest that, at least based on this task, the processes involved are relatively well established in 9- to 10-year-olds and may be similar across this age range (see also Czernochowski et al., 2005). Nonetheless, because memory performance was reduced in the children and adolescents relative to the young adults, we cannot rule out the possibility, as mentioned earlier, that other processes, such as those underlying executive control, contribute to the overall poorer performance of the younger participants.

Some of the data that support the contention that improvements in executive-control processes contribute to the maturation of episodic-memory performance will be provided in the following paragraphs in which I describe the results of a study of source memory conducted with children, adolescents, and young adults (Cycowicz et al., 2003; de Chastelaine et al., 2007). In this initial neurodevelopmental investigation of the recollection of contextually based memories, we used the exclusion-memory paradigm described originally by Jacoby (1991). Unlike the simple old/new recognition-memory (or inclusion) task, during exclusion testing a selective response is made to only one class of studied items (target old), whereas the other class of studied items (nontarget old) and new items receives the same response. It is generally thought that above-chance performance on the exclusion task can be maintained only if the two classes of old items can be distinguished.

That is, simple, old/new discrimination will not suffice. Moreover, the assumption is made that, unlike performance during inclusion testing, familiarity-based responding will not yield accurate performance, because target old and nontarget old items are equally familiar. During the exclusion test, recollection is pitted against familiarity, and participants must make covert source judgments in order to perform well. That is, participants are assumed to base their recognition decisions on the retrieval of contextual or source information.

A schematic of the experimental design that was used in this investigation appears in Figure 10.5. In our implementation of this paradigm, 16 children (mean age = 10 years), 16 adolescents (mean age = 13 years), and 16 young adults (mean age = 24 years) encoded pictures of common objects that were outlined in either green or red. During the encoding phase, our volunteers were told that their memories for the objects would be tested but they were not instructed about the nature of the subsequent memory test until after the study series. To emphasize the perceptual aspects of the "source" (i.e., the color in which the objects were outlined), participants were asked to make red/green choice decisions to each item presented

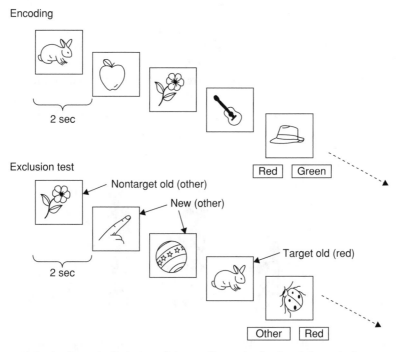

Figure 10.5. A schematic depiction of an encoding series (top) and the exclusion-memory test phase (bottom). During the former, participants made speeded and accurate red/green (see color inserts), choice RT decisions. During the latter, participants made speeded and accurate target old/other judgments. In the case illustrated here, participants pressed the target old button to any previously studied picture that they thought had been outlined in red during the encoding phase and pressed the "other" button to pictures that had been presented in green or were new

at study. During memory testing, two types of recognition block were administered. During inclusion testing, participants made simple, speeded, and accurate
old/new judgments without reference to the objects' study color. On the other
hand, during exclusion testing, volunteers were asked to discriminate between two
classes of old items, those that were studied in the target color (e.g., red) and those
that were studied in the nontarget color (e.g., green). Target responses were made
with one hand, whereas nontarget and new items were both assigned to the opposite hand. As during inclusion testing, speeded and accurate responding were
emphasized equally.

Figure 10.6 depicts the basic performance data during the exclusion or source-
memory test phases. The discrimination between targets and new items is greater
than that between target and nontarget objects in similar fashion in all three
age groups. This is not surprising because the two types of old items are equally
familiar. Hence, accurate discrimination of the two requires recollection of the
source or color in which the item was outlined at study. Nonetheless, as might be
expected based on prior performance-oriented studies, there are reliable increments in memory sensitivity from middle childhood through adolescence into
young adulthood in both the Pr (new) and Pr (nontarget) memory indices, suggesting increments in source-memory performance across this age range. What
are the neurophysiologic underpinnings of the increment in source-memory performance that presumably depend on recollection-based processes?

For a preliminary answer, Figure 10.7 depicts the ERP data recorded during the
retrieval phase of the exclusion task. Correctly recognized targets and nontargets

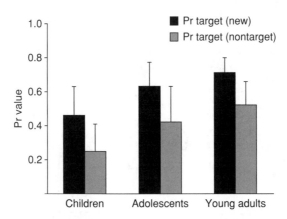

Figure 10.6. Grand-mean memory sensitivity, Pr, values averaged across subjects within
each age group. Pr to targets was computed in two ways: (a) using the false alarm rate
to new items, yielding a measure of memory discrimination between targets and new
items (Pr Target [New] in the figure); and (b) using the false alarm rate to nontargets
(e.g., calling a nontarget item studied in green outline a target red item), yielding an
index of memory discrimination between target and nontarget items (Pr Target
[Nontarget] in the figure). Vertical error bars represent the standard error
of the mean

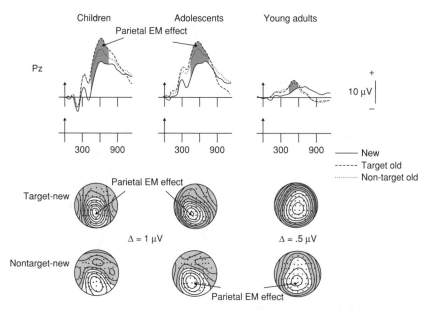

Figure 10.7. Grand-mean ERP waveforms averaged across subjects within the child, adolescent, and young adult groups to pictures of common objects that were correctly recognized as targets (dashed-line ERPs), nontargets (dotted-line ERPs), or correctly identified as new (solid-line ERPs) during the exclusion task. Time lines every 300 ms; arrows mark stimulus onset. The scalp topographies of the old-new differences during the putative recollection-based region of the ERPs are depicted below each age group's waveforms. Small dots represent the electrode locations. Isopotential lines are separated by 1.0 μV for the children and adolescents and 0.5 μV for the young adults. Negative activity is indicated by shaded areas and positive activity by unshaded areas

are superimposed along with correctly rejected new items at the mid-parietal (Pz) scalp location. The difference between the ERPs to targets and new items and nontargets and new items is the parietal EM effect, which is shaded in dark gray. Measurement of the target-new and nontarget-new differences revealed reliable parietal EM effects in each of the three age groups. Below the waveforms, I have depicted the target-new and nontarget-new scalp topographies for the region in which the parietal EM effect was active (shaded in dark gray). Notably, in all age groups, the scalp distributions are characterized by tightly focused, parietal maxima, entirely in accord with a very large number of investigations of this ERP memory-related phenomenon (Friedman & Johnson, 2000; Mecklinger, 2000; Paller et al., 2009; Rugg & Yonelinas, 2003). Based on the well-documented evidence that the parietal EM effect reflects recollection-based processes, the ERP data indicate that all groups were able to retrieve the contextual (i.e., color) or source information associated with target and nontarget memories.

Nevertheless, it is clear from the behavioral data that children and adolescents did not perform source retrievals at the same level of accuracy as the young adults.

Hence, although these groups undoubtedly engaged recollection in order to discriminate target and nontarget old objects, immature or inefficient executive-control processes may also have played a role in the children's lower source-memory performance relative to young adults.

For example, it is well known that supervisory processes that exert control over what is encoded and direct the search for that information during retrieval (Badre & Wagner, 2007; Blumenfeld & Ranganath, 2007; Shallice & Burgess, 1996; Thompson-Schill et al., 1997; Wagner et al., 2001) are required for efficient epi-sodic remembering. Furthermore, like episodic-memory performance, tasks that require the recruitment of these cognitive-control processes show relatively long maturational courses (Bunge, Dudukovic, Thomason, Vaidya, & Gabrieli, 2002; Friedman, Nessler, Cycowicz, & Horton, 2009; Zelazo, 2004), but little is known about how they putatively contribute to the well-documented developmental enhancement in episodic-memory performance (Schneider, 2002). During a source-memory task, for example, it is thought that such control processes are critical to strategically guide and monitor the retrieval of task-relevant contextual attributes. In fact, the results from extant developmental studies, though rare, sug-gest that immaturity in prefrontally based, cognitive-control systems may influ-ence the poorer source, relative to item, memory performance of younger versus older children and young adults that has typically been observed (Cycowicz et al., 2003; Cycowicz, Friedman, Snodgrass, & Duff, 2001; Drummey & Newcombe, 2002; Rybash & Colilla, 1994; Zelazo, Craik, & Booth, 2004).

Moreover, recent ERP data from this laboratory (de Chastelaine et al., 2007) suggest that these kinds of executive-control processes are slower to unfold and may not yet be mature in 9- to 10-year-old children. We came to this conclusion based on data that, rather than being time-locked to the stimulus, were time-locked to the response (Friedman et al., 2009; Johnson, Henkell, Simon, & Zhu, 2008; Nessler, Friedman, Johnson, & Bersick, 2007b). Importantly, it can be the case that reaction-time (RT) variability obscures the ERP activity associated with late-occurring cognitive processes (i.e., those more closely related to response onset than to stimulus onset; Friedman, 1984). For instance, whereas onset of memory search operations is likely more closely linked to the copy cue in recognition-memory testing situations, those related to postretrieval executive processes such as the implementation of attentional control to enhance target memories and facilitate response selection are likely more tightly coupled to the occurrence of the response (de Chastelaine et al., 2007).

Figure 10.8 depicts the response-locked data corresponding to the stimulus-locked data illustrated in Figure 10.7. The data are shown at midline parietal (Pz) and right frontopolar (FP2) scalp locations for a 1000-ms interval prior to RT and 250 ms following it. At the parietal and frontopolar sites, all age groups generally show more positive-going waveforms to target- and nontarget-old objects relative to correctly rejected new items (the regions shaded in dark gray at Pz and light gray at FP2). Nonetheless, the temporal differentiation between target, nontarget, and new items is different at the two scalp locations. At the parietal scalp site, target and nontarget items are more positive than new items, but can be seen to

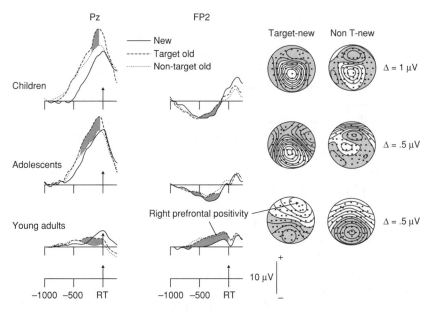

Figure 10.8. Grand-mean response-locked ERP waveforms averaged across subjects within the child, adolescent, and young adult groups to pictures of common objects that were correctly recognized as targets (dashed-line ERPs), nontargets (dotted-line ERPs), or correctly identified as new (solid-line ERPs) items during the exclusion task. The target-new and nontarget-new scalp topographies are depicted to the right of each age group's waveforms for the 200-ms period prior to RT. Small dots represent the electrode locations. For the children, isopotential lines are separated by 1.0 μV; for the adolescents and young adults they are separated by 0.5 μV. Negative activity is indicated by shaded areas and positive activity by unshaded areas. NonT = nontarget

diverge from each other (targets are more positive) at different time points for the three groups. The target–nontarget differentiation begins earliest for the young adults (at about 600 ms prior to RT), followed by the adolescents, and onsets latest for the children. At the right frontopolar scalp site, by contrast, target and nontarget items are not different from one another, but diverge from new objects at approximately 600 ms prior to the RT response in young adults (Figure 10.8). Hence, on this basis, the electrical activities observed at parietal and right prefrontal scalp locations appear to reflect different cognitive processes (see following discussion). The target–nontarget divergence at about 600 ms pre RT is equivalent to about 250 to 300 ms poststimulus, suggesting, at least for young adults, that mnemonic processing is sensitive to different aspects of the study context very early in the information-processing sequence. Therefore, these data suggest that, although all age groups appear to differentiate previously studied from new items, it takes longer for this to occur in the youngest children.

Furthermore, the timing of the divergence of target and nontarget items relative to RT would have consequences for the processes involved in response selection. That is, the sooner one can differentiate items from the two study contexts, the greater will be the time available for control processes to organize, prepare, and select the appropriate response. On these bases, the data in Figure 10.8 indicate that children may not have had sufficient time to adequately prepare their responses, whereas young adults and adolescents would have. This temporal difference may, at least in part, account for the poorer source-memory performance in the children. Moreover, the maps of the scalp distributions depicted to the right of the waveforms allow further inferences concerning the development of source memory. Note that, for young adults, the target-new and nontarget-new scalp topographies appear to be quite distinct, suggesting that the processing of correctly identified targets and nontargets may have involved different intracranial generators and, hence, at least partially nonoverlapping cognitive processes. Figure 10.8 shows that, for young adults, target items elicit a right-lateralized prefrontal positivity, whereas nontargets elicit a bilaterally symmetrical frontal positivity. By contrast, for the children, the scalp distributions are both posteriorly focused and quite similar, suggesting analogous processing of both targets and nontargets. For adolescents, the target and nontarget topographies appear somewhat different, but dissimilar from those of the young adults. Hence, the adolescents may have differentiated the two classes of old items better than the children (as evinced by their higher memory-sensitivity scores to both classes of old item; Figure 10.6), but appeared to utilize different processes than those of the young adults.

These response-locked data suggest that a series of processes that operate on the products of retrieval downstream from those underlying the initial recovery of information display a developmental trajectory. Developmental change in these postretrieval processes may, therefore, account, at least in part, for improvement in source-memory performance often observed across this age range (Cycowicz et al., 2001; de Chastelaine et al., 2007; Drummey & Newcombe, 2002; Rybash & Colilla, 1994). For example, the greater-magnitude target compared to nontarget parietal activity could reflect the consequence of greater allocation of attentional resources to task-relevant target versus nontarget information. Indeed, some models propose that retrieval involves the focus of attention on internally generated mnemonic information (Anderson & Bjork, 1994) and could, therefore, support an account of selectively focusing attention on a targeted subset of information that has been retrieved initially (de Chastelaine et al., 2007). More recent accounts based on hemodynamic data suggest that focusing attention on internal representations may be initiated in the parietal cortex (Cabeza, 2008; Cabeza, Ciaramelli, Olson, & Moscovitch, 2008; Wagner, Shannon, Kahn, & Buckner, 2005), although other interpretations of parietal activations during memory tasks, such as reflecting an episodic-memory buffer (Baddeley, 2000), have also been advanced (Vilberg & Rugg, 2008). Nonetheless, the parietal maximum of the ERP target–nontarget difference described earlier would be consistent with the attention to internal representations hypothesis advanced by some investigators (Cabeza, 2008; Cabeza et al., 2008; Wagner et al., 2005) and would further suggest that the internal control of the attentional focus develops over the childhood and adolescent years.

Other executive processes, such as monitoring and checking the products of retrieval, might also be expected to occur in close proximity to the behavioral decision, because these processes would be necessary to inform that decision. Indeed, in studies with young adults, a right-lateralized, prefrontal positive activity in stimulus-locked averages has often been associated with these types of postretrieval control operations (ERP reviews by Friedman, 2000; Wilding & Sharpe, 2002; see Rugg, Otten, & Henson, 2002, for fMRI studies). Importantly, in the current, response-locked data, this activity precedes RT by a sufficient time period to have been instrumental in guiding the behavioral decision (Figure 10.8; de Chastelaine et al., 2007). Moreover, in the current data, the prefrontal-positive activity was right-lateralized to targets, but bilaterally distributed to nontargets (Figure 10.8), which is consistent with several studies of the exclusion paradigm in which stimulus-locked averaging has been used (Wilding, Fraser, & Herron, 2005). As noted by de Chastelaine et al. (2007), the topographic distinction between targets and nontargets at frontal locations in young adults suggests the possibility that postretrieval monitoring processes may be triggered exogenously by the stimulus (in a bottom-up fashion; evident in stimulus-locked ERPs) and/or endogenously (i.e., internally) according to behavioral goals (i.e., top-down control; evident in response-locked ERPs). Nonetheless, as argued by others on the basis of ERP (Hayama, Johnson, & Rugg, 2008) as well as fMRI (Cabeza et al., 2003) data, these processes may not be distinctly mnemonic, but may reflect more generic attentional mechanisms and/or monitoring and decisional processes. Hence, on the basis of the current data, it is not yet clear which of these sets of processes shows developmental improvement. Clearly, this is one area of developmental memory research that would benefit from further psychophysiological and hemodynamic investigation.

CONCLUDING REMARKS

In this chapter, I have provided a brief overview of developmental ERP and behavioral findings primarily from my own laboratory. This was necessitated by the very limited number of developmental investigations of episodic memory in which ERPs have served as dependent measures. Similarly, there are barely a handful of developmental fMRI investigations of episodic-memory phenomena. Nonetheless, even at this very early stage in the accumulation of knowledge, some general points can be made, although more definitive statements await further work.

It has been known (via behavioral research) for some time that children have difficulty in spontaneously semantically elaborating to-be-remembered material. Nevertheless, the extant ERP and hemodynamic encoding-related data suggest that it is the LIPFC that plays a crucial role in the maturation of the transformation of experience via semantic elaboration into contextually rich memories and that the processes reflected unfold relatively late in the information processing sequence. Presumably, these processes ensue after the to-be-remembered item has been retrieved from semantic memory, thus accounting for their late onset even in young adults (Figure 10.2). To the best of my knowledge, the waveforms depicted in Figure 10.2 are the only encoding-related ERP data available in which children have been compared with either adolescents or young adults. Hence, they require replication and extension to other, more traditional, stimulus materials such as pictures of common objects and their verbal equivalents.

Repetition is a tried and true technique for increasing memory performance and, as demonstrated here, benefited children, adolescents, and young adults (Table 10.1, Figure 10.4). Importantly, repetition appeared to modulate recollection-based processing, putatively reflected by the parietal EM effect, and did so in similar fashion in all three age groups. This result suggests that recollection-based processing is relatively mature in 9- to 10-year-old children and, at least in the task used here, does not appear to develop further. Nonetheless, in both the symbol-recognition and exclusion, source-memory tasks, children performed more poorly than adolescents and young adults, despite showing evidence of recollection-based processing. As noted earlier, this suggests that factors other than recollection per se may have been responsible for the children's poorer performance. Indeed, as demonstrated here (Figure 10.8), control processes (whether generic or mnemonic) that direct the search for previously experienced episodes during retrieval appear to play important roles in the maturation of episodic memory (see also Czernochowski, Mecklinger, & Johansson, 2009). This is perhaps the most important, though preliminary, conclusion of the brief overview provided here.

Finally, it is most likely the case that the prolonged maturation of the frontal lobes and their interconnections play a role in the increasing ease, across the developmental lifespan, with which older children, adolescents, and young adults exert control over what they encode and how this task-relevant information is retrieved. However, as noted herein, there are still large gaps in our understanding of the precise nature of these processes, their temporal sequencing, and how they are instantiated in the brain. The ERP provides fine-grained temporal precision currently unavailable with fMRI methods. In the ERP investigations described in the current paper, the critical neural events reflecting either developmental or condition-related differences occurred within the first 250 to 800 ms poststimulus. On the other hand, fMRI affords excellent spatial resolution, whereas the intracranial sources of scalp-recorded activity are more difficult to infer based on scalp distribution alone. Hence, an approach in which both techniques are combined will most likely lead to significant advances in knowledge. This kind of approach has been successful in other domains (for discussions, see Luck, 1999; Rugg, 1998) but, to date, has not been applied to the study of the development of episodic memory. New techniques for relating ERP and hemodynamic measures are becoming available (Debener et al., 2005; Goldman et al., 2009) and will undoubtedly aid in a better understanding of the processes, timing, and neural networks that underlie developmental improvements in episodic memory.

ACKNOWLEDGMENTS

I thank my current and former collaborators and assistants for their contributions to the work reported here: Ms. Brenda Malcolm, Mr. Cort Horton, and Drs. Yael M. Cycowicz, Marianne de Chastelaine, Alberto Manzi, and Doreen Nessler. I thank

Mr. Charles L. Brown III for computer programming and technical assistance and all of the volunteers for their participation in these studies. The writing of this chapter was supported in part by grant HD014959 from National Institute of Child Health and Human Development and by the New York State Department of Mental Hygiene. Address correspondence to: David Friedman, Cognitive Electrophysiology Laboratory, Division of Cognitive Neuroscience, New York State Psychiatric Institute, 1051 Riverside Drive, Unit 50, New York, New York 10032; E-mail: df12@columbia.edu.

REFERENCES

Anderson, M. C., & Bjork, R. A. (1994). Mechanisms of inhibition in long term memory. In D. Dagenbach & T. H. C. I (Eds.), *Inhibitory processes in attention, memory, and language* (pp. 265–325). San Diego, CA: Academic Press.

Baddeley, A. (2000). The episodic buffer: A new component of working memory? *Trends in Cognitive Science, 4,* 417–23.

Badre, D., & Wagner, A. D. (2007). Left ventrolateral prefrontal cortex and the cognitive control of memory. *Neuropsychologia, 45,* 2883–901.

Berman, S., & Friedman, D. (1993). A developmental study of ERPs during recognition memory: Effects of picture familiarity, word frequency, and readability. *Journal of Psychophysiology, 7,* 97–114.

Blumenfeld, R. S., & Ranganath, C. (2007). Prefrontal cortex and long-term memory encoding: An integrative review of findings from neuropsychology and neuroimaging. *Neuroscientist, 13,* 280–91.

Brainerd, C. J., Holliday, R. E., & Reyna, V. F. (2004). Behavioral measurement of remembering phenomenologies: So simple a child can do it. *Child Development, 75,* 505–22.

Brown, M. W., & Aggleton, J. P. (2001). Recognition memory: What are the roles of the perirhinal cortex and hippocampus? *Nature Reviews: Neuroscience, 2,* 51–61.

Bunge, S. A., Dudukovic, N. M., Thomason, M. E., Vaidya, C. J., & Gabrieli, J. D. (2002). Immature frontal lobe contributions to cognitive control in children: Evidence from fMRI. *Neuron, 33,* 301–11.

Cabeza, R. (2008). Role of parietal regions in episodic memory retrieval: The dual attentional processes hypothesis. *Neuropsychologia, 46,* 1813–27.

Cabeza, R., Ciaramelli, E., Olson, I. R., & Moscovitch, M. (2008). The parietal cortex and episodic memory: An attentional account. *Nature Reviews Neuroscience, 9,* 613–25.

Cabeza, R., Dolcos, F., Prince, S. E., Rice, H. J., Weissman, D. H., & Nyberg, L. (2003). Attention-related activity during episodic memory retrieval: A cross-function fMRI study. *Neuropsychologia, 41,* 390–9.

Chi, M. T. H. (1976). Short-term memory limitations in children: Capacity or processing deficits? *Memory and Cognition, 4,* 559–72.

Chiu, C. Y., Schmithorst, V. J., Brown, R. D., Holland, S. K., & Dunn, S. (2006). Making memories: A cross-sectional investigation of episodic memory encoding in childhood using fMRI. *Developmental Neuropsychology, 29,* 321–40.

Craik, F. I. (2002). Levels of processing: Past, present, and future? *Memory, 10,* 305–18.

Craik, F. I. M., & Lockhart, S. (1972). Levels of processing: A framework for memory research. *Journal of Verbal Learning and Verbal Behavior, 11,* 671–84.

Cramer, P. (1976). Changes from visual to verbal memory organization as a function of age. *Journal of Experimental Child Psychology, 22,* 50–7.

Cycowicz, Y. M. (2000). Memory development and event-related brain potentials in children. *Biological Psychology, 54,* 145–74.

Cycowicz, Y. M., Friedman, D., & Duff, M. (2003). Pictures and their colors: What do children remember? *Journal of Cognitive Neuroscience, 15,* 759–68.

Cycowicz, Y. M., Friedman, D., Snodgrass, J. G., & Duff, M. (2001). Recognition and source memory for pictures in children and adults. *Neuropsychologia, 39,* 255–67.

Czernochowski, D., Brinkmann, M., Mecklinger, A., & Johansson, M. (2004). When binding matters: An ERP analysis of the development of recollection and familiarity. In A. Mecklinger, H. Zimmer, & U. Lindenberger (Eds.), *Bound in memory. Insights from behavioral and neuropsychological studies* (pp. 93–128). Aachen: Shaker.

Czernochowski, D., Mecklinger, A., & Johansson, M. (2009). Age-related changes in the control of episodic retrieval: An ERP study of recognition memory in children and adults. *Developmental Science, 12,* 1026–40.

Czernochowski, D., Mecklinger, A., Johansson, M., & Brinkmann, M. (2005). Age-related differences in familiarity and recollection: ERP evidence from a recognition memory study in children and young adults. *Cognitive Affective and Behavioral Neuroscience, 5,* 417–33.

de Chastelaine, M., Friedman, D., & Cycowicz, Y. M. (2007). The development of control processes supporting source memory discrimination as revealed by event-related potentials. *Journal of Cognitive Neuroscience, 19,* 1286–301.

de Chastelaine, M., Friedman, D., Cycowicz, Y. M., & Horton, C. (2009). Effects of multiple study-test repetition on the neural correlates of recognition memory: ERPs dissociate remembering and knowing. *Psychophysiology, 46,* 86–99.

Debener, S., Ullsperger, M., Siegel, M., Fiehler, K., von Cramon, D. Y., & Engel, A. K. (2005). Trial-by-trial coupling of concurrent electroencephalogram and functional magnetic resonance imaging identifies the dynamics of performance monitoring. *Journal of Neuroscience, 25,* 11730–7.

Demb, J. B., Desmond, J. E., Wagner, A. D., Vaidya, C. J., Glover, G. H., & Gabrieli, J. D. E. (1995). Semantic encoding and retrieval in the left inferior prefrontal cortex: A functional MRI study of task difficulty and task specificity. *Journal of Neuroscience, 15,* 5870–8.

Diana, R. A., & Ranganath, C. (2011). Neural basis of recollection: Evidence from neuroimaging and electrophysiological research. In S. Ghetti & P. J. Bauer (Eds.), *Origins and development of recollection: Perspectives from psychology and neuroscience* (pp. 168–87). New York: Oxford University Press.

Dobbins, I. G., Foley, H., Schacter, D. L., & Wagner, A. D. (2002). Executive control during episodic retrieval: Multiple prefrontal processes subserve source memory. *Neuron, 35,* 989–96.

Drummey, A. B., & Newcombe, N. S. (2002). Developmental changes in source memory. *Developmental Science, 5,* 502–13.

Emmerich, H. J., & Ackerman, B. P. (1979). The effect of orienting activity on memory for pictures and words in children and adults. *Journal of Experimental Child Psychology, 28,* 499–515.

Fabiani, M., Gratton, G., Chiarenza, G. A., & Donchin, E. (1990). A psychophysiological investigation of the von Restorff paradigm in children. *Journal of Psychophysiology, 4,* 15–24.

Fletcher, P. C., & Henson, R. N. (2001). Frontal lobes and human memory: Insights from functional neuroimaging. *Brain, 124,* 849–81.

Fletcher, P. C., Stephenson, C. M., Carpenter, T. A., Donovan, T., & Bullmorel, E. T. (2003). Regional brain activations predicting subsequent memory success: An event-related fMRI study of the influence of encoding tasks. *Cortex, 39,* 1009–26.

Friedman, D. (1984). P300 and slow wave: Effects of reaction time quartile. *Biological Psychology, 18,* 49–71.

Friedman, D. (1990). ERPs during continuous recognition memory for words. *Biological Psychology, 30,* 61–87.

Friedman, D. (1991). The endogenous scalp recorded brain potentials and their relationship to cognitive development. In J. R. Jennings & M. G. H. Coles (Eds.), *Psychophysiology of human information processing: An integration of central and autonomic nervous system approaches* (pp. 621–56). New York: Wiley.

Friedman, D. (1992). Event-related potential investigations of cognitive development and aging. *Annals of the New York Academy of Sciences, 658,* 33–64.

Friedman, D. (2000). Event-related brain potential investigations of memory and aging. *Biological Psychology, 54,* 175–206.

Friedman, D., de Chastelaine, M., Nessler, D., & Malcolm, B. (2010). Changes in familiarity and recollection across the lifespan: An ERP perspective. *Brain Research, 1310,* 124–41.

Friedman, D., & Johnson, R. (2000). Event-related potential (ERP) studies of memory encoding and retrieval: A selective review. *Microscopy Research Techniques, 51,* 6–28.

Friedman, D., Nessler, D., Cycowicz, Y. M., & Horton, C. (2009). Development of and change in cognitive control: A comparison of children, young and older adults. *Cognitive and Affective Behavioral Neuroscience, 9,* 91–102.

Ghatala, E. S., Carbonari, J. P., & Bobele, L. Z. (1980). Developmental changes in incidental memory as a function of processing level, congruity and repetition. *Journal of Experimental Child Psychology, 29,* 74–87.

Ghetti, S., & Angelini, L. (2008). The development of recollection and familiarity in childhood and adolescence: Evidence from the dual-process signal detection model. *Child Development, 79,* 339–58.

Goldman, R. I., Wei, C. Y., Philiastides, M. G., Gerson, A. D., Friedman, D., Brown, T. R., & Sajda, P. (2009). Single-trial discrimination for integrating simultaneous EEG and fMRI: Identifying cortical areas contributing to trial-to-trial variability in the auditory oddball task. *Neuroimage, 47,* 136–47.

Hayama, H. R., Johnson, J. D., & Rugg, M. D. (2008). The relationship between the right frontal old/new ERP effect and post-retrieval monitoring: Specific or non-specific? *Neuropsychologia, 46,* 1211–23.

Jacoby, L. L. (1991). A process dissociation framework: Separating automatic from intentional uses of memory. *Journal of Memory and Language, 30,* 513–41.

Jacoby, L. L., Bishara, A. J., Hessels, S., & Toth, J. P. (2005). Aging, subjective experience, and cognitive control: Dramatic false remembering by older adults. *Journal of Experimental Psychology: General, 134,* 131–48.

Johnson, R. (1995). Event-related potential insights into the neurobiology of memory systems. In F. Boller & J. Grafman (Eds.), *Handbook of neuropsychology* (Vol. 10, pp. 135–63). Amsterdam: Elsevier.

Johnson, R., Henkell, H., Simon, E., & Zhu, J. (2008). The self in conflict: The role of executive processes during truthful and deceptive responses about attitudes. *Neuroimage, 39,* 469–82.

Johnson, R., Kreiter, K., Russo, B., & Zhu, J. (1998). A spatio-temporal analysis of recognition-related event-related brain potentials. *International Journal of Psychophysiology, 29,* 83–104.

Kohler, S., Paus, T., Buckner, R. L., & Milner, B. (2004). Effects of left inferior prefrontal stimulation on episodic memory formation: A two-stage fMRI-rTMS study. *Journal of Cognitive Neuroscience, 16,* 178–88.

Luck, S. J. (1999). Direct and indirect integration of event-related potentials, functional magnetic resonance images, and single-unit recordings. *Human Brain Mapping, 8,* 115–20.

Mandler, G. (1980). Recognizing: The judgement of previous occurrence. *Psychological Review, 87,* 252–71.

McAuley, T., Brahmbhatt, S., & Barch, D. M. (2007). Performance on an episodic encoding task yields further insight into functional brain development. *Neuroimage, 34,* 815–26.

Mecklinger, A. (2000). Interfacing mind and brain: A neurocognitive model of recognition memory. *Psychophysiology, 37,* 565–82.

Mecklinger, A., Brunnemann, N., & Kipp, K. (2010). Two processes for recognition memory in children of early school age: An event-related potential study. *Journal of Cognitive Neuroscience, 23,* 435–46.

Nessler, D., Friedman, D., Johnson, R., & Bersick, M. (2007a). Does repetition engender the same retrieval processes in young and older adults? *Neuroreport, 18,* 1837–40.

Nessler, D., Friedman, D., Johnson, J., & Bersick, M. (2007b). ERPs suggest that age affects cognitive control but not response conflict detection. *Neurobiology of Aging, 28,* 1769–82.

Nessler, D., Johnson, R., Bersick, M., & Friedman, D. (2006). On why the elderly have normal semantic retrieval but deficient episodic encoding: A study of left inferior frontal ERP activity. *Neuroimage, 30,* 299–312.

Ofen, N., Kao, Y. C., Sokol-Hessner, P., Kim, H., Whitfield-Gabrieli, S., & Gabrieli, J. D. (2007). Development of the declarative memory system in the human brain. *Nature Neuroscience, 10,* 1198–205.

Ornstein, P. A., & Haden, C. A. (2001). Memory development or the development of memory? *Current Directions in Psychological Science, 10,* 202–5.

Paller, K. A. (1990). Recall and stem-completion priming have different electrophysiological correlates and are modified differentially by directed forgetting. *Journal of Experimental Psychology: Learning, Memory, and Cognition, 16,* 1021–32.

Paller, K. A., Kutas, M., & Mayes, A. R. (1987). Neural correlates of encoding in an incidental learning paradigm. *Electroencephalography and Clinical Neurophysiology, 67,* 360–71.

Paller, K. A., McCarthy, G., & Woods, C. C. (1988). ERPs predictive of subsequent recall and recognition performance. *Biological Psychology, 26,* 269–76.

Paller, K. A., Voss, J. L., & Boehm, S. G. (2007). Validating neural correlates of familiarity. *Trends in Cognitive Science, 11,* 243–50.

Paller, K. A., Voss, J. L., & Westerberg, C. E. (2009). Investigating the awareness of remembering. *Perspectives on Psychological Science, 4,* 185–99.

Paller, K. A., & Wagner, A. D. (2002). Transforming experience into memory: Observations of mind and brain. *Trends in Cognitive Sciences, 6,* 93–102.

Perlmutter, M. (1980). A developmental study of semantic elaboration and interpretation in recognition memory. *Journal of Experimental Child Psychology, 29,* 413–27.

Rugg, M. D. (1998). Convergent approaches to electrophysiological and hemodynamic investigations of memory. *Human Brain Mapping*, 6, 394–8.

Rugg, M. D., & Curran, T. (2007). Event-related potentials and recognition memory. *Trends in Cognitive Science*, 11, 251–7.

Rugg, M. D., Mark, R. E., Walla, P., Schloerscheidt, A. M., Birch, C. S., & Allan, K. (1998). Dissociation of the neural correlates of implicit and explicit memory. *Nature*, 392, 595–8.

Rugg, M. D., Otten, L. J., & Henson, R. N. (2002). The neural basis of episodic memory: Evidence from functional neuroimaging. *Philosophical Transactions of the Royal Society of London B: Biological Sciences*, 357, 1097–110.

Rugg, M. D., & Yonelinas, A. P. (2003). Human recognition memory: A cognitive neuroscience perspective. *Trends in Cognitive Sciences*, 7, 313–9.

Rybash, J. M., & Colilla, J. L. (1994). Source memory deficits and frontal lobe functioning in children. *Developmental Neuropsychology*, 10, 67–73.

Sanquist, T. F., Rohrbaugh, J. W., Syndulko, K., & Lindsley, D. B. (1980). Electrocortical signs of levels of processing: Perceptual analysis and recognition memory. *Psychophysiology*, 17, 568–76.

Schneider, W. (2002). Memory development in childhood. In U. Goswami (Ed.), *Blackwell handbook of childhood cognitive development* (pp. 236–56). Malden, MA: Blackwell Publishing.

Shallice, T., & Burgess, P. (1996). The domain of supervisory processes and temporal organization of behaviour. *Philosophical Transactions of the Royal Society of London*, 351, 1405–11.

Snodgrass, J. G., & Corwin, J. (1988). Pragmatics of measuring recognition memory: Applications to dementia and amnesia. *Journal of Experimental Psychology: General*, 117, 34–50.

Sophian, C., & Hagen, J. W. (1978). Involuntary memory and the development of retrieval skills in young children. *Journal of Experimental Child Psychology*, 26, 458–71.

Thaiss, L., & Petrides, M. (2003). Source versus content memory in patients with a unilateral frontal cortex or a temporal lobe excision. *Brain*, 126, 1112–26.

Thompson-Schill, S. L., D'Esposito, M., Aguirre, G. K., & Farah, M. J. (1997). Role of left inferior prefrontal cortex in retrieval of semantic knowledge: A reevaluation. *Proceedings of the National Academy of Sciences*, 94, 14792–7.

Tulving, E. (1985). Memory and consciousness. *Canadian Psychologist*, 26, 1–12.

Vilberg, K. L., & Rugg, M. D. (2008). Memory retrieval and the parietal cortex: A review of evidence from a dual-process perspective. *Neuropsychologia*, 46, 1787–99.

Wagner, A. D., Pare-Blagoev, E. J., Clark, J., & Poldrack, R. A. (2001). Recovering meaning: Left prefrontal cortex guides controlled semantic retrieval. *Neuron*, 31, 329–38.

Wagner, A. D., Schacter, D. L., Rotte, M., Koutstaal, M. R. W., Maril, A., Dale, A. M., . . . Buckner R. L. (1998). Building memories: Remembering and forgetting of verbal experiences as predicted by brain activity. *Science*, 281, 1188–91.

Wagner, A. D., Shannon, B. J., Kahn, I., & Buckner, R. L. (2005). Parietal lobe contributions to episodic memory retrieval. *Trends in Cognitive Science*, 9, 445–53.

Werkle-Bergner, M., Muller, V., Li, S. C., & Lindenberger, U. (2006). Cortical EEG correlates of successful memory encoding: Implications for lifespan comparisons. *Neuroscience and Biobehavioral Reviews*, 30, 839–54.

Wilding, E. L. (2000). In what way does the parietal ERP old/new effect index recollection? *International Journal of Psychophysiology*, 35, 81–7.

Wilding, E. L., Fraser, C. S., & Herron, J. E. (2005). Indexing strategic retrieval of colour information with event-related potentials. *Brain Research: Cognitive Brain Research, 25*, 19–32.

Wilding, E. L., & Sharpe, H. (2002). Episodic memory encoding and retrieval: Recent insights from event-related potentials. In A. Zani & A. M. Proverbio (Eds.), *The cognitive electrophysiology of mind and brain* (pp. 169–96). New York: Academic Press.

Yonelinas, A. P. (2002). The nature of recollection and familiarity: A review of 30 years of research. *Journal of Memory and Language, 46*, 441–517.

Zelazo, P. D. (2004). The development of conscious control in childhood. *Trends in Cognitive Science, 8*, 12–7.

Zelazo, P. D., Craik, F. I., & Booth, L. (2004). Executive function across the life span. *Acta Psychologica (Amsterdam), 115*, 167–83.

11

Memory Development Following Early Medial Temporal Lobe Injury

MICHELLE DE HAAN

Memory is central to our everyday lives, allowing us to amass a knowledge base of facts, rules, and skills and to retain details about personal experiences that are central to our sense of who we are as individuals. Adults' reliance on memory is clearly illustrated when it is compromised following brain injury or disease. A classic example is patient H.M., who suffered severe memory loss following surgical removal of a large part of both temporal lobes as treatment for medication-resistant epilepsy. H.M. was unable to form new long-term memories for facts or events, forgetting such things within minutes. Even so, he remained able to remember things from his life before the surgery and to form new long-term memories under some circumstances, such as in conditioning or priming tasks. The case of HM had an important impact on our understanding of memory, both by illustrating that memory is not a unitary function and by illustrating that different subtypes of memory rely on different brain networks. In particular, this case highlighted the difference between *cognitive memories*, which are those memories that we can bring to mind, and *noncognitive memories*, which are memories typically expressed as changes in performance; only the former type of memory is affected in H.M. and dependent on the medial temporal lobes (MTL; Cohen & Squire, 1980).

While H.M.'s memory loss was undoubtedly devastating, he did retain most of his memories from before the surgery. What would happen if brain regions mediating memory were damaged in infancy or childhood, before an individual has the opportunity to amass a store of knowledge and personal memories? This is the topic of the present chapter, focusing on how injury during childhood to brain regions known to underlie cognitive memory in adults affects the functional development of cognitive memory. The aim is to review such cases, with an eye toward how they contribute to the debate regarding the neural correlates of a further subdivision within the cognitive memory system—that between semantic and episodic memory. The chapter will conclude with discussion of how understanding the impact of brain injury on memory development contributes to our understanding of the brain bases of normal memory development.

BRIEF NEUROANATOMY OF COGNITIVE MEMORY IN ADULTS.

To set the context for understanding memory development following brain injury or disease, this section provides a brief overview of brain regions important for cognitive memory in adults. In adults, it is accepted that structures in the MTL, including the perirhinal, parahippocampal, and entorhinal cortices and the hippocampus are critical for the formation and consolidation of new cognitive memories (Squire, Stark & Clark, 2004; Vargha-Khadem, Gadian, & Mishkin, 2001; see also Diana & Ranganath, Chapter 7, this volume; St. Jacques & Cabeza, Chapter 8, this volume). One current debate is regarding functional subdivision within this system. From a behavioral point of view, most agree that cognitive memory can be further subdivided into *episodic memory* for personal experiences (e.g., I went to Paris last summer and the airline lost my luggage) and *semantic memory* for general knowledge and facts (e.g., Paris is the capital of France). Recall of items from episodic memory is by definition associated with retrieval of contextual details related to the encoding, whereas recall from semantic memory is not. A similar distinction applies to recognition, whereby it can occur with retrieval of contextual details related to encoding ("recollection-based recognition") or without these additional details ("familiarity-based recognition"). From a neuroanatomical point of view, there is some disagreement regarding brain correlates of these different forms of cognitive memory. According to one hierarchical view, perceptual information first enters the parahippocampal regions mediating semantic memory (and familiarity-based recognition) and only then passes to hippocampal regions necessary for episodic memory (and recollection-based recognition; Mishkin, Suzuki, Gadian & Vargha-Khadem, 1997; Vargha-Khadem et al., 2001). Other views acknowledge the possibility of a division of labor within the MTL but argue that the hippocampus itself is involved in both semantic and episodic memory (Squire et al., 2004; see Figure 11.1a).

Although the focus of this chapter will be on the MTL, other brain regions have been implicated in cognitive memory (see Figure 11.1b). In particular, the amygdala plays a role in processing of emotional information in memories (Buchanan, 2007); the prefrontal cortex plays a role in memory retrieval and monitoring of the success of the retrieval process (Ranganath, Heller & Wilding, 2007; see also Hanten & Levin, Chapter 12, this volume); and the temporal pole may be a convergence zone for interactive processing semantic memories across modalities (Paterson, Nestor & Rogers, 2007). Subcortical structures such as the mamillary bodies (Cai, 1990), anterior and medial-dorsal thalamic nuclei (Aggleton & Brown, 1999; Van der Werf, Jolles, Witter, & Uylings, 2003), and connecting pathways such as the fornix (Aggleton & Brown, 1999) also contribute to cognitive memory.

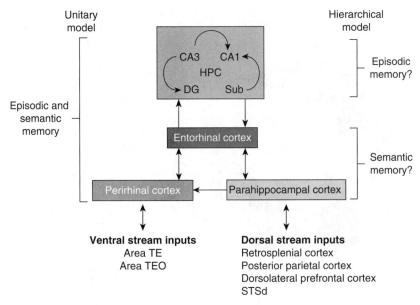

Figure 11.1. The hierarchical and unitary models provide different accounts for the neural basis of the semantic and episodic components of cognitive memory. According to the hierarchical model, information from the *what* (ventral) and *where* (dorsal) visual streams first enters the perirhinal and parahippocampal cortices, respectively, and then can pass via the entorhinal cortex to the hippocampus. In this model, semantic memory is mediated by the perirhinal, entorhinal, and posterior parahippocampal regions, whereas episodic memory relies on the hippocampus; thus, information is first encoded in semantic memory before it can pass on in the hierarchy to be encoded in episodic memory. Therefore, this model predicts that selective damage to the hippocampus can result in impaired episodic memory but that semantic memory can remain intact, whereas damage to the surrounding cortical regions would impair both types of memory. In the unitary model, both semantic and episodic memory rely on the hippocampus and the surrounding cortices. Thus, damage to any of these components should affect both semantic and episodic memory. Reprinted from de Haan, M., Mishkin, M., Baldeweg, T., & Vargha-Khadem, F. (2006). Human memory development and its dysfunction after early hippocampal injury. *Trends in Neurosciences, 29*, 374–81, with permission from Elsevier. Area TE and Area TEO = regions of the inferior temporal cortex; DG = dentate gyrus; HPC = hippocampal complex; STSd = dorsal superior temporal sulcus; Sub = subiculum

EFFECT OF BRAIN INJURY ON THE DEVELOPMENT OF COGNITIVE MEMORY

This section will examine memory ability in four groups of children with documented MTL injury or who are considered at risk for such injury: (a) developmental amnesia, (b) hypoxic-ischemic injury, (c) premature birth, and (d) temporal lobe epilepsy

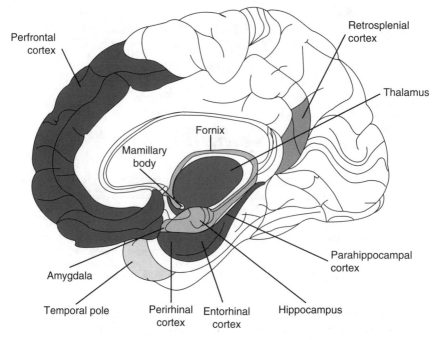

Figure 11.2. A sketch showing the approximate locations of MTL and extra-MTL regions involved in cognitive memory

Developmental Amnesia

MEMORY AND NEUROANATOMIC CHARACTERISTICS

Historically there have not been many reports of selective memory impairment following brain injury in children (for an exception, see Wood, Brown, & Felton, 1989). This might be because it was believed that memory impairments occurring so early in life would result in a global developmental delay, or it might be due to the belief that brain plasticity would allow for functional compensation. However, a report in 1997 by Vargha-Khadem and colleagues brought this issue to the forefront by describing a group of children with a specific memory impairment related to a well-documented, focal brain injury within the MTL. Cases Beth, Jon, and Kate all had difficulty remembering information after a delay in spite of normal performance on tests of immediate memory and of memory span. Even though they were unable to retain much information for more than a minute or so, all three children performed in the normal range on tests of academic achievement (with the exception of spelling) and on the subtests of IQ that tap general knowledge. In other words, the children appeared to have a selective impairment in episodic memory, with relatively intact semantic memory. This pattern of memory impairment occurred together with bilateral reduction of the volume of the hippocampus to a level ~40% to 60% of normal size. Elevated T2 values bilaterally indicated that even the little remaining hippocampal tissue was abnormal. Subsequent reports with additional patients used voxel-based morphometry to evaluate the whole brain and confirmed that the bilateral gray matter reductions were selective to the hippocampus within the MTL, and additionally identified reductions outside the temporal lobe including bilateral reductions in the putamen (Gadian et al., 2000; Vargha-Khadem et al., 2003), caudate and thalamus, and right-sided reductions in the retrosplenial cortex (Vargha-Khadem et al., 2003). Generally, this pattern of brain injury is associated with hypoxic-ischemic episodes and was interpreted as consistent with the children's medical histories (Gadian et al., 2000).

HOW CAN CHILDREN WITH SEVERELY IMPAIRED EPISODIC MEMORY STILL LEARN?

From a cognitive point of view, it is puzzling to imagine how children with severe problems in retaining information for more than a few minutes can progress in school and amass an extensive factual knowledge base. It is even more puzzling given that studies of new semantic learning in adults with temporal lobe amnesia have not provided strong evidence of such learning. Overall results are mixed, with some studies concluding that such learning does not occur (e.g., Bayley & Squire, 2005). Studies that do find evidence of learning indicate that it may be more likely to occur if tasks are set within a framework of retained premorbid semantic knowledge but that, even then, learning is limited (Kan, Alexander & Verfaellie, 2009; Moses, Ostreicher, Rosenbaum & Ryan, 2008; O'Kane, Kensinger & Corkin, 2004). Children with amnesia as a consequence of brain injury early in life do not have the help of a premorbid knowledge base to facilitate the learning, yet remain able to acquire a vast store of semantic knowledge postinjury. This is illustrated by several recent reports showing that children with severe deficits in episodic memory still have at least partially preserved skills to acquire new semantic knowledge (Brizzolara, Cassalini, Montanaro, & Posteraro, 2003; Gardiner, Brandt, Baddeley, Vargha-Khadem & Mishkin, 2008; Guillery-Girard, Martins, Parisot-Carbuccia, & Eustache, 2004; Martins, Guillery-Girard, Jambaqué, Dulac & Eustache, 2006; Vicari et al., 2007; Wood et al., 1989). For example, Case Jon has a severe impairment in delayed episodic recall yet is able to learn new facts presented orally in a question-and-answer format over repeated trials (Gardiner et al., 2008).

Although this is impressive, a few points about the nature of semantic learning and memory in individuals with severely impaired episodic memory have been highlighted: (a) semantic learning may occur more slowly and require more repetitions than it normally would do (Gardiner et al., 2008; Martins et al., 2006); (b) the level of learning attained within experiments may not reach the level attained by control subjects (Gardiner et al., 2008; Martins et al., 2006), even with extra learning trials (Martins et al., 2006); and (c) measures of existing semantic knowledge are not always entirely normal. These findings suggest that, whereas semantic learning can occur in developmental amnesia, and possibly may do so more easily than reported in adult amnesics, it does not so absolutely normally. This may reflect the greater difficulty in acquiring semantic knowledge without the full support of episodic memory. For example, the loss of episodic memory can be seen as a direct cause of the greater intertrial forgetting observed in developmental amnesia; in other words, it is more difficult to acquire new semantic knowledge if information cannot be retained from one encounter to the next (Gardiner et al., 2008). One study that compared two cases with differing degrees of residual episodic-memory skill also found better semantic acquisition in the case with greater residual episodic memory (Martins et al., 2006).

From a neuroanatomical view, understanding the neural bases of new semantic learning in amnesia is important because the hierarchical and unitary models make different predictions on this point. Hierarchical models predict that dissociations occur between episodic memory and semantic memory because of their different neural correlates (Miskin et al., 1997). Perceptual representations formed in the cortex are first processed in the parahippocampal regions to form semantic memories, and are then further processed by the hippocampus to add contextual richness to form episodic memories. Thus, selective damage to the hippocampus can result in a selective impairment in episodic memory. By contrast, the unitary model predicts that episodic and semantic memory should be equally impaired following MTL damage because of their common neural correlates within the MTL (Squire et al., 2004). To support their hierarchical model, Vargha-Khadem and colleagues used quantitative neuroimaging to establish that damage in their cases of developmental amnesia was restricted to the hippocampus and did not encroach on surrounding cortices (Gadian et al., 2000; Vargha-Khadem, 2003). Whole-brain analysis using voxel-based morphometry[1] showed bilateral reduction of gray matter selective to the hippocampus within the MTL, and T2 relaxometry[2] in the temporal cortex surrounding the hippocampus did not reveal major abnormalities. To further support their claim that parahippocampal cortical areas were intact in their cases, Vargha-Khadem and colleagues (1997) demonstrated that the amnesic children performed normally on tasks of item recognition and associative recognition that, in monkeys, are sensitive to parahippocampal, but not hippocampal, injury. In other reported cases of children with impaired episodic memory but relatively intact semantic memory, the pattern of brain injury has not been identical or always as selective as in the cases reported by Vargha-Khadem and colleagues. However, injuries did always seem to affect a component of the diencephalic-MTL memory circuit (Vicari et al., 2007, Case C.L.—fornix, thalamus, hippocampus; Martins et al., 2006, Case R.H.—mamillary bodies, Case K.F.—hippocampus) with no observable effect on the parahippocampal regions (except possibly Case K.F., where mild general atrophy was noted, but with hippocampus much more affected). Thus, the findings to date are consistent with the view that the integrity of the parahippocampal regions could allow for semantic memory to remain relatively intact even when episodic memory is severely impaired. It is relevant to note here that semantic memory is believed to be mediated by a distributed system (Patterson et al., 2007) and this focus on the integrity

1. Voxel-based morphometry is a quantitative neuroimaging analysis technique that allows investigation of differences in the volume of gray or white matter across the whole brain.

2. T2 relaxometry is a magnetic resonance imaging technique sensitive to alterations in tissue microstructure. Thus, it would allow assessment of whether any remaining hippocampal tissue was abnormal.

of parahippocampal regions is in the context of understanding division of labor within the MTL and not because this region is the only one responsible for semantic memory.

Proponents of the unitary view argue against the interpretation provided by the hierarchical view for several reasons. They point out that most all reported cases of developmental amnesia have had some degree of residual episodic-memory ability that accounts for semantic learning. As mentioned, there is evidence that episodic memory does support semantic learning (Gardiner et al., 2008; Martins et al., 2006). Thus, a strong test between the hierarchical and unitary views would be a case with no residual episodic memory. The hierarchical view would predict that semantic learning could still occur, whereas the unitary view would predict it would not occur. Proponents of the unitary view also take issue with the interpretation that semantic memory is intact or relatively preserved. Even in cases with no evidence of episodic memory on laboratory tests (Vicari et al., 2007), it is difficult to prove that semantic memory has reached the full potential that it would if episodic memory were normal. Moreover, because there are no standardized tests of episodic and semantic memory that allow a direct comparison of the two abilities, it is difficult to establish conclusively if one type of memory is more affected than another because other task-related variables, such as difficulty, could account for any observed differences. A final point is that the plasticity of the developing brain might allow for some functional recovery and thereby result in a memory profile in developmental amnesia that does not directly reflect the typical functional organization of the adult system.

EFFECTS OF AGE AT INJURY

Only one study has directly addressed this last question of whether there is greater plasticity and compensation of memory function if hippocampal injury occurs earlier rather than later in childhood (Vargha-Khadem et al., 2003). This study examined individuals with developmental amnesia who sustained their injuries within a few months of birth (birth to 3 months) and those who sustained their injuries later in childhood (6 to 14 years). Both groups showed the same pattern of brain injury, with bilateral hippocampal volume reductions of about 40%. There were no differences in semantic or episodic memory related to age at injury, with both groups showing impaired episodic memory with relatively spared semantic memory. This suggests that age at injury, at least into adolescence, does not have an impact on the profile of long-term memory impairment observed after selective bilateral hippocampal injury. This conclusion should be taken cautiously, however, due to the small sample size (5 to 6 per group) and the large age range in the late-lesion group. The only effect of age at injury was that earlier injury allowed better performance on some tests of immediate memory (delays of 15 to 30 s) and was associated with a higher rate of memory intrusions (falsely "recalled" items). The interpretation of the superior immediate memory in the early lesion group is not entirely straightforward. On the one hand, this seems possible evidence of greater compensation following earlier injury. On the other hand, this might suggest a greater impairment in retention following earlier injury since both groups were equally impaired at delay. The finding of greater intrusions in memory recall in the early injury group may be a sign of dysfunction in prefrontal regions or MTL-prefrontal connections, because intrusions have been linked to perturbations of prefrontal strategic monitoring processes (Desgranges et al., 2002).

Overall the results of this study are generally consistent with the view that the greater plasticity of the developing brain may not account for the relatively good semantic memory observed in children with severe episodic memory impairments. A more conclusive study in which a larger group of individuals sustaining injuries in childhood and those sustaining similar injuries in adulthood are directly compared remains to be carried out.

RECOGNITION AND RECALL

In addition to their relatively intact semantic memory, there is some evidence that children with developmental amnesia show relatively intact recognition memory but more severely impaired recall memory. For example, Case Jon performed in the normal range on several tests of recognition despite severely impaired recall (Baddeley, Vargha-Khadem & Mishkin, 2001). One difficulty with this and many other studies comparing performance on recognition and recall tasks is that recognition tasks are typically easier than recall tasks; thus, better performance on recognition in amnesic participants might occur because it is easier and not because of a true dissociation between recognition and recall. The Doors and Peoples test was designed to address this problem by providing measures of recognition and recall for both verbal and visual materials that take into account such task-related differences. A recent study using this task in a group of 10 participants with developmental amnesia supported the pattern observed with Jon (Adlam, Malloy, Mishkin & Vargha-Khadem, 2009). The patients with developmental amnesia showed a much greater impairment in recall than recognition. It is relevant to note that patients, compared with control subjects, did show impairments in visual, but not verbal, recognition; thus recognition was not totally preserved. This retention of a relatively good ability to recognize may be explained by appealing to the distinction between recollection-based and familiarity-based recognition (Adlam et al., 2009). In this interpretation, recognition in developmental amnesia is based mainly on familiarity in the absence of recollection of contextual information. This is possible because perirhinal-entorhinal regions support familiarity-based recognition and these regions remain intact in developmental amnesia (Duzel, Vargha-Khadem, Heinze & Mishkin, 2001). This view is supported by results from an event-related potential study of Patient Jon. Event-related potential studies of typical memory have linked an increased late positive component to recollection and modulation of the N400 component to familiarity (Rugg et al., 1998). Jon shows an absence of late positive component effect, but an intact N400 effect (Duzel et al., 2001). Jon also is reported to have a lack of the phenomenological experience of recollecting (Baddeley et al., 2001). Together, these results support the view that recollection-based recognition is impaired but familiarity-based recognition is intact following early bilateral selective hippocampal injury.

DELAYED ONSET OF MEMORY IMPAIRMENT IN EARLY INJURY CASES

An interesting characteristic of developmental amnesia is that, in cases of injury in infancy, memory difficulties are typically not noticed until some years later (Gadian et al., 2000). One possible explanation is that this delayed emergence of the impairment reflects the pattern of maturation of neurocognitive systems underlying cognitive memory (de Haan, Mishkin, Baldeweg & Vargha-Khadem, 2006). In this explanation, cognitive memory develops hierarchically, with semantic memory unfolding first and normally in both healthy children and those with selective bilateral hippocampal pathology. Episodic memory emerges later during childhood in healthy individuals, but fails to develop normally in those with early onset hippocampal damage, because this injury prevents its continued development. Thus, memory impairments would only become noticeable at an age when the hippocampus would normally become mature enough to support episodic-memory function. The small number of existing studies using functional magnetic resonance imaging to look at the brain correlates of episodic memory in children have also suggested that, at least with respect to episodic encoding in children above 8 years of age, the prefrontal cortex also plays an increasing role with age (Chiu, Schmithorst, Brown, Holland, & Dunn, 2006; Menon, Boyett-Anderson & Reiss, 2005; Ofen, et al., 2007). Thus, the development of communication between MTL and prefrontal memory regions could also contribute to the emergence of the memory impairment in developmental amnesia.

It is possible that signs of memory impairment in individuals with hippocampal damage are actually detectable early in life, but that such impairments are initially relatively subtle and become more pronounced with age. According to one view, the hippocampus mediates an immature form of cognitive memory in infancy (recent review in Richmond & Nelson, 2007). This form of memory is best demonstrated in the visual paired comparison memory test. In this task, participants are first familiarized with one visual stimulus and then their memories tested by presenting the familiar stimulus alongside a novel one. Adult humans (McKee & Squire, 1993) and monkeys (Pascalis & Bachevalier, 1999) with bilateral MTL lesions, including those restricted to the hippocampus (Pascalis, Hunkin, Holdstock, Isaac, & Mayes, 2004; Zola et al., 2000) show the normal pattern of looking for longer times at novel than at familiar stimuli when there is little or no delay between familiarization and test, but their responses are impaired if a delay is imposed. Unlike these adults with lesions, human infants show evidence of delayed memory: 3- to 4-day-old children look longer at a novel face than a familiar one even if a 2-min delay is imposed (Pascalis & de Schoen, 1994), and 3-month-olds can do so even with a 24-hr delay (Pascalis, de Haan, Nelson & de Schonen, 1998). It is possible that, if individuals with developmental amnesia had been assessed as infants using such tasks that are sensitive to infant MTL functioning, impairments would have been observed. Early identification of infants at risk for developmental amnesia would obviously have potential clinical benefits. It would also be useful from an empirical point of view, as it would allow a better characterization of the emergence of the condition. Even in existing reports, there have been no systematic longitudinal investigations to document how developmental amnesia evolves once identified. Does the deficit remain equally severe across further development once identified? Does the condition show evidence of improvement or deterioration with age? How might any change observed be related to brain development or reorganization? Such questions remain open for future investigation.

SUMMARY

In summary, dissociations within cognitive memory can occur following childhood injury to the diencephalic-MTL circuit, with greater impairment in episodic than in semantic memory. Available evidence is consistent with the view that the cortices surrounding the hippocampus must be spared for semantic memory to be spared. However, a theoretically important test case in which relevant parahippocampal regions are injured with the hippocampus remaining intact has not been reported. In cases of selective bilateral hippocampal injury, recognition appears less affected than recall because of sparing of familiarity-based recognition, again possibly due to the sparing of perirhinal-entorhinal cortices.

Hypoxic-Ischemic Injury

Although the exact circumstances that lead to developmental amnesia are not known, one factor that appears to play a role in at least some cases is a hypoxic-ischemic episode (HIE). There is often a medical history involving such episodes and the neuropathology documented in the cases reported by Vargha-Khadem and colleagues (1997) is consistent with the pattern of injury expected following hypoxic-ischemic insult. Although hypoxia-ischemia is a global insult that can potentially affect the whole brain, there is evidence that the hippocampus is particularly vulnerable to such injury (Cervós-Navarro & Diemer, 1991). These are some of the factors that have led to an increased interest in examining memory in populations of infants and children exposed to or at risk for HIEs. This section will focus on children who experienced HIEs at full-term birth (for discussion of similarity in memory outcomes in HIE and children with diabetic ketoacidosis, see Ghetti, Lee, Sims, DeMaster & Glaser, 2010).

Hypoxia-ischemia occurs in approximately 1 to 6 per 1000 live term births. It is associated with neonatal encephalopathy, a clinical syndrome in which neurological function is disturbed in the first days of postnatal life in term infants (MacLennan, 1999). If the neonatal encephalopathy is severe, then cognitive and motor outcome are generally poor. If the neonatal encephalopathy is moderate or mild, then by 2 years of age, the majority of children will have good motor function, will appear to be making good cognitive, linguistic, and social progress and so will be considered normal and discharged from follow-up. However, the tendency of most studies to focus on identifying major developmental abnormalities at a young age may mean that subtler consequences emerging at older ages might be missed.

Detailed neuropsychological assessments at school age in term-born children, who experienced neonatal encephalopathy are still scarce (reviewed in de Haan, Wyatt, et al., 2006; Rennie, Hagmann & Robertson, 2007; van Handel, Swaab, de Vries & Jongmans, 2007). Marlow, Rose, Rands, and Draper (2005) examined 50 children aged 7 years without motor impairments who had experienced moderate or severe neonatal encephalopathy using the Developmental Neuropsychological Assessment (NEPSY) and British Ability Scales-II criteria. Children with moderate neonatal encephalopathy performed generally similar to classmate control subjects with the exception of a lower performance on the sensorimotor and language domains of the NEPSY and verbal memory items only within the memory domain. Children with severe neonatal encephalopathy performed more poorly than classmate control subjects on most all measures from the NEPSY and British Ability Scales-II; when compared to those with moderate neonatal encephalopathy, they were still generally poorer on the British Ability Scales-II scales but were poorer only on the memory and attention–executive function domains of NEPSY. These findings are similar to those by Mañeru, Junque, Botet, Tallada, and Guardia (2001), who examined 15-year-old children with a history of moderate neonatal encephalopathy ($n = 20$), mild encephalopathy ($n = 8$), and comparison children without such a histories ($n = 28$). They found evidence of memory, perceptuo-motor and executive function deficits in those with moderate neonatal encephalopathy compared with control subjects. They found few differences between the mild and moderate groups or between the mild and control groups, though this might be due to the small number of mild cases tested. By contrast, Viggedal, Lundälv, Carlsson, and Kjellmer (2002) found few differences between mild, moderate, and control groups, who showed no neurological signs at 18 months and who were tested on a comprehensive task battery as adults. They did report that 1 of 11 participants in the moderate group showed an isolated memory deficit for verbal and visual materials, associated with bitemporal hypoperfusion revealed throughsingle photon emission computed tomography. This later finding is similar to that reported by de Haan et al. (2002), who found that, in a group of 12 adolescents who had experienced severe birth asphyxia but showed no neurological signs at 1 or 4 years of age, 1 patient showed a specific memory impairment associated with reduced hippocampal volumes bilaterally.

SUMMARY

Hypoxic-ischemic injury at term birth and associated with mild or moderate neonatal encephalopathy may result in cognitive impairment in moderate and mild cases even when there is no striking motor impairment. There is as yet not strong evidence that selective memory impairments are a common characteristic in this group, though memory is often among the skills affected. There is some evidence that a subset (a very rough estimate of 0.09% to 0.08% of reported cases, but these are very small groups) may show specific memory impairment related to MTL abnormality. Further studies combining neuroimaging with sophisticated cognitive testing will help to better characterize the cognitive nature and brain correlates of any memory impairments observed.

Prematurity

Infants born prematurely can face a variety of biomedical and psychosocial risk factors in addition to the simple fact that their brains are exposed to a sensory environment not species-typical for their state of development. There has been an interest in studying memory development on infants born preterm both because of reported brain abnormalities, including hippocampal injury (Isaacs et al., 2000; Nosarti, et al., 2002), and because of cognitive reports suggesting that memory may be affected (reviewed in de Haan, 2010).

There is some evidence that immediate memory may be affected in infants who were born preterm. They show reduced novelty preferences at 5 to 12 months corrected age compared with the performance of full-term infants (e.g., Rose, Feldman, & Jankowski, 2001; Rose, Feldman, McCarton, & Wolfson, 1988). Novelty preference scores are particularly affected in preterm infants who suffer respiratory distress syndrome postnatally, especially if they also required prolonged mechanical ventilation (Rose et al., 1988). Event-related potential studies of auditory recognition memory also suggest impairments. Event-related potentials recorded at term show that preterm infants fail to recognize the mother's voice (Therien, Worwa, Mattia & de Regnier, 2004), and event-related potentials at 4 months of age show that novelty detection is present but to a lesser degree (Tokioka, Pearce & Crowell, 1995; but see O'Connor, 1980, for evidence of intact auditory recognition in a behavioral task). However, none of the studies imposed a delay between familiarization and memory test. Because novelty preferences are thought to require the hippocampus only if a delay is involved, the impairments observed in immediate tests might be due to damage in surrounding cortices or other brain regions. The finding of impaired novelty preference at immediate test also suggests a more general impairment in information processing, as such impairments have been linked to impaired speed of processing and to later IQ (Rose & Feldman, 1997).

In full-term normally developing infants, recall memory can be assessed by approximately 6 to 9 months of age (e.g., Carver & Bauer, 2001; Herbert, Gross & Hayne, 2006). This has been done using a task called *deferred imitation*, where recall is inferred from better production of single actions or action sequences after observation of an experimenter modeling actions compared with a premodeling baseline. Two studies demonstrate that memory in this task involves the MTL, one showing impairments in amnesic adults with MTL damage (but not in adults with frontal lobe damage; McDonough, Mandler, McKee & Squire, 1995) and the other in individuals who sustained selective bilateral hippocampal lesions during infancy or early childhood (Adlam, Vargha-Khadem, Mishkin & de Haan, 2005).

Two studies have found that children born preterm are impaired on recall in deferred imitation tasks. In one study, toddlers tested at 19 months corrected age, compared with their full-term counterparts, showed poorer recall of three-step sequences at immediate recall and after a 15-min delay (de Haan, Bauer, Georgieff & Nelson, 2000). Memory performance was related to gestational age at birth in this low risk sample. Another study using a similar procedure found that deficits are present by 12 months corrected age and persist until at least 36 months (Rose, Feldman & Jankowski, 2005). Although performance improves considerably from 12 to 36 months for both children born full term and those born preterm, there was no evidence of preterm "catch-up." The deficits detected at 12 months did not diminish with age. This study also found links between performance and medical risk factors. Lower birth weight and lengthier postnatal hospitalization were associated with poorer performance in preterm children at 24 and 36 months. It is important to note that in neither study was the specificity of the memory impairment assessed, so it is not clear whether it reflects a particular difficulty with memory or whether it is part of a more widespread impairment of cognitive abilities.

Studies with preschool and school-aged children who have been born preterm have primarily used standardized neuropsychological assessments of memory abilities. Generally, these studies have suggested that there are either no impairments in long-term memory (Briscoe, Gathercole, & Marlow, 2001; Rushe, et al., 2001) or that any impairments observed are in line with level general intellectual function and do not reflect specific memory deficits (Hoff Esbjørn, Hansen, Greisen & Mortensen, 2006; Narberhaus et al., 2007). Generally, impairments in working memory or attention-executive tasks are more consistent and striking than the impairments in long-term memory (reviewed in de Haan, 2010).

As mentioned previously, there is some direct evidence from magnetic resonance imaging studies indicating that the hippocampus is abnormal in children born preterm. In general, reductions of roughly 10% have been observed in long-term follow-up studies (Isaacs et al., 2000; Nosarti et al., 2002). This reduction is considerably smaller than that typically reported in developmental amnesia and may not be sufficient to cause a severe episodic-memory impairment. One study directly compared adolescents born preterm with those with developmental amnesia (Isaacs et al., 2000). Hippocampal volumes were reduced by about 40% in developmental amnesia but only by about 8% in preterms. IQ was similar in the two patient groups and generally a bit lower than control subjects though scores still fell in the normal range. On measures of memory, the general pattern was for preterms to perform as well as control subjects and for both preterms and control subjects to do better than children with developmental amnesia. One exception was for measures of verbal working memory where the children born preterm obtained lower scores than those with developmental amnesia.

SUMMARY
There is some evidence that the hippocampus may be smaller in children born preterm, though not to the degree observed in developmental amnesia. Studies of infants and toddlers born preterm have documented poorer performance on memory tasks thought to tap MTL function, though it is not clear from these studies whether this result reflects a specific memory impairment or is a reflection of a more global decrease in cognitive function. In studies of older children, deficits observed in memory are often consistent with children's general level function rather than selective to memory, and deficits are often more striking for working memory tasks than delayed recall tasks.

Pediatric Temporal Lobe Epilepsy

Epilepsy is a brain disorder involving recurrent seizures that have a unilateral focus. In adults, epilepsy affecting the temporal lobes (TLE) is most often due to hippocampal sclerosis and, when medication-resistant, can be treated by surgical resection of the affected brain tissue. Although unilateral TLE does not result in amnesia even when temporal lobe tissue is removed, it is commonly associated with some impairment in episodic memory. These impairments are often material-specific and related to side of injury. Verbal memory impairments are common when TLE affects the language-dominant hemisphere (usually the left), whereas visual-spatial impairments occur, though less consistently so, when TLE affects the nondominant hemisphere (usually the right). There has been less focus on documenting semantic memory in adult TLE, and some have suggested that it is not affected (Helmstaedter, 2002). However, recent reports suggest that semantic memory is compromised in TLE (Messas, Mansur & Castro, 2008), with some reports linking such impairments to left TLE (Giovagnoli, 1999; 2005; Giovagnoli, Erbetta, Villani & Avanzini, 2005).

Given this background, pediatric TLE would seem to provide potential for further understanding the role of the MTL in cognitive memory development. Althoug this is true, it is important to note that the causes and clinical profile of TLE are more variable in children than in adults. In adults the most common cause of TLE is mesial temporal sclerosis. However, in children there are several common causes, including mesial temporal sclerosis but also low-grade tumors and malformations of cortical development. Furthermore, dual pathology occurs more commonly in children than in adults (Bocti et al., 2003). Given this greater variability in neuropathology in children compared with adults, results concerning memory may also be expected to be more variable. Numerous other factors, such as the duration and frequency of seizures, age of onset of seizures, and type of treatment, may also influence memory outcome in this population.

Documenting material-specific deficits in memory in children with TLE speaks to the question of the development of brain hemispheric specialization. Findings of adultlike material specificity would provide support for the view that such specialization is already established early in life, whereas a lack of such findings would be more consistent with the view that development of specialization is a more prolonged and possibly experience-dependent process. There is to date not a clear relationship between type of memory impairment and lateralization of TLE in children. Although some studies have observed the same pattern of material-specific impairment as reported for adults (Jambaqué, Dellatolas, Dulac, Ponsot & Signoret, 1993; Jambaqué et al., 2007), others have observed no differences in verbal memory for right versus left TLE (Nolan et al., 2004). There is also a suggestion that in children the link between verbal memory impairment and left TLE is less pronounced (Helmstaedter & Lendt, 2001) and between visual memory impairment and right TLE more pronounced (Jambaqué et al., 1993; Mabbott & Smith, 2003; Nolan et al., 2004) than in adults. These variable results may well be due to the great etiological, clinical, and electroencephalographic diversity seen in children compared with adults (Guimaraes et al., 2006).

Few studies of memory in children with TLE have set out to specifically examine both semantic and episodic memory. However, the issue of semantic memory has been more prominent in children than in adults, probably because of the more frequent occurrence of neocortical lesions in children. A recent study examined both types of memory in 20 children with TLE postsurgery (Jambaqué et al., 2007). Most children had a poor everyday memory as documented by the Rivermead Behavioural Memory Test. Children with left TLE showed both poor verbal episodic memory and verbal semantic knowledge particularly on a naming task. This result is consistent with prior findings of impairments in both semantic and episodic memory in nonsurgical cases of pediatric TLE (Temple, 1984, 1997). Performance on the naming task was better with later onset of epilepsy, suggesting earlier temporal lobe injury has a greater impact on acquisition of semantic knowledge of words. Children with right TLE showed poor visual episodic memory but showed no impairment in semantic memory. This link between left TLE and impaired semantic memory is consistent with some adult studies (Giovagnoli, 1999. 2005; Giovagnoli et al., 2005). However, it may also have occurred because all the semantic memory tests in this study were verbally based.

Given this evidence for difficulties with semantic memory, it is perhaps not surprising to note that there is also evidence that general intellectual ability is affected by pediatric unilateral TLE. One recent study reported that 57% of children show IQs below 79 (where IQ has a population mean of 100 and standard deviation of 15; Cormack et al., 2007). The best predictor of level of intellectual function was age of epilepsy onset, with early onset linked to lower levels of function. Epilepsy with onset in the first year was particularly disruptive to intellectual development, with 82% of children showing impairment.

Few studies of children with TLE have examined more closely the pattern of memory impairment with brain structure and function using neuroimaging methods. There is evidence that reductions in gray matter occur not only to the hippocampus ipsilateral to the seizure focus but also to ipsilateral lateral temporal cortex and bilateral extratemporal regions (Cormack et al., 2005; Guimarães et al., 2007). The pattern of affected areas generally reflects the pattern of hippocampal connections. The gray matter reductions may be caused by the disruptive effect of seizures on cortical development as well as by loss of input from the affected hippocampus. In one study to directly compare children and adults, the pattern of gray matter atrophy was milder and less distributed in children (Guimarães et al., 2007).

SUMMARY

In summary, children with TLE usually experience some memory impairment but not amnesia. The memory impairment may affect only visual or only verbal materials, though the exact pattern of memory and its relation to side of injury has not been conclusively defined. There is evidence that both semantic and episodic memory are affected, which would be consistent with the fact that childhood TLE may originate neocortically and with evidence that, even in cases of hippocampal sclerosis, atrophy extends to other regions of the temporal lobes and beyond. However, the data are still limited and as yet would not allow a dissociation of the contributions of medial and lateral temporal lobe regions to different types of memory.

DISCUSSION AND CLOSING REMARKS

Studying how memory is affected when the developing brain is injured is one approach for understanding the neural bases of memory development. The studies reviewed in this chapter point to an important role for the hippocampus in episodic memory in children. If the hippocampus is mildly damaged, such as has been observed in preterms, episodic memory may not be affected, but if it receives a more serious injury, such as has been observed in developmental amnesia or TLE, then episodic memory is compromised. There is little evidence of plasticity and compensation of function related to earlier injury to the hippocampus, although there is still only limited information on this point. It is possible that the hippocampus shows less plasticity than has sometimes been observed following neocortical lesions because of differences between the phylogenetically older hippocampus and more recent neocortex.

Though the role of the hippocampus has been emphasized, it is important to note that in all of the conditions discussed in this chapter, injury has not been completely isolated to the hippocampus. Even in the relatively selective lesions observed in developmental amnesia, areas related to memory function, such as the thalamus and retrosplenial cortex, are also affected. This highlights the importance of considering brain memory systems as networks rather than isolated regions, particularly when study development, understanding connections, and communication within brain memory systems will likely be important for understanding how they normally develop and are affected by injury. For example, the studies in TLE illustrated how injury within the MTL can have more widespread effects that may be related to the altered outputs of the injured areas.

In general, the findings are consistent with the hierarchical view that the hippocampus is important for episodic memory but that, if it is injured, the surrounding cortices may still support semantic memory and possibly also familiarity-based recognition. The findings from developmental amnesia are consistent with this view, and the results of studies of TLE could be seen as consistent in that semantic memory appears affected in the context of more widespread MTL injury.

Although the existing literature provides a window into developing brain memory systems, one aspect that is missing is a closer investigation of the unfolding consequences of early brain injury. When investigating childhood brain injury, it is important to remember that the injury is imposed on a system that is changing and developing. Thus, the true consequences of the injury on memory may not be apparent by studying isolated time points, but may only be apparent by tracking the development of the system over time.

REFERENCES

Adlam, A. L., Malloy, M., Mishkin, M., & Vargha-Khadem, F. (2009). Dissociation between recognition and recall in developmental amnesia. *Neuropsychologia, 47*, 2207–10.

Adlam, A. L., Vargha-Khadem, F., Mishkin, M., & de Haan, M. (2005). Deferred imitation of action sequences in developmental amnesia. *Journal of Cognitive Neuroscience, 17*, 240–8.

Aggleton, J. P., & Brown, M. W. (1999). Episodic memory, amnesia, and the hippocampal-anterior thalamic axis. *Behavioral and Brain Sciences, 22,* 425–44.

Baddeley, A., Vargha-Khadem, F., & Mishkin, M. (2001). Preserved recognition in a case of developmental amnesia: Implications for the acquisition of semantic memory? *Journal of Cognitive Neurosciences, 13,* 357–69.

Bayley, P. J., & Squire, L. R. (2005). Failure to acquire new semantic knowledge in patients with large medial temporal lobe lesions. *Hippocampus, 15,* 273–80.

Bocti, C., Robitaille, Y., Diadori, P., Lortie, A., Mercier, C., Bouthillier, A., & Carmant, L. (2003). The pathological basis of temporal lobe epilepsy in childhood. *Neurology, 60,* 191–5.

Briscoe, J., Gathercole, S. E., & Marlow, M. (2001). Everyday memory and cognitive ability in children born very prematurely. *Journal of Child Psychiatry and Psychology, 42,* 749–54.

Brizzolara, D., Casalini, C., Montanaro, D, & Posteraro, F. (2003). A case of amnesia at an early age. *Cortex, 39,* 605–25.

Buchanan, T. W. (2007). Retrieval of emotional memories. *Psychological Bulletin, 133,* 761–79.

Cai, Z. J. (1990). The neural mechanisms of declarative memory consolidation and retrieval: A hypothesis. *Neuroscience and Biobehavioral Reviews, 14,* 295–304.

Carver, L. J., & Bauer, P. J. (2001). The dawning of a past: The emergence of long-term explicit memory in infancy. *Journal of Experimental Psychology: General, 130,* 726–45.

Cervós-Navarro, J., & Diemer, N. M. (1991). Selective vulnerability in brain hypoxia. *Critical Reviews in Neurbiology, 6,* 149–82.

Chiu, C. Y., Schmithorst, V. J., Brown, R. D., Holland, S. K., & Dunn, S. (2006). Making memories: A cross-sectional investigation of episodic memory encoding in childhood using fMRI. *Developmental Neuropsychology, 29,* 321–40.

Cohen, N. J., & Squire, L. R. (1980). Preserved learning and retention of pattern analyzing skill in amnesia: Dissociation of knowing how and knowing that. *Science, 210,* 207–9.

Cormack, F., Cross, J. H., Isaacs, E., Harkness, W., Wright, I., Vargha-Khadem, F., & Baldeweg, T. (2007). The development of intellectual abilities in pediatric temporal lobe epilepsy. *Epilepsia, 48,* 201–14.

Cormack, G., Gadian, D. G., Vargha-Khadem, F., Cross, J. H., Connelly, A., & Baldeweg, T. (2005). Extra-hippocampal grey matter density abnormalities in paediatric mesial temporal sclerosis. *Neuroimage, 27,* 635–43.

de Haan, M. (2010). A cognitive neuroscience perspective on the development of memory in children born preterm. In C. Nosarti, R. M. Murray, & M. Hack (Eds), *Neurodevelopmental outcomes of preterm birth: From childhood to adult life* (pp. 185–94). Cambridge : Cambridge University Press.

de Haan, M., Bauer, P. J., Georgieff, M. K., & Nelson, C. A. (2000). Explicit memory in low-risk infants aged 19 months and born between 27 and 42 weeks gestation. *Developmental Medicine and Child Neurology, 42,* 304–12.

de Haan, M., Mishkin, M., Baldeweg, T., & Vargha-Khadem, F. (2006). Human memory development and its dysfunction after early hippocampal injury. *Trends in Neurosciences, 29,* 374–81.

de Haan, M., Wyatt, J, Roth, S., Gadian, G., Vargha-Khadem, F., & Mishkin, M. (2002, March). *Effects of birth asphyxia on memory development and hippocampal volume during childhood*. Poster presented at the Meeting of the Cognitive Neuroscience Society, San Francisco, CA.

de Haan, M., Wyatt, J. S., Roth, S., Vargha-Khadem, F., Gadian, D., & Mishkin, M. (2006). Brain and cognitive-behavioural development after asphyxia at term birth. *Developmental Science, 9,* 350–8.

Desgranges, B., Baron, J. C., Giffard, B., Chételat, G., Lalevée, C., Viader, F., . . . Eustache, F. (2002). The neural basis of intrusions in free recall and cued recall: A PET study in Alzheimer's disease. *Neuroimage, 17,* 1658–64.

Diana, R. A., & Ranganath, C. (2011). Neural basis of recollection: Evidence from neuroimaging and electrophysiological research. In S. Ghetti & P. J. Bauer (Eds.), *Origins and development of recollection: Perspectives from psychology and neuroscience* (pp. 169–87). New York: Oxford University Press.

Duzel, E., Vargha-Khadem, F., Heinze, H. J., & Mishkin, M. (2001). Brain activity evidence for recognition without recollection after early hippocampal damage. *Proceedings of the National Academy of Sciences USA, 98,* 8101–6.

Gadian, D. G., Aicardi, J., Watkins, K. E., Porter, D. A., Mishkin, M., & Vargha-Khadem, F. (2000). Developmental amnesia associated with early hypoxic-ischaemic injury. *Brain, 123,* 499–507.

Gardiner, J. M., Brandt, K. R., Baddeley, A. D., Vargha-Khadem, F., Mishkin, M. (2008). Charting the acquisition of semantic knowledge in a case of developmental amnesia. *Neuropsychologia, 46,* 2865–8.

Ghetti, S., Lee, J. K., Simms, C. E., De Master, D. M., & Glaser, N. S. (2010). Diabetic ketoacidosis and memory dysfunction in children with Type 1 Diabetes. *Journal of Pediatrics, 156,* 109–14.

Giovagnoli, A. R. (1999). Verbal semantic memory in temporal lobe epilepsy. *Acta Neurologica Scandinavia, 99,* 334–9.

Giovagnoli, A. R. (2005). Characteristics of verbal semantic memory impairment in left hemisphere epilepsy. *Neuropsychology, 19,* 501–8.

Giovagnoli, A. R., Erbetta, A., Villani, F., & Avanzini, G. (2005). Semantic memory in partial epilepsy: Verbal and non-verbal deficits and neuroanatomical relationships. *Neuropsychologia, 43,* 1482–92.

Guillery-Girard, B., Martins, S., Parisot-Carbuccia, D., & Eustache, F. (2004). Semantic acquisition in childhood amnesic syndrome: A prospective study. *Neuroreport, 15,* 377–81.

Guimarães, C. A., Bonilha, L., Franzon, R. C., Li, M. L., Cendes, F., & Guerreiro, M. M. (2007). Distribution of regional gray matter abnormalities in a pediatric population with temporal lobe epilepsy and correlation with neuropsychological performance. *Epilepsy & Behavior, 11,* 558–66.

Guimaraes, C. A., Min, L. L., Rzezak, P., Fuentes, D., Franzon, R. C., Montenegro, M. A., . . . Guerreiro, M. M. (2006). Memory impairment in children with temporal lobe epilepsy: A review. *Journal of Epilepsy & Clinical Neurophysiology, 12,* 22–5.

Hanten, G., & Levn, H. S. (2011). Memory development and frontal lobe insult. In S. Ghetti & P. J. Bauer (Eds.), *Origins and development of recollection: Perspectives from psychology and neuroscience* (pp. 286–308). New York: Oxford University Press.

Helmstaedter, C. (2002). Effects of chronic epilepsy on declarative memory systems. *Progress in Brain Research, 135,* 439–53.

Helmstaedter, C., & Lendt, M. (2001). Neuropsychological outcome of temporal and extratemporal lobe resections in children. In I. Jambaqué, M. Lassonde, & O. Dulac, (Eds.) *Neuropsychology of childhood epilepsy: Advances in behavioral biology.* (pp. 215–27). New York: Kluver Academic Publishers.

Herbert, J., Gross, J., & Hayne, H. (2006). Age-related changes in deferred imitation between 6 and 9 months of age. *Infant Behavior and Development, 29,* 136–9.

Hoff Esbjørn, B., Hansen, B. M., Greisen, G., & Mortensen, E. L. (2006). Intellectual development in a Danish cohort of prematurely born preschool children: Specific or general difficulties? *Journal of Developmental and Behavioural Pediatrics, 27,* 477–84.

Isaacs, E., Lucas, A., Chong, W. K., Johnson, C. L., Marshall, C., Vargha-Khadem, F., & Gadian, D. G. (2000). Hippocampal volume and everyday memory in children of very low birth weight. *Pediatric Research, 47,* 713–20.

Jambaqué, I., Dellatolas, G., Dulac, O., Ponsot, G. & Signoret, J. L. (1993). Verbal and visual memory impairment in children with epilepsy. *Neuropsychologia, 31,* 1321–37.

Jambaqué, I., Dellatolas, G., Fohlen, M., Bulteau, C., Watier, L., Dorfmuller, G., . . . Delalande, O. (2007). Memory functions following surgery for temporal lobe epilepsy in children. *Neuropsychologia, 45,* 2850–62.

Kan, I. P., Alexander, M. P., & Verfaellie, M. (2009). Contribution of prior semantic knowledge to new episodic learning in amnesia. *Journal of Cognitive Neuroscience, 21,* 938–44.

Mabbott, D. J., & Smith, M. L. (2003). Memory in children with temporal or extra-temporal excisions. *Neuropsychologia, 41,* 995–1007.

MacLennan, A. (1999). A template for defining a causal relation between acute intrapartum events and cerebral palsy: International consensus statement. *BMJ, 319,* 1054–9.

Mañeru, C., Junqué, C., Botet, F., Tallada, M., & Guardia, J. (2001). Neuropsychologial long-term sequelae of perinatal asphyxia. *Brain Injury, 15,* 1029–39.

Marlow, N, Rose, A. S., Rands, C. E., & Draper, E. S. (2005). Neuropsychological and educational problems at school age associated with neonatal encephalopathy. *Archives of Disease in Childhood: Fetal and Neonatal Ed., 90,* F380–7.

Martins, S., Guillery-Girard, B., Jambaqué, I., Dulac, O., & Eustache, F. (2006). How children suffering severe amnesic syndrome acquire new concepts? *Neuropsychologia, 44,* 2792–805.

McDonough, L, Mandler, J. M., McKee, R. D., & Squire, L. R. (1995). The deferred imitation task as a nonverbal measure of declarative memory. *Proceedings of the National Academy of Sciences USA, 92,* 7580–4.

McKee, R. D., & Squire, L. R. (1993). On the development of declarative memory. *Journal of Experimental Psychology: Learning Memory and Cognition, 19,* 397–404.

Menon, V., Boyett-Anderson, J. M., & Reiss, A. L. (2005). Maturation of medial temporal lobe response and connectivity during memory encoding. *Cognitive Brain Research, 25,* 379–85.

Messas, C. S., Mansur, L. L., & Castro, L. H. M. (2008). Semantic memory impairment in temporal lobe epilepsy associated with hippocampal sclerosis. *Epilepsy & Behavior, 12,* 311–6.

Mishkin, M., Suzuki, W. A., Gadian, D. G., & Vargha-Khadem, F. (1997). Hierarchical organization of cognitive memory. *Philosophical Transactions of the Royal Society of London B: Biological Sciences, 352,* 1461–7.

Moses, S. N., Ostreicher, M. L., Rosenbaum, R. S., & Ryan J. D. (2008). Successful transverse patterning in amnesia using semantic knowledge. *Hippocampus, 18,* 121–4.

Narberhaus, A., Pueyo-Benito, R., Segarra-Castells, M. D., Perapoch-López, J., Botet-Mussons, F., & Junqué, C. (2007). Long-term cognitive dysfunctions related to prematurity. *Revista de Neurologia, 45,* 224–8.

Nolan, M. A., Redoblado, M. A., Lah, S., Sabaz, M., Lawson, J. A., Cunningham, A. M., . . . Bye, A. M. (2004). Memory function in childhood epilepsy syndromes. *Journal of Paediatric Child Health, 40,* 20–7.

Nosarti, C., Al-Asady, M. H., Frangou, S., Stewart, A. L., Rifkin, L., & Murray, R. M. (2002). Adolescents who were born very preterm have decreased brain volumes. *Brain, 125,* 1616–23.

O'Connor, M. J. (1980). A comparison of preterm and full-term infants on auditory discrimination at four months and on Bayley Scales of Infant Development and eighteen months. *Child Development, 51,* 81–8.

Ofen, N., Kao, Y-C, Hessner-Sokol, P., Kim, H., Whitfield-Gabrieli, S., & Gabrieli, J. D. E. (2007). Development of the declarative memory system in the human brain. *Nature Neuroscience, 10,* 1198–205.

O'Kane, G., Kensinger, D. A., & Corkin, S. (2004). Evidence for semantic learning in profound amnesia: An investigation with patient HM. *Hippocampus, 14,* 417–25.

Pascalis, O., & Bachevalier, J. (1999). Neonatal aspiration lesions of the hippocampal formation impair visual recognition memory when assessed by paired-comparison task but not by delayed nonmatching-to-sample task. *Hippocampus, 9,* 609–16.

Pascalis, O., de Haan, M., Nelson, C. A., & de Schonen, S. (1998). Long-term recognition memory for faces assessed by visual paired comparison in 3- and 6-month-old infants. *Journal of Experimental Psychology: Learning Memory and Cognition, 24,* 249–60.

Pascalis, O., & de Schonen, S. (1994). Recognition memory in 3- to 4-day-old human neonates. *Neuroreport, 5,* 1721–4.

Pascalis, O., Hunkin, N. M., Holdstock, J. S., Isaac, C. L., & Mayes, A. R. (2004). Visual paired comparison performance is impaired in a patient with selective hippocampal lesions and relatively intact item recognition. *Neuropsychologia, 42,* 1293–300.

Patterson, K., Nestor, P. J., & Rogers, T. T. (2007). Where do you know what you know? The representation of semantic knowledge in the human brain. *Nature Reviews Neuroscience, 8,* 976–87.

Ranganath, C., Heller, A. S., & Wilding, E. L. (2007). Dissociable correlates of two classes of retrieval processing in prefrontal cortex. *Neuroimage, 35,* 1663–73.

Rennie, J. M., Hagmann, C. F., & Robertson, N. J. (2007). Outcome after intrapartum hypoxic ischaemia at term. *Seminars in Fetal Neonatology, 12,* 398–407.

Richmond, J., & Nelson, C. A. (2007). Accounting for change in declarative memory: A cognitive neuroscience perspective. *Developmental Review, 27,* 349–73.

Rose, S. A., & Feldman, J. F. (1997). Memory and speed: Their role in the relation of infant information processing to later IQ. *Child Development, 68,* 630–41.

Rose, S. A., Feldman, J. F., & Jankowski, J. J. (2001). Attention and recognition memory in the 1st year of life: A longitudinal study. *Developmental Psychology, 37,* 135–51.

Rose, S. A., Feldman, J. F., & Jankowski, J. J. (2005). Recall memory in the first three years of life: A longitudinal study of preterm and term children. *Developmental Medicine and Child Neurology, 47,* 653–9.

Rose, S. A., Feldman, J. F., McCarton, C. M., & Wolfson, J. (1988). Information processing in seven-month-old infants as a function of risk status. *Child Development, 59*, 589–603.

Rugg, M. D., Mark, R. E., Walla, P., Schloerscheidt, A. M., Birch, C. S., & Allan, K. (1998). Dissociation of the neural correlates of implicit and explicit memory. *Nature, 392*, 595–8.

Rushe, T. M., Rifkin, L., Stewart, A. L., Townsend, J. P., Roth, S. C., Wyatt, J. S., & Murray, R. M. (2001). Neuropyschological outcome at adolescence of very preterm birth and its relation to brain structure. *Developmental Medicine and Child Neurology, 43*, 226–33.

Squire, L. R., Stark, C. E., & Clark, R. E. (2004). The medial temporal lobe. *Annual Review of Neuroscience, 27*, 270–306.

St. Jacques, P. L., & Cabeza, R. (2011). Neural basis of autobiographical memory. In S. Ghetti & P. J. Bauer (Eds.), *Origins and development of recollection: Perspectives from psychology and neuroscience* (pp. 188–288). New York: Oxford University Press.

Temple, C. M. (1984). Surface dyslexia in a child with epilepsy. *Neuropsychologia, 22*, 569–76.

Temple, C. M. (1997). Cognitive neuropsychology and its application to children. *Journal of Child Psychology and Psychiatry, 38*, 27–52.

Therien, J. M., Worwa, C. T., Mattia, F. R., & de Regnier, R. A. (2004). Altered pathways for auditory discrimination and recognition memory in preterm infants. *Developmental Medicine and Child Neurology, 46*, 816–24.

Tokioka, A. B., Pearce, J. W., & Crowell, D. H. (1995). Endogenous event-related potentials in term and preterm infants. *Journal of Clinical Neurophysiology, 12*, 468–75.

Van der Werf, Y. D., Jolles, J., Witter, M. P., & Uylings, H. B. (2003). Contributions of thalamic nuclei to declarative memory functioning. *Cortex, 39*, 1047–62.

van Handel, M., Swaab, H., de Vries, L. S., & Jongmans, M. J. (2007). Long-term cognitive and behavioral consequences of neonatal encephalopathy following perinatal asphyxia: A review. *European Journal of Pediatrics, 166*, 645–54.

Vargha-Khadem, F., Gadian, D. G., & Mishkin, M. (2001). Dissociations in cognitive memory: The syndrome of developmental amnesia. *Philosophical Transactions of the Royal Society of London. Series B: Biological Science, 356*, 1435–40.

Vargha-Khadem, F., Gadian, D. G., Watkins, K. E., Connelly, A., Van Paesschen, W., & Mishkin, M. (1997). Differential effects of early hippocampal pathology on episodic and semantic memory. *Science, 277*, 276–380.

Vargha-Khadem, F., Salmond, C. H., Watkins, K. E., Friston, K. J., Gadian, D. G., & Mishkin, M. (2003). Developmental amnesia: Effect of age at injury. *Proceedings of the National Academy of Sciences USA, 100*, 10055–60.

Vicari, S., Menghini, D., Di Paola, M., Serra, L., Donfrancesco, A., Fidani, P., . . . Carlesimo, G. A. (2007). Acquired amnesia in childhood: A single case study. *Neuropsychologia, 45*, 704–15.

Viggedal, G., Lundälv, E., Carlsson, G., & Kjellmer, I. (2002). Follow-up into young adulthood after cardiopulmonary resuscitation in term and near-term newborn infants: II Neuropsychological consequences. *Acta Paediatrica, 91*, 1218–26.

Wood, F. B., Brown, I. S., & Felton, R. H. (1989). Long-term follow-up of a childhood amnesic syndrome. *Brain & Cognition, 10*, 76–86.

Zola, S. M., Squire, L. R., Teng, E., Stefannaci, L., Buffalo, E. A., & Clark, R. E. (2000). Impaired recognition memory in monkeys after damage limited to the hippocampal region. *Journal of Neuroscience, 20*, 451–63.

12

Memory Development and Frontal Lobe Insult

GERRI HANTEN AND HARVEY S. LEVIN

Injury to the brain is among the most frequent causes of mortality and morbidity among children in the United States, with traumatic brain injury (TBI) affecting approximately 70 of 100,000 children per year (Langlois et al., 2003). Impaired memory is among the most common cognitive sequelae of TBI in children and adults.

The trajectory of general recovery after TBI follows a predictable pattern of immediate decline in performance, followed by recovery for 6 months or more until, after about a year, performance levels reach asymptote (Jaffe, Polissar, Fay, & Liao, 1995). Although many children who sustain TBI recover intellectual functioning to within the normal range on standard tests (Levin, Eisenberg, Wiggs, & Kobayashi, 1982), cognitive deficits, including memory, frequently persist in children with severe TBI (Jaffe et al., 1995). Further, recent studies have revealed effects of injury severity that increase over time, suggesting the performance gap between uninjured children and children with severe TBI may increase with age (Levin et al., 2004).

Impairments of memory after childhood TBI may arise from compromise of existing memory systems or by interruption of normal development of memory. Different from adults, the pattern of memory impairment in children may change over time as cognitive skills that support memory fail to develop because of damage to the underlying neural substrate. For example, a child with a brain injury at an early age may appear to recover well until reaching the age at which a particular skill (e.g., rehearsal strategy) normally develops, but if the neural substrate supporting that particular skill is damaged, then the skill may fail to develop, and the child will show a deficit where none was previously apparent. Currently, models that allow for the prediction of specific deficits are in the early stages. Progress in this area will be facilitated by further understanding of the trajectory of memory skill development, which, though fairly well characterized in broad strokes, continues to be refined in terms of specific skills. In addition, rapid advances in neuroimaging technology are beginning to yield more accurate knowledge of the patterns of brain structure development. Although the dialectic concerning the relation of behavioral and neural mechanisms underlying the development of memory continues, the integration of neuroimaging with developmental behavioral science offers cause for optimism for increased accuracy of prediction of acute and latent deficits and, therefore, enhanced prospects for remediation of childhood TBI.

This chapter addresses the effect of TBI on memory skills in children. To provide a framework for our discussion of the neurobehavioral consequences of TBI in children, we first offer a very brief overview of memory development and some findings regarding the relation between neural structure and memory performance in children, both of which subjects are addressed in other sections of this volume. Our focus, however, will be on studies of the consequence of TBI in children to domains of learning and memory and the factors that have been found to affect outcome.

DEVELOPMENT OF MEMORY SKILLS

Investigations of infant memory, though unable to directly index conscious recollection, have used indirect behavioral measures to demonstrate the rudiments of recognition memory in newborn infants (DeCasper & Fifer, 1980; Purhonen, Kilpelainen-Lees, Valkonen-Korhonen, Karhu, & Lehtonen, 2005). Paradigms purportedly measuring declarative memory have revealed that memory for objects and actions is present in early infanthood, but it is context-limited until around 18 months of age when representational flexibility becomes apparent (Hayne, Boniface, & Barr, 2000). However, it should be noted that measurement of declarative memory, which usually relies on explicit measures, remains somewhat controversial in preverbal infants (Richmond & Nelson, 2008). Studies of infants using event-related potentials have linked development of visual paired comparison skill with increases in speed of processing (Webb, Long, & Nelson, 2005). These studies each demonstrate that the ability to maintain a representation over time develops at a very early age.

A great deal of research has been directed at uncovering the bases of age-related changes in memory skills beyond infanthood (Appel et al., 1972; Bjorklund, 2004; Cowen, 1999; Flavell, Beach, & Chinsky, 1966; Ghetti, Lyons, Lazzarin, & Cornoldi, 2008; Keeney, Cannizzo, & Flavell, 1967). Memory span in children increases approximately 3.5-fold from the age of 2.5 years to college age, and increases are negatively accelerated, especially after the age of 7 years (Dempster, 1985), with the mechanisms responsible for these gains still under discussion. Procedural memory appears to mature early, reaching adultlike levels as early as 7 to 8 years. In contrast, declarative memory continues to develop after the age of 12 years (DiGiulio, Seidenberg, O'Leary, & Raz, 1994), possibly reflecting a greater contribution of later-developing strategic skills.

The self-regulatory, strategic, and metacognitive control activities that are closely associated with the central executive in models of working memory, and which have been implicated in increases in declarative memory skills, seem to appear in early childhood (Brown & DeLoache, 1978). For example, within the domain of verbal memory, children start to use rehearsal as a memorization strategy around the age of 6 or 7 years (Keeney et al., 1967; Kennedy & Miller, 1976), and by around the age of 9 years, they have acquired the concept of semantic strategies (Moynahan, 1973; Worden & Sladewski-Awig, 1982). Similarly, on tests of spatial memory, children transition from simple cue-based strategies to more sophisticated place-based strategies between the ages of 7 to 9 years (Lehnung et al., 1998). Interestingly, in studies of metamemory development, consistent increases in memory performance seem to be associated less with spontaneous use of strategies, than with the awareness of the utility of strategy use (Ghatala, Levin, Pressley, & Lodico, 1985; Justice, 1985), suggesting the importance of self-monitoring and evaluation in memory development, although the exact mechanisms involved (neural substrate vs. representation) merit further discussion (Ceci, Fitneva, & Williams, 2010). The specifics of metamemory have been investigated in studies of the development of awareness of memory strength (Ghetti et al., 2008) and the ability to discriminate false from true memories (Ghetti, 2008), as well as the development of understanding the bases of memory failure (Jaswal & Dodson, 2009) and the use of mnemonic heuristics (Koriat, Ackerman, Lockl, & Schneider, 2009). Further, relations between development of these metamemorial skills has been linked to development of other metalevel skills, such as language competence and social perspective taking (Lockl & Schneider, 2007).

BRAIN MATURATION AND DEVELOPMENT
OF MEMORIAL PROCESSES

Age-related differences in intellectual abilities have been tied to the development and maturation of brain structures (Bauer, 2009; Casey, Tottenham, Liston, & Durston, 2005; Diamond, 2002; Reiss, Abrams, Singer, Ross, & Denckla, 1996; Schmithorst, Wilke, Dardzinski, & Holland, 2005; Sowell, Delis, Stiles, & Jernigan, 2001). Consistent with the pattern of developing memory skills, the most dramatic structural changes in the brain occur before the age of 5 years. Increased electrical activity in cortical frontal regions is associated with development of working memory and inhibitory control in infants and in preschoolers, with the pattern of activity appearing to become more specialized with age (Wolfe & Bell, 2004), and linked to emotional development (temperament) in young children (Wolfe & Bell, 2007). Maturation of the medial temporal region has also been associated with development of declarative memory in infants, with evidence suggesting that improvements in encoding may be attributed to rapid myelination during the first year, but prolonged increases in maintenance of representations and retrieval more related to extended maturation of the dentate gyrus (Richmond & Nelson, 2007). Although few studies have examined the relation of developing brain structure to procedural memory, adult studies have suggested a lesser role of frontal regions in procedural skill acquisition, depending on task demand (Schmidtke, Manner, Kaufmann, & Schmolck, 2002; Torriero et al., 2007).

In functional neuroimaging studies of working memory, increased recruitment of the prefrontal, striatal, and parietal regions is associated with improvements in working memory and, perforce, cognitive control (Bunge & Wright, 2007). A similar pattern has been observed with visuospatial working memory tasks, during which young children recruit regions primarily associated with core demands of working memory (i.e., dorsolateral prefrontal regions), adolescents show a more extended network of recruitment, including more specialized regions such as premotor response areas, and adults showed the most specialized regional recruitment, including stimulus-specific regions (Scherf, Sweeney, & Luna, 2006).

Recent evidence has shown that although cerebral volume does not change dramatically after 11 or 12 years of age, there are distinct developmental changes in white and gray matter that continue until late adolescence (Giedd et al., 1999; Wilke, Krågeloh-Mann, & Holland, 2006) and that have been related to gains in intellectual function. Several studies, longitudinal and cross-sectional, have examined brain development (Giedd et al., 1999; Gogtay et al., 2004; Reiss et al., 1996; Sowell, Trauner, Gamst, & Jernigan, 2002), with consistent findings. The general pattern is that between the ages of 4 years and 22 years, volume of white matter increases linearly with age and uniformly across brain regions, with greater changes in males than females. Cortical gray matter shows nonlinear and regionally specific development, with early increases in gray matter followed by decreases, usually in adolescence. In the frontal and parietal lobes, the maximum volume occurs at around 12 years for males and 11 years for females, but temporal gray matter lags slightly behind. These data point out that measurement of relationships between neural structure maturity and development of cognitive ability is influenced by the type of structure measured (white matter vs. gray), the nature of the measurement (integrity of microstructure vs. changes in volume), and the region of interest. For example, in the frontal lobes, early increases in volume may be expected to correspond to better performance on tests of cognition, but in adolescence, with decreases in volume signaling maturity and presumably greater efficiency, a negative relationship may emerge. In the context of our topic, such findings illustrate the complications in linking specific regional damage to developing cognitive skills.

PATHOPHYSIOLOGY OF CHILDHOOD TBI AND IMPACT ON MEMORY FUNCTION

Brain imaging studies (Levin et al., 1997; Wilde et al., 2005) have shown that TBI associated with closed head injury in children frequently involves both focal lesions and diffuse injury to the prefrontal region. The proximity of the sphenoidal ridges and bony protrusions on the base of the skull to the frontal lobes contributes to the vulnerability of the orbitofrontal area and other prefrontal regions to injury (Adams, 1980; Bigler, 1990). In children with TBI, gray matter in the orbitofrontal and dorsolateral cortices is reduced even in the absence of focal lesions (Berryhill et al., 1995). Shearing and stretching of axons at the time of impact, secondary injury due to excitotoxicity, inflammation, dysregulation of the intracellular and extracellular environment, and subsequent degenerative changes over the ensuing months all contribute to the multifocal and diffuse injury to prefrontal gray and white matter (Kochanek et al., 2000). Degenerative changes have been detected after periods as long as three years postinjury, suggesting that TBI influences brain development in white matter structures such as the corpus callosum (Levin, Benavidez, et al., 2000).

Poorer performance with verbal memory has been most often associated with frontal lobe lesions, as compared to extrafrontal lesions (Levin et al., 1994) although extrafrontal lesion volume has also been predictive of memory impairment (Salorio et al., 2005) when widespread extrafrontal damage suggests extensive diffuse axonal injury (DAI). With the assumption of a high proportion of children with TBI having frontal lobe damage, these findings are consistent with studies of the neurobehavioral correlates of brain maturational changes, in which frontal lobe gray matter is more strongly predictive of verbal memory functioning than the mesial temporal lobe gray matter volume (Sowell et al., 2001). The relation of frontal pathology to memory task performance has been demonstrated in several studies. For example, in a study comparing children with mild and severe TBI, Di Stefano and colleagues (2000) used hierarchical regression of lesion size to predict performance on the California Verbal Learning Test (CVLT; Delis, Kramer, Kaplan, & Ober, 1994), a test of verbal memory. When frontal lesion size was entered into the regression equation after the Glasgow Coma Scale score (a widely used index of brain injury severity; Teasdale & Jennett, 1974) and age at test, prediction was improved for measures of recall. In contrast, bilateral extrafrontal, and left and right extrafrontal lesion size did not predict performance, nor did hippocampus volume relate to performance (Di Stefano et al., 2000). Albeit with a small sample size, the lack of relations between hippocampus volume and verbal memory was corroborated by Serra-Grabulosa et al. (2005), who found only cerebral-spinal fluid volume, an indirect index of diffuse axonal injury, was related to verbal memory in a sample of 16 patients with severe TBI in a long-term outcome study (Serra-Grabulosa et al., 2005). It should be noted that the CVLT word lists comprise four exemplars of each of four categories, which encourages the use of semantic strategies, so it may be particularly sensitive to frontal damage (Alexander, Stuss, & Fansabedian, 2003).

Consistent with the view that frontally guided, distributed networks subserve memory functions, disruption of these connections by diffuse axonal injury has been implicated in recent brain imaging studies using diffusion tensor imaging (DTI), which is especially sensitive to disruption of white matter microstructure, and in functional magnetic resonance imaging (MRI) studies linking circuitry to memory functioning (Kraus et al., 2007; Kumar, et al., 2009). However, it should be noted that not all studies linking diffusion tensor imaging findings to memory function show a relationship, especially with mild or moderately injured patients (Wozniak et al., 2007).

In concert with diffusion tensor imaging findings, functional brain imaging studies (Newsome et al., 2007; Newsome et al., 2008) have disclosed that the pattern of frontal and parietal activation during performance of memory tasks is altered in patients with moderate to severe TBI. Taken together, structural and functional brain imaging research indicates that prefrontal tissue loss and disruption are frequent sequelae of TBI, which contribute to persisting memory problems.

DOMAINS OF MEMORY IMPAIRMENT AFTER CHILDHOOD TBI

Many studies have shown that children with TBI have relatively poor memory skills. However, not all memory domains are affected equally (Anderson, Morse, Catroppa, Haritou, & Rosenfeld, 2004; Levin et al., 1994). Further, a number of factors not directly related to injury (e.g., demographics) have been found to interact with injury variables to predict recovery of cognitive function (Lajiness-O'Neill, Erdodi, & Bigler, 2010). In the next section, we cover patterns of memory impairment after childhood TBI as well as the major factors that have been identified as predictors of memory impairment and recovery, including nature and severity of injury, age variables, and environmental factors.

In recent years, memory theorists have come to substantial agreement that human memory is not a unitary construct, but rather is made up of dissociable components sensitive to differing stimulus characteristics and demands (Baddeley, 1998). Recently, neuroimaging studies have elucidated relations among brain structures and memory skills (Cohen et al., 1993). The precise nature and relation of components of memory have yet to be completely specified, and discussion of the various theories relating to memory components and systems are beyond the scope of this chapter. However, in reporting research concerning the effects of TBI on memory, we will conform to commonly accepted functional domains of memory (Alexander & Mayfield, 2005; Mottram & Donders, 2005). Although we tried to cover the major domains, the section is by no means exhaustive.

The specific relationship between localization of traumatic focal lesions and memory disorder is complicated by individual variation in type and size of lesions, as well as differences in age and age at injury, which relate to stages of brain maturation and cognitive development. Nonetheless, recent research relating to specific memory deficits after TBI indicates that certain types of memory disorders occur more frequently than others. The following section reports general findings of the consequences of traumatic injury of the brain to specific domains of memory. The literature on effects of childhood TBI on domains of memory is sparse as compared to the adult literature. However, recent work has begun to fill the gaps, allowing a more complete picture to emerge.

Auditory-Verbal Memory and Learning

Probably the most common of memory impairments after TBI, as well as the most thoroughly characterized area of cognitive impairment, is auditory-verbal memory. A long-term outcome study of children with TBI found impairment persisted beyond 5 years for complex verbal memory, but not for simple digit span, backward digit span, or block-pattern span (Anderson & Catroppa, 2007). Many studies have directly or indirectly investigated the characteristics of auditory-verbal memory after TBI using recall, cued recall, or recognition tests. The tests employed have frequently been standardized list-learning tests using the repeated presentation and recall of a single list of words, such as the CVLT (Delis et al., 1994) or the Auditory-Verbal Learning Test (Schmidt, 2003), which have the advantage of being widely accessible and familiar both to researchers and clinicians, but which may be less sensitive to the mechanisms of impairment than experimental tasks designed to test specific hypotheses.

The general finding is that children who have had severe TBI are likely to show deficits in verbal memory, including delayed recall (Anderson, Catroppa, Rosenfeld, Haritou, & Morse, 2000; Yeates, Blumenstein, Patterson, & Delis, 1995), verbal working memory (Levin et al., 2002; Roncadin, Guger, Archibald, Barnes, & Dennis, 2004), word list learning (Catroppa & Anderson, 2002; Yeates et al., 1995), auditory-verbal selective learning (Hanten et al., 2004; Hanten, Zhang, & Levin, 2002) and, less consistently, for recognition memory (Roman et al., 1998). In addition, within verbal memory tasks, intrusions and perseverations as well as impairment in the ability to utilize semantic information to aid recall have been reported (Hanten & Martin, 2000; Levin et al., 1996). Deficits in verbal learning and immediate serial recall relative to controls may exist despite relatively unimpaired vocabulary and nonverbal intelligence (Gupta, MacWhinney, Feldman, & Sacco, 2003). Deficits are more likely to be observed on complex memory tasks, which presumably depend on integration of different intellectual domains (thus require intact connectivity), than on simple span tasks (Anderson & Catroppa, 2007; Catroppa & Anderson, 2002; Serra-Grabulosa et al., 2005). Further, there is some evidence that impaired verbal learning may be mediated by slowed speed of processing (Mottram & Donders, 2006). Impairments are greatest during the first few months after injury and are most consistently present in children with severe injury (Levin & Eisenberg, 1979a; Roman et al., 1998). Later, performance may decline in relation to age norms, especially as children injured at a younger age "grow into" their deficits (Anderson et al., 1997).

Spatial Memory and Nonverbal Memory

As compared to studies of verbal memory and learning, fewer studies have specifically considered the impact of childhood TBI on spatial and location memory and nonverbal memory. However, such studies that have been done suggest that spatial, location, and nonverbal memory are relatively spared beyond the acute stages of TBI (Lehnung et al., 2003). In one prospective study of spatial learning and cognitive mapping skills, children with severe TBI were assessed on the ability to learn to negotiate a maze in a room both at baseline (during acute recovery phase) and 4 years later. Although children were impaired at the baseline evaluation, deficits in spatial learning had resolved 4 years later. However, deficits in the ability to use more complex mapping skills remained impaired (Lehnung et al., 2003). Studies requiring recall of unnamable (thus unverbalizable) objects in children with TBI fail to show effects of injury severity on nonverbal memory (Levin, Song et al., 2000), or visuospatial memory (Anderson & Catroppa, 2007; Donders, 1993) beyond the acute stages of recovery. In a recent study of mild TBI (Slobounov, et al., 2010) using a combination of virtual reality technology and functional neuroimaging to investigate spatial navigation abilities in adolescents and young adults, no performance differences were observed between the TBI group and an uninjured comparison group. However, the imaging data revealed that, though unimpaired on performance, the TBI patients nonetheless recruited more extensive regions of the brain during task performance (Slobounov et al., 2010). Thus, current evidence suggests that spatial and nonverbal memory may be less vulnerable to TBI than is verbal memory, but that there may be mild effects that are overcome by neural adaptation.

Semantic Memory

Long-term memory and semantic knowledge also appear to be relatively spared after brain injury in children, although deficits may be present in the early stages of recovery for some measures of semantic processing (Levin et al., 1996). In adolescents and young adults, some studies suggest that deficits observed in the early stages of TBI may reflect impaired access to knowledge, rather than the loss of semantic representation (McWilliams & Schmitter-Edgecombe, 2008). Other studies investigating persistent effects of TBI on semantic representation have found preservation of knowledge acquisition, knowledge base, speed of knowledge access (Barnes & Dennis, 2001; Dimoska, McDonald, Pell, Tate, & James, 2010), and vocabulary (Gupta et al., 2003). However, evidence suggests that the ability to use semantic knowledge in the service of more complex tasks may be impaired in children with severe TBI, especially within the domain of language processing (Chapman et al., 2004; Chapman et al., 2006; Dennis & Barnes, 1990) and executive function (Levin et al., 1996).

Implicit and Procedural Memory.

Within the procedural memory domain, studies with TBI patients have generally shown intact procedural learning, even in the presence of impaired verbal learning. Though studies directly comparing conscious recollection (explicit tests of memory) to memory in the absence of conscious awareness (implicit tests of memory) in TBI patients are relatively sparse, findings suggest that implicit memory in children is more resistant to impairment after TBI than is explicit memory (Shum, Jamieson, Bahr, & Wallace, 1999; Ward, Shum, Wallace, & Boon, 2002; Yeates & Enrile, 2005). For example, Shum, Jamieson, et al. (1999) investigated the abilities of 12 children with severe TBI and 12 matched uninjured children on a picture fragment completion task under conditions of explicit or implicit instructions. In the study phase of both conditions, the children were shown complete pictures in a naming task followed by a filled delay. Under implicit instructions, the children were asked to identify pictures from fragments of pictures presented in the study phase, which were intermixed with nonstudied picture fragments. Under explicit instructions, the children were given the same instructions, but were also told that they had seen the pictures earlier in the testing session. The investigators found that the children with TBI performed similarly to the uninjured control children in the implicit task, but were significantly impaired on the explicit task. Consistent with these data, in a interview study of everyday memory function (Ward, Shum, Dick, McKinlay, & Baker-Tweney, 2004), parents endorsed preserved procedural memory in their children after TBI. A developmental perspective suggests that because implicit and explicit declarative memory skills have different developmental trajectories, with implicit memory skills maturing relatively early and explicit memory continuing to improve with age, at least until 12 years old (DiGiulio et al., 1994), they may be differentially vulnerable to disruption during the developmental period (Yeates & Enrile, 2005).

Prospective Memory

Prospective memory, the recall of future intentions or actions to be performed, is a complex or multicomponent form of memory. Prospective memory has a declarative component (sometimes called the *what* element), and a temporal-contextual component (the *when* or *where* elements). Although the adult TBI literature suggests that prospective memory is affected after TBI (Hannon, Adams, Harrington, Fries-Dias, & Gipson, 1995; Shum, Valentine, & Cutmore, 1999), relatively little research has been conducted on children's prospective memory skills after TBI. Using a parent interview to assess memory functioning in children and adolescents, Ward et al. (2004) reported declines in prospective memory performance in day-to-day living after TBI. These data are supported by a descriptive study of prospective memory after childhood TBI reporting that under event-based cueing conditions, children with severe TBI were less likely than orthopedic control subjects to respond to a cue when instructions had been given earlier in the session and less likely to respond to monetary incentive (McCauley et al., 2010), which may have implications for remediation. Taking a more theoretical approach, Ward, Shum, McKinlay, Baker, and Wallace (2007) explored the underlying mechanisms of prospective memory deficits in terms of frontal lobe development and the effect of increasing cognitive load on performance of an event-based prospective memory task. They found that at younger ages, thus during earlier stages of frontal lobe maturation, children with TBI did not differ from their uninjured peers in the effect of increasing cognitive load on task performance, but the two adolescent groups (in whom, presumably frontal lobe development would be approaching maturity in the absence of brain injury) differed significantly in the decrease in performance from low to high cognitive load. Further, the study also demonstrated that performance on tests of executive function were predictive of prospective memory performance (Ward et al., 2007), thus raising the question of the mediation of prospective memory by executive function.

Working Memory

The term *working memory* refers to a multicomponent limited capacity system for the temporary storage of information held for further manipulation or goal attainment (Baddeley, 1992), which is neither dedicated, nor localizable to a specific region. Working memory has recently been conceptualized as an emergent system of interactions between the prefrontal cortex and other task-specific regions of the brain (D'Esposito, 2007). Early functional imaging studies with adults revealed the importance of the prefrontal cortex to working memory (Braver et al., 1997), and more recent studies have refined and extended understanding of the multicomponent and multiregional nature of working memory performance (Ranganath, Cohen, Dam, & D'Esposito, 2004). Given the importance of the prefrontal cortex to working memory and the frontal-biased pathophysiology of TBI in children, it is perhaps expected that working memory be impaired in children with severe TBI (Levin et al., 2002; Roncadin et al., 2004). Levin et al. (2002) investigated working memory performance in children who had sustained mild, moderate, or severe TBI using an N-back task, in which a long string of upper- and lowercase letters appeared one at a time on a computer screen. Children monitored the letters for a letter match one position back (... P-k̲-**K**-o -V ...), 2 positions back (... P-k̲-o-**K**-V ...), or 3 positions back (... P-k̲-o-V-**K** ...) (Braver et al., 1997). As illustrated in Figure 12.1, as compared to children with mild TBI, children with moderate and severe TBI showed persistent deficits that became more pronounced over a 2-year period (Levin et al., 2004).

Functional neuroimaging studies have provided insight into the neural correlates of such deficits. For example, using a version of the N-back task, Newsome et al. (2007) studied children with moderate-to-severe TBI and typically developing children. Children with TBI who performed more poorly on the task than age- and gender-matched control subjects showed a pattern of lesser frontal activation than did the control subjects. However, children with TBI who were equated

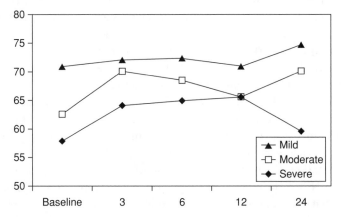

Figure 12.1. Changes over a 2-year interval in N-back working memory performance in terms of percentage of net correct (hits – false alarms) for children with mild, moderate, and severe TBI. Levin, H. S., Hanten, G., Zhang, L., Swank, P. R., Ewing-Cobbs, L., Dennis, M., et al. (2004). Changes in working memory after traumatic brain injury in children. *Neuropsychology, 18*, 240–7. Reprinted with permission from APA

to the control subjects on performance showed the reverse pattern; that is, achieving the same level of performance required recruitment of more widespread frontal regions (Newsome et al., 2007). In a different functional MRI study, Newsome et al. (2008) illuminated the impact of pediatric TBI on discrete stages of memory processing and the relation to frontal functioning. Using a task in which memory sets of one and four items were presented, followed by a short delay and an item-recognition probe (Sternberg, 1966), the investigators observed a dissociation between typically developing adolescents and those with moderate-to-severe TBI in patterns of frontal and parietal activation associated with the encoding, maintenance, and retrieval stages of memory. Relative to controls, adolescents with TBI showed a pattern of load-related increases in activation at the encoding and retrieval stages, but not during maintenance. Typically developing adolescents showed greater load-related increases (relative to TBI patients) in the maintenance stage only. These findings suggest that deficits in working memory may depend on faulty strategy deployment (i.e., maintenance stage), rather than impaired capacity, and that diffuse damage after TBI may result in overrecruitment of frontal lobe structures, which may have implications for the role of neural plasticity in rehabilitation.

Other studies of childhood TBI have looked at the relation between specific subcomponents of working memory to other intellectual deficits. For example, Mandalis, Kinsella, Ong, and Anderson (2007) determined that impaired performance on tasks tapping the phonological component of working memory predicted poor performance on new word learning, whereas deficits in the executive component were related to general memory dysfunction in acquisition, retrieval, and recognition memory (Mandalis et al., 2007). In another study of the relation of components of working memory to sentence processing in children after TBI, Hanten and Martin (2000) reported that children with a specific deficit in either phonological working memory or semantic working memory showed differing patterns of impairment on sentence processing tasks (Hanten & Martin, 2000). Conklin, Salorio, and Slomine (2008) investigated the relation between a performance measure of working memory (backward digit span) and the working memory subscale of a widely used parent report, the Behavior Rating Inventory of Executive Function. They found that the two measures of working memory were not related statistically. They also found that although the injury variable (length of coma) did predict performance on digit span, it did not predict the Behavior Rating Inventory of Executive Function working memory score. However, variables related to age were predictive of scores. In a study relating memory to higher language function, Chapman et al. (2006) found that working memory (as measured by an N-back task), but not simple immediate word list recall, was significantly correlated with summarization ability and ability to recall discourse content. The findings of these studies reveal both the broader impact of deficits in working memory as a consequence of TBI, and the importance of research linking specific mechanisms to dysfunction. They also highlight the need to be circumspect in selecting appropriate measures for working memory, and that measurement of working memory may be to some degree task-specific.

Metamemory, Strategy Development, Strategic Learning

Successful memorial performance involves more than the passive registration and retrieval of information. It also involves strategic manipulation of information, assessment of ongoing processes, monitoring of performance, and appraisal of feedback. There is a rich tradition of research relating to the metacognitive and strategic aspects of memory in children (Bjorklund, 2004; Flavell, Friedrichs, & Hoyt, 1970; Ghetti et al., 2008), which has been extended to neuropsychological research (Mazzoni & Nelson, 1998; Metcalfe & Shimamura, 1994). Studies of individuals with TBI have revealed that in performance of memory tasks they may fail to apply the appropriate metacognitive processes. For example, studies of verbal learning using the CVLT have shown that children with TBI show increased numbers of intrusions and perseverations in list recall (Levin et al., 1996), suggesting impaired control processes. Studies with both verbal and nonverbal materials have shown decreased ability to monitor frequency and recency of item representation (Levin, Song, et al., 2000), suggesting impaired metacognitive monitoring. In studies directly addressing metamemory in children with TBI, deficits have been reported in feeling-of-knowing judgments (Hanten, Bartha, & Levin, 2000), which results differ from similar studies in adults (Anderson & Schmitter-Edgecombe, 2009). Even when verbal recall is relatively preserved after childhood TBI, deficits in the ability to strategically manipulate processes that support performance on complex memory tasks have been reported, both with simple word lists (Hanten et al., 2002) and in text (Gamino, Chapman, & Cook, 2009; Hanten et al., 2004).

VARIABLES THAT AFFECT RECOVERY

Severity of Injury and Chronicity

Impact of acute TBI severity on verbal memory in children has been demonstrated with measures of word list recall such as the selective reminding test (Levin & Eisenberg, 1979b; Levin et al., 1982) and the CVLT (Roman et al., 1998). As mentioned, the typical pattern of impact and recovery is a steep decline in functioning immediately after the injury, followed by an acute recovery phase that may last several months. Afterward, recovery is slower, and perceived increases in function may be confounded with development. The extent and rate of recovery have been shown to interact with injury severity, such that mild TBI, as compared with severe TBI, results in few long-term sequelae (Levin et al., 2004). Longitudinal studies with follow-up intervals extending as late as 5 years have shown that injury severity predicts impairment on complex memory tasks, but not necessarily on simple span tasks (Anderson & Catroppa, 2007). As well, severity effects on residual deficits in working memory have been reported, with evidence for a late decline (after 1 year) in relation to age (Levin et al., 2004). Recently, Catroppa, Anderson, Ditchfield, and Coleman (2008) found effects of severity on residual impairment of complex memory 5 years after injury, with MRI findings implicating disruption of distributed neural circuitry involving the frontal and temporal regions as predictive of late outcome (Catroppa et al., 2008). It should be noted that these findings on the relation of injury severity to outcome refer to single instances of injury, as most studies exclude children with previous history of TBI. And, although most children with mild TBI recover fully, recent studies of sports-related head injury suggest that multiple mild head injuries occurring within short time frames may have long-term consequences if not managed properly (Buzzini & Guskiewicz, 2006; Kirkwood, Yeates, & Wilson, 2006).

Age at Injury

In spite of the persistent notion that a younger brain retains plasticity and, therefore, recovery is greater for children injured at a younger age, studies have confirmed that the opposite relation is the case after severe traumatic brain injury, which has diffuse effects. That is, when matched for severity of injury, children injured earlier appear to have poorer recovery in terms of general outcome (Kriel, Krach, & Panser, 1989), as well as memory function (Anderson et al., 2000; Donders & Warschausky, 2007), although children with mild and moderate injuries show less of an effect than do children with severe injuries (Anderson, Catroppa, Morse, Haritou, & Rosenfeld, 2006). In a study of working memory after childhood TBI, Levin et al. (2002) found left frontal lesions were related to working memory deficit in older children and adolescents, but not in young children, suggesting that the degree to which age at injury influences outcome may depend on the region affected and its state of maturity along the developmental time course. These findings are consistent with studies of nonhuman primates, in which infant monkeys showed memory impairment with orbitofrontal, but not dorsolateral prefrontal lesions, whereas juvenile monkeys showed impairment after both orbitofrontal and dorsolateral prefrontal lesions, which was interpreted as evidence for earlier functional commitment of the orbitofrontal region (Goldman, 1974).

Premorbid factors

A number of interrelated preexisting factors, including premorbid function, family functioning (Yeates, Taylor, & Drotar, 1997), and prior (and family) history of psychiatric disorder (Max et al., 1998) appear to be related to outcome after childhood TBI, though few studies have looked specifically at effects on memory. One of the impediments to assessing the effect of premorbid memory functioning on outcome is lack of direct comparisons of pre- and postmorbid functioning. Studies that have compared pre- to postinjury function have used standard academic test scores, which may not be sensitive to specific effects of injury on cognition. In fact, in a study of childhood TBI in which premorbid predictors of cognitive and academic functioning after TBI was assessed, parental evaluation of change in functioning was a better predictor of outcome than standardized measures of premorbid academic function (Arroyos-Jurado, Paulsen, Ehly, & Max, 2006).

One of the interesting findings about recovery from traumatic brain injury is that it is strongly affected by the environment of the child, especially family functioning. However, it should be noted that the environment may reflect differences in independent environmental variables, such as economic resources, education level, and family support, but may also reflect inherited individual factors, such as premorbid IQ, or cognitive reserve (Dennis, Yeates, Taylor, & Fletcher, 2007). Genetics aside, studies of the role of family support in recovery from brain injury in children have demonstrated its importance, both as a predictor of outcome (Anderson, Catroppa, Dudgeon et al., 2006; Keenan & Bratton, 2006; Nadebaum, Anderson, & Catroppa, 2007), and as a factor in successful intervention and functional recovery (Taylor et al., 1995; Wade, Carey, & Wolfe, 2006).

IMPLICATIONS FOR REHABILITATION

Evaluation of remedial techniques for memory disorder in children with TBI has been limited to a small number of controlled studies and case reports (see Laatsch, Thurlborn, Krisky, Shobat, & Sweeney, 2004; Ylvisaker et al., 2005, for recent reviews of the literature on cognitive rehabilitation of children with TBI). Positive effects of 17 weeks of daily training in 30-min sessions with attention and memory techniques was reported by Van't Hooft et al. (2005) in a randomized controlled study of children who had sustained TBI. Van't Hooft et al. found gains 2 weeks after training on measures of verbal memory relative to a control group who underwent nonspecific activities with their family (Van't Hooft et al., 2005). Limitations of this study include the lack of longer term follow-up assessment and lack of detail concerning the randomization procedure. However, it is an initial step toward clinical trials for cognitive rehabilitation in children with TBI. Based on earlier adult studies (Wilson, Baddeley, Evans, & Shiel, 1994), Landis et al. (2006) compared an errorless learning technique (in which the subject is prevented from committing errors due to guessing during learning, thus decreasing competition for the target item during encoding and retrieval) with a trial and error approach to memory training in children with memory problems following a TBI. Using a within-subject design in which the child underwent training with both techniques in each session, Landis et al. did not find evidence that errorless learning was uniformly superior to the trial-and-error technique (Landis et al., 2006).

From a methodological perspective, it is questionable whether training techniques can resolve a memory deficit, but there are indications that they can facilitate compensation (Glang et al., 2008). With a dearth of well-controlled clinical trials in children with memory deficit secondary to TBI, it is appropriate to offer these techniques to patients with the caveat that this methodology is promising, but evaluation is still in progress.

CONCLUSIONS

Despite advances in critical care and acute neurosurgical management of pediatric TBI, residual impairment of memory is still common especially on verbal recall and working memory, and for complex rather than simple tests of memory. The multicomponent nature of memory interacts with injury variables, including the severity of impaired consciousness and associated multifocal and diffuse brain insult, together with focal lesions in the frontotemporal region, to contribute to persistent memory deficit after severe TBI in children. Prefrontal dysfunction during working memory performance has also been demonstrated, with the suggestion that active maintenance of representations is especially altered in children with TBI, implicating compromised strategy use. Early age at the time of severe TBI is also related to persistent impairment of declarative memory possibly due to diffuse axonal injury and disruption of the neural network mediating development of this ability. Nonverbal declarative memory and implicit memory are relatively spared, but further research is indicated in these areas. Interventions to enable the child to compensate for memory deficit after traumatic brain injury are promising, but randomized clinical trials of innovative techniques are needed.

ACKNOWLEDGMENT

The authors were supported by grant NS-21889 from the National Institutes of Health (USA).

REFERENCES

Adams, J. H. (1980). Brain damage in fatal non-missile head injury. *Journal Clinical Pathology, 33*, 1132–45.

Alexander, A. I., & Mayfield, J. (2005). Latent factor structure of the Test of Memory and Learning in a pediatric traumatic brain injured sample: Support for a general memory construct. *Archives of Clinical Neuropsychology, 20*, 587–98.

Alexander, M. P., Stuss, D. T., & Fansabedian, N. (2003). California Verbal Learning Test: Performance by patients with focal frontal and non-frontal lesions. *Brain, 126*, 1493–503.

Anderson, J. W., & Schmitter-Edgecombe, M. (2009). Predictions of episodic memory following moderate to severe traumatic brain injury during inpatient rehabilitation. *Journal of Clinical and Experimental Neuropsychology, 31*, 425–38.

Anderson, V., & Catroppa, C. (2007). Memory outcome at 5 years post-childhood traumatic brain injury. *Brain Injury, 21*, 1399–409.

Anderson, V., Catroppa, C., Dudgeon, P., Morse, S., Haritou, F., & Rosenfeld, J. V. (2006). Understanding predictors of functional recovery and outcome 30 months following early childhood head injury. *Neuropsychology, 20*, 42–57.

Anderson, V., Catroppa, C., Morse, S., Haritou, F., & Rosenfeld, J. (2006). Functional plasticity or vulnerability after early brain injury? *Pediatrics, 116*, 1374–82.

Anderson, V. A., Catroppa, C., Rosenfeld, J., Haritou, F., & Morse, S. (2000). Recovery of memory function following traumatic brain injury in pre-school children. *Brain Injury, 14*, 679–92.

Anderson, V. A., Morse, S. A., Catroppa, C., Haritou, F., & Rosenfeld, J. V. (2004). Thirty month outcome from early childhood head injury: A prospective analysis of neurobehavioral recovery. *Brain, 127*, 2608–20.

Anderson, V. A., Morse, S., Klug, G., Catroppa, C., Haritou, F., Rosenfeld, J., & Pentland, L. (1997). Predicting recovery from head injury in young children: A prospective analysis. *Journal of the International Neuropsychological Society, 3,* 568–80.

Appel, L. F., Cooper, R. B., McCarrell, N., Sims-Knight, J., Yussen, S., & Flavell, J. H. (1972). The development of the distinction between perceiving and memorizing. *Child Development, 43,* 1365–81.

Arroyos-Jurado, E., Paulsen, J. S., Ehly, S., & Max, J. (2006). Traumatic brain injury in children and adolescents: Academic and intellectual outcomes following injury. *Exceptionality, 14,* 125–40.

Baddeley, A. D. (1992). Working memory. *Science, 255,* 556–59.

Baddeley, A. D. (1998). Recent developments in working memory. *Current Opinion in Neurobiology, 8,* 234–38.

Barnes, M. A., & Dennis, M. (2001). Knowledge-based inferencing after childhood head injury. *Brain and Language, 76,* 253–65.

Bauer, P. (2009). Neurodevelopmental changes in infancy and beyond: Implications for learning and memory. In O. A. Barbarin & B. Hanna (Eds.), *Handbook of child development and early education: Research to practice* (pp. 78–102). New York: Guilford Press.

Berryhill, P., Lilly, M., Levin, H. S., Hillman, G. R., Mendelsohn, D., Brunder, D. G., . . . Eisenberg, H. M. (1995). Frontal lobe changes after severe diffuse closed head injury in children: A volumetric study of magnetic resonance imaging. *Neurosurgery, 37,* 392–400.

Bigler, E. D. (1990). Neuropathology of traumatic brain injury. In E. D. Bigler (Ed.), *Traumatic brain injury* (pp. 13–49). Austin, TX: PRO-ED.

Bjorklund, D. F. (2004). Memory development in the new millennium [Special issue]. *Developmental Review, 24,* 343–6.

Braver, T. S., Cohen, J. D., Nystrom, L. E., Jonides, J., Smith, E. E., & Noll, D. C. (1997). A parametric study of prefrontal cortex involvement in human working memory. *Neuroimage, 5,* 49–62.

Brown, A. L., & DeLoache, J. S. (1978). Skills, plans, and self-regulation. In R. S. Siegler (Ed.), *Children's thinking: What develops?* (pp. 3–35). Hillsdale, NJ: Lawrence Erlbaum Associates, Inc.

Bunge, S. A., & Wright, S. B. (2007). Neurodevelopmental changes in working memory and cognition. *Current Opinion in Neurobiology, 17,* 243–50.

Buzzini, S. R., & Guskiewicz, K. M. (2006). Sport-related concussion in the young athlete. *Current Opinion in Pediatrics, 18,* 376–82.

Casey, B. J., Tottenham, N., Liston, C., & Durston, S. (2005). Imaging the developing brain: What have we learned about cognitive development? *Trends in Cognitive Sciences, 9,* 104–10.

Catroppa, C., & Anderson, V. (2002). Recovery in memory function in the first year following TBI in children. *Brain Injury, 16,* 369–84.

Catroppa, C., Anderson, V., Ditchfield, M., & Coleman, L. (2008). Using magnetic resonance imaging to predict new learning outcome at 5 years after childhood traumatic brain injury. *Journal of Child Neurology, 23,* 486–96.

Ceci, S. J., Fitneva, S. A., & Williams, W. M. (2010). Representational constraints on the development of memory and metamemory: A developmental-representational theory. *Psychological Review, 117,* 464–95.

Chapman, S., Sparks, G., Levin, H. S., Dennis, M., Roncadin, C., Zhang, L., & Song, J. (2004). Discourse macrolevel processing after severe pediatric traumatic brain injury. *Developmental Neuropsychology, 25,* 37–60.

Chapman, S. B., Gamino, J. F., Cook, L. G., Hanten, G., Li, X., & Levin, H. S. (2006). Impaired discourse gist and working memory in children after brain injury. *Brain and Language, 97,* 178–88.

Conklin, H. M., Salorio, C. F., & Slomine, B. S. (2008). Working memory performance following paediatric brain injury. *Brain Injury, 22,* 847–57.

Cohen, J. D., Forman, S. D., Braver, T. S., Casey, B. J., Servan-Schreiber, D., & Noll, D. C. (1993). Activation of the prefrontal cortex in a nonspatial working memory task with functional MRI. *Human Brain Mapping, 1,* 293–304.

Cowen, N. (1999). The differential maturation of two processing rates related to digit span. *Journal of Experimental Child Psychology, 72,* 193–209.

D'Esposito, M. (2007). From cognitive to neural models of working memory. *Philosophical Transactions of the Royal Society of London, 362,* 761–72.

DeCasper, A. J., & Fifer, W. P. (1980). Of human bonding: newborns prefer their mothers' voices. *Science, 208,* 1174–6.

Delis, D. C., Kramer, J. H., Kaplan, E., & Ober, B. (1994). *The California Verbal Learning Test—Children's Version.* San Antonio, TX: Harcourt Assessment, Inc.

Dempster, F. (1985). Short-term memory development in childhood and adolescence. In C. J. Brainerd & M. Pressley (Eds.), *Basic processes in memory development.* New York: Springer-Verlag.

Dennis, M., & Barnes, M. A. (1990). Knowing the meaning, getting the point, bridging the gap, and carrying the message: Aspects of discourse following closed head injury in childhood and adolescence. *Brain and Language, 39,* 428–46.

Dennis, M., Yeates, K. O., Taylor, G. H., & Fletcher, J. M. (2007). Brain reserve capacity, cognitive reserve capacity, and age-based functional plasticity after congenital and acquired brain injury in children. In Y. Stern (Ed.), *Cognitive reserve: Theory and applications* (pp. 53–83). Philadelphia: Taylor and Francis.

Di Stefano, G., Bachevalier, J., Levin, H. S., Song, J. X., Scheibel, R. S., & Fletcher, J. M. (2000). Volume of focal brain lesions and hippocampal formation in relation to memory function after closed-head injury in children. *Journal of Neurology, Neurosurgery and Psychiatry, 69,* 210–6.

Diamond, A. (2002). Normal development of prefrontal cortex from birth to young adulthood: Cognitive functions, anatomy, and biochemistry. In D. T. Stuss & R. T. Knight (Eds.), *Principles of frontal lobe function* (pp. 466–503). London: Oxford University Press.

DiGiulio, D. V., Seidenberg, M., O'Leary, D. S., & Raz, N. (1994). Procedural and declarative memory: A developmental study. *Brain and Cognition, 25,* 79–91.

Dimoska, A., McDonald, S., Pell, M. C., Tate, R. L., & James, C. M. (2010). Recognizing vocal expressions of emotion in patients with social skills deficits following traumatic brain injury. *Journal of the International Neuropsychological Society, 16,* 369–82.

Donders, J. (1993). Memory functioning after traumatic brain injury in children. *Brain Injury, 7,* 431–7.

Donders, J., & Warschausky, S. (2007). Neurobehavioral outcomes after early versus late childhood traumatic brain injury. *Journal of Head Trauma Rehabilitation, 22,* 296–302.

Flavell, J. H., Beach, D. R., & Chinsky, J. M. (1966). Spontaneous verbal rehearsal in a memory task as a function of age. *Child Development*, *37*, 283–99.

Flavell, J. H., Friedrichs, A., & Hoyt, J. (1970). Developmental changes in memorization processes. *Cognitive Psychology*, *1*, 324–40.

Gamino, J. F., Chapman, S. B., & Cook, L. G. (2009). Strategic learning in youth with traumatic brain injury: Evidence for stall in higher-order cognition. Topics in Language Disorders, 29, 224–35.

Ghatala, E. S., Levin, J. R., Pressley, M., & Lodico, M. G. (1985). Training cognitive strategy-monitoring in children. *American Educational Research Journal*, *22*, 199–215.

Ghetti, S. (2008). Rejection of false events in childhood: A metamemory account. *Current Directions in Psychological Science*, *17*, 16–20.

Ghetti, S., Lyons, K. E., Lazzarin, F., & Cornoldi, C. (2008). The development of metamemory monitoring during retrieval: The case of memory strength and memory absence. *Journal of Experimental Child Psychology*, *99*, 157–81.

Giedd, J. N., Blumenthal, J., Jeffries, N. O., Castellanos, F. X., Liu, H., Zijdenbos, A., . . . Rapoport, J. L. (1999). Brain development during childhood and adolescence: A longitudinal MRI study. *Nature Neuroscience*, *2*, 861–3.

Glang, A., Ylvisaker, M., Stein, M., Ehlhardt, L., Todis, B., & Tyler, J. (2008). Validated instructional practices: Application to students with traumatic brain injury. *The Journal of Head Trauma Rehabilitation*, *23*, 243–51.

Gogtay, N., Giedd, J. N., Lusk, L., Hayashi, K. M., Greenstein, D., & Vaituzis, A. C. (2004). Dynamic mapping of human cortical development during childhood through early adulthood. *Proceedings of the National Academy of Sciences of the United States of America*, *101*, 8174–9.

Goldman, P. S. (1974). Functional recovery after lesions of the nervous system. 3. Developmental processes in neural plasticity. Recovery of function after CNS lesions in infant monkeys. *Neurosciences Research Program Bulletin*, *12*, 217–22.

Gupta, P., MacWhinney, B., Feldman, H. M., & Sacco, K. (2003). Phonological memory and vocabulary learning in children with focal lesions. *Brain and Language*, *87*, 241–52.

Hannon, R., Adams, P., Harrington, S., Fries-Dias, C., & Gipson, M. T. (1995). Effects of brain injury and age on prospective memory self-rating and performance. *Rehabilitation Psychology*, *40*, 289–98.

Hanten, G., Bartha, M., & Levin, H. S. (2000). Metacognition following pediatric traumatic brain injury: A preliminary study. *Developmental Neuropsychology*, *18*, 383–98.

Hanten, G., Chapman, S. B., Gamino, J. F., Zhang, L., Benton, S. B., Stallings-Roberson, G., . . . Levin, H. S. (2004). Verbal selective learning after traumatic brain injury in children. *Annals of Neurology*, *56*, 847–53.

Hanten, G., & Martin, R. C. (2000). Contributions of phonological and semantic short-term memory to sentence processing: Evidence from two cases of closed head injury in children. *Journal of Memory & Language*, *43*, 335–61.

Hanten, G., Zhang, L., & Levin, H. S. (2002). Selective learning in children after traumatic brain injury: A preliminary study. *Child Neuropsychology*, *8*, 107–20.

Hayne, H., Boniface, J., & Barr, R. (2000). The development of declarative memory in human infants: Age-related changes in deferred imitation. *Behavioral Neuroscience*, *114*, 77–83.

Jaffe, K. M., Polissar, N. L., Fay, G. C., & Liao, S. (1995). Recovery trends over three years following pediatric traumatic brain injury. *Archives of Physical Medicine and Rehabilitation, 76,* 17–26.

Jaswal, V. K., & Dodson, C. S. (2009). Metamemory development: Understanding the role of similarity in false memories. *Child Development, 80,* 629–35.

Justice, E. M. (1985). Categorization as a preferred memory strategy: Developmental changes during elementary school. *Developmental Psychology, 21,* 1105–10.

Keenan, H. T., & Bratton, S. L. (2006). Epidemiology and outcomes of pediatric traumatic brain injury. *Developmental Neuroscience, 28,* 256–63.

Keeney, T. J., Cannizzo, S. R., & Flavell, J. H. (1967). Spontaneous and induced verbal rehearsal in a recall task. *Child Development, 38,* 953–66.

Kennedy, B. A., & Miller, D. J. (1976). Persistent use of verbal rehearsal as a function of information about its value. *Child Development, 47,* 566–9.

Kirkwood, M. W., Yeates, K. O., & Wilson, P. E. (2006). Pediatric sport-related concussion: A review of the clinical management of an oft-neglected population. *Pediatrics, 117,* 1359–71.

Kochanek, P. M., Clark, R. S. B., Ruppel, R. A., Adelson, P. D., Bell, M. J., Whalen, M. J., . . . Jenkins, L. W. (2000). Biochemical, cellular, and molecular mechanisms in the evolution of secondary damage after severe traumatic brain injury in infants and children: Lessons learned from the bedside. *Pediatric Critical Care Medicine, 1,* 4–19.

Koriat, A., Ackerman, R., Lockl, K., & Schneider, W. (2009). The memorizing effort heuristic in judgments of learning: A developmental perspective. *Journal of Experimental Child Psychology, 102,* 265–79.

Kraus, M. F., Susmaras, T., Caughlin, B. P., Walker, C. J., Sweeney, J. A., & Little, D. M. (2007). White matter integrity and cognition in chronic traumatic brain injury: A diffusion tensor imaging study. *Brain, 130,* 2508–19.

Kriel, R. K., Krach, L. E., & Panser, L. A. (1989). Closed head injury: Comparison of children younger and older than 6 years of age. *Pediatric Neurology, 5,* 296–300.

Kumar, R., Husain, M., Gupta, R. K., Hasan, K. M., Haris, M., Agarwal, A. K., . . . Narayana, P. A. (2009). Serial changes in the white matter diffusion tensor imaging metrics in moderate traumatic brain injury and correlation with neurocognitive function. *Journal of Neurotrauma, 26,* 481–95.

Laatsch, L. K., Thurlborn, K. R., Krisky, C. M., Shobat, D. M., & Sweeney, J. A. (2004). Investigating the neurobiological basis of cognitive rehabilitation therapy with fMRI. *Brain Injury, 18,* 957–74.

Lajiness-O'Neill, R., Erdodi, L., & Bigler, E. D. (2010). Memory and learning in pediatric traumatic brain injury: A review and examination of moderators of outcome. *Applied Neuropsychology, 17,* 83–92.

Landis, J., Hanten, G., Levin, H. S., Li, X., Ewing-Cobbs, L., Duron, J., & High, W. M. Jr. (2006). Evaluation of the errorless learning technique in children with traumatic brain injury. *Archives of Physical Medicine and Rehabilitation, 87,* 799–805.

Langlois, J. A., Kegler, S. R., Butler, J. A., Gotsch, K. E., Johnson, R. L., Reichard, A. A., . . . Thurman, D. J. (2003). Traumatic brain injury-related hospital discharges. *MMWR Surveillance Summaries, 52,* 1–18.

Lehnung, M., Leplow, B., Ekroll, V., Benz, B., Ritz, A., Mehdorn, M., & Ferstl, R. (2003). Recovery of spatial memory and persistence of spatial orientation deficit after traumatic brain injury during childhood. *Brain Injury, 17,* 855–69.

Lehnung, M., Leplow, B., Friege, L., Herzog, A., Fersti, R., & Mehdorn, M. (1998). Development of spatial memory and spatial orientation in preschoolers and primary school children. *British Journal of Psychology*, 89, 463–80.

Levin, H. S., Benavidez, D. A., Verger-Maestre, K., Perachio, N., Song, J. X., Mendelsohn, D., & Fletcher, J. M. (2000). Reduction of corpus callosum growth after severe traumatic brain injury in children. *Neurology*, 54, 647–53.

Levin, H. S., Culhane, K. A., Fletcher, J. M., Mendelsohn, D., Lilly, M., Harward, H., . . . Eisenberg, H. M. (1994). Dissociation between delayed alternation and memory after pediatric head injury: Relationship to MRI findings. *Journal of Child Neurology*, 9, 81–9.

Levin, H. S., & Eisenberg, H. M. (1979a). Neuropsychological outcome of closed head injury in children and adolescents. *Child's Brain*, 5, 281–92.

Levin, H. S., & Eisenberg, H. M. (1979b). Neuropsychological impairment after closed head injury in children and adolescents. *Journal of Pediatric Psychology*, 4, 389–402.

Levin, H. S., Eisenberg, H. M., Wiggs, C. L., & Kobayashi, K. (1982). Memory and intellectual ability after head injury in children and adolescents. *Neurosurgery*, 11, 668–73.

Levin, H. S., Fletcher, J. M., Kusnerik, L., Kufera, J. A., Lilly, M., Duffy, F. F., . . . Bruce, D. (1996). Semantic memory following pediatric head injury: Relationship to age, severity of injury, and MRI. *Cortex*, 32, 461–78.

Levin, H. S., Hanten, G., Chang, C. C., Zhang, L., Schachar, R. J., Ewing-Cobbs, L., & Max, J. E. (2002). Working memory after traumatic brain injury in children. *Annals of Neurology*, 52, 82–8.

Levin, H. S., Hanten, G., Zhang, L., Swank, P. R., Ewing-Cobbs, L., Dennis, M., . . . Hunter, J. V. (2004). Changes in working memory after traumatic brain injury in children. *Neuropsychology*, 18, 240–7.

Levin, H. S., Mendelsohn, D., Lilly, M., Yeakley, J., Song, J. X., Scheibel, R. S., . . . Bruce, D. (1997). Magnetic resonance imaging in relation to functional outcome of pediatric closed head injury: A test of the Ommaya-Gennarelli model. *Neurosurgery*, 40, 432–40.

Levin, H. S., Song, J., Scheibel, R. S., Fletcher, J. M., Harward, H., & Chapman, S. B. (2000). Dissociation of frequency and recency processing from list recall after severe closed head injury in children and adolescents. *Journal of Clinical and Experimental Neuropsychology*, 22, 1–15.

Lockl, K., & Schneider, W. (2007). Knowledge about the mind: Links between theory of mind and later metamemory. *Child Development*, 78, 148–67.

Mandalis, A., Kinsella, G., Ong, B., & Anderson, V. (2007). Working memory and new learning following pediatric traumatic brain injury. *Developmental Neuropsychology*, 32, 683–701.

Max, J. E., Robin, D. A., Lindgren, S. D., Smith, W. L. J., Sato, Y., Mattheis, P. J., . . . Castillo, C. S. (1998). Traumatic brain injury in children and adolescents: Psychiatric disorders at one year. *Journal of Neuropsychiatry and Clinical Neurosciences*, 10, 290–7.

Mazzoni, G., & Nelson, T. O. (Eds.). (1998). *Metacognition and cognitive neuropsychology: Monitoring and control processes*. Mahwah, NJ: Lawrence Erlbaum Associates.

McCauley, S. R., Pedroza, C., Chapman, S. B., Cook, L. G., Hotz, G., Vasquez, A. C., & Levin, H. S. (2010). Event-based prospective memory performance during sub-acute recovery following moderate to severe traumatic brain injury in children: Effects of monetary incentives. *Journal of the International Neuropsychological Society, 16*, 335–41.

McWilliams, J., & Schmitter-Edgecombe, M. (2008). Semantic organization during the early stage of recovery from traumatic brain injury. *Brain Injury, 22*, 243–53.

Metcalfe, J., & Shimamura, A. P. (1994). *Metacognition: Knowing about knowing*. Cambridge, MA: MIT Press.

Mottram, L., & Donders, J. (2005). Construct validity of the California Verbal Learning Test—Children's version after pediatric traumatic brain injury. *Psychological Assessment, 17*, 212–7.

Mottram, L. & Donders, J. (2006). Cluster subtypes on the California Verbal Learning Test—Children's version after pediatric traumatic brain injury. *Developmental Neuropsychology, 30*, 865–83.

Moynahan, E. D. (1973). The development of knowledge concerning the effect of categorization upon free recall. *Child Development, 44*, 238–46.

Nadebaum, C., Anderson, V., & Catroppa, C. (2007). Executive function outcomes following traumatic brain injury in young children: A five year follow-up. *Developmental Neuropsychology, 32*, 703–28.

Newsome, M. R., Scheibel, R. S., Hunter, J., Wang, Z. J., Chu, Z., Li, X., & Levin, H. S. (2007). Brain activation during working memory after traumatic brain injury in children. *Neurocase, 13*, 16–24.

Newsome, M. R., Steinberg, J. L., Scheibel, R. S., Troyanskaya, M., Chu, Z., Hanten, G., . . . Levin, H. S. (2008). Effects of traumatic brain injury on working memory-related brain activations in adolescents. *Neuropsychology, 22*, 419–25.

Purhonen, M., Kilpelainen-Lees, R., Valkonen-Korhonen, M., Karhu, J., & Lehtonen, J. (2005). Four-month-old infants process own mother's voice faster than unfamiliar voices—electrical signs of sensitization in infant brain. *Cognitive Brain Research, 24*, 627–33.

Ranganath, C., Cohen, M. X., Dam, C., & D'Esposito, M. (2004). Inferior temporal, prefrontal, and hippocampal contributions to visual working memory maintenance and associative memory retrieval. *Journal of Neuroscience, 24*, 3917–25.

Reiss, A. L., Abrams, M. T., Singer, H. S., Ross, J. L., & Denckla, M. B. (1996). Brain development, gender, and IQ in children. A volumetric imaging study. *Brain, 119*, 1763–74.

Richmond, J., & Nelson, C. A. (2007). Accounting for change in declarative memory: A cognitive neuroscience perspective. *Developmental Review, 27*, 349–373.

Richmond, J., & Nelson, C. A. (2008). Mechanisms of change: A cognitive neuroscience approach to declarative memory development. In C. A. Nelson & M. Luciana (Eds), *Handbook of developmental cognitive neuroscience* (2nd ed., pp. 541–52). Cambridge, MA: MIT Press.

Roman, M. J., Delis, D. C., Willerman, L., Magulac, M., Demadura, T. L., de la Pena, J. L., . . . Kracun, M. (1998). Impact of pediatric traumatic brain injury on components of verbal memory. *Journal of Clinical and Experimental Neuropsychology, 20*, 245–58.

Roncadin, C., Guger, S., Archibald, J., Barnes, M., & Dennis, M. (2004). Working memory after mild, moderate, or severe childhood closed head injury. *Developmental Neuropsychology, 25*, 21–36.

Salorio, C. F., Slomine, B. S., Grados, M. A., Vasa, R., Christensen, J. R., & Gerring, J. (2005). Neuroanatomic correlates of CVLT-C performance following pediatric traumatic brain injury. *Journal of the International Neuropsychological Society, 11*, 686–96.

Scherf, K. S., Sweeney, J. A., & Luna, B. (2006). Brain basis of developmental change in visuospatial working memory. *Journal of Cognitive Neuroscience, 18*, 1045–58.

Schmidt, M. (2003). *Rey Auditory Verbal Learning Test: A handbook.* Lutz, FL: Psychological Assessment Resources, Inc.

Schmidtke, K., Manner, H., Kaufmann, R., & Schmolck, H. (2002). Cognitive procedural learning in patients with fronto-striatal lesions. *Learning and Memory, 9*, 419–29.

Schmithorst, V. J., Wilke, M., Dardzinski, B. J., & Holland, S. K. (2005). Cognitive functions correlate with white matter architecture in a normal pediatric population: A diffusion tensor MRI study. *Human Brain Mapping, 26*, 139–47.

Serra-Grabulosa, J. M., Junque, C., Verger, K., Salgado-Pineda, P., Maneru, C., & Mercader, J. (2005). Cerebral correlates of declarative memory dysfunctions in early traumatic brain injury. *Journal of Neurology, Neurosurgery & Psychiatry, 76*, 129–31.

Shum, D., Jamieson, E., Bahr, M., & Wallace, G. (1999). Implicit and explicit memory in children with traumatic brain injury. *Journal of Clinical and Experimental Neuropsychology, 21*, 149–58.

Shum, D., Valentine, M., & Cutmore, T. (1999). Performance of individuals with severe long-term traumatic brain injury on time-, event-, and activity-based prospective memory tasks. *Journal of Clinical and Experimental Neuropsychology, 21*, 49–58.

Slobounov, S. M., Zhang, K., Pennell, D., Ray, W., Johnson, B., & Sebastianelli, W. (2010). Functional abnormalities in normally appearing athletes following mild traumatic brain injury: A functional MRI study. *Experimental Brain Research, 202*, 341–54.

Sowell, E. R., Delis, D., Stiles, J., & Jernigan, T. L. (2001). Improved memory functioning and frontal lobe maturation between childhood and adolescence: A structural MRI study. *Journal of the International Neuropsychological Society, 7*, 312–22.

Sowell, E. R., Trauner, D. A., Gamst, A., & Jernigan, T. L. (2002). Development of cortical and subcortical brain structures in childhood and adolescence: A structural MRI study. *Developmental Medical Child Neurology, 44*, 4–16.

Sternberg, S. (1966). High speed scanning in human memory. *Science, 153*, 652–4.

Taylor, G. H., Drotar, D., Wade, S. L., Yeates, K. O., Stancin, T., & Klein, S. (1995). Recovery from traumatic brain injury in children: The importance of the family. In S. H. Broman & M. E. Michel (Eds.), *Traumatic head injury in children* (pp. 188–216). New York: Oxford University Press.

Teasdale, G., & Jennett, B. (1974). Assessment of coma and impaired consciousness: A practical scale. *Lancet, 2*, 81–4.

Torriero, S., Oliveri, M., Koch, G., Lo Gerfo, E., Salerno, S., & Caltagirone, C. (2007). Cortical networks of procedural learning: Evidence from cerebellar damage. *Neuropsychology, 45*, 1208–14.

Van't Hooft, I., Andersson, K., Bergman, B., Sejersen, T., von Wendt, L., & Bartfai, A. (2005). Beneficial effect from a cognitive training programme on children with acquired brain injuries demonstrated in a controlled study. *Brain Injury, 19*, 511–8.

Wade, S. L., Carey, J., & Wolfe, C. R. (2006). The efficacy of an online cognitive-behavioral family intervention in improving child behavior and social competence following pediatric brain injury. *Rehabilitation Psychology, 51*, 179–89.

Ward, H., Shum, D., Dick, B., McKinlay, L., & Baker-Tweney, S. (2004). Interview study of the effects of pediatric traumatic brain injury on memory. *Brain Injury, 18*, 471–95.

Ward, H., Shum, D., McKinlay, L., Baker, S. & Wallace, G. (2007). Prospective memory and pediatric brain injury: Effects of cognitive demand. *Child Neuropsychology, 13,* 219–39.

Ward, H., Shum, D., Wallace, G., & Boon, J. (2002). Pediatric traumatic brain injury and procedural memory. *Journal of Clinical and Experimental Neuropsychology, 24,* 458–70.

Webb, S., Long, J., & Nelson, C. (2005). A longitudinal investigation of visual event-related potentials in the first year of life. *Developmental Science, 8,* 605–16.

Wilde, E. A., Hunter, J. V., Newsome, M. R., Scheibel, R. S., Bigler, E. D., Johnson, J. L., . . . Levin, H. S. (2005). Frontal and temporal morphometric findings on MRI in children after moderate to severe traumatic brain injury. *Journal of Neurotrauma, 22,* 333–44.

Wilke, M., Krågeloh-Mann, I., & Holland, S. K. (2006). Global and local development of gray and white matter volume in normal children and adolescents. *Experimental Brain Research, 178,* 296–307.

Wilson, B. A., Baddeley, A. D., Evans, J., & Shiel, A. (1994). Errorless learning in the rehabilitation of memory impaired people. *Neuropsychological Rehabilitation, 4,* 307–26.

Wolfe, C. D., & Bell, M. A. (2004). Working memory and inhibitory control in early childhood: Contributions from physiology, temperament, and language. *Developmental Psychobiology, 44,* 68–83.

Wolfe, C. D., & Bell, M. A. (2007). Sources of variability in working memory in early childhood: A consideration of age, temperament, language, and brain electrical activity. *Cognitive Development, 22,* 431–55.

Worden, P. E. & Sladewski-Awig, L. J. (1982). Children's awareness of memorability. *Journal of Educational Psychology, 74,* 341–50.

Wozniak, J. R., Krach, L., Ward, E., Mueller, B. A., Muetzel, R., Schnoebelen, S., . . . Lim, K. O. (2007). Neurocognitive and neuroimaging correlates of pediatric brain injury: A diffusion tensor imaging (DTI) study. *Archives of Clinical Neuropsychology, 22,* 555–68.

Yeates, K. O., Blumenstein, E., Patterson, C. M., & Delis, D. C. (1995). Verbal learning and memory following pediatric closed-head injury. *Journal of the International Neuropsychological Society, 1,* 78–87.

Yeates, K. O., & Enrile, B. G. (2005). Implicit and explicit memory in children with congenital and acquired brain disorder. *Neuropsychology, 19,* 618–28.

Yeates, K. O., Taylor, H. G., & Drotar, D. (1997). Preinjury family environment as a determinant of recovery from traumatic brain injuries in school-age children. *Journal of the International Neuropsychological Society, 3,* 617–30.

Ylvisaker, M., Adelson, P. D., Braga, L. W., Burnett, S. M., Glang, A., Feeney, T. J., . . . Todis, B. (2005). Rehabilitation and ongoing support after pediatric TBI: Twenty years of progress. *Journal of Head Trauma Rehabilitation, 20,* 95–109.

Index

Note: Page numbers followed by "*f*" and "*t*" denote figures and tables, respectively.

autobiographical memory (*Cont'd*)
functional neuroimaging for
investigating, 188–90, 189*f*
hippocampus and
vividness of, 208–9
interlocking systems in, 30
neural activations in, 192–95, 194*f*
organization of, 198, 199*f*
parietal cortex damage and deficits in,
196–97
quality differentiation for, 154–55
recollection importance
to, 27, 50, 188
recollection modulation for, 203–4,
205*f*, 206–10
recollection research paradigms from,
50
remoteness modulating recollection of,
207–9
retrieval and construction
of, 198–203
retrieval length of, 199–201, 200*f*
retrieval phases for, 201–2
semantic, 191–92, 191*f*, 195–98, 199*f*,
201
social and self functions of, 38
temporal range of, 207–8
vividness modulating, 206–7
autonoetic consciousness, 5, 87,
89, 191
autonoetic memory, 76
axons, 221
diffuse injury to, 290
shearing and stretching of, 289

Back to the Future hypothesis, 91
basic memory, 22–24
Bauer, Patricia, 62
behavioral dual-process
models, 8
behavioral paradigms, 51
Behavior Rating Inventory of Executive
Function, 296
BIC model. *See* binding of items
and contexts model
bilateral finger tapping, 229
binding
in animals, 89

behavioral and neural development
related to, 147–50
bound representations
from, 145
changeable features and, 86
controlled processes interaction with,
150
development of, 82–87, 147–50
in early childhood, 83–85, 84*f*
episodic (contingent), 74
in episodic memory
development, 77–80, 145–50
extrinsic, 77
feature memory development
compared with, 86
hippocampus and, 147
in human aging, 80–82, 81*f*, 82*f*
interobject, 77
intraobject, 77
intrinsic, 77
lifespan studies of, 85–86
rate of development
differences in, 150
in recollection, 76–77
retrieval and deficiencies in, 84
in school-aged children, 85
semantic (lawful), 74
in visual short-term memory, 76
in working memory, 77
binding of items and contexts model (BIC
model), 177–80
binding problem, 73–75
phenomena described by, 76–77
block designs, 229, 230
Blood Oxygenated Level Dependent signal
(BOLD), 242
bound representations, 145, 146, 147
brain
memory skill related to, 288–89, 291
prefontal region injury, 289–90
structural changes of, 288–89
structural imaging of, 224–27
brain development
cellular and molecular, 223–24
growth in study of, 235–36
of memory-related regions, 223–27
neurobiology of, 219–23
brain imaging studies, 289